Encyclopedia of Hell

Encyclopedia of Hell

Miriam Van Scott

St. Martin's Press
New York

A THOMAS DUNNE BOOK.
AN IMPRINT OF ST. MARTIN'S PRESS.

Design by Jennifer Ann Daddio

Frontispiece: *The Inferno.*
GIRAUDON/ART RESOURCE, N.Y.

Library of Congress Cataloging-in-Publication Data
Van Scott, Miriam.
Encyclopedia of hell / Miriam Van Scott
p. cm.
Includes bibliographical references.
ISBN 0-312-18574-X
1. Hell—Encyclopedias. I. Title.
BL545.V26 1998
291.2'3—dc21 98-13705
CIP

First Edition: September 1998

1 3 5 7 9 10 8 6 4 2

This book is dedicated to

Tara Lynn Swank

fulfilling a promise made two decades ago

acknowledgments

I extend my deepest gratitude and sincere appreciation to the following for invaluable contributions to this project:

Daniel Timothy Corcoran, Jr.
John Schulte and the staff at Toynetwork
Clive Barker
Joe Daley
Mary Ann Sullivan of the Blue Army of Our Lady of Fatima USA, Inc.
Harris McCarty Design Group of Manassas, Virginia
Michael Gariepy of *Art Today*
Alison Gallup of *Art Resource*
Linda Hassani
Leon Fletcher
Staff and personnel of the Prince William County
and Fairfax County, Virginia, library systems
Dolores and Cornelius Van Scott

Introduction

Humankind has been fascinated with the concept of hell from time immemorial. The custom of sitting around the campfire telling ghost stories dates back centuries, even millennia, to the first cave dweller who timidly speculated about the fate of our souls. With the threat of death lurking around every corner, early peoples had to wonder, What happens next? Struggling to unravel these vast mysteries in a strange and unknowable world, our ancestors weaved all manner of fantastic tales about underworld deities and perilous journeys the dead must take on the way to the afterlife. The stories were passed from parent to child by word of mouth, with every generation adding a little of its own spice to the mix.

As time passed, pictures scratched into clay pots and drawn on parchment scrolls brought these legends alive. The old tales soon grew into complex belief systems of gods, heroes, villains, and rites and rituals, giving each culture its own identity and ultimately defining its values and goals. And though the specifics of these supernatural myths differ, one thing is clear: Belief in a hell is universal. From humanity's most ancient legends, afterlife beliefs have been tinged with the crimson threat of everlasting punishment.

People became more civilized, and so did their beliefs. Organized religion fine-tuned these theories into elaborate cause-and-effect scenarios. Good behavior meant salvation; evil, damnation. Details about what those terms mean rages on to this day, with no real consensus. Art, literature, and drama brought hell into the common experience. Modern technology has made it come alive before our very eyes in films, television programs, and even music videos. And yet, there is still little agreement on what awaits us beyond the grave.

The *Encyclopedia of Hell* gathers these diverse descriptions of the netherworld from myth, religion, literature, visions, theater, art, music, film, television, and pop culture in a single comprehensive volume. It offers a broad range of interpretations from hundreds of different sources, highlighting areas of similarity and contrast between theories. The *Encyclopedia of Hell* also explains the origins of underworld concepts and examines the impact of these ideas on literature, history, and cultural development. All information is relayed without subjective interpretation and includes cross-references for further explanation.

Recent research shows that more than 60 percent of Americans believe in the existence of hell, although most are not quite sure of the specific details. Today, most people currently derive an understanding of the underworld from religious teachings, horror movies, rock videos, and other fragments of information. This volume puts these scattered concepts in context and traces connections among evolving suppositions.

In addition to describing various images of the underworld, *The Encyclopedia of Hell* includes hundreds of fascinating facts relating to the great below. Illuminated herein are such tales as the origin of the first mummy, the reason why only a wooden stake can kill a vampire, and why the number thirteen is considered unlucky. The book also explores the question, Is the gate of hell located in Long Island, or—as ancient myth tells us—in France? and many other amusing infernal theories.

Despite the modern obsession with solving the mysteries of life through science, interest in hell remains dynamic and pervasive. Perhaps it is because death is the great equalizer of all ages, uniting contemporary peoples with those long-ago cave dwellers huddled around the communal fire. And images of the afterlife, even ghastly visions of torment and agony, provide a promise of something more. In the case of hell, studying the inferno on this side of eternity is preferable to investigating damnation firsthand. *The Encyclopedia of Hell* is as close to the underworld as any of us would ever like to come.

A

ABBADON Abbadon, the Hebrew word for "destruction," is the biblical dwelling place of the dead found in both the Old and New Testaments. It is used interchangeably with SHEOL. Abbadon is the "bottomless pit" in which the damned suffer for all eternity. Over time, Abbadon also became synonymous with death and the grave.

REVELATION refers to Abbadon as the place for those who "neither repented of their murders, nor their DEVIL worship, nor their fornication, nor their thefts." Abbadon is described as a foul, smoky abyss out of which locusts, demons, and monsters emerge to destroy the earth. The ruler of Abbadon is APOLLYON, the dark angel of the underworld.

Abbadon has also been described as a DEMON in *THE PILGRIM'S PROGRESS* and *Paradise Found,* the sequel to Milton's *PARADISE LOST*. In these, and numerous other classic stories, the name refers to the personification of evil.

ACHERON The Acheron is one of the mystical rivers of ancient Greek myth. According to the legends, the waters flow directly to the underworld of King HADES. Odysseus, hero of Homer's *ODYSSEY,* offers a blood sacrifice on the banks of the Acheron in order to converse with the souls of the dead.

Acheron is also the name of the DEMON from the *Vision of TUNDAL* who guards the gates of hell.

ADAMNAN A mystic named Adamnan, an abbot of the Iona Abbey, claims to have had a horrific vision of hell that was later transcribed and distributed throughout Christendom in the tenth century. His infernal nightmare features a host of fiery tortures. The cleric reports having seen sinners lashed to burning columns with chains of molten serpents. Others are immersed to their necks in an ocean of flame. Some of the damned are beaten repeatedly with clubs or forced to cross red-hot rocks while DEMONS shoot flaming arrows at them. The vilest offenders are pierced through the tongue with scalding spikes. And those who manage to avoid these blazing tortures are devoured by packs of wild dogs.

Adamnan offers his gruesome vision as a warning to Christians of what awaits the evil in the afterlife. His story became a popular example of VISION LITERATURE and was widely circulated and discussed during the Middle Ages.

ADAMUS EXUL *Adamus Exul,* a seventeenth-century Latin drama written by Dutch playwright Hugo Grotius, proposes that nonexistence is preferable to damnation in hell. It shows a vengeful LUCIFER determined to hurt God by dragging his new, precious creation—humanity—into eternal suffering. This is as close as he could ever come to forcing God himself into the abyss.

The play opens as Lucifer, after being expelled from heaven for his pride and rebelliousness, devises a plan for taking vengeance on God. Knowing he cannot force God into hell, he schemes to draw humans into the underworld by tempting people away from the Creator. This is the next best thing, he decides, since people have been fashioned in God's own image. Lucifer succeeds in causing Adam to sin in the Garden of Eden, but his triumph is short-lived. Unwilling to abandon humankind, God gives Adam hope of salvation by promising a future Messiah who will one day redeem humanity.

According to the drama, the worst suffering of hell is not merely lack of union with God, who encompasses beauty and joy, but also imprisonment in self-importance. Lucifer discovers that entangling man in his own evil manipulations does not reduce his agony. In fact, his wicked machinations only intensify the pain of being exiled to the underworld. He is eternally mired in his own empty, hollow self-pity and the damnation of humanity does not lessen that suffering. This is the true agony of hell.

ADLIVUN Adlivun is Eskimo for "those beneath us" and refers to the region for spirits unworthy of departing to the Land of the Moon (paradise) upon death. It is a dark, dank, shadowy realm located at the bottom of the ocean. Souls in Adlivun are not tortured; their punishment is simply the loss of paradise and the separation from the living.

Adlivun is ruled by the Sedna, Eskimo goddess of the underworld. She is a one-eyed giant so hideous that only a shaman (medicine man) can bear to look directly at her. Sedna came to rule Adlivun after being cast to the bottom of the sea by her parents. On the ocean floor, Sedna guards the ungrateful dead who have displeased her, her dead parents among them.

The underworld is associated with all bodies of water, which are believed to be quite dangerous due to Sedna's grim influence. Dormant lakes and standing pools are considered especially hazardous, as they contain evil spirits waiting to devour human souls.

Myths differ on why Sedna's mother and father drowned their daughter. Some stories say she was once a great beauty who angered her parents by refusing many offers of marriage from wealthy and powerful tribesmen. Unwilling to accept any man as her mate, Sedna elected instead to wed a dog. This decision, her parents felt, deprived them of great riches and social status and brought shame and ridicule instead. They avenged this offense by hurling their child into the ocean.

Another legend claims that Sedna had an insatiable appetite and ate constantly. One night, her parents awoke to find the girl gnawing on their arms and legs as they slept. Still another tale says she was thrown out of her father's boat as a sacrifice during a raging storm to keep his boat from capsizing. Trying to appease angry gods, he flung her over the side, cutting off her fingers as she clung to the vessel. She immediately sank to the murky depths and took up rule in Adlivun.

The entrance to the underworld is guarded by Sedna's husband, a ferocious dog who sits at the gate of a razor-thin bridge. His job is to keep the living from raiding Adlivun and to prevent the dead from escaping. Under certain circumstances, such as during a plague or famine, the canine will allow a shaman to enter the land of the dead to offer sacrifice to Sedna and plead for her assistance.

Occasionally, an evil spirit eludes the guard, successfully negotiates the dangerous passage, and returns home to terrorize the living. Eventually, however, Sedna retrieves the ghoul and returns it to her dark underworld kingdom.

ADVERTISING Hell has been used as an advertising tool for centuries. The underworld has long fired people's imaginations and piqued their curiosity, making it an attractive venue for peddling wares. Carefully used in commercial ads, depictions of the place of the damned provide alluring, sometimes even glamorous, glimpses into a forbidden world. Savvy ad executives have turned this naughty fascination into a powerful medium for selling their products, ranging from perfumes to military service to athletic shoes.

One of the first instances of a printed ad featuring a carnal, seductive hell occurred in an 1880 poster advertising a posh French café. The text invites Paris's elite to "A Party in Hell." The illustration shows bejeweled ladies in evening gowns and their tuxedo-clad escorts dining and dancing as a smiling DEVIL nods approvingly from his blazing throne. Several decades later, a World War I Allied Forces recruiting poster offers the darker side of damnation. This call to arms transforms Kaiser Wilhelm II into SATAN, complete with horns and tail, towering over a burning empire. The implication to eager young patriots was clear: Join the army and help send the DEMON back to hell. Similar diabolical images have been used in print advertisements over the past decades to peddle home safes, FOOD NOVELTIES, and even children's toys.

The invention of television opened

An early American political ad depicts the "1812 Imperial Devil." ART TODAY

a whole new outlet for using infernal appeal. One of the first commercials to mix underworld allusions with a sales pitch was a 1950s cosmetics ad. The thirty-second spot depicts a mousy housewife who turns into a sultry, seductive devil after donning a few drops of perfume. The gorgeous blond, now a horned vixen, cuddles up to her enthusiastic husband. The tag line informs viewers that even the most demure woman needs to get in touch with her dark side once in a while.

Today, most hellish television advertisements use a touch of wit to soften the realm of the damned. A 1993 ad for a Roy Rogers fast-food restaurant shows a man who has just been killed in a traffic accident appearing before a celestial review board. In the background are two escalators, one going up to heaven, the other going down to the smoky abyss. When the recently deceased asks if they "cook anything" in heaven, his winged escort quickly interrupts, telling him he must be "thinking of the *other* place." At this, a blast of smoke and fire erupts from a black chimney emanating from the depths, and a distant voice howls, "Yow! I *hate* this place!"

Digital, a renowned technology corporation, goes a step further in embracing the underworld. In one ad campaign, the high-tech company proudly lists the great inferno as one of its customers. The commercial shows a burning landscape interspersed with a collage of scenes of mass destruction. The line that follows this barrage of devastation reads simply, "Hell has our phone number."

Other commercials offer damnation tailored to their particular target audience. A British Knights advertisement for athletic shoes, for example, features basketball star Derrick Coleman having a nightmare about Fullcourt Hell. In the dream, the athlete finds himself in a steamy world where chubby, middle-aged opponents can play the game as well as he can with the aid of BK shoes. A sneering, horned devil laughs at Coleman from a smoldering cloud of murky smoke. Coleman bolts upright in bed as the last sulfurous fumes fade away, while the sound of the demon's laughter echoes through his room.

California Milk Producers has created one of the most amusing hellish promotions ever presented. The advertisement shows a ruthless power broker, currently in the process of firing his mother via cellular phone, being run down by a bus. The disoriented man suddenly finds himself in a brilliant realm where a soft, feminine voice coos, "Welcome to eternity." Declaring that this must be heaven, the newly deceased finds a plate of gigantic chocolate chip cookies, shoves one in his mouth, then heads for a huge refrigerator. Upon opening the door, the man finds that it is packed with milk cartons. He gleefully grabs one, only to find it empty. He snatches a second, but it too contains nothing. The man frantically pulls down carton after carton only to discover that *all* are empty. At this point, the terrified snacker looks into the camera and screams, "Where *am* I?" realizing that he is damned to spend eternity eating dry cookies without being able to wash them down with a swig of ice-cold milk. The screen goes black before sizzling red letters burn across the screen asking viewers, "Got milk?"—and reminding them to stock up on dairy products while they still have the chance.

Appropriately enough, some of the most elaborate and frightening depictions of hell appear in advertisements for COMPUTER GAMES about the underworld. The commercial for Doom II features a preacher offering a HELL-FIRE SERMON filled with grisly images of a treacherous afterlife. The sweaty reverend thrusts his fist onto the pulpit, shouting that "hell is a dark prison of lost souls" as graphics of the infernal adventure flash on screen.

Representations of the underworld are not confined to print and television advertising. Radio commercials can create fascinating visions of hell through sound effects, dialogue, and implication. In a 1997 ad for Cool Iced Tea, comic Penn Jillette opens by announcing, "I'm in Hell," perched on a molten iron bench "next to some former IRS auditors." The cries of the damned, shrieks of demons, and crackling flames are audible in the background. But despite "walls of fire" and sizzling temperatures, Penn stays comfortable in the inferno by sipping his refreshing beverage.

These ad campaigns, and others like them, underscore the pervasive and timeless infatuation human beings have with the place of the damned. Even those who do not want to view hell in person are fascinated and captivated by infernal images. Advertisers have turned this morbid curiosity into successful promotions.

AENEID Virgil's epic *Aeneid* chronicles the adventures of Aeneas, a great soldier of the Trojan War who founds the city of Rome after his homeland of Troy is destroyed. (It is in many ways the Latin counterpart to the Greek *ODYSSEY*; each describes the aftermath of the war from opposing perspectives.) Virgil's poem was unfinished at the time of his death in 19 B.C., and he had left instructions that the manuscript be destroyed. But Roman Emperor Caesar Augustus demanded that copies be kept intact. As a result, the *Aeneid* has become a classic of Western literature and has provided inspiration for numerous works, including Purcell's opera *Dido and Aeneas* and Dante's *DIVINE COMEDY: THE INFERNO*.

The *Aeneid* opens as its hero searches for purpose in his life after his beloved city of Troy has been conquered. Confused and near despair, Aeneas decides to travel to the underworld and ask his deceased father, Anchises, what to do now that he cannot return home. A sibyl (priestess of Apollo) serves as Aeneas's guide to DIS, the land of the dead. The two set out on their perilous, gloomy journey to the realm of deceased spirits.

Aeneas adventure begins at LAKE AVERNUS (located outside Naples, Italy), a flaming black pool in the heart of a dense forest. A pitch-dark cavern leads down to the gates of the netherworld, where the two must face monsters of Disease, Fear, Old Age, Hunger, Poverty, Death, Trials, Sleep (called "Death's brother"), War, and Strife. Aeneas and his guide must then pass the monstrous hydra, a beast with fifty heads, and other fiends before coming to the banks of the river STYX.

While making his descent, Aeneas sees many of the familiar fixtures of the mythological Greek underworld: the rivers Chaos and Phlegethan, the ERINYES (Furies), CHARON the ferryman, and CERBERUS, the fierce guardian of the gates of the HADES. He also witnesses a number of agonies suffered by the dead and is moved to sorrow by their plight.

Aeneas is particularly disturbed by a "swarming" of wilted spirits (SHADES) wandering aimlessly along the marshes of the Styx. He asks the sibyl why Charon will not ferry them to the underworld. She explains that these men have not had a proper burial and are thus "helpless and unburied . . . . They wander for a hundred years and hover about these banks before they gain their entry." Aeneas is heartbroken to see several of his friends, Trojan sailors lost at sea during a storm, among these marooned souls.

One fallen comrade begs Aeneas to "cast earth upon my body" when he returns to the upperworld, or use his influence with the gods to release him from this fate. The dead soldier longs for relief, so that "in death I might find a place of rest." The sibyl promises to ease his sorrow, assuring him that his death will be avenged and that his enemies' land will be conquered and one day bear the deceased warrior's name.

As the journey continues, the two come upon further obstacles. Charon is skeptical of their intentions, remembering how living men had once tried to storm the underworld to kidnap Prosperpine (PERSEPHONE), queen of the dead. He refuses to ferry the pair to the abyss. But Aeneas offers a magic golden bough as tribute to Prosperpine, assuring Charon that he only wishes to speak with his father who is among her subjects. Hearing this, Charon agrees to transport them to their destination.

When they reach the underworld, Aeneas discovers a new variety of horrors. The priestess agrees, claiming, "If I had a hundred tongues and a hundred mouths and a voice of iron, I still could not describe all the crimes and all the varieties of punishment" awaiting the dead. These tortures include being hanged in the wind and purged by fire. The sound of wailing and shrieking of the damned is unbearable, adding to the torment.

One of Aeneas's greatest moments of sorrow comes as he meets Dido, his wife, who committed suicide when he left her to fulfill his destiny of founding a new city. Dido had been the queen of Carthage and had loved Aeneas deeply. But the god Mercury warned Aeneas he must not remain in her kingdom but venture on to build a new city for the surviving Trojans. He set sail before hearing of her death and is moved by guilt and pity to find her in the land of the dead. Aeneas approaches her, but Dido turns her back on him and refuses to hear his apology.

More dejected than ever, Aeneas finally reaches his father. The elder cheers his son by telling Aeneas that he will one day found a great city (Rome) and will father a line of glorious warriors and kings. Arenas is even given a glimpse of his regal descendants, the future Caesars of the Roman Empire. At this, Aeneas joyfully returns to the land of the living to live out his destiny.

Virgil's description of the realm of the dead features many elements found in other classic works, including Homer's *ODYSSEY* and Plato's *GORGIAS*. He lists the brutal King MINOS as the "magistrate" who "shakes the urn and calls on the assembly of the silent, to hear the lives of men and their misdeeds" in determining each shade's place in the underworld. The poet likewise alludes to the legend of THESEUS, a foolhardy mortal who storms the dark depths to restore its queen to the land of the living. His Latin background is apparent in the assigning of names. In the *Aeneid,* Hades is replaced by Pluto, the Roman equivalent of hell's ruler, and his wife Persephone is called Prosperpine.

AGAINST THE SECTS A fifth-century text titled *Against the Sects* describes an underworld oratory between Christ and SATAN. According to the story, the two debate on whether humans, inherently prone to sin and constantly offending God, should receive justice or mercy in the afterlife.

Since Satan cannot ascend to heaven, Christ journeys to hell to address the issue. Satan argues that humans should be punished severely for their transgressions, as he and the rebel angels have been punished. The demon claims it is only fair that these mortal creatures be held to the same high standards. He even quotes Scripture passages about divine retribution.

Christ refuses this assertion, claiming that humans were tempted, perhaps even tricked into sinning against the Almighty. They were outwitted by beings far superior in intelligence and understanding. Christ reminds Satan that he and the rebel angels had not been lured into sin as humans had, but were motivated by arrogance and pride. Humans, therefore, deserve divine compassion.

Against the Sects was distributed throughout Europe and became a favorite topic of lectures and sermons. It has been rewritten and embellished over the centuries and is still a popular subject for conjecture.

AGRIPPA Agrippas are sorcerer's books that contain ancient secrets, rites, and spells of the occult. The texts were named for the sixteenth-century philosopher Heinrich Cornelius Agrippa von Nettesheim, who was said to have conspired with underworld

A sorcerer summons the powers of hell with the aid of an agrippa. ART TODAY

forces as part of his dark studies. He believed that the physical body was "the chariot of the soul" and that the spirit could leave its shell and travel to other realms. Legend holds that agrippas can be used to transport spirits to and from hell and that each has the "heat and fury of Hellfire bounded within its pages."

Agrippas are huge volumes, usually more than five feet tall, with pages made of human skin. Each contains the names of all known DEMONS and lists spells for conjuring the fiends. Using the agrippa in black magic ceremonies leaves the smell of "sulfurous breath" and "smoke of hell" in the summoner's hair and clothes. The books themselves are considered living demons and must be handled very carefully to avoid provoking an angry spirit. When not in use, agrippas are wrapped in chains and suspended from beams in empty rooms to prevent the evil from escaping.

Amateurs foolish enough to dabble with the demonic texts could face horrible retribution. Each agrippa has an intimate, personal relationship with its owner and will strike out against an unauthorized user. According to age-old tales, the agrippas can cause madness, disfigurement, and even death. Stories of young apprentices being mutilated while practicing the master's art have been circulated among disciples of the occult for centuries.

When the owner of an agrippa dies, the book senses abandonment. The more powerful volumes unleash a rampage of terror in response to the death. In such cases, family members and friends of the deceased often suffer mysterious illnesses or are killed in freak accidents. (One story claims a mourning agrippa caused its dead owner's house to collapse on itself, trapping his wife and children inside. The fallen structure burst into flames before anyone could escape. When the smoke cleared, the undamaged agrippa was found amid the scorched bones and charred ruins.) The only way to control the raging abomination is to have the book exorcised—burn the unholy volume, then scatter its ashes on consecrated ground.

AHRIMAN Ahriman is the Zoroastrian equivalent of the Christian LUCIFER, the King of darkness and death. He is the despicable demon in ZOROASTRIANISM, the Middle Eastern faith that predates Islam. Ahriman rules the underworld and torments the souls of the wicked. He is frequently referred to as the "Lord of Lies" and is blamed for causing evil in the world. His twin brother is the good god Ohrmazd. The two are locked in an ongoing battle for control over the world, although it is believed that Ohrmazd will ultimately prevail.

The name of Ahriman first appears in the *Gathas*, or *Songs of Zoroaster*, dating back to the seventh-century B.C. Zoroastrianism centers on religious dualism, teaching that the created universe is the product of two equally powerful gods rather than one supreme being. According to the story, the deity Zurvan wanted a son and made sacred offerings in hopes of becoming a father. After years without a child, he begins to doubt that his prayers will ever be answered. At this instant, both Ohrmazd and Ahriman are conceived: Ohrmazd in response to Zurvan's faithfulness and Ahriman as punishment for his doubts. Zurvan decides that the firstborn child will be given rule over the earth.

Upon hearing this, Ahriman tears his way out of the womb and demands his birthright. Zurvan weeps, realizing that this child is dark and evil, while Ohrmazd is good and beautiful. Reluctantly, Zurvan agrees to keep his word—but only for nine thousand years. When that time is over, Ohrmazd will defeat his twin, and Ahriman will face ANNIHILATION. The underworld will then be emptied and Ohrmazd will rule in peace for all eternity, a destiny similar to the Christian doctrine of the LAST JUDGMENT. Until that time,

Ahriman reigns over both earth and hell, causing unceasing pain and suffering.

AL AARAAF Al Aaraaf is the LIMBO of Islamic faith, a middle ground that offers neither pleasure nor pain. It lies between JAHANNAM (hell) and Djanna (paradise) and is ruled by a beautiful and just maiden. Her task is to oversee the souls of those who can be judged neither good enough to merit heaven nor evil enough to be damned. These spirits must remain in this intermediate realm for all eternity. Inhabitants of Al Aaraaf include children who die in infancy, the insane, and the morally neutral. In Al Aaraaf, spirits suffer only the loss of heaven and the inability to see Allah, but they endure no physical pain.

ALA The Ibo of eastern Nigeria believe in Ala, the melancholy goddess of the underworld. She is the child of Mother Earth goddess Chuku. In addition to ruling the land of the dead, Ala is overseer of the harvest and of fertility. The deity combines elements of both natural and supernatural worlds as the eternal guardian of deceased spirits.

When a person dies, Ala takes the soul into her womb. The spirit feels no pain or torture but must endure a monotonous existence without the joys of earthly life. Souls in the care of Ala are lethargic, nebulous beings without the freedom and individuality they knew before death. They are similar in description to SHADES, the sullen souls of Greek myth.

ALBERIC OF SETTEFRATI A monk at the abbey of Monte Cassino during the eleventh century, Alberic of Settefrati experienced a truly nightmarish vision of hell. After succumbing to fever and illness, the monk fell into a nine-day coma from which he was not expected to recover. During this time, he claimed that he was escorted to the underworld by St. Peter and a pair of angelic guides. There he witnessed a litany of supernatural horrors.

Alberic was shown a number of torments prepared for the damned, including a river of erupting fire and an oven that burns without ceasing. St. Peter then took the terrified cleric to a valley ringed with piercingly cold ice, a thorny forest, and a lake of boiling blood. Further into the depths of hell he saw a red-hot ladder with rungs of razor-sharp teeth and a caldron of fiery pitch at its foot. An endless line of sinners is forced to climb the ladder, without falling, to prove they should not be damned. Most fail this task and plunge, screaming, into the fire.

The guides explained to Alberic that the suffering in hell corresponded to the evil of each soul's life. Those who had indulged their flesh while on earth are roasted in a pot of human excrement. The most vile sinners, including Judas Iscariot, betrayer of Jesus Christ, are imprisoned in a deep canyon that is guarded by a monstrous beast. As Alberic gaped at the spectacle, a huge vulture snatched him up and tried to drop him into the inferno, but St. Peter intervened and restored the monk to life.

Upon awakening from the coma, Alberic related this story to another monk who then transcribed it during the early 1100s. Several decades later the story was rewritten, and this second version is believed to have inspired some of the horrors in Dante's *DIVINE COMEDY: THE INFERNO.*

ALBUM COVER ART With the rise of modern rock and roll music came a new category of popular art: album cover illustrations. The typical photographs of smiling singers dressed in formal attire that had adorned the musical releases of the 1940s and 1950s were quickly replaced by eerie paintings, altered photos, and surreal collages. Like the music itself, the art of the post-Woodstock generation reflected an attitude of defiant irreverence toward traditional values. Hell quickly became a favorite inspiration.

The daring and innovative illustrations on many records became as important to browsing teens as the albums' musical content. Responding to the rebellious mood of the 1960s and 1970s, pop singers began allying themselves with the devil, showing the ultimate rejection of conformity and exhibiting a reckless, irreverent fearlessness. An increasing number of albums offered pictures of horned musicians standing amid smoldering landscapes while bloodthirsty DEMONS gleefully torture the damned. The underworld immediately grew into a sort of trademark for bands catering to morose teens who felt alienated and misunderstood by their elders. (This continues to be true especially of the HEAVY METAL MUSIC genre.)

Some artists, such as Blue Oyster Cult, Ozzy Osbourne, and Black Sabbath have used images of Satan, hell, and other occult symbols on virtually every record they produced. British bad boys Iron Maiden went one step further, creating an "undead" character named Eddie to appear on album covers and at concert performances. He is shown emerging from the underworld in various stages of decomposition, becoming more decrepit and ghastly with each progressive album. The group became further identified with Satan after releasing its 1982 album *Number of the Beast.* The cover shows thousands of souls writhing in agony silhouetted against the flames of a raging inferno. A gigantic, glowering LUCIFER stands above them, while the decrepit Eddie towers over *him.*

Fringe performers are not the only ones who use graphics of the underworld to boost sales. Many mainstream artists have also featured depictions of the damned on their covers. Top 40 soloist Meatloaf released his *Bat Out of Hell* album in 1977 with illustrations to match the record's title. The cover shows a motorcycle rogue rocketing out of a graveyard in a fiery explosion as a winged demon watches approvingly from above. In 1993, Meatloaf went *Back Into Hell.* For this follow-up, the same cyclist eludes ghouls who pursue him through a haunted city of charred ruins. The million-selling group Asia, who peaked in popularity during the 1980s, includes a toothy LEVIATHAN on its self-titled 1982 release. And a variety of other artists, from Led Zepplin to Queen, have used infernal imagery to peddle music and increase visibility.

Over the years, these diabolical images became increasingly outrageous as the popularity of infernal album art grew, eventually prompting concerned parent groups to protest that these "shock rock" albums should not be seen *or* heard. Reproductions of the most offensive illustrations were soon being passed out at religious and social gatherings along with warnings about the dire effects these demonic icons have on young minds. Many parents, who had never taken a close look at album graphics, were shocked to find depictions of hell, Satan, devils, black mass altars, human sacrifices, zombies, and other atrocities plastering the covers of their kids' favorite musical releases. But in the end, the controversy had the usual effect: Sales increased as hellbent performers received an unprecedented amount of free publicity.

The most commercially successful album to be caught up in the hellish debate was the Eagles's *Hotel California.* Its title song describes a gloomy inn where guests "can never leave." The record's cover opens to reveal a panoramic shot of the lobby of the grim hotel. It is an eerie, dark chamber crammed with slinky blonds, musclebound gents, and sweaty revelers. At the center of the photograph is a blurry figure that many believe is supposed to represent SATAN. Fans and critics alike claimed that this is the demon described in the song as "the beast" who cannot be killed. The form seems to be overseeing the debauchery at the hotel from a balcony above the crowd. Eagles lead singer Don Henley has repeatedly stated that the picture is not of a stylized DEVIL but of a young black model and that her murky appearance is just a trick of the lens. Despite this explanation, the controversy over *Hotel California*'s art persists two decades later. (The incident did, however, convince many that the attack on album cover illustrations was merely paranoia on the part of a few extremists.)

In spite of the furor (or perhaps because of it), art of the abyss remains popular. A number of performers, recognizing that selling hell can be quite profitable, have transformed the demonic scenes from their album covers into performance sequences for their live stage shows. And as technology progressed, these depictions of the underworld have leaped from record jackets to the screen in the form of MUSIC VIDEOS.

AL JASSACA Al Jassaca is the Islamic monster who will mark souls damned to hell at the LAST JUDGMENT, which will occur at the end of the world. The monstrous beast has the head of a bull, the body of a lion, and legs of a camel. Al Jassaca's mission is to separate the saved from the condemned, labeling each with a sacred seal. Those who bear the mark of damnation will be tortured physically and emotionally before ultimately facing ANNIHILATION.

ALL DOGS GO TO HEAVEN

The animated feature film *All Dogs Go to Heaven* traces the adventures of Charlie B. Barkin, a wily mutt who tries to cheat death. After being murdered by a rival pooch, Charlie finds himself in paradise but soon discovers that it is too boring and predictable for his tastes. He prefers his old life of challenges, cunning, and surprises. Charlie then outwits heaven's gatekeeper and returns to earth, ignoring the canine angel's warning that anyone who exits the Pearly Gates "can never come back."

At first, Charlie enjoys being back home. But the angel's dire words come back to him in a nightmare, where he envisions himself in Doggy Hell. The sequence includes rivers of molten lava, fiery explosions, and tiny demon dogs who tear at Charlie's flesh and fur. This canine underworld is overseen by a huge, dark fiend with piercing eyes and sharp claws called Evil Dog. He greets Charlie with a grin, claiming, "Now you are mine!"

The nightmare seems to be coming true as Charlie faces death for the second time. Evil Dog comes to claim Charlie, demanding that the twice-dead canine surrender himself. But the forces of heaven intervene and force Evil Dog back into the underworld. Charlie, who met his latest demise while helping save the life of an orphan girl, has redeemed himself. His selfless courage has saved him from spending eternity as a hound of hell.

AMBROSIO, THE MONK

Matthew Gregory Lewis penned a shocking tale of seduction, murder, and sacrilege in his Gothic novel *Ambrosio, The Monk.* The tale is loosely based on the legend of BARSISA, an Islamic monk who entered into a pact with SATAN after murdering his pregnant lover. In Lewis's account, the cleric's crimes are richly embellished and his fate more graphically described.

The story opens as Ambrosio, abbot of a Capuchian monastery in Madrid, prides himself on his exemplary life. His holiness is known and revered across Spain and even throughout Europe. Satan vows to strip Ambrosio of this virtue and sends Matilda, a DEMON disguised as a young noblewoman, to tempt him. The monk is fascinated by her seemingly pious demeanor and is soon seduced by her charms. Together the two embark upon a crime spree involving desecration of churches, vandalism, rape, and eventually murder. Ambrosio realizes, too late, that he must repent and return to a life of virtue. But by this time his crimes have been discovered by the magistrate, and he is called before the Inquisition to account for his actions.

During his trial, Ambrosio is reviled for his hypocrisy as well as his evil deeds. Since he despairs that God has abandoned him, the monk turns to

Satan for help. The DEVIL promises to deliver Ambrosio to sanctuary if the fallen cleric will renounce Christianity and pay homage to the beast. Ambrosio somberly agrees, only to be transported to a blazing desert wasteland. Ashamed and frightened, Ambrosio declares that he is ready to repent and begs for divine mercy. But upon hearing this, Satan tears the monk's body to bits and bears his soul away to hell for eternal torment.

AMITYVILLE 3: THE DEMON

Although this 1983 film was a commercial flop, *Amityville 3: The DEMON* (originally titled *Amityville 3-D* during its cinematic run) broke new ground in hell cinematography by having the horrors of the underworld leap out at the theater audience.

Amityville 3 follows the misadventures of a dour journalist (played by Tony Roberts) obsessed with discovering the truth about his supposedly haunted house. Roberts refuses to believe that "ghosts" are responsible for the odd happenings in his new home, even after a coworker researching the house's past is brutally—and mysteriously—killed. Only after his daughter (played by Lori Loughlin) drowns in a boating accident while her disembodied spirit roams the hallways does Roberts take action. He calls in a team of "paranormal" experts who soon learn that an odd cistern in the basement is actually the gate of hell. Once opened, the passage spews forth a variety of gory surprises, including foul-smelling slime, ominous locusts, and bug-eyed DEMONS.

Amityville 3-D was revised for television and aired under the title *Amityville: The Demon,* although the scenes of hell were not as impressive when viewed in two dimensions. And unlike other films exploring passages to the underworld (such as *THE GATE, THE SENTINEL, GHOST TOWN,* and *DEVIL'S RAIN*), *Amityville 3* offers no explanation of how or why this supernatural conduit exists. This lack of coherent plot, and the lackluster infernal effects, led to the film's demise both at the box office and on television.

AMMUT Ammut is the Egyptian "eater of the dead." The monster is part crocodile, part lion, and part hippopotamus. He (the sex of this god is ambiguous; in some versions Ammut is female) sits at the feet of King OSIRIS in the Hall of Justice where the recently departed must face final judgment. As the soul gives an account of its life, Ammut tries to trick and confuse it, hoping to bring about an unfavorable ruling. If the soul is judged unworthy to enjoy the splendors of the afterlife—or if it does not know the right hymns and incantations—Ammut devours it, sometimes with slow cruelty.

Spells listed in the Egyptian BOOK OF THE DEAD could be helpful in thwarting Ammut; however, only priests and pharaohs had access to this mystic writ. Inexpensive copies were eventually made available to all Egyptians, but these had no pictures and were so heavily edited that they contained very little useful information. They offered almost no protection from Ammut and other terrors of the world to come.

ANAON The people of Brittany (an area in western France and parts of Great Britain settled by the Britons around 500 B.C.) believe that unpurified souls are delivered to Anaon, the ruler of a cold realm of suffering and misery. Damnation to the kingdom of Anaon means an eternity of unrelenting physical torment. Spirits are taken to the underworld by ANKOU, "Reaper of the Dead" and servant of the cruel Anaon.

Anaon's empire is sometimes referred to as the Marsh of Hells, and it includes some parts of the earth. The heart of hell is said to be located on the Armorican peninsula. This area is surrounded by hills on three sides and by sharp sandstone formations on the fourth. Due to its ominous geology, this place is considered to be the entrance to the underworld of Anaon.

Britons believe that a condemned soul can be rescued from Anaon by performing dark rituals, especially exorcism. (This is not done for the benefit of the damned but rather to protect the living from being haunted by an unhappy ghost.) The exorcist presides over an elaborate rite, after which the exorcised spirit appears in the form of a black dog. The dog is released at Youdig ("where Hell opens its gates"), no longer capable of terrorizing the living. Such souls cannot be "saved" since they are unworthy of heaven, but exorcism releases them from the eternal punishment administered by Anaon.

ANASTASIS FRESCO One of the last examples of religious art of the Byzantine period is the *Anastasis (Resurrection) Fresco* in the Church of the Savior in Chora, Istanbul. The early fourteenth-century work shows Christ's HARROWING OF HELL, when the savior descended into the underworld to retrieve the souls of the patriarchs. The painting is located in the funerery chapel where it offers hope and comfort to mourners that their deceased loved one is in the arms of a loving savior. Although it shows hell, the *Anastasis Fresco* is a powerful affirmation of the glories of the Christian afterlife.

The fresco features the image of a Christ, robed in dazzling white and bearing a halo of shimmering gold, storming the gates of the underworld. Hell is dark and gloomy, a stark contrast to the Lord's gleaming presence. This use of color symbolizes the triumph of light over dark, good over evil, truth over lies. Christ is shown pulling Adam and Eve out of hell by the hand while John the Baptist, King David, and the rest of the patriarchs rush forward to join them. The conquered SATAN is bound with ropes at the wrists, ankles, and neck. His broken body lies under the smashed gates of the abyss at Christ's feet. He is left alone in the gloomy pit amid scores of locks, bolts, and hasps. These implements of imprisonment symbolize that the DEMON will be confined in hell until the LAST JUDGMENT, at which time he will be forced to appear before God to account for his depravity.

ANGEL HEART The 1987 film *Angel Heart* is a cinematic blend of voodoo, witchcraft, and the FAUST legend. Based on the 1978 novel *Falling Angel* by William Hjortsberg, *Angel Heart* stars Mickey Rourke as Harry Angel, a small-time private detective in 1950s New York. He is hired by Lou Cyphre (a play on the name LUCIFER; played by Robert De Niro) to track down Johnny Favorite, a famous singer who entered into a mysterious bargain with De Niro but has managed to vanish, seemingly without a trace. De Niro is determined to find Favorite and claim his due.

Rourke's search takes him through a maze of bleak and gloomy locales, from the grimy backstreets of Harlem to Louisiana's marshlands. His journey eventually brings him to the disturbing world of New Orleans voodoo ceremonies where reality and hallucination become inextricably mingled.

The film contains several scenes of bloody slaughter, which allude to the story's conclusion. Religion and violence are frequently intermixed. In an opening scene, a man commits suicide in the upstairs room of a church. Another character stores his gun next to his Bible, and it is later revealed that the Bible's interior has been hollowed out to hold a cache of bullets. A black magic altar hosts an inverted cross alongside a pair of human eyeballs. During a brawl involving Rourke, the statue of a cherub is smashed to pieces. And when De Niro comes to New Orleans to check Angel's progress, the two meet in a church to discuss the recent grisly murders associated with the search. The hymns of the choir can be heard in the background as Rourke gives De Niro the gory details.

There is also a disturbing undertone of impending doom. Throughout the movie, Rourke has recurring visions of an ominous elevator shaft in an abandoned building. He sees himself in the lift's small cage, going down, down, past innumerable floors, toward some unknown horror. De Niro teases him with hints about what might lie in that infernal cellar. He holds up a hard-boiled egg, telling Rourke that some people consider it to be the representation of the human soul. So saying, De Niro bites the egg in half and slowly grinds it between his teeth.

Rourke ultimately discovers the horrible truth about Johnny Favorite: The detective himself is actually the elusive singer who has sold his soul to the devil, believing he could outwit the fiend. The elevator shaft of his nightmares is the transport to hell. Having seen the bloody tortures that surely await him, Rourke goes quietly to the gate of damnation. *Angel Heart*'s final scene is a chilling trip to the edge of the grisly underworld, with final horrors left to the viewers' imagination.

ANGEL ON MY SHOULDER
The 1946 comedy *Angel on My Shoulder* is part of the modern cinematic revival of the classic FAUST story. In this version, Paul Muni stars as a murdered gangster who is unwilling to surrender his soul to hell. He strikes a deal with the DEVIL (played by Claude Rains):

Muni agrees to return to earth as a judge so that he can free evil criminals to prey on society. The film was cowritten by Harry Segall, author of *Here Comes Mr. Jordan,* another supernatural fantasy about negotiations in the afterlife.

Angel on My Shoulder was remade for television in 1980 with Peter Strauss in the role of the resurrected convict. Similar films about bartering human souls include *THE DEVIL AND MAX DEVLIN, HIGHWAY TO HELL, THE DEVIL AND DANIEL WEBSTER, INVITATION TO HELL,* and *HELLRAISER.* The Faust theme is also revisited in a number of theatrical productions such as *DAMN YANKEES* and in a variety of ANIMATED CARTOONS.

ANHANGA Anhanga is the DEVIL of the Amazon Indians of Brazil. According to the myth, Anhanga is a formless shape-shifter who can assume many identities to deceive and torment humans. Similar to the Norse god LOKI, Anhanga is a prankster who delights in tricking humans. He is most notorious for stealing children. The dark god is also adept at filling people's minds with horrific visions of the supernatural, including frightening images of a horrific afterlife.

ANIMATED CARTOONS
Virtually hundreds of cartoons have included images of hell, DEMONS, and the DEVIL in their drawings. Animated characters from Tom and Jerry to 2 Stupid Dogs have visited the underworld; some have even faced SATAN. Music Television's original series *Liquid Television* includes various portrayals of hell, including one sketch about a cruel baker who is damned to spend eternity baking on a cookie sheet in a huge oven. Usually, however, the excursion to the realm of the dead is a round-trip, and the cute and quirky characters return—unscathed—from the wretched inferno.

Galtar, Hanna and Barbera's medieval superhero series from the mid-1980s, includes numerous examples of demonic IMAGERY. The cartoon features scenes in both the "Cavern of Death" and "Skull Forest," infernal regions of doom. The heroic Galtar must battle a range of ghoulish creatures, including winged demons and flesh-eating dragons, as he navigates a burning landscape of fire.

The 1988 blockbuster film *BEETLEJUICE* inspired a cartoon of the same name with the movie's creative genius Tim Burton as its executive producer. The animated series is set in the "Neitherworld," a surreal realm of mildly menacing oddities and supernatural puns. Lydia, the morose teen from the film, enjoys endless adventures in this ghoulish mirror world. The *Beetlejuice* cartoon lampoons everything from Shakespeare (the sign on his front door reads "Beware of Doggerel") to the Wild West in an afterlife existence that is certainly no paradise.

Matt Groening's series *The Simpsons* uses scenes of hell in a number of episodes. One features a frightening lesson in Sunday school where the children are told that in hell the damned will have "maggots in their sheets" and that the underworld is so horrible that "if you saw it, you'd be so frightened you'd die." One rascal thinks hell sounds "cool," since it would be filled with such interesting characters as pirates and other rambunctious rogues. But young Lisa, terrified that her father will be damned for stealing cable through an illegal splitter, is horrified at this description of the underworld. After leaving Sunday school she envisions her living room transforming into a flaming lake of fire while her family members mutate into grotesque demons. A red, pitchfork-wielding Satan sits with them, inviting Lisa to come join them in watching the stolen signals.

Another episode has the local minister passing out literature to teens titled "It Isn't Cool to Fry in Hell." Homer, head of the dysfunctional Simpson family, tells his son Bart there is a doggy heaven, so there must be a doggy hell. When the boy asks who is there, Homer replies that Hitler's dog and Nixon's Checkers are now dwelling in the canine abyss.

Stephen Vincent Benét's classic short story "THE DEVIL AND DANIEL WEBSTER" is parodied in a *Simpson* Halloween special. In the cartoon adaptation, Homer sells his soul to the devil in exchange for a raspberry glazed doughnut. After gobbling up the last bite, a flaming portal to the underworld opens up in the Simpson kitchen, and Homer is seized by Satan and hurled into hell. Falling past rivers of fire, molten cliffs, and horned demons, Homer remarks that "this isn't so bad"—that is, until he is chopped into bits by a laughing GHOUL. Homer then faces the "Ironic Retribution" torture chamber, where his punishment is to have doughnuts constantly shoved into his mouth by a mechanical pastry launcher. The torture backfires, however, when Homer enjoys the never-ending stream of snacks. His long-suffering wife eventually retrieves Homer from the abyss by proving that he had promised his soul to her long ago and so it was not his to trade for a doughnut in the first place.

The 1994 *Tiny Toons Night Ghoulery* also lambastes Benét's story. In this revision, the man who regrets selling his soul hires Plucky Duck to defend him against the diabolic Mr. Scratch. Unfortunately, the fowl barrister turns out to be a charlatan more interested in collecting his fee than in clearing his client. In the end, both are sent to hell, depicted as a fiery orange canyon dotted with pitchforked demons. Unable to believe his situation, Plucky asks Mr. Scratch why he has been banished to the underworld. The devil laughs, telling him, "Sooner or later, most lawyers end up here."

The Critic, a made-for-adults series that follows the adventures of a chubby, unfulfilled New York movie reviewer, also features scenes of the underworld. In one episode, the title character places a quick phone call to Satan to ask him if he had anything to do with Marisa Tomei winning an Oscar for her role in *My Cousin Vinny.* The horned demon sits at a desk in the steaming pit chatting with his fiendish secretary. Another glimpse of the fiery abyss shows the devil warning cast members of the television show *Wings* that there is only so much he can do to keep their series on the air.

Animated sketches of hell can also be seen in major motion pictures, such as *HEAVY METAL*, the Disney classic *FANTASIA*, the 1997 release *HERCULES*, and *ALL DOGS GO TO HEAVEN*. And the eternal abyss is described in "Hellfire," a song from Disney's *The Hunchback of Notre Dame,* in a sequence rife with flames, demonic symbolism, and inferences to terrible torture.

ANKOU Ankou is the figure in Briton myth who collects spirits of the dead and brings them to hell. His name means "Reaper of the Dead," and he is the forerunner of our Grim Reaper, appearing as a skeleton draped in a black cloak and holding a scythe. Ankou can also be portrayed as a tall, impossibly thin man wearing a black undertaker's suit.

During the dark of the moon, Ankou drives a cart drawn by skeletal horses across the countryside to fetch the souls of the sick and dying. (His rig is grimly reminiscent of the corpse carts that circulated during the worst days of the medieval plagues.) At dawn, Ankou delivers his cargo to ANAON, the dour king of the underworld.

Legends vary on the details of Ankou's identity. Some believe that the last person to die during the calendar year will serve as Ankou for the following year. Others say that Ankou is the very personification of death and that his identity does not change. Disagreement also exists over exactly what Ankou does with the souls he collects. One tale holds that Ankou bears them across the seas or to the parish cemetery before judgment. But most fear that he delivers them directly to the infernal kingdom of Anaon.

According to the myth, Ankou empties his cart into a desolate pit at the Bois de Huelgoat, the entrance to hell. People can avoid being seized by Ankou by departing during the daylight hours, their spirits escaping before the reaper and his grotesque cart can arrive.

There are many folktales regarding Ankou and his dark mission. One popular English tale tells of an ironsmith who refuses to show proper respect for the Christmas Eve holiday. The smith disregards the Christmas bells and continues working well into the night. At midnight, an old man appears and asks the smith to replace a nail in his broken scythe. When the smith finishes the job, the old man reveals himself as Ankou, slays the worker, and drags his soul to Anaon to pay for his sacrilege.

ANNIHILATION Annihilation, the ultimate destruction of the damned soul in the afterlife, is a fiercely debated concept of hell. The theory of annihilation holds that the fires of the underworld are not punitive but consumptive. This means that condemned souls are cast to the underworld not for punishment but for eradication. All spirits dispatched to the inferno will eventually be burned out of existence, making the agony of damnation temporary. Annihilation is offered by many preachers as a kinder alternative to the seemingly harsh doctrine of a suffering in hell that continues for all eternity.

The theory that hell is a place of spiritual annihilation has been debated by theologians for centuries. Ancient legends about the Zoroastrian demon AHRIMAN claim that he will one day be purged out of existence. The Egyptians also believed that the soul could die a second time in the afterlife, especially if it was judged unclean. In such cases, the monster AMMUT would destroy the spirit by swallowing it whole.

Annihilation was first promoted in the Christian church by the second-century philosopher Origen, who claimed that eventually even SATAN himself would be annihilated. His teachings were condemned by Christian authorities as heresy, but the controversy continued. Defenders of his hypothesis asserted that a plausible case for annihilation could be made using quotes from Scripture and that there is no conflict between traditional Christian doctrine and annihilation. They agreed that the fires of hell may be everlasting, but souls cast into it are not.

Scholars point to specific verbiage in the Bible that refers to "consuming fire" and to the "second death," both of which have been interpreted as indicating a final eradication of the spirit. An especially powerful argument is found in a passage of Ezekiel that reads "the soul that sins shall surely die." This implies that not just the body but also the spirit of the sinner will ultimately perish. And in the New Testament, Christ himself says: "And fear not them which kill the body, but are not able to kill the soul: but rather fear him which is able to destroy both soul and body in hell" (Matt. 10:28). But this evidence seems to be contradicted by biblical descriptions of hell as a place of eternal torment and unending regret. The Gospel of St. Matthew quotes Christ as warning his followers against falling into "everlasting fire." In the letters of St. Paul, hell is repeatedly described as a realm where sinners will suffer for all time. And many Doctors of the Church (most notably SAINT AUGUSTINE) have written extensive treatises denouncing annihilation theory as incorrect and incompatible with Christ's teaching.

For many Christians, the purging of evil souls seems a viable interpretation of damnation. Belief in the annihilation of the damned has recently gained popularity among many twentieth-century Protestants who feel that eternal exile to a place of agony is in conflict with the idea of a loving, forgiving God. They find the doctrine of eternal suffering inconsistent with their idea of a compassionate Creator. A term of physical or spiritual punishment followed by ultimate extermination seems a much more merciful means of divine retribution. Critics, however, argue that this solution denies the principle of divine justice, which is also an important facet of humanity's relationship with the Supreme Being. Thus the debate continues.

ANWNN Anwnn, also called the Kingdom of Shades, is the underworld of Celtic myth. It is a series of coexisting realms containing many different life-forms. In addition to housing the souls of the damned, Anwnn includes areas belonging to the gods and to benevolent spirits. These different sectors are separated by mountain ranges, rivers, and impassable chasms. Uffern is the realm identified as hell and is associated with fear and punishment.

The Spoils of Anwnn, an old Welsh epic, describes a disastrous trip that King Arthur and his knights made to the dark hell in hopes of stealing a magic caldron. According to the poem, Anwnn is an island of "twilight underworld" riddled with gloom and despair. The expedition runs into a variety of obstacles, including an impenetrable "fortress of glass" and a series of dire warnings against continuing farther. Every step is a battle, claiming scores of soldiers. Of the three shiploads of men who had set sail with Arthur, only seven remained alive at the journey's end. Discouraged, angry, and exhausted, King Arthur and the few survivors finally abandon their quest and return home empty-handed, vowing never again to invade the Kingdom of Anwnn.

APOCALYPSE OF PAUL The Apocalypse of Paul, a fourth-century apocrypha, is a complex prosaic work about the horrors of hell. It became even more popular than the APOCALYPSE OF PETER, which had been written and circulated two centuries earlier during the first days of Christianity. This unauthenticated account was not considered credible and was therefore excluded from the Bible; however, it enjoyed great popularity among Christ's early followers. The text contained a number of elements never before suggested in relation to the netherworld, including a brief repose from suffering for the damned every year on Easter Sunday. Scholars believe that the apocrypha was heavily influenced by Virgil's *AENEID,* an epic poem about a warrior's trek to the land of the dead written in the first century A.D.

The geographic details of hell corresponded to many contemporary concepts of the underworld. The Apocalypse of Paul describes rivers of pitch, snow, and blood and pits of cold fire where DEMONS inflict torment upon the damned. In addition to the tortures of the evil spirits, condemned souls must endure gnawing by a variety of toothy demons and bloodthirsty monsters. The fiend TARTARUCHUS rules in hell until SATAN is returned to the abyss at the LAST JUDGMENT.

According to the Apocalypse of Paul, the northernmost side of hell is bounded by a deep chasm of that gives off the bitter stench of death. Within the pit, pagans and those who have rejected the words of Christ are fed upon by "the worm that sleepeth not." Their suffering is compounded by the deafening wail of constant screeching. The hideous canyon is a place of punishment for both the wicked and for heretics who attack Christian doctrine.

APOCALYPSE OF PETER The Apocalypse of Peter, an apocrypha written by an unknown author around A.D. 160, became one of the most popular second-century Christian texts despite the fact that early church leaders did not consider it worthy of inclusion in the Bible. (Most authorities believe that it was authored by believers in GNOSTIC HELL, a heretical concept that life on earth is no different from damnation.) Unable to authenticate the writ, authorities declined to proclaim the book the true word of God, and the work soon became an underground classic. It was especially popular since Christians at the time were facing fierce persecution and hatred, and the Apocalypse of Peter offered hope, validation, and even a promise of revenge against their enemies in the afterlife.

Focusing on the terrors of the LAST JUDGMENT and the punishments of hell, the Apocalypse of Peter offers a ghastly picture of a brutal underworld where each specific sin garners a corresponding punishment. Christ takes Peter to hell and shows him dark angels punishing the immoral between rivers of fire and pits of ice where "the color of the air of place is also dark." For every offense against God there is a particular torture, which is outlined in graphic detail.

The pages tell of blasphemers hanging over a pit of fire by their tongues, of disobedient children eaten by ravenous birds, and of fornicators having their flesh repeatedly torn to shreds. The "unrighteous" are drowned in a lake of fetid pitch. Murderers are feasted on by worms and insects. Women who had abortions are immersed up to the neck in a river of human feces. Those who persecuted Christians are burned alive, flogged, and gnawed by maggots. Homosexuals are repeatedly thrown off cliffs into a dark abyss. Masters of witchcraft and the "dark arts" are lashed to spinning wheels of fire. The Apocalypse's catalog of horrors continues: "And there were also others, women hanged by their hair above that mire which boiled up; and these were they that adorned themselves for adultery. . . . And in another place were gravelstones sharper than swords or any spit, heated with fire, and men and women clad in filthy rags rolled upon them in torment. And these were they that were rich and trusted in their riches. . . ." The black angel TARTARUCHUS holds rule over these souls, mocking them and delighting in their agony. When a damned spirit calls out to him for relief, he answers by increasing its suffering. The time to ask for mercy, he laughingly replies, has long since passed.

Moved to tears by the terrors he has witnessed, Peter asks Christ if it would not have been better if these pitiful sinners had never been created in the first place. Christ responds that they were made by God to enjoy paradise but instead freely chose the path of evil. Justice demands this retribution. The author intends his book serve as a warning to keep sinners from falling to this terrible place where the full weight of divine wrath will be inescapable in the "last days."

APOLLYON Apollyon, the destroyer, is the Greek name for the biblical angel who rules in hell. He is mentioned in REVELATION: "And he opened the bottomless pit; and there arose a smoke out of the pit, as the smoke of a great furnace; and the sun and the sky were darkened by reason of the smoke of the pit. . . . And they had a king over them, which is the angel of the bottomless pit . . . whose name in the Greek tongue is Apollyon" (Rev. 9:2, 11).

Apollyon is portrayed as the fierce DEMON in *THE PILGRIM'S PROGRESS* who does battle with the book's hero, Christian. Author John Bunyan describes the GHOUL as a monstrous mixture of lion's mouth, dragon wings, and fish scales. He calls Apollyon "hideous to behold," a despicable servant of evil and master of darkness.

Robert Browning's haunting poem "CHILDE ROLAND TO THE DARK TOWER CAME" also includes mention of Apollyon, a fierce and vile fiend.

ARALU The oldest known myths of the underworld are Sumerian, with records dating at least as far back as 2000 B.C. Babylonian hell is known as Aralu, the "LAND OF NO RETURN." Aralu is a hot, dusty desert realm at the base of a huge mountain. In Aralu, the damned are heaped in a mass grave and forced to eat dirt. Ancient myths refer to this place as a "domain of darkness" filled with horrific monsters and mutant beasts.

To enter the Land of No Return, a spirit must pass through seven portals, each guarded by a DEMON. ERESHKIGAL, goddess of the underworld, rules Aralu with her husband, NERGAL, and enjoys afflicting her subjects with all manner of chastisements.

ASURAS The Asuras are the fifteen deities of the JAIN religion (derived from the Hindu Asuras, DEMONS who were in constant conflict with the good gods) noted for their dark character and ominous origins. Called "antigods," the Asuras "take fiendish delight" in torturing the damned in the many hells of Jain belief. But they do not determine a soul's fate; they simply mete out punishment.

According to ancient teachings, there is no Supreme God and thus no judge who condemns spirits in the afterlife. A person's actions carry automatic consequences: Evil souls turn dark and heavy and "sink" to the underworld, while good souls rise with their beauty and light. Souls in hell have no memory of their former lives and do not know why they are being tormented. Eventually, the spirit's sins will be purged and it will be reincarnated in the never-ending cycle of transmigration. The Asuras oversee this process and make sure all evil is burned away before the spirit is incarnated in another form.

AUCASSIN AND NICOLETTE The twelfth-century drama *Aucassin and Nicolette* sketches a picture of an appealing, vibrant hell that is preferable to the monotonous, somber heaven. The plot follows the attempts of the rich nobleman Aucassin to win the hand of

Nicolette, a young maiden with "eyes gray and laughing, and a slender face . . . and lips redder than the cherry or the rose in summertime." Both families are against the union, so Aucassin considers taking Nicolette as his mistress. He is warned by an elder, however, that should he take her to his bed without the benefit of marriage, "for all the days of the world your soul will be in Hell because of it." Aucassin replies that he would rather be damned than have to spend eternity in dreary heaven: "What would I be doing in Paradise? . . . For to Paradise go only . . . the old priests, the old cripples and maimed ones . . . and those who wear old worn-out clothes and are dressed in tattered rags . . . dying of hunger and thirst and of cold and of misery. . . . But to Hell I wish indeed to go; for to Hell go the handsome clerics, the fine knights who have died in the tourneys and great wars, and the good soldiers and brave men; . . . there also go the fair and courteous ladies who have two or three lovers besides their husbands. And there go the gold and silver and miniver and gray furs. . . . With them, I wish to go."

Steadfast, Aucassin resolves to have Nicolette. The two finally overcome all obstacles and marry, "then they lived for many days, and much pleasure did they have." For "now has Aucassin his joy," for which he was willing to face eternal damnation.

AUGUSTINE, SAINT

St. Augustine of Hippo (A.D. 354–430), a bishop and doctor of the Christian church, was a brilliant writer who wrote many texts defending Christianity (and its doctrines about hell and damnation) from its critics. Among these works is CITY OF GOD, which contains elaborate descriptions of the pains of the underworld. In this book, Augustine presents hell as a place of both great physical agony and unrelenting mental torture. *City of God* asserts that the worst agony of the damned is the loss of union with God. The theories Augustine presents in this volume have greatly influenced current concepts of CHRISTIAN HELL.

Augustine drew from his own diverse experiences when formulating ideas on humanity, God, salvation, and damnation. The son of a Christian mother and pagan father, Augustine spent much of his youth involved in debauchery, drunkenness, and self-serving pursuits. He then spent almost a decade as a Manichaean. This heretical sect embraced GNOSTIC HELL, the belief that life on earth is equivalent to damnation to the underworld and that all matter is evil. Augustine converted to Christianity after finding many logical problems with Manichaeanism that could not be reconciled to his satisfaction.

After his conversion, Augustine spent several years studying and debating Christian doctrine. In addition to clarifying the church's concept of hell, he took on the subject of the LAST JUDGMENT. According to his interpretation, the human soul does not truly enter into its afterlife existence until this final adjudication, which occurs at the end of the world. He believed that human spirits are created to spend eternity celebrating the goodness of God in paradise. For this truly to occur, people must be manifest in both body and soul. Thus, not until the flesh is reunited with the spirit at the Last Judgment is one able to fulfill one's destiny.

Augustine thus believed that the soul is judged twice: once at the time of death and again at the Last Judgment. So existence in heaven (or damnation to hell) is only an interim state until the end of time. Real pleasure, or eternal pain, truly begins then. Once God renders his final decision, the damned soul's suffering in hell is commensurate with its wickedness: The more atrocities committed during life, the worse agonies it experiences in the afterlife.

The writings of St. Augustine have had a far-reaching impact. Both Martin Luther and John Calvin used his theories when forming their own Christian denominations. And his postulations continue to be studied and discussed even today. The bishop also makes an appearance in a popular song by artist Sting. The British singer's 1993 "St. Augustine in Hell" touches on several of the man's beliefs and even features a "welcome to the underworld" speech from the DEVIL.

AVICI Avici is the lowest realm of the 136 Buddhist underworlds, each one dedicated to a specific punishment for a particular offense. Avici, the grisliest BUDDHIST HELL, is reserved for the most egregious offenders, those who have rejected Buddha and his teachings. While in the underworld, souls purge their sins before being reincarnated and receiving another chance at attaining spiritual perfection. Such sentences are measured in "hell years." Every day in hell is equivalent to fifty years on earth, and banishment to one of these realms lasts a minimum of five hundred hell years. YAMA, lord of the dead and a wicked tormentor, rules Avici and metes out punishment.

One ancient Indian legend recounts how the heroic RADISH journeys to Avici to reclaim the soul of his damned mother. He does not recognize her at first because she has been turned into a dog as punishment for her offenses. But Radish convinces the gods to allow her to return to her human form if she vows to dedicate herself to performing good deeds in her next incarnation. She is freed from Avici and becomes a faithful disciple of Buddha.

B

BARDO THODOL The Bardo Thodol, or Tibetan Book of the Dead, is an ancient text that contains graphic descriptions of the terrors of the underworld. The book dates back centuries before Christ and offers details

Mask and costume of a Tibetan underworld deity. ART TODAY

about the doctrinal origins of Eastern religions. It remains one of the most grisly ancient writs concerning the horrors of damnation ever written.

According to the book, there is no supreme being who judges souls in the afterlife; iniquitous spirits sink to the underworld from the weight of their own evil. They are then forced to look into a mirror that reflects their vile deeds, and this determines their fate. Once condemned, such souls face a variety of torments. The Bardo Thodol paints a rather grim picture of what awaits the wicked at the time of death: "YAMA, The Lord of Death, will place round thy neck a rope and drag thee along; he will cut off thy head, extract thy heart, pull out thy intestines, lick up thy brains, drink thy blood, eat thy flesh, and gnaw thy bones; but thou wilt be incapable of dying. Although the body be hacked to pieces, it will revive again. The repeated hacking will cause intense pain and torture. Thy body, being a mental body, is incapable of dying even though beheaded and quartered."

The Bardo Thodol further describes eight "hot hells," eight "cold hells," eight "crushing hells," and eight "cutting hells." Damned souls can also suffer "hells of mental torture" or "hungry ghost realms," in which punishment directly suits the offense. The greedy, for example, are tortured by having insatiable appetites but very tiny mouths and impossibly long throats. When they do find food, it is difficult to eat and burns as it is consumed, intensifying the pain rather than alleviating it.

Buddhist tradition is based largely on the Bardo Thodol, which teaches that humans are constantly in flux between "excessive pain and excessive pleasure." This continues into the afterlife, at which time spirits needing to be purged of their evil must face grueling tortures that epitomize "excessive pain."

According to the Bardo Thodol, a soul can avoid damnation by properly preparing for death. This is accomplished through spiritual reflection, meditation, and living a life of virtue. The book also offers advice on easing the pains of the afterlife. One prayer, for relief of "Terrors of the Between," invokes divine assistance for freeing oneself of evil:

Now when I suffer by the power of
negative evolution
May the Archetype Deities dispel that
suffering!

Parts of the Bardo Thodol have been incorporated into later Eastern religions; however, emphasis on reincarnation has greatly diluted the impact of these frightening images.

BARK OF DANTE Eugène Delacroix drew inspiration from Dante's *DIVINE COMEDY: THE INFERNO* to create his 1822 painting *Bark of Dante.* The artist frequently based his compositions on works of Western literature, interpreting the text through his own creative medium. *Bark of Dante* is one of his most compelling accomplishments.

The work shows the poets Virgil and Dante sailing across a fetid river to the underworld city of DIS. In the background, the towers of a city in flames glow ominously, sending spirals of dark smoke into the murky sky. The two sailors try desperately to keep the frail rowboat from capsizing as bodies of the damned rise from the river and tug at the tiny craft. The condemned men are pale, muscular fiends with fierce faces and evil grins. One reaches a hand into the boat as another pauses to smash the skull of one of his damned companions. The dark spirits claw at each other, each trying to overtake the threatened ship.

Delacroix uses sharp contrasts to create a mood of danger and doom for his underworld. The living men, Virgil and Dante, are depicted as well-dressed scholars, while the damned are naked beasts. A vast river makes the small boat appear impossibly vulnerable to both the tides and the advances of the GHOULS. And the stark conflict of light and dark colors demonstrates the sharp difference between hope and despair. The overall effect is striking: Hell is the place of utter anguish, underscoring the inscription Dante offers above the gates of the underworld, "Abandon hope, all ye who enter here."

BARKER, CLIVE British author Clive Barker (1952–) has virtually built a career on transcribing his fascinating concepts of hell. His works include novels, plays, short stories, films, paintings, COMIC BOOKS, and even COMPUTER GAMES set in the underworld. Barker has also penned his own version of the FAUST story, called *The Damnation Game.* Best-selling horror writer Stephen King was so impressed with the artist's work that King dubbed Barker "the future of horror." But Barker rejects the label, telling an interviewer that he is simply "a writer who works in my imagination." The young genius cites the works of artist WILLIAM BLAKE and author C. S. Lewis *(THE SCREWTAPE LETTERS, THE GREAT DIVORCE)* among his sources of inspiration.

Barker burst onto the horror scene in the 1980s with *The Book of Blood,* a collection of ghoulish SHORT STORIES.

Author/Filmmaker Clive Barker.
PHOTO BY LANCE STAEDLER

The book includes "The Midnight Meat Train," a grisly tale describing how the dead eat human bodies delivered to them via a diabolical subway. This first foray into the realm of the damned was followed by dozens of equally gory underworld fantasies. *The Books of Blood* series currently contains six volumes.

The Inhuman Condition, another collection of short works, offers "Down, Satan," a piercing tale about a despairing millionaire who tries to gain God's attention by putting his soul in grave jeopardy. He accomplishes this by hiring a madman to create "Hell on earth"—a rambling structure of ghastly crematoriums, pools of human feces, and torture devices of every kind. His plan backfires when the ghastly palace, rather than affecting his salvation, plunges him into the depths of depravity and seals his doom.

Barker took up the subject of hell in a number of novels as well. In his *Rawhead Rex,* the author presents a DEMON imprisoned in an underworld chamber located below a field in Ireland. When a farmer disregards the warnings about plowing this forbidden ground, he accidentally breaks the seal and releases the GHOUL into the world. The flesh-eating fiend goes on a ravenous rampage until a visiting historian finds a way to send it back to hell.

Barker has also enjoyed great success in America in feature films. He wrote and directed the 1987 horror cult classic *HELLRAISER,* adapted from his novella *The Hellbound Heart.* Upon its release the film was well received by both viewers and critics and in the past decade has become an icon of supernatural cinema. (Its sequels, *Hellbound, Hell on Earth,* and *Bloodline,* however, were disappointments, perhaps because Barker left the writing and directing to others.) The underworld of the original is an innovative maze where danger lurks around every corner, inhabited by bloodthirsty creatures called Cenobites who delight in inflicting sadistic torture. *Hellraiser* offers an abyss of agony where the damned are subject to unimaginable mutilations, impalements, and disembowelments.

And though *Hellraiser* did not generate fantastic profits for its author (production costs were exorbitant), the film launched Barker's international career and earned him worldwide fame. His name became synonymous with modern metaphysical fiction. Barker quickly won the reputation of being a great contemporary philosopher, posing probing questions about life, death, and the afterlife. His works attracted the attention of philosophy scholars and horror buffs alike.

Hellraiser was followed by a number of less successful, but comparably imaginative, films. *Nightbreed,* a 1990 adaptation of Barker's novel *Cabal,* depicts a lost city of the dead called Midian that lies below the "waking world." The inhabitants of Midian are doomed souls dwelling underneath a frozen Canadian cemetery. *Candyman,* released in 1992, recounts the story of a lynched black man whose ghost is back from the underworld for revenge. Barker's 1995 *Lord of Illusions* sends a private investigator into the ominous world of the occult, only to discover that a diabolical cult leader has been mysteriously resurrected.

The prolific author's interpretations of the underworld are not limited to books and films. Several of Barker's infernal projects have been converted into other media. *Hellraiser* is available as the computer game *Virtual Hell,* patterned after the cinematic horrors of the nether region as depicted in the movie. Players are greeted by Pinhead, leader of the Cenobites, who groans "welcome to hell" before delivering them to the depths of the abyss for a variety of dark adventures. (Barker had little input in designing the format of this cyber adventure, as his energies went into creating his own underworld computer game, *Ectosphere.*)

Horror fans can also experience Barker's macabre visions in a number of comic books. The Pinhead series sends the prickly Cenobite across space and time to bring hell to unsuspecting victims everywhere. Each issue highlights a unique set of tortures ranging from decapitations to complete dismemberment. In *Razorline: Super Heroes from the Mind of Clive Barker,* readers share the adventures of dozens of supernatural victors and villains as they battle across the dimensions.

In 1992, Barker experimented with composing an infernal fable. His allegorical tale *The Thief of Always* tells of a fiend who traps children in time. "Hood's Prison" is a hell for little ones who become lost and accidentally wander into the misty realm. A demonic magic hides the house from the sight of adults and keeps the children from being rescued.

Barker has also created a nonfiction tour de force of the macabre, titled *Clive Barker's A–Z of Horror.* This demonic reference book offers information on hundreds of supernatural films and includes interviews with writers, actors, directors, and special effects crews who specialize in the genre. *A–Z* also features otherworldly FANTASY ART and other eerie oddities. And the works and words of Clive Barker are featured in *Fear in the Dark,* a 1991 British documentary on modern horror. The film includes footage from *Hellraiser* and other projects, as well as behind-the-scenes insights from Barker. When asked why he believes people have such an appetite for grisly fare, the author replies that tales of supernatural terror are actually quite reassuring. After all, he asserts, if hell exists, so too must heaven.

BARSISA Barsisa is the Islamic counterpart of FAUST, the scholar who entered into a bargain with SATAN and surrendered his soul in exchange for material gain. Like the doctor, Barsisa turns his back on his faith in order to indulge his vices. And he suffers the same ultimate fate: damnation to hell.

Barsisa's tale is recounted in various legends, most notably in the *History of the Forty Viziers*, a fifteenth-century compilation of Turkish literature. According to the legend, Barsisa is a devout monk whose piety attracts the attention of Satan. The DEVIL vows to corrupt the man and tempts him with a beautiful virgin (or, in some versions, a young princess). After several attempts, the girl succeeds in seducing him. Barsisa soon regrets his sin and returns to his life of holiness, but he panics when he discovers the girl is pregnant with his child. In a fit of desperation he murders the girl and buries her body to hide his crime. It is not long, however, before her body is found, and Barsisa's sins are revealed. The monk is sentenced to death by decapitation.

Before the execution is carried out, the devil appears to Barsisa and offers to free him on one condition: Barsisa must renounce Allah and swear eternal allegiance to Satan. Barsisa accepts this pact and utters dark blasphemies against the deity he once served. Laughing, the devil quotes the KORAN, Islam's holy book, rebuking the monk for failing to "fear Allah, the Lord of the World!" For if only Barsisa had put his faith in Allah, he would have been spared. Satan then seizes Barsisa's soul and drags him down to hell to pay for his atrocities.

The story of Barsisa was translated into Spanish by the Moors and became the basis for Matthew Gregory Lewis's phenomenally popular novel, *AMBROSIO, THE MONK*.

BARTÓK, BÉLA Hungarian composer Béla Bartók (1881–1945) is considered a master at "dark" and "spectral" music. He dedicated his career to creating spiritually unnerving musical works, which have been called "ghoulish and ghastly." Bártok was a genius at forcing infernal sounds from instruments and in chilling audiences with diabolical melodies.

Bartók wrote only one opera during his long career; however it has been dubbed a masterpiece of supernatural terror. The 1911 musical drama *Bluebeard's Castle* includes such hellish components as a torture chamber, halls drenched in blood, and maniacal devices of pain. His allegory conjures images of the sufferings of the damned while intimating that madness may not be far off, for both the subject of the opera and its author. The work uses growls, screams, and bangs to build a mood of mounting terror and mortal fear.

Bartók's ballet, *The Miraculous Mandarin,* is equally horrifying. The odd tale of prostitution, extortion, and murder features a villain who cannot be killed despite many gruesome attempts. His hunger for a young prostitute provides him with supernatural protection from death. Bartók blurs the line between the DEMON and the damned in this ghoulish composition. The music is as terrifying as the story, and the ballet caused quite a controversy when it premiered in 1918.

The composer's music has also been used in contemporary tales of horror. Bartók's works are featured in the horror film *The Shining* to underscore the movie's visual atrocities. His compositions continue to be regarded as among the most successful attempts at bringing spiritual fear and terror into the soul through music.

BAUDELAIRE, CHARLES Poet Charles Baudelaire (1821–1867) explored the duality of human nature through his numerous works concerning the human connection to the supernatural. Baudelaire firmly believed in the DEVIL, although it is unclear as to whether he was a Satanist. His religious beliefs fluctuated wildly, prompting many to decry him as evil and dismiss his work as immoral propaganda. Others asserted that his seemingly diabolical poems, such as "Litanies to *SATAN*," were written as irony and prove his disgust with the forces of the underworld.

Baudelaire's most controversial book was *The Flowers of Evil,* published in 1857. This collection of poems (several of which were censored from early editions) has been called the beginning of the modernism movement in literature. The work was heavily criticized as scandalous, and Baudelaire was convicted for offenses against the public morals after the book's publication. (The conviction was posthumously overturned in 1947, years after the writer's death.)

In *The Flowers of Evil* as well as in his other works, Baudelaire expresses his restlessness and hunger for death, though he considered his own damnation imminent. Bored with life, he believed that even hell would be an improvement over his monotonous existence on earth. In one poem, "Hymn to Beauty," the writer begs for comforting visions whatever their origin. The work cries out for fellowship from SATAN's "dark gulf" or God's celestial home in the "stars"; it makes no difference to the tormented author. A similar sentiment is echoed in "Sad Madrigal," in which Baudelaire writes that anyone whose dreams have not "been reflections of Hell" is simply a lost prisoner of "irresistible Despair."

Baudelaire seemingly surrenders himself to the powers of the abyss in several compositions praising "Great LUCIFER." "The Irreparable" describes a great memory in which he sees "a fairy light up in the skies of Hell, a dawn miraculous." The poem repeatedly asks, "Beloved Sorceress, love you the damned?" An introductory passage to a collection of works claims, "The devil holds our strings in Puppetry." And in "Possessed," the poet states that there is "not a fibre" in his tormented being that does not cry out to the Lord of Hell, *"Satan, I worship thee!"*

These glorifications of hell and of its rulers seem to attest to Baudelaire's diabolical beliefs. Some scholars, however, maintain that the poet is simply using such flamboyance to express his style, not his personal beliefs. Supporters cite his many traditional compositions, including a touching tribute to the VIRGIN MARY, the mother of Jesus Christ, who is reputed to have power over hell, as evidence of his true faith.

BEDAZZLED Comedians Dudley Moore and Peter Cook share writing as well as acting credits in this comedic update of the FAUST story. In the 1967 *Bedazzled,* Moore is an awkward short-order cook who longs to win the affections of his restaurant's beautiful waitress. Despairing that she will never be his, Moore tries to commit suicide by hanging himself. Instead, he manages to conjure Mr. Spiggott, a debonair DEVIL, played by Cook, who offers to grant seven wishes in exchange for Moore's soul.

But the bumbling Moore keeps stumbling into foolish predicaments, wasting his opportunities and his wishes. He finds himself becoming a trampoline-bouncing nun, a hapless ladies' man, and even the proverbial "fly on the wall." To summon Cook for diabolical assistance, Moore must shout the magic words "Julie Andrews!" Needless to say, Bedazzled offers a MERRY HELL where the worst torment the damned suffer is having to wear atrocious fashion ensembles. Similar theatrical treatments of deals with SATAN as comic foils include *DAMN YANKEES* and *THE DEVIL AND MAX DEVLIN.*

BEDE The Venerable Bede (Baeda, Beda, Bebe) (673–735) was an Anglo-Saxon theologian, writer, and historian who broke new ground in VISION LITERATURE with his *Historia Ecclesiastica Gentis Anglorum* (Ecclesiastical History of the English Nation) in 731. The text (which scholars call "the beginning of English literature") includes several apparitions of hell adapted from a variety of sources. Bede collected these stories from old records or mutual acquaintances, embellished them considerably, then compiled them in his *History.* The book quickly became the topic of debate and conjecture among clerics and a valuable reference for world historians.

The first vision of the inferno described in *History* is that of an Irish monk named FURSEUS. The cleric claimed to have had many supernatural apparitions, ranging from visits with angels to horrible trips to the burning underworld. In his vision of hell (which occurred around 630), Furseus witnesses the tortures of the damned. He sees a great chasm, a horde of cruel DEMONS, and a sea of spirits enveloped in flames being tortured by vicious fiends. An angel protects Furseus from being harmed by these GHOULS. However, the charred soul of a man Furseus had known in life hurls himself into the monk's face, leaving a black scar. Bede reports that the dreadful experience haunted Furseus for the rest of his life.

Another vision of the afterlife recounted by Bede regards a landowner named DRITHELM who "dies" and is taken to a great abyss. The farmer sees a valley of suffering souls and an ocean where damned spirits roll in and out on black waves, screeching in hysterics. Demons try to seize Drithelm, but his angelic guide protects him from their bloodlust. After being revived, Drithelm sells all his property and joins a local monastery where he spends the rest of his life in meditation and prayer.

Bede's *History* greatly contributed to both the popularity and the credibility of vision literature. The writer had a gift for stylish, compelling prose, which made his text especially appealing to a vast audience. Since he claimed to have based his accounts on the reports of people who knew Furseus and Drithelm, readers were willing to accept the tales as authentic. Clerics quickly adapted these eyewitness accounts of hell into their sermons, offering them as unimpeachable proof of the horrors of the underworld. Bede's work also earned him a reputation as a prominent historian, as he is credited with devising the system for dating events from the birth of Christ.

BEETLEJUICE One of the most innovative movies about the land of the dead is surrealist Tim Burton's 1988 comedy smash *Beetlejuice*. The view of the afterlife presented in this film is unlike anything Hollywood had ever produced. *Beetlejuice* depicts a confusing and somewhat disjointed netherworld in which the dead can, and do, interact with the living and in which damnation and salvation are inextricably linked to these interrealm relationships.

Geena Davis and Alec Baldwin star as a young couple killed in a car accident. After realizing that they are indeed deceased, the two make another unpleasant discovery: They must share their home with its new owners. The traditional New Englanders are disgusted by the repulsive socialite, her pantywaist husband, and his morbid teenage daughter who now inhabit their house. Finding the new arrangements intolerable, the dead couple seeks help from a netherworld "case worker" assigned to help them make the supernatural transition. This entails spending interminable hours in the "Afterlife Waiting Room" where the two encounter a variety of oddities and GHOULS.

In the celestial holding cell, Baldwin and Davis see a hit-and-run victim who glides through the afterlife as flattened "road kill" with a tire track running down his middle. The charred corpse of a man who fell asleep while smoking still puffs away. And a green-faced ex–beauty queen shows the couple her slit writs, commenting that "death is a personal thing," which is different for each individual. But after meeting with their "afterlife case worker," the two are simply sent back to the house with instructions to solve the problem themselves.

Condemned to remain with the obnoxious new residents, Baldwin and

Davis decide to try HAUNTING the newcomers away. The two discover that they have unsettling new powers that allow them to mutate into frightening monsters. They proceed to put on a flamboyant display of their supernatural abilities. But their plan backfires when the tacky new tenants are delighted to be living in a haunted house and begin inviting their garish friends over to witness the apparitions.

With nowhere else to turn, the duo hires the offensive yet intriguing ghoul Beetleguese, played by Michael Keaton, to get rid of the unwanted persons. He summons all the powers of hell to terrorize the superficial New Yorkers. But they fight back, staging an exorcism that turns Davis and Baldwin into shriveled, crumbling corpses.

In addition to innovative concepts of the not-so-great beyond, *Beetlejuice* contains scenes reminiscent of traditional hell. For the deceased couple, everything outside the house is an endless desert of terrors. The afterlife exterior, a barren wasteland of vile fiends and vicious torments, is a familiar component of infernal visions. When Davis runs out the front door, she finds herself the prey of gigantic Sand Worms that wait to devour wandering spirits, similar to the Hebrew sea serpent LEVIATHAN. And even the title character himself eventually faces retribution for his trickery, another common element of afterlife speculation.

The wildly successful movie spawned a COMPUTER GAME, and ANIMATED CARTOON series, and a wealth of MOVIE MERCHANDISING trinkets and toys.

BELIAL Belial, a name meaning "worthless," is a DEVIL named in both the Hebrew Old Testament and the Christian New Testament. Debate exists among religious scholars on whether Belial is another name for SATAN or if he is in fact a separate DEMON, one of the angels who joined in the rebellion against God. But all agree he is a lord of hell, firmly committed to evil and to the frustration of God's will.

The patriarch Samuel refers to charlatans and rogues as "men of Belial," indicating that they are allied with the forces of hell. St. Paul, in his letters to the Corinthians, uses Belial as a contrast to Christ, saying that the two are as different as darkness is from light. Belial is also named in the DEAD SEA SCROLLS, called an "angel of destruction" whose "dominion is darkness."

In the 1463 *Das Buch Belial* (Book of Belial), the fiend serves as the attorney for the underworld. He brings a case against Jesus for meddling in the affairs of the world through his incarnation. According to Belial, the demon holds dominion over the underworld *and* over the earth. This makes Jesus' redemption of humanity and HARROWING OF HELL unfair offenses against him. The wise King Solomon serves as judge and renders a verdict exonerating Jesus. Belial presses the suit and is eventually assured that after the LAST

JUDGMENT he will be given exclusive powers over the damned in hell. Illustrations from the fifteenth-century manuscript show the underworld as a gaping HELLMOUTH from which demons and flames spew forth.

The fiend Belial also appears in Milton's *PARADISE LOST,* as an indulgent GHOUL who delights in "vice for its own sake," and in Joost van den Vondel's drama *LUCIFER* as a leader of the rebel angels in the war on heaven.

BEYOND, THE The 1981 film *The Beyond* explores what happens when the portal to the underworld is accidentally opened. The movie puts the gateway to hell in a decrepit Southern mansion that has been converted into a hotel. It is a dank, smoky passage of flickering flames and murky steam. Once disturbed, spirits of the damned slip back among the living to spread their evil, pausing only to feast on the hotel's unsuspecting guests. Desperate to end the grisly practice, the inn's proprietor must force the GHOULS back into the underworld and seal the passage forever.

Speculation on a passageway between earth and the underworld dates back to ancient myths and religions. The Greeks believed that they could reach the place of the dead through LAKE AVERNUS; medieval Christians placed this portal at the CAVE OF CRUACHAN in Ireland. During the Middle Ages, locating this mysterious gateway became a fascination of many adventurists, similar to the quest for the Holy Grail. This search still captivates the collective imagination, as is evident in the many films about this mystic portal. Others include *AMITYVILLE 3-D, THE DEVIL'S RAIN, THE GATE, THE SENTINEL, HIGHWAY TO HELL,* and *THE DEVIL'S DAUGHTER.*

BIKERS In their ongoing attempt to prove their unflinching fear while simultaneously flouting traditional social standards, motorcycle gangs have adopted hell as their home base. Biker attire is heavily adorned with smoking landscapes, horned fiends are among the favorite TATTOOS, and the cycles themselves often sport airbrushed illustrations of grinning DEMONS being licked by flames. A visit to any reputable Harley-Davidson dealership reveals racks of hell-stamped merchandise peddled by staffers covered in demonic "body art."

The biker lifestyle is inherently hard on the body; intimacy with the damned makes it equally dangerous to the soul. The embrace of eternal evil serves to reinforce both the disdain for the conventional and the aura of fearlessness. Not surprisingly, the most notorious gang in America is the Hell's Angels, founded in 1950 by a group of riders in San Bernardino, California. Allegiance to the underworld is not a despicable prospect but rather the ultimate badge of rebellion against society.

Bikers have never been embraced by mainstream America, but they became truly infamous after the ill-fated Rolling Stones concert at Altamont in 1969. Despite warnings against such an imprudent move, the group used members of the Hell's Angels—paid with alcohol—as security guards and crowd control for the show. The event ended in disaster when the bikers' use of brute force against audience members resulted in dozens of injuries and one fatality. A young fan, Meredith Hunter, was stabbed to death while trying to climb on stage as Mick Jagger crooned "Sympathy for the Devil." This grim incident later inspired singer Don McLean to condemn the episode in his hit "American Pie." Lyrics refer to the California concert, declaring that "no angel born in Hell could break that Satan spell" and that he "saw Satan laughing with delight" at the spectacle.

The debacle at Altamont was captured on film and later included in *Gimme Shelter,* a promotional film for Rolling Stones albums. For millions of shocked viewers, this was their first exposure to biker gangs. The groups were immediately condemned as evil, even diabolical, a label that endures.

BILE Bile is the ancient Celtic lord of the dead. He is evil and vicious, requiring human sacrifices to appease his violent nature. The kingdom of Bile is a vast wasteland of crushed spirits and broken bodies who must pay the deity eternal homage.

BILL & TED'S BOGUS JOURNEY The 1991 comedy hit *Bill & Ted's Bogus Journey* made damnation to hell seem downright laughable. The film features the dense but lovable duo from *Bill & Ted's Excellent Adventure* (played by Alex Winter and Keanu Reeves) in a bizarre romp through the afterlife. *Bogus Journey* sends the high school buddies who changed history with their HEAVY METAL MUSIC to the DEVIL, where they must face their own personal adolescent hell. On their supernatural quest, the two meet the Grim Reaper, SATAN, and even the Supreme Being.

Winter and Reeves begin their underworld travels after evil robots sent from the future kill the hapless lads. The pair tries to contact the living through an amateur New Age medium to explain what has happened. But she panics, believing them to be evil spirits, and performs an exorcism that sends them both to hell.

After a lengthy fall through a dark chasm, Winter and Reeves land in the abyss. Surprised by the appearance of the fiery orange pit, the two comment that they were "totally lied to by our album covers" about what hell looks like. They are greeted by an enormous Satan, who tries to send them into a flaming HELLMOUTH. But the two escape the burning portal and find themselves in a metallic maze of endless corridors and confrontational phatasms. Here they find that the punishments of the inferno are specific to each individual.

The devil shouts "choose your eternity!" then uses ugly images from their own memories to torment the boys. Winter is pursued by Granny Preston, a hideous, wart-covered hag who wants a kiss from her terrified grandson. Meanwhile, Reeves is stalked by a killer Easter Bunny who wants vengeance against the teen for stealing his little brother's basket of goodies years ago. And both are terrorized by the commandant of an Alaskan military school who sees the pair as new recruits in need of massive training. "Drop and give me infinity!" he tells the boys, who immediately begin doing push-ups at his command.

Luckily, however, their damnation is not permanent. Winter and Reeves are given the opportunity to challenge the Grim Reaper (played by William Sadler) to a test of skills, with the promise of release if they win. Should they lose, the two must remain in hell forever. But when the duo defeats Sadler at the board game Battleship, he angrily demands that they go "two out of three!" This contest is followed by a round of Clue, a Twister match, and finally a bout of mechanical football, all of which are won by the dead teens. The Grim Reaper reluctantly agrees to take the pair to heaven to seek advice on how to return to life on earth. As they leave hell, Winter quips, "Don't fear the Reaper!" a homage to a HEAVY METAL MUSIC classic by Blue Oyster Cult.

BLACK HOLE, THE Disney's first PG-rated film, *The Black Hole* is a science fiction adventure about an out-of-control explorer obsessed with probing the mysteries of deep space. This 1979 project stars Maximilian Schell as the demented scientist whose obsession eventually takes him to the depths of hell.

Marooned at the edge of the cosmic oddity, Schell commandeers the ship of a passing space patrol to continue his expedition. Despite the inherent danger of entering the unexplored entity, Schell pilots the stolen craft directly into the heart of the black hole, hoping finally to unravel this seemingly impenetrable secret of space. What he finds instead is his own dark destiny. Schell dies before the ship enters the hole, but his captive crew watches as the craft tours a harsh, rocky, flaming landscape reminiscent of the Greek underworld of HADES.

Within the black hole, lost spirits wander the vast chasms, bounded by a river similar to the STYX. Valleys of fire erupt into smoky chaos. Before being catapulted back out of the black hole, the crew sees the recently deceased Schell's eyes starring out from the metallic body of his maniacal robot. The ruthless villain has been transformed into a high-tech DEVIL, damned to spend eternity in the bubbling abyss.

BLACK ROSES The 1988 film *Black Roses* clumsily explores the connection between hell and HEAVY METAL MUSIC. Set in the quiet village of Mill Basin, *Black Roses* offers a sinister rock band whose lead singer is actually SATAN in disguise. The group supposedly comes to town to put on a series of concerts, but it is actually opening a portal to the underworld and bringing up toothy DEMONS to attack and devour critical parents.

One of the movie's songs describes the band's "hometown" as a place "way down deep" where an unquenchable "fire is burning." Another ditty offers a musical invitation to "tear down the walls of hell" and kill family members, which the teens do with much glee. As the passage between the underworld and middle America widens, the young metal fans transform into fearsome GHOULS with a taste for human flesh. Satan himself eventually reveals his true form, looking suspiciously like a scaled-down Godzilla with a few extra teeth. But Satan's plan to use Mill Basin as a "test case" before taking over the earth in the name of hell is finally thwarted by a sensitive English teacher who saves the kids from falling into the abyss.

Though *Black Roses* is hampered with inane dialogue, ridiculous plot twists, and shabby special effects, it does illustrate the popular belief that Heavy Metal is the music of hell. The rebellion of teens against their parents' ideals is juxtaposed against the fall of the rebel angels, and both groups ultimately face dire consequences for their actions. A similar theory is developed in *TRICK OR TREAT,* an earlier depiction of the link between Satan and "his music."

BLAKE, WILLIAM Artist, poet, and philosopher William Blake (1757–1827) dedicated decades of creative energies to interpreting his concept of the supernatural, including many vivid illustrations of hell. Blake claimed to be both a Christian and a polytheist, believing in a number of powerful gods or "Zoas." He was a follower of EMANUEL SWEDENBORG and mentions the philosopher's teachings in many of his own works, although he eventually transcended and abandoned many of Swedenborg's doctrines. Blake drew upon his free-form ideas on religion and philosophy and his own visions of the supernatural as inspiration for a host of poems, paintings, and theories.

Blake detested reason and cherished imagination and creativity. He claimed to have seen a "tree filled with angels" at age eight and wrote that such mystic apparitions continued throughout his life, giving him a unique perspective on the mysteries of the hidden world. To Blake, hell is of a realm of specters, souls who are spiritually dead through their lack of creativity.

Blake uses ambiguous terms to define good and evil, each being related to artistic expression rather than morality. Creativity is good; obstruction of the creative force is evil. Using this philosophy, Blake identifies the traditionally worshiped God as evil, since he is too controlling and interferes with human passions. He paid a great compliment to fellow writer John Milton (author of *PARADISE LOST*), claiming that Milton could better describe hell and DEMONS than he could God and angels because Milton "was a true Poet and of the Devil's party without knowing it."

Blake's works refer to "Jesus the Imagination" and "SATAN the selfhood," asserting that true salvation rests in eternal creativity, while damnation is fruitless indulgence. He calls Satan's realm the "Kingdom of Nothing," which contains no originality, no beauty, no artistic energy. In his 1794 *Book of Urizen,* the creation of religion itself stems from the failure of the human imagination. Evil is a result of there being too many rules to follow. And the soul is threatened in eternity by the crushing lack of artistic sense:

Lo, a shadow of horror is risen
In Eternity! Unknown, unprolific,
self-closed, all repelling: what Demon
Hath formed this abominable void,
This soul-shuddering vacuum?

Blake's *Last Judgment,* 1808, depicts the damned being cast into everlasting torment.
NATIONAL TRUST/ART RESOURCE, N.Y.

Blake offers his most extensive interpretations of the Christian afterlife in *The Marriage of Heaven and Hell.* The work offers a description of Jesus as impulsive and energetic, brimming with creativity. This, Blake asserts, is the true savior: a man of passion and fire, not the tedious "law giver" preached by contemporary reverends.

In *Marriage,* angels are "vain" and preoccupied with their own wisdom. One angel shows Blake the "infinite abyss" of fire and smoke that is intended for the author upon his death. The beautiful spirit warns that unless he reforms, Blake faces an eternity of agony "between black and white spiders." The artist laughs at this, telling the angel that damnation and salvation are simply a matter of perspective and that he does not fear eternal anguish. Another angel renounces God and becomes a "great friend" of Blake's. The two "read the Bible together in its infernal or diabolic sense." They also share enjoyment of what Blake fleetingly refers to as the "Bible of Hell."

Based in part on Swedenborg's models of heaven and hell, Blake's *Marriage* describes hell as a place of passionate inspiration and boundless creativity. The work denies that people ultimately choose good or evil, insisting instead that there are only good and evil "states." These are permanent, and humanity passes through them on the journey of life but is itself morally neutral. (This assertion inspired C. S. Lewis's *THE GREAT DIVORCE,* which soundly rejects this concept of the afterlife.) Blake offers details of his "visits" to hell, which he describes as a realm filled with horrors that would undo a "conventional mind." But Blake is unharmed and in fact relishes this underworld tour: ". . . I was walking among the fires of Hell, delighted with the enjoyments of Genius, which to angels look like torment and insanity."

In "Proverbs of Hell," Blake provides "infernal wisdom" derived from the lower depths. One decries prudence as "a rich, ugly, old maid." Another advises that "the road of excess leads to the palace of wisdom." To the author, the greatest sin is to resist or ignore the impulses of one's own heart. Blake condemns inaction as hateful, saying he should "sooner murder an infant in its cradle than nurse unacted desires." This inertia, he claims, is true damnation.

In *Milton,* Blake offers a Satan who is rebuked for his self-righteousness but praised for asserting himself against God. This work, and many others, incorporates images of the LAST JUDGMENT. To Blake, this is not a time for punishment or reward but rather an eradication of all error that previously existed in the universe. His theories and interpretations of heaven and hell as states of selfhood greatly inspired the poet WILLIAM BUTLER YEATS, who penned a number of works reflecting Blake's ideas.

In addition to being a prolific writer, Blake created many intriguing paintings with religious, mythic, and literary themes. He began working as an artist while apprenticed to an engraver who specialized in etching Gothic tombstones, using his visions as inspiration. Blake's paintings include many representations of the damned, such as *Satan Arousing the Rebel Angels* (an illustration from Milton's *PARADISE LOST*), *Valley of Dry Bones,* and *Satan Before the Throne of God.* He also illustrated Dante's *DIVINE COMEDY: THE INFERNO* with a number of haunting portraits patterned after the horrors described in the underworld classic.

Biblical themes, too, served as inspiration for many of Blake's artistic creations. His *Death on a Pale Horse* is a haunting depiction of the end of the world drawn from REVELATION. Blake's *Last Judgment,* an incredibly complex illumination of humanity's final accounting, is the most recent depiction of this cataclysmic event to be painted by a major artist.

BOBBY GOULD IN HELL

Playwright David Mamet presents a trip to the infernal regions as the means of redeeming a hellbound cad in *Bobby Gould in Hell.* The one-act play features the boorish and brooding Gould, an insensitive rouge, who is called to the underworld to answer for his sins; most recently exploiting then deserting women who trust him. The DEVIL accuses Gould of being "cruel without being interesting" and of deluding himself into believing that his actions are actually morally beneficial. Gould's defense is that people sin because "we want God to notice us."

Unable to explain away his selfishness, Gould tries to shift blame to his most recent lover, claiming that the woman is unbearable and he could no longer stand her company. The devil brings her to hell to "testify" and does indeed find her rather unpleasant. But this does not justify Gould's betrayal, nor does it answer the devil's question: Why does Gould (representing humanity) waste so much energy making excuses for his evil behavior rather than channeling that energy into improving himself? It takes more effort to be damned than to be salvaged, yet this is the path so often chosen.

The infernal atmosphere for *Bobby Gould in Hell* is created through a variety of sights and sounds, including a ring of flames and the sound of DEMONS howling in the distance. Hell's gatekeeper spews insulting ethnic jokes over the roar of distant explosions. And whenever Gould tries to escape hell, he is met by a burst of smoke that forces him to retreat. But the real ugliness of the abyss, in the final analysis, is the despicable attitude of the damned.

An illustration of hell from the *Book of Hours of Catherine of Cleves*. THE PIERPONT MORGAN LIBRARY/ART RESOURCE, N.Y.

BOOK OF HOURS During the Middle Ages, Christians trying to keep up with their religious duties began commissioning books of hours. These are programs that schedule specific rites to be performed each day by the faithful. The book is usually named for its patron. (Since early editions had to be printed and illustrated entirely by hand, almost all were commissioned by royalty or wealthy nobles.) A typical book of hours contains a calendar of saints' feast days, prayers and meditations, and illustrations of religious themes.

These illuminated manuscripts routinely feature pictures of hell, SATAN, and DEMONS. The *Hours of Catherine of Cleves*, created during the mid-1400s, offers several grisly portraits of the damned. One drawing shows three weeping sinners languishing in a fiery HELLMOUTH. Another offers a bleak astral fortress where the damned are reduced to bloody skeletons. Similar graphics (and warnings against heresy, lechery, and other immoral behavior) are found in the *Rohan Book of Hours*, commissioned around the same time.

A volume composed for the Duke of Berry, *LES TRÈS RICHES HEURES DU DUC DE BERRY*, includes one of the most gruesome depictions of hell ever conceived. It shows a blue-gray Satan belching up the souls of devoured sinners while grotesque demons stab, strangle, and beat the damned.

The depictions of a horrific hell and the ever-present threat of damnation were instrumental in emphasizing the importance of obeying moral codes, and such vivid images went a long way in encouraging Christians to keep to the strict schedule. Illustrations of the terrors of the underworld also fed the morbid curiosity of readers hungry for a taste of the inferno. These books of hours, referred to every day, served as constant reminders to their owners that eternal damnation was an ever-present danger that must be guarded against through prayer, penance, and sacrifice. They remained popular for centuries and even became showcases for brilliant craftsmanship and artistic imagination.

BOOK OF THE DEAD The Egyptian Book of the Dead dates back to approximately 1600 B.C., when Egyptians began placing scrolls of text beside entombed bodies. The Book lists the horrors that await spirits unprepared for the afterlife and offers methods for avoiding and overcoming these dangers.

The ancient Egyptians were the first to believe that souls would be judged after death, and no culture was more obsessed with the question of immortality. Their complex mythology turns the afterlife into the ultimate private club, a place where one has to know a whole series of secret passwords and complicated rituals to negotiate an intricate supernatural maze. The great beyond is fraught with dangers, and souls who lose their way face numerous terrors. Directions for escaping these horrors became so involved that they eventually had to be transcribed in manuscript form, and the text became known as the Egyptian Book of the Dead.

The Book of the Dead lists a variety of catastrophes that await spirits in the afterlife, including lakes of flame, harsh deserts, and the ravenous Four Crocodiles of the West. Even if the soul follows every rule for eluding these terrors, it can still run into problems. Souls of those who have not been buried properly can suffer unbearable hunger. Spirits can also be attacked by snakes, locusts, or monstrous DEMONS. They can even die a second death. (One reference in the Book of the Dead says that the wicked are tortured in pits of fire in the afterlife; however, most Egyptians generally believe that truly evil souls eventually face ANNIHILATION.)

According to the myth, when a person dies, the soul travels in the boat of Ra (the sun god) along the river of the sky with scores of other newly dead toward DUAT, the Valley in the Sky. It must then pass through seven gates, but passage is granted only if the spirit knows all seven gatekeepers by name. He or she must also be able to tell which paths are safe and which hold hidden dangers.

If the departed makes it past the tangle of perilous roads, a dog-headed deity named Anubis delivers the spirit to the Hall of Justice. Anubis, called by Latin poet Apuleius the "messenger between Heaven and Hell," helps the soul find its way into the king's court. Here, King OSIRIS asks the soul for a

A chart from the Book of the Dead shows souls in the underworld. ART TODAY

complete account of both its good and bad acts. He then weighs the deceased's heart against the "feather of truth" to validate the soul's account. The scales tip toward good or evil, at which time Osiris renders final judgment.

During the judgment, a hideous monster named AMMUT sits at Osiris's feet and tries to distract and confuse the soul to negatively affect the outcome. In order to survive this test, the spirit must also recite a specific series of invocations, prayers, and magic words to appease Osiris. If it fails at any of these tasks, or if Osiris renders an unfavorable verdict, then Ammut savagely devours the soul. (This image is associated with the HELLMOUTH in later art and literature.) An illustration from a copy of the Book of the Dead dating from around 1310 B.C. titled *The Last Judgment Before Osiris* shows Ammut drooling hungrily as Osiris places a dead man's heart on the mystical scales, anxious to consume the unfortunate spirit.

With so much to remember, Egyptians began burying scrolls of instructions with their deceased loved ones. These texts, at first called Chapters Coming Forth by Day, were eventually compiled under the title Book of the Dead. The Book also lists ideas on human nature and destiny, magic spells, funeral rites, and incantations. Unfortunately, only priests and pharaohs were considered worthy of such information, so the common folk were condemned to wander the afterlife without the benefit of instruction. Eventually, cheap copies were made available to the peasantry, but these no-frills editions contained only the bare essentials and had no maps nor illustrations. The best a commoner could hope for in the next world was to serve as a slave to pharaoh, where at least it would be protected from further supernatural horrors.

BOSCH, HIERONYMUS

Flemish painter Hieronymus Bosch (born Jerom van Aeken) (1450–1516) spent his entire artistic career interpreting hell and depicting supernatural agonies. He gained a reputation during the fifteenth and sixteenth centuries as a visionary obsessed with showing humanity's fallen nature and tendency to sin and the morbid tortures of the underworld.

Bosch grew up in an isolated village that was behind the times, still lingering in the throes of the Middle Ages. His works reflect this, using images drawn from medieval legends, alchemy, sorcery, and rudimentary religion. Bosch was a member of the Brotherhood of Our Lady, a religious society dedicated to decorating churches and presenting MORALITY PLAYS. The painter certainly participated in these endeavors, perhaps even designing sets and costumes for the church dramas. This involvement with traditional ceremonies and stories is apparent in his paintings.

Bosch was an innovator who broke with tradition by illustrating the dark side of people and their sinful nature rather than depicting their beauty and hope of salvation. Previous artisans usually focused their religious works on the splendor of Christ, the VIRGIN MARY, and the virtuous saints. Their depictions of the afterlife featured rosy scenes of souls rejoicing in heaven, with less emphasis placed on the torments of hell. Bosch took the opposite tack, showing the fall in the Garden of Eden, the tendency to give in to carnal pleasures, and the horrors of the underworld. Most of Bosch's works offer representations of evil, its triumph in the world and the ultimate punishments awaiting sinners in hell.

The artist often shows a progression from innocence to sin to damnation, using separate panels to depict each concept. In *Hay Wain,* Bosch leads a ghoulish cart through a throng of murderers, adulterers, and thieves into hell where the spirits of the damned are dumped into the inferno. His *GARDEN OF EARTHLY DELIGHTS,* also presented in three stages, offers a bleak depiction of hell alongside the luscious Eden, creating a stark visual as well as moral contrast.

This detail from the *Garden of Earthly Delights* shows a surreal hell. ART TODAY

A black mass in honor of SATAN appears in his *Temptation of Saint Anthony,* a visual interpretation of the saint's legendary confrontations with the DEVIL. Years later, Bosch created a softened version of this same topic, this time presenting a much more serene scene of St. Anthony's problems with the forces of evil. His *Death of a Miser* offers an ambiguous account of the afterlife, showing both angels and DEMONS vying for the dead man's soul.

All of Bosch's works portraying hell include graphic and imaginative images unlike anything the European art world had ever seen. His compositions show the damned being mauled by demons, vomited on, eaten by bird-headed monsters, and defecated in the stool of beasts. He envisioned a nightmarish realm of mutant animals and grisly demons cavorting in mind-boggling chaos. Bosch mixed traditional depictions of fiends administering physical torture with surreal images of huge, fire-breathing giantesses, rat-faced winged ghouls, and robotlike metallic creatures raping the damned. His unusual use of color also set Bosch's works apart from those of similar themes. Bosch typically set bright, vivid images against black, murky backgrounds. The splashes of jewel tones among dark smudges create a powerful statement about the battle between good and evil.

During his lifetime, Bosch's original works were lauded as masterpieces of the macabre and could be found in the finest homes and palaces of Spain, Austria, and the Netherlands. The artist also painted several altarpieces for Saint John's Cathedral in the village of Hertogenbosch (the town from which he derives his name). All of these have since been lost or destroyed. Among his greatest surviving accomplishments is a LAST JUDGMENT altarpiece commissioned by the Spanish royal family in the early 1500s.

Bosch gained newfound popularity in the twentieth century as the surrealist style emerged. His works, painted centuries earlier, bear striking similarities to the compositions of the modern era. The painter also was ahead of his time in portraying supernatural images that are now commonplace. One painting in particular, a depiction of purgatory, features a "tunnel of light" that eerily parallels the luminescent corridor described in many modern NEAR-DEATH EXPERIENCES.

BRAN Bran is the lord of the dead in Welsh mythology. His symbol is the raven, an image associated with death and the grave. He was a deified mortal who angered the gods, was beheaded, and then was banished to the underworld as punishment for his transgressions. Bran's kingdom of the dead is filled with failed heroes who must spend eternity in angst and regret.

One legend claims that King Arthur located and unearthed Bran's severed head (called Uther Ben, the "wonderful head"). It had been used as a talisman to prevent evil from befalling Britain, but King Arthur claimed that the kingdom was strong enough to triumph without magic or charms. He declared that the living, not the damned, must steer the course of the country's future and forbade his men from paying tribute to Bran.

BRENDAN, SAINT St. Brendan, also called Brendan the Navigator (484–577), is the subject of many legends regarding the supernatural, including a mystic expedition to the underworld. According to the *Navigatio Brendani* (Travels of Brendan), written in the tenth century, Brendan was searching for the Island of Earthly Paradise and the Land Promised to the Saints when he came instead upon the gate of hell.

The story tells that Brandan had gone off course and was drifting on uncharted seas. His crew then catches sight of a rocky wasteland of slag and pitch, and Brendan steers toward the island. As the boat draws closer, Brendan hears the sounds of a hammer striking an anvil and of a fuming bellows. He records coming upon a "dark country full of stench and smoke" where he sees Judas Iscariot "naked and in great misery and pain" hovering over a rock. The ravages of the sea have torn away all Judas's flesh, leaving only ribbons of skin over his pale skeleton. Overwhelmed by pity, Brendan stops to hear the traitor's sad tale.

Judas tells Brendan that he is eternally condemned to suffer the horros of hell (located inside the mouth of a volcano) but is allowed to leave on certain feast days for a brief respite. During the rest of the year, Judas endures "lying in burning fire with Pilate, Herod, Annas and Caiaphas" (all adversaries of Jesus Christ) in the depths of the abyss. This is punishment for taking part in Christ's crucifixion. As the two are talking, a horde of DEMONS comes to drag Judas back to hell, declaring that his time of rest is over.

The *Navigatio Brendani* was widely read across Europe during the centuries following its publication. It contained extensive maps and illustrations of Brendan's travels and is believed to have influenced explorer Christopher Columbus and inspired sections of Dante's *DIVINE COMEDY: THE INFERNO*.

BRIDGET OF SWEDEN, SAINT Bridget of Sweden (1302–1373), a wealthy noblewoman, experienced many mystic visions during her lifetime, including grim apparitions of hell. She kept a record of these frightening episodes and offered them as a warning to Christians about the punishments of the afterlife.

Bridget was born of nobility in 1302. She married at age fourteen and bore eight children, including a second-generation saint, Catherine of Sweden. After her husband's death, Bridget lived a quiet, secluded life devoted to improving the plight of the poor. Her maid said of Bridget that she was "kind and meek to every creature" and had "a laughing face." Always willing to extend aid to those in need, Bridget was well loved by the community and had a reputation for being compassionate, generous, and gentle.

Throughout her life, Bridget experienced mystic visions and revelations about the future. Word of her ability spread, and she soon found herself being approached by kings, noblemen, and political leaders for advice and counsel. She corresponded regularly with a number of powerful rulers, although many officials were angered when Bridget suggested that they were abusing their power and should mend their ways.

Among her visions were many terrifying images of a fiery hell where sinners faced violent torments. Bridget continually cautioned against incurring divine justice, as the price for leading an immoral life is horribly high. Sinners who disregard the warning should be prepared to endure excruciating agonies. According to her accounts of hell: "The fire of the furnace boiled upward under the feet of the soul like water rising through a pipe to a point where it bursts . . . so that its veins seem to flow with the blaze. The ears were like a smith's bellows blasting through the brain. The eyes seemed reversed, looking to the back of the head. The mouth hung open and the tongue was drawn through the nostrils. . . . The teeth had been driven like nails into the palate." These torments are amplified by an "icy cold" that emits a discharge "like that which oozes from an infected ulcer," creating a "stench worse than anything in this world."

Hoping to help others avoid these terrors by encouraging virtuous living, Bridget used property left to her by King Magnus II to found a convent and monastery. She died in 1373 and was declared a saint of the Roman Catholic church. Bridget is still dearly loved by the people of Sweden, who have adopted her as the country's patron saint.

BROTHERS KARAMAZOV, THE Russian author Feodor Dostoevsky wrote the classic novel *The Brothers Karamazov* in 1880. This epic describes the struggle between good and evil through the complex trials of the troubled Karamazov family. The story's characters are constantly struggling with questions of meaning, purpose, and relevance of their own lives. And there are numerous warnings against seeking knowledge and power without love, an offense that has led many to misery, frustration, and ultimate damnation.

Central to this struggle is the question of whether the family members believe in God. Father Zossima, a gentle and compassionate priest, cautions the brothers that God is love itself, and thus hell is "the suffering of being unable to love" through alienation from the divine. Ivan Karamazov challenges this assertion by insisting that humanity does not need a hell, since it has perverted the world with ugliness and evil. He cites several examples of recent local atrocities, such as tales of children being murdered and of animals being cruelly abused. Ivan concludes that the world is already "without love," no different from Zossima's description of hell.

Still grappling with his unresolved doubts about the afterlife, Ivan has a nightmarish vision of the infernal depths. SATAN parades before him. At first beautiful and appealing, the evil shape-shifter transforms himself into a series of frightening animals before taking on the form of humankind personified. Finally, the DEVIL appears in the figure of Ivan himself. The two have a lengthy dialogue about the nature of humanity, Satan takes every opportunity cleverly to twist and trick Ivan. But Ivan ultimately rejects the force of hell, deciding that love truly is the greater power. Despite the ugliness he has witnessed in his lifetime, Ivan believes that true beauty does exist and that the damned will be forever denied that splendor.

BRUEGHEL The Brueghel family of artists lived in Flanders during the mid-1500s to early 1600s. Patriarch Pieter Brueghel (Brueghel the Elder) and his sons Jan and Pieter were prolific painters who specialized in illustrating the supernatural. Young Pieter earned the nickname "Hell Brueghel" due to his love of creating scenes of the underworld. Jan distinguished himself by depicting affluent noblemen robed in rich velvet. His greatest work is a picture of the Greek musician ORPHEUS, a grief-stricken lover who journeys to HADES (the hell of ancient myth) to retrieve the spirit of his dead wife.

The most gifted of the three was Brueghel the Elder. He had a flamboyant style and a sense of humor that set his works apart. The celebrated artist offered interpretations of *THE FALL OF THE REBEL ANGELS* and the HARROWING OF HELL as well as several visions of the underworld drawn from folktales. One unique portrait of the damned is *Dulle Griet* (Angry Gretchen), a proverbial housewife who is so fearsome that even the DEMONS of hell cringe as she passes. Brueghel shows the furious frau stomping through the netherworld while infernal beasts scamper away. Gretchen, carrying home sacks of wares from the market, is oblivious to the fires that rage about her. Nor does she seem to notice the legions of demons and ranks of the damned who writhe in agony throughout the landscape.

Brueghel the Elder also composed

fantastic paintings of the *Seven Deadly Sins* and the *Triumph of Death* over humanity at the end of the world. His works are considered masterpieces.

BUDDHIST HELL Buddhism, like many Eastern religions, teaches that souls are reincarnated into other life-forms after death and therefore suffer no eternal damnation. The Buddhist tradition does, however, include many temporary hells where bad KARMA is burned away. The belief is that the spirit itself is not evil; it must simply atone for wicked acts performed during its time on earth. A soul's ultimate goal is to reach Nirvana, a state of collective universal bliss.

On this cosmic pursuit, a soul may spend time in one of many Buddhist hells. These include places of extreme heat, swamps of pitch, torture chambers, and cold regions of icy suffering. Details about the specifics vary from region to region, with as many as 136 hells described in some traditions. The most gruesome realm of Buddhist hell is AVICI, the lowest circle where the worst of the damned are punished.

Chinese Buddhists believe in an intricate system of hells, each overseen by a distinct YAMA (king) who is both judge and punisher of the dead. The underworld is run much like the mortal world: It is a huge bureaucracy where the dead are sentenced in a courtlike atmosphere. One painting shows the court of Yama where souls await trial. Some make offerings of food and riches to the judge (possibly as a bribe) while others are beaten by monstrous green and red DEMONS. In the foreground are the damned, their battered and bloodied bodies confined in a flaming pool infested by huge serpents.

EMMA-O is the underworld ruler of Japanese Buddhist tradition. He is also a judge and tormentor, usually shown wearing the robes of a Chinese magistrate. Two decapitated heads aid him in his decisions, since no sin can be hidden from their piercing eyes. Tortures in the realm of Emma-O include being roasted on a spit, sliced with spears, or beaten with an enormous hammer. Some Japanese texts include mention of JIGOKU, an underworld complex of eight cold and eight hot hells.

Tibetan Buddhists believe in a much more extensive collection of infernal horrors, outlined in the BARDO THODOL (Tibetan Book of the Dead). There is no ultimate judge in Tibetan belief; a soul damns itself by its evil. Punishment in the afterlife consists of having to face one's own moral ugliness.

A rare example of VISION LITERATURE from Burmese Buddhist tradition describes how the wicked will be treated in the underworld. According to the text, one unrepentant sinner is buried to his neck in human feces while huge worms gnaw at his flesh. Other evildoers are forced to climb a tree covered with razor-sharp thorns. As they attempt this, their feet are mutilated into bloody ribbons, but they must continue climbing.

The damned can take comfort in the knowledge that their situation is not permanent. Buddhist doctrine teaches that souls go through numerous incarnations on their journey through eternity, with brief detours to hell when necessary. And even the few, rare souls deemed irrevocably evil are not made to suffer unending torture. These dark spirits eventually face ANNIHILATION and are eradicated from existence.

BUMPER STICKERS Americans delight in advertising their feelings, beliefs, politics, and interests on the backs of their motor vehicles. Among the sugary notes about wonderful grandchildren and obnoxious outlets for inner hostility are a host of messages concerning hell. These range from warnings against damnation to boasts about being chummy with the DEVIL.

One popular sticker brags, "See you in Hell—I'll be working the bar." Other motorists want to proclaim, "Heaven doesn't want me and Hell is afraid I'll take over," "Don't follow me, I'm on the Highway to Hell," and "I've been married—I no longer fear Hell." A particularly cavalier sticker announces, "Hell was full, so I came back." There is also an offshoot of invitations to report safety violations: "If you don't like the way I'm driving, go to Hell."

On the other side of the spectrum are cautionary suggestions on how to avoid damnation to the fiery underworld. "The road to Hell is paved with good intentions" reads one sticker. Another tells fellow motorists, "It's never too late for the Hellbound to make a U-turn." Witty spiritualists have even developed a clever twist on the national fire safety campaign. Against a background of red and orange flames, the text of this bumper sticker advises, "Learn not to burn—read the Bible."

C

CAESARIUS OF HEISTERBACH The sermons and exempla of Caesarius of Heisterbach (c. 1230) are filled with vivid, terrifying images of SATAN and the accursed abyss. The thirteenth-century Christian cleric also heavily preached about the LAST JUDGMENT, routinely filling his parishioners' minds with images of grisly DEMONS, bloody tortures, and everlasting fire that await evildoers in the world to come. He warned them of the eventual end of the world, a time at which Christ will return to judge the souls of all people, living and dead, and cast the irrevocable sinners into the depths of hell. His doctrines were repeated at pulpits throughout every Christian nation and became the basis for countless HELLFIRE SERMONS during the following century.

Caesarius encouraged devotion to the VIRGIN MARY for protection against damnation. He believed that Christ's mother had the power not only to save souls from being condemned but also to visit hell to retrieve sinners from the underworld. His writings include the example of a corrupt monk who had died, been damned, but was restored to life through Mary's intercession. The man repented, led a devout life, and eventually became a saint. This case history was spread throughout Chrisendom and was cited to convince the wicked to mend their ways. Caesarius's teachings also became instrumental in securing the Virgin's reputation as intercessor for human souls.

CAIN Lord Byron displays his self-proclaimed contempt for traditional morals in his poem *Cain.* The work is sympathetic to both LUCIFER and to Adam and Eve's wicked son Cain, the biblical figure who murders his brother Abel out of jealousy. Byron's *Cain* turns the killer into a hero for asserting his independence and God into a vain despot who demands an unreasonable amount of tribute and adoration to feed his massive ego.

In *Cain,* Byron (who had recently learned of the first discoveries of dinosaur fossils) depicts the extinct reptiles as superhuman creatures who once inhabited the earth. After falling from grace, they are damned to a hell located somewhere in outer space. Young Cain is transported there by his host, Lucifer, an energetic fiend who has been unfairly banished from paradise. Byron describes these ancient beasts as sadly beautiful, inhabiting the "gloomy realms" of the dark abyss. He feels sorrow for the "immense serpent" (an Enlightenment LEVIATHAN) and the other monsters languishing in their exile.

Cain celebrates the rebellious creatures and their fiery bravado. Not surprisingly, Byron's poem was immediately condemned as blasphemous for elevating Lucifer to the level of supernatural hero while decrying the Creator as a petty tyrant. Byron relished this condemnation—it was exactly the reaction he had wanted. He believed that this rebuke was proof that his intellect frightened and intimidated "superstitious" believers. The poet gave similar favorable treatment to the legendary rogue DON JUAN, an unscrupulous scoundrel for whom Byron has nothing but praise.

CARNIVAL ATTRACTIONS
Amid the Ferris wheels, cotton candy stands, and pitch-till-you-win games at many roadside carnivals, revelers often find scary attractions that promise to thrill and chill brave patrons. These "haunted houses" are also mainstays at many major amusement parks, from Coney Island to Disneyland. And every Halloween brings scores of part-time underworld concessions to neighborhoods across the country. Spooky enticements with names such as The Bottomless Pit, Dante's Inferno, Hell Hole, Chamber of Horrors, Village of the Damned, and The Devil's Den often take their themes from the depths—and horrors—of hell.

These forbidding attractions draw ideas for frightening images from myth, literature, and art. Most exteriors include pictures of menacing a DEVIL, GHOULS, skeletons, corpses, and witches languishing in hellfire.

Carnival haunted houses feature such icons of hell as Satan, demons, and Leviathan.

Inside, patrons find both live figures, usually dressed as DEMONS or familiar fiends such as Dracula and Frankenstein, and gory displays of severed body parts, open graves, and bloody implements of torture. Sound effects of howling devils and screaming souls underscore the infernal atmosphere.

Another popular feature is the oversized statue of a threatening demon. SATAN and LUCIFER are most common, usually shown as red fiends with horns and claws, wielding razor-sharp pitchforks. Mythic underworld beasts such as the guard dog CERBERUS and ferryman CHARON are also perennial favorites. Monsters of modern American pop culture (child killer Freddy Kruger of *NIGHTMARE ON ELM STREET,* for example) have begun showing up in more and more spook houses.

The popularity and prevalence of these attractions reinforce the fact that people are fascinated with hell and are interested in a brief visit. Proprietors have discovered that the suffering of the damned is sensual and darkly stimulating. The sinister appeal of such concessions has been captured in horror stories and movies as well, including the suspense novel *HIDEAWAY* and motion picture *DANTE'S INFERNO*.

CARNIVAL OF SOULS The 1962 film *Carnival of Souls* depicts a grim afterlife where the dead continue on in a sort of faded existence, similar to the SHADES of ancient Greek myth.

Originally a low-budget independent, the movie has attracted quite a cult following. Filmed almost entirely in Kansas (at a cost of less than $100,000), *Carnival of Souls* offers an unsettling look at the supernatural realm through the eyes of Mary Henry (played by Candace Hilligoss), a young organist whose recent brush with death leaves her haunted by a recurring specter.

Carnival of Souls opens with the scene of a two cars drag racing, speeding recklessly down a rural lane. When the race continues onto a narrow bridge, the vehicle containing Hilligoss and her friends goes out of control and plunges into the river below. She emerges from the water seemingly unscathed but soon begins having frightening visions of a pale, grinning stranger who is stalking her. Hilligoss quickly arranges to leave town, dispassionately telling acquaintances, "I'm never coming back."

The organist drives across the country to take a job as soloist at a new church. Her hallucinations continue as she travels, and Hilligoss quickly realizes that the smirking man is following her. When she arrives to assume her new position, the pastor of the church finds her to be cold and "soulless." Her maniacal organ playing horrifies him, sounding more like a diabolical dirge than a joyous hymn. The minister gently suggests that she "accept help" in the form of spiritual guidance to remedy her "profane" behavior. He then asks her to resign. She quietly agrees, not knowing what inspired her eerie outburst.

The bizarre events of her life continue after she flees the church. As a new boyfriend bends to kiss her, she sees him reflected in the mirror as the sinister GHOUL who has been menacing her since the auto accident in her hometown. Hilligoss tries to buy a bus ticket out of town, but no one at the station can see or hear her. Scrambling onto one of the waiting buses, she discovers that the passengers are all pale corpses, led by the familiar phantom. She runs screaming from the scene, unable to comprehend—or stop—the horrible visions.

Confused and terrified, Hilligoss heads for an abandoned lakeside pavilion on the edge of town that seems somehow to be connected to the strange events. Inside she discovers a ghostly gathering of vacant-eyed zombies dancing lethargically to an unearthly tune. None of them speak; they swirl endlessly in a slow, morbid waltz. Before she can escape this macabre prom, Hilligoss sees herself, also a vacuous ghost, dancing in the arms of the ghoul who has been pursuing her. Horrified, she turns and runs out onto the lakeshore. The dancers run after her, overtaking her on the wet sand at the water's edge.

Carnival of Souls concludes with a scene at the riverside back in Hilligoss's hometown, where the car accident initially occurred. The smashed vehicle is pulled from the water with her drowned body still trapped in the wreckage. Hilligoss's misadventures and ultimate arrival at the haunted pavilion have been part of her bleak afterlife, a somber realm of gloomy existence. Her journey has not been to a new town and a second chance at life, but to a bitter, monotonous eternity. Hilligoss has at last embraced her destiny.

CAVE OF CRUACHAN The Cave of Cruachan in Connaught, Ireland, has been called the "Gateway to Hell" by early Christian folklorists. Its reputation derives from ancient pagan stories linking the cavern with the underworld. The old legends claim that Cruachan is actually a portal through which dead armies of zombies come to attack the living. Christians updated the tales, asserting that the harsh geologic formation is where human souls enter the abyss of the damned.

CERBERUS Cerberus is the Greek mythological guardian of the underworld. He is a ferocious three-headed dog with serpents' tails and a body entwined with vipers. Cerberus sits at the gates of HADES, gnawing on human bones. His duty is to prevent the dead from escaping and the living from invading the underworld. Cerberus's fierce howling and putrid stench are so frightening that few even dare approach the passageway.

Only two mortals, ORPHEUS and HERCULES, have ever bested Cerberus. Orpheus charmed him to sleep with his enchanted music; Hercules wrestled him into submission as part of one of his legendary labors.

Cerberus appears in scores of artwork, in Dante's *DIVINE COMEDY: THE INFERNO,* and in the motion picture *HIGHWAY TO HELL.*

CERNUNNOUS Cernunnous (the Horned One) is the ancient Celtic god of the underworld and ruler of the dead. Images of the dark sorcerer etched into cave walls in France date back to 9000 B.C. He is portrayed as a horned deity surrounded by fearsome animals. Also associated with hunting and fertility, Cernunnous became identified with the Antichrist when Christianity spread to the Celtic regions. After the conversion of Ireland, Cernunnous was increasingly linked with a dark and foul underworld, the dwelling place of evil spirits and souls of the damned.

CHARON Charon is the escort who ferries the dead to HADES, the underworld of ancient Greek myth. Souls must pay him for this service; otherwise they will be left to wander aimlessly the banks of the river STYX throughout eternity.

The mythic Charon appears in hundreds of plays, poems, paintings, films, and other creative works. Homages to the ferryman can be seen in the movie *HIGHWAY TO HELL,* in MUSIC VIDEOS, and on centuries-old MEMORIALS to the dead.

CHARON ON THE RIVER STYX Joachim Patinir's sixteenth-century painting *CHARON on the River STYX* exemplifies the lasting influence of ancient Greek myths on the art world. Created more than two millennia after the demise of Helenic civilization, Patinir's composition employs underworld images and icons that have endured through the centuries. The work is a brilliant blaze of blues and greens illuminating paradise, a stark contrast to the dark and sinister colors of the land of the damned.

In *Charon on the River Styx,* Patinir offers a naked, gaunt Charon perched in a tiny rowboat ferrying souls across the river Styx to a grim fortress of torture. The underworld looms in the background, a burning city choked with black smoke. The gates of HADES await on the opposite bank, guarded by the three-headed beast CERBERUS. Broken bodies dangle limply over the walls, still being tormented by DEMONS. Farther on, souls are thrown into a raging fire by gleeful fiends. The faces of the damned are upturned in agony, longing for relief that will never come.

"CHILDE ROLAND TO THE DARK TOWER CAME" Poet Robert Browning told his contemporaries that his existential poem "Childe Roland to the Dark Tower Came" "came upon me as a kind of dream." He denied that there was any specific allegorical meaning; however, the work includes a chilling passage that invokes images of a treacherous CHRISTIAN HELL. One line declares that the "LAST JUDGMENT's fire must curse this place," a clear allusion to the spiritual grotesqueness of the underworld. Browning also makes several explicit references to the DEVIL and to APOLLYON, the angel of the abyss.

Childe (a title indicating a young gentleman who is awaiting knighthood) Roland is a feisty warrior in search of adventures and glory who embarks upon a grim quest to storm the mysterious Dark Tower. During this bleak adventure, he comes to a river of writhing bodies groaning in utter agony. Its "black eddy" could have "been a path for the fiend's glowing hoof." The ravaged spirits in this mire are held there by some ominous power, for there is "no footprint leading to that horrid mews, none out of it."

As he crosses the river, the speaker is horrified by the ghastly carnage beneath his feet:

Which, while I forded, good saints, how I
feared
To set my foot upon a dead man's cheek,
Each step, or feel the spear I thrust to seek
For hollows, tangled in his hair or beard!
It may have been a water-rat I speared,
But, ugh! it sounded like a baby's shriek.

This repugnant stream extends far into the distance, "a furlong on," to a gruesome engine that perpetually would "reel men's bodies out like silk." He is chilled not only by this aberration but also by the unseen force that keeps these damned souls from escaping. The narrator gratefully reaches the opposite bank but cannot escape the haunting specter of this dark, hideous river. Yet Roland's worst vision is yet to come.

When he reaches the courtyard of the Dark Tower, Roland is horrified to see among the castle's occupants the faces of fallen friends who have died during battles. They look out at their former companion with vacant, haunted eyes. Roland laments "in a sheet of flame I saw them" before pity forces him to turn away. Rather than invigorating his spirit and whetting his taste for such feats, the trip to the Dark Tower has left him broken and desolate, questioning the very nature of his own purpose in the world.

CHILDREN'S LITERATURE A number of children's stories involve the land of the damned, either directly or allegorically. Some are cautionary tales designed to help young ones follow the path of righteousness; others are simply satirical whimsies that downplay the horror of the underworld. The oldest date back centuries; the most recent have been around for less than a decade, demonstrating the timeless appeal of infernal yarns.

Throughout the ages, overanxious zealots, eager to begin saving tender young souls, composed stories designed specifically to frighten children into behaving in an acceptable manner. Children around the world have listened breathlessly to tales of naughty children who defy their elders or thwart societal rules, then end up in a ghastly underworld where they must pay for their offenses. Such stories are followed by a not so subtle warning: Do as you're told and this won't happen to you. One of the most extreme examples is "Sight of Hell," penned by Rev. Joseph Furniss in the late 1800s. His work details the horrors of the inferno in simple-to-understand terms, vividly describing a young child writh-

An 1864 illustration from *The History of Our Lord: Vol I* shows wicked children suffering the fires of hell. ART TODAY

ing in a "red hot oven." Furniss admonishes young followers against such juvenile offenses as disobeying parents, telling tales, and missing Sunday services.

Secular stories, too, could be downright horrifying for youngsters. Among the most disturbing examples of hellish literature for children is Hans Christian Andersen's "The Girl Who Trod on a Loaf." The tale describes the damnation of Inger, an "arrogant" child who fails to appreciate her parents' love and is ultimately sent to hell. Inger seals her doom when she throws a cake of bread that was to be a gift for her mother into a mud puddle to use as a stepping stone. More concerned about soiling her shoes than about her impoverished parents, Inger immediately sinks into the "black bubbling pool" full of "noisome toads" and "slimy snakes." In this murky underworld, Inger experiences "icy cold," "terrible hunger," and other severe pains. Inger's mother weeps for her lost child, but her tears only "burn and make the torment fifty times worse." Eventually, Inger is released from hell through her sainted mother's prayers, but only to exist as a songbird.

Few fables are as harsh as this; most use gentle metaphor to warn children about the consequences of sin. In *Pinocchio,* for example, naughty boys who disobey their parents are transformed into donkeys. This reflects the common belief that damned souls become beastlike in the afterlife. Likewise, the burning of the witch in "Hansel and Gretel" symbolizes the fires that await evildoers in the underworld. And the story of the "Billy Goats Gruff" contains several examples of infernal IMAGERY. The innocent animals must pass over a dangerous bridge while a wicked troll waits below to devour them. Only by knowing the correct words to outsmart the monster can the little goats escape. The hellish images of a perilous bridge, an evil fiend, and magic spells are components of a number of ancient myths and religious doctrines regarding the afterlife.

Hell continues to be used in children's tales, although contemporary stories are usually more humorous than allegorical. *The* DEVIL *and Mother Crump,* written in 1987 by Valerie Scho Carey, tells of a cantankerous woman who outsmarts the DEMONS of the underworld by proving herself more despicable than the fiends. For when Mother Crump dies and LUCIFER calls her to hell, she so enrages the devils sent to claim her that they finally give up trying. Eventually, Mother Crump decides that she is old, exhausted, and ready for death. But heaven won't have her, and the angels send her down to hell. Lucifer, remembering the beating he took from her years ago, refuses to let her in. Instead he gives her a coal and tells her to create a hell of her own. Mother Crump ultimately maneuvers her way into paradise, providing a happy ending for young readers.

Child-oriented tales of the underworld—both terrifying and trivial—can also be found in ANIMATED CARTOONS, COMIC BOOKS, and COMPUTER GAMES. There are also numerous feature films designed for children that include depictions of the great below, such as *ALL DOGS GO TO HEAVEN, THE DEVIL AND MAX DEVLIN,* and Disney's 1997 animated version of *HERCULES.*

CHIMAERA Chimaera is a mythical underworld beast that appears in a variety of legends and works of Western literature. He has a lion's head, goat's body, and serpent's tail. Chimaera also figures in ETRUSCAN mythology as a fierce underworld DEMON.

In *PARADISE LOST,* John Milton describes Chimaera as a fire-breathing monster who inhabits hell. He is a guardian of the gates of HADES according to the poets Homer and Virgil. In the *AENEID,* Virgil depicts Chimaera as "armed with flames" and horrible to behold. And the beast is referred to as the father of the DEVIL in the *Faerie Queene,* a sixteenth-century tale of goblins, FAIRIES, and other figures of the "otherworld."

CHINVAT BRIDGE According to ancient Persian myth, when a person dies, the soul remains by the body for three days. On the fourth, it travels to Chinvat Bridge (the Bridge of the Separator, also called Al-Sirat), accompanied by gods of protection. The bridge is "finer than a hair and sharper than a sword" and spans a deep chasm teeming with monsters. On the other side of the bridge is the gateway to paradise.

DEMONS guard the foot of the bridge and argue with the gods over the soul's fate. The actions of the dead person, both good and bad, are weighed, and the soul is either allowed to cross or denied access to the bridge. Spirits whose evil outweighs their good fall into the demon-infested pit to face eternal torment. In this abyss of the damned, each soul is tortured by a GHOUL that represents its sins in life. Once fallen into the gulf, no soul can escape the horrors of hell through its own power.

Zoroaster, a sixth-century B.C. religious leader, had warned his followers of this obstacle to heaven but promised to lead his flock safely across. The ancient manuscript *Gathas* (Songs of Zoroaster) explains that the Bridge of the Separator "becomes narrow for the wicked," whereas the holy can easily pass unharmed. (In *Gathas,* the fair god Rashnu is named as the judge who helps determine who is worthy of salvation and who must be damned.) All infidels (nonbelievers) fall into hell, which the prophet says has been created especially for the "followers of the lie."

The legends are sketchy but assert that Chinvat Bridge is located somewhere in the far north. It is a place of filth where the damned endure physical tortures and spiritual agony. Souls who are unsuccessful in crossing Chinvat Bridge suffer these torments until AHRIMAN, the evil god of ZOROASTRIANISM, is destroyed by the good god Orzmahd during the LAST JUDGMENT. At this time, lost spirits are restored to the truth since "the lie" has been eradicated, or they face final ANNIHILATION.

"CHRIST AND SATAN" The Old English poem "Christ and Satan" provides a frightening description of the underworld. It also offers an estimation of the SIZE OF HELL, a mystery that has occupied philosophers and scholars since the inception of underworld mythology.

According to the work, hell is a "horrible cavern underground" that is impermeably dark, where fires continuously burn but give off no light. Those in hell, creatures who once sang hymns of joy, now wail and shriek in everlasting mourning, bound in chains of fire. Their ultimate misery is their refusal to accept their fate. They are damned to spend eternity raging against God and seething at their predicament.

The fallen angels in hell blame SATAN for causing their damnation. They accuse him of lying and misleading them by claiming he could replace God and reward them with places of honor in paradise. Remembering the beauty of heaven causes them unbearable agony since that glory is now forever outside their grasp. They lament "alas that I am deprived of eternal joy" and left with unending sorrow.

"Christ and Satan" also includes an account of the HARROWING OF HELL, when Jesus raids the underworld and frees the souls of the patriarchs. As he appears at hell's gate, a song of rejoicing erupts from the faithful. Satan, powerless to stop him, must stand idly by as Jesus delivers the just to heaven. Before leaving, Jesus warns Satan that this is not his final defeat, for a larger battle is waiting at the time of the LAST JUDGMENT. This will occur at the end of the world, when Satan will be vanquished for eternity.

CHRISTIAN HELL Christian hell is a place of final justice for the wicked who have offended God and have died without seeking forgiveness. The Bible describes the realm as "everlasting fire prepared for the DEVIL and his angels" where souls of the damned suffer according to their sins. It is called a "lake of fire" and a "bottomless pit." SATAN, a former angel who rebelled against God and started a war in heaven, is hell's overlord.

There is no generally accepted information regarding the location or SIZE OF HELL, nor is there a consensus about who has been damned. In fact, most Christian leaders teach that there is no evidence that *any* souls have been condemned to this eternal abyss. (Some scholars believe that the Bible implies that Judas is in hell. Jesus is quoted as saying, "It would be better for him [Judas] if he had never been born." They theorize that the only fate worse than nonexistence is damnation to hell.)

Theologians and philosophers through the ages have attempted to offer details about the nature of the underworld; however, little doctrine has been universally accepted. As we head into the twenty-first century, the specifics of Christian hell remain unresolved. Many hold the view that the underworld is a place of sensory torture and agony; others believe that it is merely a state of mental anguish. Still another group believes that damnation to hell is a temporary punishment before ANNIHILATION. These various interpretations of the underworld are illuminated in numerous literary works by Christian authors, including Dante's *DIVINE COMEDY: THE INFERNO,* Milton's *PARADISE LOST,* and a host of MYSTERY PLAYS and MORALITY PLAYS. Visions of the land of the damned are also depicted in paintings, sculptures, and mosaics found in Christian CHURCH ART AND ARCHITECTURE.

ST. AUGUSTINE, a fourth-century doctor of the church, wrote several academic texts regarding hell. In *CITY OF GOD,* he asserts that in the underworld, the damned suffer both physically and spiritually and that this torment continues for all eternity. He cites the Bible and traditional beliefs as the basis for his deductions, such as the passage in the Gospel of St. Matthew that those who ignored Christ's words "shall go away into *everlasting* punishment." Augustine's theories were sanctioned by Christian authorities at the Synod of Constantinople in 543 and heavily influenced the teachings of both Martin Luther and John Calvin. And his conclusions about the underworld are still taught in Catholic institutions.

Yet many Christians believe that the pains of hell are metaphorical. The fires of the underworld, for example, are not actual flames but the burning pangs of a guilty conscience. The "everlasting torment" is the unending separation from God. Evangelist Billy Graham professed this belief in his *Sermons from Madison Square Garden* in 1969. He stated that "the fire Jesus talked about is an eternal search for God that is never quenched," not a true inferno. This view is shared by many Protestant denominations, which find the notion of a place of physical torment to be somewhat outdated and incompatible with the notion of a merciful God.

Modern concepts of horrors in the afterlife have also been weakened by the atrocities witnessed by recent generations. It is difficult to imagine greater terrors than the Nazi concentration camps, nuclear devastation, and the wholesale slaughter of political dissidents in China, Cambodia, and Eastern Europe. And the advances of technology have led many to believe that there is no place for traditional hell in the mind of today's educated and enlightened thinker. For this reason, some have embraced annihilation theory, which maintains that in the afterlife evil souls will be eradicated from existence.

Critics of annihilation theory claim that belief in an underworld for unrepentant sinners, whether actual or metaphorical, remains essential to the importance of Jesus Christ's redemption of humanity. Without a hell, his sacrifice and death would not have been necessary. Many further claim that existence of hell also serves as proof of free will. God does not force anyone to love him nor to spend eternity with him in heaven if that individual would rather choose evil, selfishness, and ultimately damnation.

Today, most denominations emphasize God's mercy and encourage their faithful to strive for heaven rather than try to cheat hell. They also stress that damnation is a choice made by those who reject the Almighty and not a punishment imposed on evildoers by an angry or vengeful deity. So while debate continues over the specifics of the unpleasant afterlife, most Christians retain that hell is real and that everyone is vulnerable.

CHRISTIAN TOPOGRAPHY

Sixth-century Egyptian monk Cosmas Indicopleustes offers an unusual description of hell in his treatise *Christian Topography.* According to the manuscript, Earth is completely flat, protected by the "dome of Heaven" above. Damned souls will "sleep" below the ground until the LAST JUDGMENT, when the material world will be transformed into hell. After this occurs, the earth will become harsh and barren, a perpetual desert devoid of any plant or animal life. Evil spirits will be forced to spend eternity in this wasteland, while the saved are restored to heaven to savor the abundant delights of paradise.

Indicopleustes' theories were rejected by both scientists and religious scholars of the time. However, the peasantry excitedly embraced his model of the supernatural universe. For decades, the concept of a ravaged earth serving as hell was the topic of countless sermons, lectures, and lively debate.

CHRISTINA, SAINT

St. Christina (1150–1224) was born in Brusthem and became an orphan at age fifteen. Seven years after the death of her parents, Christina had a disturbing vision of hell following a near-fatal brain seizure. The young woman fell into a comalike state, and doctors, unable to revive her, pronounced Christina dead. She was laid in her coffin and taken to the church for a Requiem Mass. During the funeral, however, she sprang up from her coffin and levitated to the church rafters. The priest told her to come down, but she refused, claiming she was sickened by the stench of people's sins.

Christina then recounted her supernatural travels, telling the stunned cleric that she had in fact died and been taken on a tour of heaven, purgatory, and hell. In the underworld, she saw sights so horrible she could not bring herself to put them into words. God invited her to remain with him in heaven but also offered her opportunity to return to life to help others avoid hell and to aid the suffering of those in purgatory through her sacrifice and intercession. Sickened by the severity of the torments she had witnessed among the damned, Christina decided to rejoin the living and help others attain heaven.

Christina lived out her life in prayer and penance, continually spreading the warning about the consequences of sin. She died in 1224 at the Convent of St. Catherine at Saint-Trond and was eventually canonized as saint of the Roman Catholic church.

CHRONICLES OF HELL, THE

Belgian dramatist Michel de Ghelderode wrote more than four dozen plays during his lifetime, most of which contain supernatural elements. His satirical treatment of the FAUST legend, called *The Death of Doctor Faust,* was well received by critics and audiences alike. However, his 1929 composition, *The Chronicles of Hell,* was by far his most adventurous and controversial work. When it was first produced in Paris in 1949, the play was condemned as sacrilegious and its author labeled a blasphemer. Despite the criticism, *The Chronicles of Hell*—a rich blend of religious satire, infernal IMAGERY, and ludicrous stereotypes—remains popular among modern audiences.

The Chronicles of Hell's setting is a Gothic cathedral in "bygone Flanders." Ghelderode describes the set as a decaying antechamber decorated with witches' masks, statues of pagan DEMONS, and brutal torture devices. In the foreground, a great table laden with succulent food and crystal goblets stands ready for a funeral banquet. Outside, a raging storm brings explosions of lightning and thunder, underscoring the eerie atmosphere of the vile place.

As the one-act play opens, six clergymen gather to mark the death of Jan Eremo, a powerful bishop. Rather than offer reverent prayers, the clerics insult both the departed man and one another, mocking their physical impediments and erupting into petty squabbles over the funeral feast. They trade opinions about the deceased—whom they loathed—and speculate on his ties with the DEVIL. When one priest suggests that the deceased bishop is bound for hell, a colleague coldly replies "he has been there" before. A third retorts, "Yes, to buy a place there for *you,* in a noxious dungeon where you will crush slugs!"

As the accursed men trade insights and insults, the storm is growing stronger and a mob of angry villagers is assembling outside the gates of the cathedral. They are mourning their beloved bishop, whom they credit with saving their town from the horrors of the plague and from starvation. His fellow clerics believe he accomplished this feat through demonic intervention, and their hatred of Jan makes them enemies of the people. The priests decry their former bishop as the Antichrist and are delighted that he is finally dead. Each flash of lightning illuminates the faces of the pagan idols that seem to be grinning in approval of the blasphemous scene.

The squabbling continues. Suddenly, at the height of the tempest, the mortuary chapel doors burst open, and Jan's towering figure lurches toward the bickering men. One demands of the corpse, "Have you seen Hell?!?" but the reanimated bishop is unable to reply. He had been given Communion just before dying, and the holy wafer chokes him, burning in his throat. Hell will not accept him while the Eucharist rests within, and heaven has long since renounced the diabolical reverend. Caught between life and death, the bishop stumbles blindly through the dark chamber of evil relics. Finally, his jealous successor runs forth and rips the communion bread from the bishop's throat, sending Jan back to his damnation.

In the aftermath of the commotion, the assembled clerics continue ridiculing one another. Several have "filled their cassocks with dung" in fits of fright at seeing the ambulatory corpse. They are chided by the others, who light up incense to mask the smell. Without warning, the mob becomes riotous and smashes into the dismal cathedral, demanding the body of the bishop. As the scene degenerates into total chaos, the priests, who have been exposed as hypocrites and nihilists, realize that they, too, are damned. The words of one minister resonate throughout the cathedral: "We are all in the abyss."

Ghelderode's *The Chronicles of Hell* explores themes common to infernal literature: deals with the devil, hypocrisy of the clergy, the seductive lure of diabolical powers. His play generated controversy mainly because it depicts the clergymen as villains rather than heroes. Such works as *AMBROSIO THE MONK,* "VATHEK," and *EPISTOLA LUCIFERI* are likewise critical of "men of the cloth" and suggest that they may in fact be among the fiercest allies of hell.

CHTHONIC The word *chthonic* means "relating to the gods of the underworld." It is from the Greek *khthonios,* "of the earth." Chthonic deities include rulers of the netherworld such as OSIRIS, HADES, HEL, YAMA, EMMA-O, and Pluto. Chthonic myth and literature include the legends of ORPHEUS, THESEUS, and HERCULES in the land of the dead, Virgil's *AENEID,* and Homer's *ODYSSEY.*

CHURCH ART AND ARCHITECTURE Images of the underworld decorate churches, temples, and places of worship throughout the world. During the days of widespread illiteracy, elaborate depictions of the damned helped illustrate the horrors of hell to congregations unable to read the sacred texts. Paintings, carvings, and statues of grisly DEMONS and damned mortals were among the most popular ornaments at religious sites.

One of the earliest examples of infernal art is Polygnotus's painting of Odysseus's visit to the kingdom of HADES inspired by Homer's epic poem the *ODYSSEY.* The picture, which dates back to the fifth century B.C., was part of a shrine to the Greek god Apollo. Unfortunately, the drawing—which showed a huge blue-black DEMON savagely eating the flesh of the damned—has been destroyed. Descriptions of the work, however, are contained in the writings of Greek scribe Pausanias.

In the Far East, graphic depictions of the gruesome horrors of BUDDHIST HELL became very popular in the Kamakura period during the twelfth century. Portraits of sinners languishing in agony and suffering a variety of ghastly tortures were etched onto hand scrolls along with text explaining the designs. These are examples of NISE-E, "likeness paintings," which took great inspiration from tales of the nether regions.

A centuries-old painting found in a Tibetan Buddhist temple includes similar images of the underworld. In this work, souls are shown writhing in the flames of hell, being beaten with clubs, gnawed upon by beasts, and jabbed with spears of fire. Wide-eyed demons delight in inflicting these and other punishments on the spirits of those sent to the underworld. Another artwork shows EMMA-O, ruler of the dead, as a green monster smashing a condemned spirit with a blood-stained mallet.

But by far the most graphic and extensive scenes of the land of the damned exist in Christian churches. As Christianity spread across the globe, artists of all backgrounds and cultures began illustrating the fiery underworld. Their works remain in chapels and cathedrals throughout the world, offering valuable insight into evolving beliefs about the horrors of CHRISTIAN HELL (as well as providing a history of the world's greatest artists).

The St. Lazare Cathedral in Autun, France, features a carving of angels weighing human souls while demons try to tip the scales in favor of damnation. This complex TYMPANUM RELIEF shows the LAST JUDGMENT when the saved are admitted to paradise and the damned cast into hell. The relief depicts horned devils taunting spirits and dragging sinners into the underworld while other condemned are being eaten by monstrous creatures. The Tympanum Relief was carved in the early twelfth century as a reminder to parishioners to heed the laws of the church.

A fourteenth-century frieze at Orvieto Cathedral in Italy shows condemned souls, bound together by thick ropes, being hauled off to hell by loathsome demons. Grinning devils, farther down in the bowels of the abyss, rapaciously devour the damned. One particular detail shows a drooling demon biting off the arm of a screeching man. The fiend's fellow GHOULS laugh approvingly at the grisly spectacle.

The *Temptation of St. Anthony* by Max Ernst, a rich oil done in royal blues and ruby reds, shows hell as a vibrant world of sensuality. Its demons are odd mutant animals: furry trunks with bird beaks and sharp claws; reptile cats with snake-weasel tongues. The background shows voluptuous nudes carved into the cliff walls of the underworld. Hell's inhabitants are beasts with human faces, their eyes dark sockets being clawed by razor-taloned devils who bite and flail at each other.

At the Monastery of St. Catherine at Sinai, a painting by St. John of Climax depicts the Ladder of Judgment. Souls try to ascend, but the evil are shot by demons' arrows or impaled on pitchforks and then pulled into hell. A sixteenth-century Russian icon shows a similar scene. Departing souls attempt to climb a ladder into heaven, but the wicked fall into waiting hell below. Winged black demons wait to snatch up the fallen spirits. The work is done in yellows and browns, creating a somber, forbidding mood of despair.

All of these artworks serve as more

than mere ornamentation: They bring dire tales of eternal suffering to life. Others, such as those of the Last Judgment and the HARROWING OF HELL, illustrate complex doctrines that might otherwise be difficult for clerics to explain to the peasantry. The tendency to adorn churches with visions of hell, demons, and damnation has faded over the centuries. However, tourists still flock to age-old chapels and cathedrals that feature such ghastly scenes, testifying to the enduring fascination we have with glimpsing a fate we hope never to suffer.

CIRCLE OF THE LUSTFUL

WILLIAM BLAKE's *Circle of the Lustful*, painted between 1824 and 1827, exquisitely illustrates a passage from Dante's *DIVINE COMEDY: THE INFERNO*. The composition shows two condemned souls, damned for their adulterous affair, telling their sad story to the poets Virgil and Dante as the scholars tour the underworld. Virgil is shown listening sympathetically as the once-lovely Francesca recalls the fateful day she and her lover succumbed to temptation. The two had been reading a tale of Sir Lancelot and his amorous adventures when they were overcome with passion. Francesca's husband, coming upon the couple in the act of adultery, killed them both. Now the pair is condemned to spend eternity swept along by the winds of desire in a never-ending storm. Dante, having heard their story, has fainted from pity and grief.

Circle of the Lustful features Blake's characteristic distorted anatomical proportions and abstract use of color and movement to illustrate the damned. He uses ink and watercolors to create the whirlwind that eternally propels sinners who, in life, were swept along by their carnal desires. He sends a legion of sensual sinners swirling through the bleak landscape and off into the distance. In contrast to the pale figures of the damned, Blake includes a vibrant portrait of the two lovers as they were in life, still full of lush color. The pair appears above the image of the damned Francesca, as in a vision. This contrast emphasizes the drab, grim realm of Dante's underworld where those who indulged their carnal desires must languish for eternity.

CITY OF GOD SAINT AUGUSTINE, a sixth-century Christian bishop and doctor of the church, penned *City of God* to address common contemporary misconceptions about hell and damnation. The text was written specifically in response to the Gnostics, a breakaway sect whose followers believe that life on earth is equivalent to existence in hell. His book refutes the concept of GNOSTIC HELL and dispels its doctrine that all matter is intrinsically evil. Augustine uses Scripture and biblical quotes to support his theories regarding the nature of matter and of the underworld.

City of God asserts that material creations are in fact beautiful and decent, having been formed by God. Augustine reminds readers that in Genesis, the Supreme Being looked directly at the new firmament and "saw that it was good." It is not until Adam disregards God's restriction and eats of the forbidden fruit that sin occurs. This free choice is a function of the human intellect and is independent of physical objects. Thus evil results not from matter but through the act of disobedience to God. Material is merely the instrument of humanity's offense, not its cause.

Damnation to hell, too, is therefore a choice. Humanity has been given the opportunity to attain salvation through the grace of God and the sacrifice of Christ, but we are not forced to accept it. Behavior during one's lifetime determines whether one is receptive to the grace necessary for redemption. Life on earth is the prelude to eternal punishment or reward rather than the bitter existence preached by the Gnostics. Equating earth with hell, according to Augustine, is not only inaccurate; it grossly underestimates the horrors that await the damned.

The bishop reiterates the distinction between matter and evil by noting that all those who suffer in hell are not material creations. Augustine points out that the fallen angels—purely spiritual beings—also endure agony in the dark underworld. He claims that "evil spirits, even without bodies, will be so connected to the fires" of hell that they, too, will be in unbearable anguish for all time. These fallen angels represent "darkness" and despair while their heavenly counterparts reflect the brilliance and sheer joy of paradise.

Augustine's *City of God* describes hell as a lake of FIRE AND BRIMSTONE and asserts that torments of the abyss are physical as well as spiritual. He denies the concept of ANNIHILATION, that souls damned to the great inferno will one day cease to exist. Augustine declares that damnation is eternal and that the nature and severity of the suffering in hell directly correspond to the evil a person has committed during his or her lifetime. *City of God* also addresses the question of the LAST JUDGMENT, noting that at this time the body and soul will be reunited, resulting in agonies of both the flesh and spirit for the damned. (An illustration from a fifteenth-century edition of *City of God* shows DEMONS of the underworld jabbing souls with black spears and boiling them in bubbling caldrons.)

Augustine's conclusions on hell were officially sanctioned by Christian authorities at the Synod of Constantinople in 543. Church leaders decreed that anyone who taught that hell is temporary or that the damned will one day be redeemed would be excommunicated for spreading heresy. (The Synod also rejected the popular notion that anyone calling himself or herself Roman Catholic would be saved from hell simply through affiliation with Christ's church. Those who live immoral, wicked, or wasted lives were advised that they could not hide behind a label and expect to attain automatic salvation.)

CLICHÉS The lingering cultural importance of hell is evident in the number and variety of common clichés about the underworld. These range from the whimsical to the profane. And most modern infernal phrases have their origins in classic works of literature, ancient myths, or religious teachings.

The expression "going to hell in a handbasket" is actually a derivative of "headed to heaven in a handbasket." The original phrase referred to one who had special, and perhaps undeserved, protection from unpleasant realities. Its infernal counterpart began as a pun but immediately became a popular way of indicating that an idea or project was doomed.

"All hell broke loose" comes from Milton's classic *PARADISE LOST.* The epic tells the tale of Adam and Eve, their sin in the Garden of Eden, and the tragic consequences of their act. Nowadays, the phrase is used to describe a situation that has gotten out of hand or gone terribly awry. "Better to reign in hell than serve in heaven" also originates with Milton.

The military has been the source of a number of infernal clichés. A World War I British army song gives us the term "hell's bells." The ditty, crooned by soldiers as they marched into battle, was a satirical tune mocking the enemy. One line claims, "The bells of hell go ting-a-ling-a-ling for you but not for me!"

General Sherman is credited with authoring the quip "War is hell." What he actually said to his troops was, "There is many a boy here today who looks on war as all glory. But boys, it is all hell." The popular line "I've done my time in hell" likewise derives from a military writ. The tombstone of a Marine killed in battle asks that St. Peter allow the soldier to enter heaven immediately, since he has already served his term in the underworld.

Love, like war, also spawned its share of hellish clichés, such as "hell has no fury like a woman scorned." This astute observation comes from a love poem by William Congreve. In his 1693 play *The Old Bachelor,* the poet notes that there is no greater horror, in this world or in the realm of the damned, than a lady who has been wronged. Commenting on charitable love between brethren, St. Frances de Sales noted in a letter that "hell is full of good intentions." The paved road was later added to complete the popular expression.

COMIC BOOKS Hell has served as a backdrop for comic book action for almost a century. Current titles include *Hellbound, Dances with Demons, Hell Blazer, Specter, Dark Dominion, Harrowers—Raiders of the Abyss,* and *Hell Storm.* The underworld is also the setting of innumerable stories contained in other pulps, such as *TWILIGHT ZONE MAGAZINE, Ellery Queen Mysteries,* and *Alfred Hitchcock Magazine.* And in the computer age, the inferno is available on-line via electronic books and "virtual toys." In the comic world, hell is both glamorized as a fascinating realm of mystery and depicted as a grisly prison for the wicked.

The history of using hell in such publications goes as far back as the early 1920s, when *Weird Tales* was first published. This innovative pulp featured the talents of such up-and-coming writers as Ray Bradbury, August Derleth, and Robert Bloch. Stories routinely involved the damned and portrayed hell as everything from a fiery pit to a plush bordello. These early tales whetted the reader's appetite for unconventional illustrations of the underworld and served as the forerunners of today's comic series. Imitators soon followed, and horror comics quickly took their place among the most popular titles in America.

Infernal comic books reached their zenith in the 1950s, when Entertaining Comics (E.C.) and a number of smaller presses couldn't keep *Fate, Haunt of Fear, Tales from the Crypt,* and a host of other spooky pulps on the shelves. By 1953, horror comics accounted for 25 percent of total sales, split almost evenly between adult and child purchasers. The craze was so popular that it prompted the government—still in the throes of McCarthyism—to produce a film warning parents about the dangers of these publications. According to narrator Ron Mann, these evil texts were part of a Communist plot to corrupt the youth of America by turning bright, patriotic children into "masses of jangled nerves" incapable of functioning in school or society. Mann showed an assortment of titles that parents should "look out for" and even interviewed a darling little eleven-year-old who tearfully told viewers how he "threw up" after reading one of these horrible comics.

In April of 1954, the United States Senate called for subcommittee hearings on the problem. Dr. Frederic Wertham, a German-born psychiatrist, testified that these demonic tales were corrupting the American psyche. Restrictions were imposed on comics as a result of these hearings, and many "offensive" words, including *horror* and *terror,* were censored from the titles. Authorities also disallowed inclusion of any "undead" creatures in the stories, including VAMPIRES and damned souls languishing in hell.

The strategy backfired: Sales soared. Critics realized that they were giving infernal comics an incredible amount of free publicity, arousing the curiosity of every prepubescent child in the country. To further aggravate the situation, the restrictions on comic books spawned a whole new cult fascination: monster television shows. Fans of the supernatural who could no longer satisfy their cravings through printed comics quickly tuned in to the new wave of programs hosted by underworld GHOULS.

Since the Establishment couldn't eradicate the desire for this type of entertainment, it decided to join them instead. The guardians of public morals adapted the horror comic format for their own purposes. Over the next few years, religious publishers put out thousands of pulps featuring grisly pictures of hell that depicted all manner of unpleasant tortures awaiting the damned. At the end of each tale was an invitation to read the Bible, repent, and return to Christian values to avoid such a fate. By the 1970s, these pulps were also incorporating into their stories warnings about the connection between drug use and damnation. One of the most successful was Hal Linsey's *There's A New World Coming,* a 1973 comic showing teens witnessing the torments of the damned as outlined in the New Testament book REVELATION.

Today, most underworld comic books feature "HADES raiders," heroes who try to save souls from hell while placing themselves in grave peril. Others, such as *Hell Hound,* are tales of guardians of the gate: champions who keep loathsome ghouls from escaping the underworld or who hunt down runaway fiends who are terrorizing the living. *Dances with Demons, Vault of Horror,* and *Lord of the Pit* all highlight the everyday adventures of life in hell. And still others are examples of devilish MOVIE MERCHANDISING, reviving damned villains and victims from feature films. These include comic books based on *HELLRAISER, NIGHTMARE ON ELM STREET,* and *BEETLEJUICE.*

Modern comics such as these feature adventures in hell.

In the Information Age, computer users can find infernal comics on the Internet. The entertainment development group Toynetwork offers a variety of electronic comic books, "virtual toys," and supernatural illustrations online. Toynetwork's latest underworld creation is *The Brotherhood,* a group of fallen angels who are "too good to be bad" and are "purged from Hell" and sent to earth to battle the wicked INCUBUS. Browsers can read the strips, view graphics, and even download and print their favorite images. If the characters generate enough interest, they can be developed into action figures, ANIMATED CARTOONS, COMPUTER GAMES, or printed comic books.

The standard depiction of hell in most modern comics is of a rocky, harsh landscape bounded by flames and deep chasms. Winged or hooded DEMONS usually preside over the dark realm and delight in inflicting pain upon the damned. Often, the newly dead are unaware of their situation or are in denial and slowly come to realize their fate as their surroundings become increasingly horrific. Torments include physical, emotional, and psychological agonies. Overall, comic book hells are depicted as instruments of justice, inescapable abysses where villains ultimately pay for their vile deeds. They offer a sense of power, of retribution, to a society feeling increasingly overwhelmed—and outgunned—by violence.

COMICS For those who can laugh in the face of danger, hell serves as a basis for a host of dark gags. The inferno below has been the setting of literally thousands of comics, ranging from weekly strips to political cartoons to whimsical quips on GREETING CARDS.

Syndicated cartoonist Gary Larson offers the lighter side of damnation in a number of his *Far Side* cartoons. His collection includes dozens of sketches lampooning the underworld. One shows a split screen with an angel in the top half greeting new arrivals to paradise with, "Welcome to Heaven, here's your harp," while the bottom portion shows a demonic counterpart telling newcomers, "Welcome to Hell, here's your accordion." Another depicts a group of the inferno's sweaty inhabitants watching a televised weather report, only to have the DEVIL inform them, "That cold front I told you about yesterday is just baaaaaaaaarely going to miss us."

Another syndicated comic, *Dilbert* by Scott Adams, features a series of strips about the red-suited, horned DEMON Phil, the "Ruler of Heck." This soft-boiled SATAN describes himself as the "Prince of Insufficient Light" and punisher of "minor offenses." In one episode, Phil offers a dissatisfied employee one of two torments: either Dilbert will receive "eternal high pay" but be forced to watch all his hard work destroyed in front of him at the end of every day, or he will be appreciated and productive but endure "eternal poverty." Phil's attempt at punishing Dilbert backfires, however, when the long-suffering worker gleefully exclaims that either option is "better than my current job!"

Hell's humorous side appears in a number of other publications. *Rolling Stone* magazine offers a regular series of *Heaven and Hell* cartoons by artist James T. Pendergrast. One features "Hell's Diner" where the specialty of the house is fried liver nuggets. Another shows the "Devil's cash machine," complete with a place to "insert first born" before removing money.

A 1994 cartoon in the *London Daily Telegraph* depicts two damned men chatting amid the flames about the pitchfork-wielding demon who watches over them. "I'm not sure about his morals," the speaker remarks, "but he's very good at his job." Similar devilish drawings by Charles Addams have appeared in *The New Yorker* for decades.

TWILIGHT ZONE MAGAZINE, published during the 1980s, ran numerous infernal comics, including lengthy stories told entirely in cartoon. Jim Ryan's 1985 feature *The Hook* shows the misadventures of a pathetic comedian who finds employment in hell. After being fired from every club in New York, the performer is approached by a Mr. Jones, a mysterious promoter who promises to make him a star. The only condition is that the comic must work for what Jones refers to as "my organization." He agrees and immediately catapults to superstardom. But when his two years of fame are up, the hapless comic must begin an eternal engagement at the "HADES Palladium."

His job is to torture hell's inhabitants with his awful jokes. Satan congratulates Jones, telling him, "This guy is the greatest thing since FIRE AND BRIMSTONE."

Hellish humor is a favorite among political satirists as well. A 1994 illustration by syndicated cartoonist Mike Luckovich shows a demon welcoming two terrorists—one Arab and one Israeli—to the smoldering underworld. He greets them with the salutation, "Welcome to your new homeland. You have to share it." And former president Richard Nixon's death generated a deluge of comics speculating on the controversial politician's damnation.

Most of these drawings soften hell considerably, showing the underworld as a place of annoyances and discomforts rather than a realm of unceasing torture. Their continued popularity, in a world that frequently trivializes religion, attests to the importance that hell holds even in our modern culture.

COMMENTARY ON THE APOCALYPSE *Commentary on the Apocalypse,* a 786 manuscript by Spanish monk Beatus of Liebana, is a fantastic mix of biblical images, folklore, legend, and fantasy. The manuscript, which was painstakingly copied by hand repeatedly in the days before printing, also features numerous illustrations of heaven and hell. It is based on prophecies of the LAST JUDGMENT, when Jesus will call all the dead before him for final reckoning, as foretold in REVELATION.

The most striking picture shows the battle with APOLLYON (also called ABBADON), the dark angel of the "bottomless pit." The winged DEMON wears a crown of flames as he rules an army of monstrous fiends. He and his minions are set against a patchwork of bright rectangles of red, green, burgundy, and yellow. They hungrily search the world for souls to devour. The picture's vibrant colors and simple lines create a feeling of utter evil and impending doom, sure to chill the hearts of its medieval readers.

COMPUTER GAMES One of the biggest fads to hit America in recent times is the video game craze. Since the early days of *Pong,* children (and adults) all over the country have been mesmerized by the flickering lights and beeps and buzzes of computerized games. Many of these involve adventures in hell, the ultimate in virtual surreality.

One of the earliest interactive infernal computer games is *TWILIGHT ZONE: Crossroads of the Imagination,* patterned after the classic television series. Players find themselves in bizarre situations with few clues as to how to escape back into reality. The adventures are episodic but are ultimately linked through common elements. Like the show, the *Twilight Zone* game incorporates many unexpected twists and turns, landing players in mysterious otherworlds and infernal regions of peril.

Hell: A Cyberpunk Thriller takes video games a step further. The computer quest features film star Dennis

Hopper's digitized image as Mr. Beautiful, a modernized SATAN. The game follows the exploits of this twenty-second-century horned fiend as he deals in all manner of drugs, pornography, and other contraband. He distributes his wares to the living via the gate of hell, located in Washington, D.C. This action-packed adventure allows players to take on the role of a secret agent exploring the depths of the fiery underworld. *Cyberpunk Thriller* incorporates sex, violence, and armageddon in a flashy format of burning landscapes, blood-drenched pentagrams, and toothy GHOULS. Atmosphere effects include bursts of FIRE AND BRIMSTONE, three-dimensional DEMONS, and the disturbing sound of souls wailing in torment.

Writer CLIVE BARKER's vision of hell has been adapted into *Hellraiser: Virtual Hell,* a slick adventure based on the Cenobites from Barker's horror film *HELLRAISER.* Far from replicating the plot of the underworld movie, *Virtual Hell* is an interactive adventure that truly involves the player. And the stakes are high: The goal of the game is to retrieve your soul from hell after it is snatched by Pinhead, leader of the underworld ghouls. *Virtual Hell* even features the voice of Doug Bradley, who played Pinhead in the *Hellraiser* movies. Technological advancements allow the sounds and images of hell to take on a three-dimensional quality.

Another movie adapted for the computer screen is *BEETLEJUICE,* the offbeat comedy about the world of the dead. The game offers a Graveyard, Ghoul House, Afterlife Waiting Room, and five additional infernal levels through which players must pass. Obstacles to be overcome include ravenous Sand Worms, detached limbs, deadly scorpions, and "cranky ogres," which must be eluded or diverted in order for players to advance.

The on-line computer adventure *The Brotherhood* features a band of rebel demons vanquishing hell.

PANGEA CORPORATION—JOHN SCHULTE, JOHN BESMEHN, CHERLY ANN WONG.

Cyber enthusiasts can also catch a ride on the video game *Hell Cab.* It begins in the abysmal parking lot of Kennedy Airport in New York City. Once players have hailed "Raul's taxi," the aim is to pay the fare before the meter runs out on life. Those who fail (or die in the process) face eternal damnation. This surreal trip also takes players through time and space, to the days of ancient Rome and even to the age of dinosaurs. However, while the fare is adding up, the soul is ebbing away.

One of the most popular combat video games, *Doom,* inspired an infernal sequel, *Doom II: Hell on Earth.* Ads for the adventure claim that, "This time, the entire forces of the netherworld have overrun Earth. To save her, you must descend into the stygian depths of Hell itself!" This trip to the dark regions includes howling hounds, gruesome ghouls, and a cavernous underworld of fire.

In addition to the myriad of underworld CD-ROM games for use on personal computers, a new wave of infernal challenges is cresting via the Internet. New "game servers" and "chat rooms" are appearing almost daily, dedicated to hellish adventures such as *Quake* and *Doom.* On-line competitions allow players from all over the world to challenge each other—and the denizens of the abyss—without leaving the keyboard.

Amusement developers are likewise "auditioning" ideas on-line, allowing users to electronically sample computer games and "virtual toys" and offer feedback. Browsers can read game descriptions, view graphics, and print their favorite images, then forward comments and suggestions to the games' creators. Concepts that generate enough interest can then be cultivated into computer games, toys, and other novelties.

Computer adventures set in hell offer players the ultimate thrill: saving themselves (and possibly the entire human race) from damnation. This takes the rescue motif, central to most computerized challenges, to its limit.

COUNTRY MUSIC Country music lyrics have been incorporating images of the grim afterlife into songs for decades. One of the first tuneful interpretations of the damned is the 1950s classic "Ghost Riders in the Sky." The song describes a frightening gang of astral cowboys who descend upon a young wrangler, terrifying him with their ghastly appearance. The troupe warns the man that he, too, faces a dismal eternity of "trying to catch the DEVIL's herd across an endless sky" if he does not change his ways.

More than three decades later, Confederate Railroad hit the charts with a ballad about the life and death of another hellbound rogue titled "If You Leave This Way You Can Never Go Back." This tale of woe recounts the sins of a wanderer who has made a habit of hurting and alienating people who have tried to help him. He eventually murders a man, is sentenced to death, and coldly renounces all hope of salvation. The somber verse predicts "all through eternity you'll roam alone" after living a life of such depravity and then refusing to repent.

Country music meets FAUST in the 1992 "The Devil Goes Back to Georgia" by Mark O'Connor. This song is a sequel to Charlie Daniel's "The Devil Went Down to Georgia," released a decade and a half earlier. In the reprise, SATAN returns to try once again to win the soul of Johnny, the fiddler who outperformed the dark lord in the first version. Johnny is now a "daddy" and is astonished that the devil is still determined to defeat him. This updated song includes passages from the Bible, prayers for victory, and a rebuke of the underworld ruler. In the MUSIC VIDEO for "The Devil Goes Back to Georgia," the image of hell is achieved through shots of molten lava, fire, and mass destruction. Superstar Travis Tritt even makes a cameo experience as the fiendish master of the damned.

Traditional images of CHRISTIAN HELL also appear in 4 Runner's "Cain's Blood." The song explores the inner struggle of a man who feels himself being pulled between the forces of good and evil, personified by his parents. Mama, a virtuous woman, preaches FIRE AND BRIMSTONE in hopes of preventing her son from turning out like his dad. Father, a chronic alcoholic and overall failure, freezes to death one cold night in a drunken stupor. Mama greets this news with the comment, "The devil can keep him warm," conjuring images of a blazing inferno to which he has surely departed. Her son keeps this memory close at hand to remind him of the consequences of sin. The music video for "Cain's Blood" illustrates this image with intermittent footage of flames leaping into the darkness.

Not all examples of lyrical hell are so serious. Hank Williams, Jr., makes known his feelings about the nature of the underworld in his ditty "If Heaven Ain't Alot Like Dixie." Fearing that paradise may not be a place of bass fishing, pro wrestling, and pork rinds, the singer begs instead, "Send me to Hell, or New York City, it'd be about the same to me."

CREEP TO DEATH Poet Joseph Payne Brennan offers a collection of haunting works on the nature of the afterlife in his 1984 compilation *Creep to Death.* His words are drenched with a sense of impending doom as he speculates on what the underworld must be like, especially following existence in a world that is far from paradise. In "Hell: A Variation," Brennan portrays the infernal region as a realm of ice rather than fire. He rejects the "scarlet DEVILS dancing" and "driving flames and smoke" in favor of a gloomy world of "gray and frozen hills" and the worst suffering, a "heart without hope."

Brennan revisits the idea of bleak isolation and coldness of the human spirit in "My Nineteenth Nightmare." In this poem, the speaker is condemned to relive the sorrow of his ill-fated "First Love" who is lost among "houses made of stone" on a desolate "frosty street." "Winter Dusk" likens the gray skies and "briefer sun" of the cold season to the barren landscape of hell. Brennan likewise laments that "I shall rot, a wrinkled ape" after death in "Grottos of Horror" while his spirit languishes in eternal morose.

The poems in *Creep to Death* stir images of eternal suffering linked to human weakness and sorrow. Damnation is the failure of those who live in a frigid world devoid of emotion to form substantive relationships with one another. Brennan equates hell with despair, a concept shared by the poet Dante in his *DIVINE COMEDY: THE INFERNO*. His works also reflect theories of WILLIAM BLAKE and EMANUEL SWEDENBORG that joy or suffering—in this life as well as the next—result from the individual soul's attitude rather than from a sentence imposed by some omnipotent deity.

CRIME Obsession with SATAN and with hell has been linked to nefarious crimes for centuries. During the Middle Ages, occultists were associated with grave robbing, necrophilia, desecration of sacred ground, and sometimes even human sacrifice. Confessed witch ISOBEL GOWDIE admitted to committing a number of atrocities as part of her coven activities, ranging from vandalism to murder. And although the time of widespread DEVIL worship has passed, ties to the netherworld continue to play a part in grisly acts. Allegiance to the inferno has factored into some of America's most notorious crimes.

The most infamous example of this is the Manson family's bloody murder spree in the late 1960s. Leader Charles Manson patterned his sect after the Church of the Final Judgment (also known as the Process), a Satanic cult founded by a former disciple of Scientology founder L. Ron Hubbard. The Process's California headquarters was just two blocks from the site of Manson's 1967 commune, and the diabolical guru had extensive contact with the sect's members (who continued to visit him in prison throughout the Tate–La Bianca murder trial). Manson adopted many of the Process's rituals and beliefs, even embracing the BIKER gang Hell's Angels as "soldiers of Armageddon."

During the days leading up to the killings, Manson identified himself as both Satan and Christ interchangeably. One of his favorite lecture topics was the "bottomless pit," a place he found quite glamorous. Manson described it as a "hole in Death Valley" where he would lead his chosen for their final reward. He frequently gave rambling speeches to "family members," extolling the virtues of the pit and its endless sensual delights.

Many of Manson's followers also had underworld ties. Cult member Bobby Beausoleil was a failed actor who had played the devil in the horror film *LUCIFER Rising*. Susan Atkins (who would later be convicted of participating in the murders) experienced visions of hell induced by LSD. She also claimed to be a witch who regularly took part in black masses and other infernal rituals. And one of the most frighteningly cold and unrepentant murderers, Charles "Tex" Watson, admitted that he had told his victims, "I am the Devil and I'm here to do the Devil's business" before mutilating them.

The connection between hell and drug use had been established long before the 1960s. Author Aldous Huxley's 1954 *The Doors of Perception,* and *Heaven and Hell,* clearly linked the two. Huxley concludes that many hallucinogenic drugs such as mescaline and LSD can cause powerful visions of the underworld. He cites one case where the user experiences terror "of being overwhelmed, of disintegrating under a pressure . . . greater than a mind could possibly bear." *Heaven and Hell* also notes that Americans spend more on alcohol and cigarettes than on education in an attempt to "escape from selfhood." But just as worry over contracting lung cancer does not stop us from smoking; the fear of hell does not stop us from committing evil acts. This is evident in the number, nature, and frequency of gruesome atrocities.

Author Joel McGinniss chronicles another infernal crime in his 1991 book *Cruel Doubt.* This factual account explores the murder and attempted murder of a prominent North Carolina couple. The surviving victim learned to her horror that her own son was responsible for her husband's brutal slaughter (he had been savagely bludgeoned to death). A lengthy investigation revealed that the teen and his college friends, all heavy drug users, had gotten the idea for the killing from Dungeons and Dragons (D & D), an "otherworldly" role-playing GAME. Before moving on to murder, the troupe had frequently played in "Hell tunnels" (symbolic of the realm of the dead) as part of their obsession with the mystic game that mixes magic, spells, and the "upper" and "lower" worlds of spirits.

Perhaps the most tragic act of violence associated with Satanism and hell is the recent rash of teenage suicides. Teens, often feeling misunderstood by their parents, persecuted by their teachers, and confused by their lack of direction in life, become easy prey for demonic cults. Most do not truly believe in the doctrines; they are simply seeking acceptance and identity through association with hell. This rejection of traditional values also gives many a feeling of independence from their families, since they know that Mom and Dad would certainly never approve. Unfortunately, some discover that unholy allegiance is fatal, as suicide pacts are becoming more prevalent among these quasi-Satanic sects.

In 1992, a high school student from an affluent Maryland suburb suddenly stepped in front of a train as her shocked friends watched. In the aftermath of her death, her parents discovered the girl's diary and were horrified to find numerous entries about Satan and hell. According to the account, the teenager proclaimed that Satan "is my father" and that he had taken her on tours of hell, where she longed to go permanently. Authorities at her high school learned that she was not the only student obsessed with the underworld and uncovered a free-form cult with Satanic beliefs. This led to probes throughout the country, and a startling number of high schools reported discovering demonic practices being conducted within their walls.

One of the difficulties in prosecuting crimes involving diabolical elements is the skepticism and denial by the general public. Few citizens want to admit that Satanism (and its gruesome practices) is truly a problem. It is too shocking for many mainstream Americans to contemplate, so they choose simply to deny the infernal connection and search instead for some other explanation. Only when violence erupts on a grand scale—such as with the Manson murders—does the public confront the notion that hell's influence played a role in the crime.

CUPAY The Inca (originating from what is now Peru, Ecuador, and parts of Chile, Bolivia, and Argentina) believe that evil souls must face Cupay, the vicious god of death. Cupay lives in a dark cavern inside the earth and feeds on the spirits of the dead. He is a greedy deity whose lust for evil is insatiable, and he is ever trying to increase the size of his kingdom. He obtains souls by tricking humans into killing each other and committing other atrocities, thereby assuring their damnation.

Cupay is considered extremely evil; some legends say he demanded frequent human sacrifice. Early Christian missionaries called him the equivalent of the DEVIL and his realm the Inca counterpart of hell.

D

DAI MOKUREN Dai Mokuren is the follower of Buddha credited with retrieving his mother's soul from hell. According to the legend, Dai Mokuren sees a vision of his mother starving in one of the many BUDDHIST HELLS and tries to comfort her. He sends her famished spirit food, but it bursts into flames as she tries to eat it. Horrified, Dai Mokuren calls on Buddha for an explanation. Buddha replies that the woman had coldly refused to feed a traveling priest during one of her past lives and is now being punished in the realm of hungry spirits. Dai Mokuren pleads for her release, and Buddha agrees on the condition that the devoted son perform an almost impossible feat on his mother's behalf.

Dai Mokuren is ordered to give food offerings to every priest throughout the world on the tenth day of the seventh month. If he can accomplish this task, his mother will be spared further torture. Through superhuman effort and dedication to his mother's cause, Dai Mokuren manages to make the offerings in time. Seeing his devotion, Buddha ends the mother's suffering.

Dai Mokuren is also credited with originating the Bon Odori, dances celebrating the Japanese Festival of the Dead. By performing these rituals, Buddhists believe they can offer solace to souls in hell.

DAMN YANKEES George Abbott's 1955 classic *Damn Yankees* brought the FAUST legend to the Broadway stage. The musical drama about deals with the DEVIL replaces Dr. Faust's thirst for knowledge with a disgruntled baseball fan's hunger for a winning season. When Joe, the sports devotee, declares he would sell his soul to help his beloved Washington Senators win the pennant, Mr. Applegate, a contemporary MEPHISTOPHELES, appears in a cloud of smoke and gladly obliges.

The topic of damnation is handled very gingerly by the cunning DEMON. Whenever anyone asks about hell or its unpleasant facilities, Mr. Applegate quickly changes the subject, saying there will be plenty of time to discuss that later. There are a few brief glimpses of what lies in store for Joe in the afterlife, such as JOKES about FIRE AND BRIMSTONE, a dance number featuring ominous demons, and flashes of Mr. Applegate's wicked temper. But the specific horrors of the underworld are left to Joe's imagination.

Damn Yankees, unlike the original Faust story, has a happy ending. Joe manages to escape his dire fate through the intercession of his deeply devoted wife. (This alternate conclusion is borrowed from later adaptations of the Faust legend in which the love of a good woman saves the immoral man from eternity in hell.)

Abbott's play was translated into a feature film in 1958 and in 1994 made a triumphant return to the Broadway stage with Jerry Lewis in the role of the wicked Mr. Applegate.

DAMNATION OF LOVERS
German painter Matthias Grünewald depicts hell as a place of divine retribution where the punishment fits the offense in his sixteenth-century painting *Damnation of Lovers.* The artist uses irony to show how one's sins are revisited upon him or her in the depths below. His portrait offers a pair of old, ugly, sexless creatures doomed to an eternity of regretting their earthly carnal indulgences.

In *Damnation of Lovers,* the man and woman who in life were obsessed with satisfying the flesh are transformed into grotesque cadavers stripped of all beauty and sensuality. Their skin is yellow and cracked, with worms and snakes crawling in and out of a dozen open wounds. Scorpions, fleas, and beetles pick at their rotting corpses. The woman's sallow breasts sag pathetically; a toad perches on her pubic area. Her lover is a balding, skeletal ogre with blackened teeth. There is no vestige of sexuality left in either one. Having surrendered their souls to lust on earth, in hell they have relinquished their bodies as well. The memories of erotic sins that offered so much gratification will taunt them for all eternity as each views the other, now a repulsive, putrefying GHOUL.

Grünewald's *Damnation of Lovers* implies that the sufferings of hell are not limited to physical pain. The agony is magnified by the realization that the damned have given their immortal souls for fleeting pleasures. This awareness of their tragic bargain torments the mind as surely as corporeal agony engulfs the body.

THE DAMNED Souls existing in hell are called damned, derived from the Latin *damnare,* meaning "to inflict loss upon or to condemn." The term applies to both natural creatures (humans) and supernatural beings (angels, gods). Damnation also implies divine wrath or punishment originating from some higher power.

DAMNED CONSIGNED TO HELL, THE LUCA SIGNORELLI painted a forceful interpretation of hell in his composition *The Damned Consigned to Hell.* The artist spent five years on his vision, working from 1499 to 1504 on the masterpiece. His imaginative use of color and realistic portrayal of human anatomy bring haunting vibrancy to the terrible realm of the dead.

At the top of the fresco are three mighty angels dressed in armor and wielding swords. They are protecting the gates of heaven, fending off an evil invasion, and casting condemned souls into the abyss. Dark DEMONS gleefully snatch the defeated assailants and whisk them into the bowels of the underworld. There they heave the lost souls into the fiery mouth of hell as if shoveling coal into a blazing furnace.

In the foreground is a riotous mass of tangled bodies. The souls of damned people are done in pale flesh tones, while the fallen angels are painted green, purple, and orange. These ghouls have sharp horns, pointed wings, and cruel, distorted faces. They drag the naked mortals into the inferno, biting, clawing, and strangling their charges. Some demons pull the forsaken along by the hair; others bind them with ropes and haul them, screaming, to their punishment.

Signorelli's *The Damned Consigned to Hell* differs from many Christian depictions of the underworld due to its lack of SATAN or ruler of hell. The damned are tortured by an army of demons with no overall leader. However, the artist may be indicating that the worst agonies are yet to come, administered by the master of pain himself, in the unseen pits of the fiery abyss.

DANAÏDS The Danaïds are forty-nine sisters damned to suffer eternally in HADES according to Greek myth. They are the daughters of Danaüs, a bitter man who secretly despises his twin brother, Aegyptus. Danaüs had fifty daughters and Aegyptus fifty sons, and the men agreed that the cousins should be wed in a mass ceremony. Danaüs instructed his girls to murder their husbands on their wedding night in order to spite Aegyptus. Forty-nine did so, and only one, Hypermnestra, spared her husband's life.

As punishment for their crime, the Danaïds are sentenced to fill a water jug in TARTARUS, the lowest realm of the underworld. But each is given a sieve instead of a ladle, so every time they draw water it spills immediately back into the pool. Thus their task can never be accomplished.

DANTE'S INFERNO This 1935 film marks one of Hollywood's first attempts at incorporating images of the underworld into a nonreligious story line. *Dante's Inferno* stars Spencer Tracy as Jim Carter, an unscrupulous drifter who sets his sights on a concession run by a kindly old gentleman and his lovely young niece. The attractions offer exhibits based on Italian poet Dante Alighieri's fourteenth-century classic *DIVINE COMEDY: THE INFERNO*. It graphically illustrates the horrors of hell as described in Dante's work.

The Inferno is a cavernous maze depicting DEMONS and tortures directly from the pages of the poet's masterpiece of supernatural literature. Torches line its dark corridors, sending dancing shadows of DEVILS, GHOULS, and winged fiends across its gloomy hallways. Huge serpents protrude from the walls. A bust of the poet watches as patrons make their way through the grim spectacle conceived in his imagination.

The owner of the sideshow has kept his concession open as a warning for viewers against indulging in wickedness, but Tracy has other plans. He connives to take over the Inferno and turn it into a moneymaking house of horrors that exploits morbid curiosity for profit. His nefarious schemes soon result in the suicide of one employee and the eventual ruin of several lives, including that of the owner's naive niece.

While running the atrocity, Tracy experiences a ten-minute vision of hell brought on by the dismal displays. Stupefied, Tracy stumbles through the hallucination, seeing himself among the damned as a detestable monster. The inhabitants of hell seem to mock him, welcoming him as one of their own. He hears echoes of the grim passages of the book describing the torments that await sinners in the underworld. The words Dante has inscribed above the gates of hell, "Abandon hope, all ye who enter here," haunt the corrupt entrepreneur as he sees his future: eternal damnation in the pit of despair.

Tracy regains his faculties and tries to forget the ugly vision but realizes that his life has become equally abysmal. After bribing a safety inspector who had threatened to close the unsafe attraction, Tracy is arrested when Inferno collapses. His wife leaves him, the inspector commits suicide, and Tracy is held responsible for the injuries resulting from the disaster. These events, and the horrific hallucination, force him to reevaluate his life and amend his evil ways to avoid ending up in the hell of his waking nightmare.

DANTE'S VISION A sixteenth-century portrait of the poet Dante Alighieri, author of the *DIVINE COMEDY:*

THE INFERNO, offers a touching glimpse into the thoughts of the great writer. The painting (artist unknown) shows a somber, brooding Dante perched above his hometown of Florence. (Dante had been living in exile from his homeland due to political conflicts which resulted in his banishment. He wrote the *Divine Comedy* while exiled, incorporating friends and enemies into his work.) The towers and spires of Florence are illuminated by the fires of hell. Across the placid Arno River, the distant paradise looms.

As Dante looks longingly to the splendor of heaven, he holds his own book, open to a passage regarding his exile. The section begins "if ever" and recounts Dante's optimistic plans for returning to his beloved Florence. The artist captures Dante's sorrow and anger, knowing what the author could not have known when he wrote the passage: Dante would die without being permitted to return to the city he so loved.

Angela Featherstone,
as Veronica Iscariot, prepares to flee hell.
PHOTO BY CHARLOTTE STEWART

DARK ANGEL: THE ASCENT

The 1994 film noir *Dark Angel: The Ascent* offers an imaginative twist on modern hell movies: It depicts a brooding DEMON who tires of torturing damned souls and dreams of living on earth. Young Veronica, the fallen angel of the title (played by Angela Featherstone), is restless and unsatisfied with life in the inferno and tells her bloodthirsty father, Helliken Iscariot, that she longs to see the upperworld. Enraged with her insubordination, the fiend angrily draws his saber and threatens to slay the girl, telling his wife that "we can always have more children." But before he can strike, Featherstone flees the underworld and escapes to the human plane through a mysterious crevasse.

The Dark Angel emerges naked from a manhole, losing her horns, claws, and wings as she is "born" into the living world. Accompanied by her dog, HELLRAISER, Featherstone begins fulfilling her self-appointed mission of dispatching "vile sinners" to her former home. In a series of brutal encounters, the dedicated spirit rips the spine out of a would-be rapist, impales a mugger on an iron pole, and slashes the throats of a pair of racist policemen, reverting to demonic form each time the vengeful rage overtakes her. But the love of a good man helps Featherstone learn compassion, and she abandons her violent ways.

Still vowing to "obliterate evil from the face of the earth," Featherstone sets her sights on reforming a heartless politician who is victimizing the city's underclass. She accomplishes this by giving him a terrifying vision of what "awaits in eternity." After seeing the damned being beaten, burned, and disemboweled, the mayor leaves his office for a secluded monastery. Featherstone, wounded by one of his bodyguards, must then return to the underworld, where only the waters of the river STYX can heal her.

Director Linda Hassani achieves the appropriate atmosphere for the abyss through a variety of innovative filming techniques. The hell sequences were shot in an abandoned seventeenth-century Romanian castle, most notably in its unfinished dungeon carved into the base of the fortress. No electric light was used in the underworld scenes; the abyss was illuminated only by firelight from hundreds of torches, bursts of subterranean flames, and a specially designed "river of fire." The result is a frightening image of doom and despair reminiscent of the grim infernos described in medieval VISION LITERATURE.

DEAD SEA SCROLLS The Dead Sea Scrolls, a collection of ancient texts dating to the second century B.C., remains one of the most controversial archaeological finds. Discovered in Qumram (near Palestine) in 1947, the writs tell of a struggle between a group of pious Jews (Hasidim) and their religious and political rivals. But the scrolls also offer historical information that illuminates both Jewish and early Christian teachings of the era. Within the scrolls are numerous references to hell, the DEMONS BELIAL and LEVIATHAN, and the impending LAST JUDGMENT.

The works are written primarily in Hebrew, although some of the later scrolls are in Aramaic and Greek. Included among them are many copies of the books of the Old Testament, the Hebrew Bible texts. A few passages believed to be identical to New Testament sections have also been translated, attesting to the validity of the scrolls.

The War of the Sons of Light and the Sons of Darkness describes an apocalyptic battle between the forces of good and evil. It names several tribes as being on the side of heaven, while the beast Belial, ruler of the underworld, commands the armies of hell. The scroll foretells a fierce, bloody battle in which many will be killed. But the author assures readers that in the end, good will triumph and the legions of evildoers will be cast into the dismal abyss.

This is followed by *The Rout of Belial* and *The Coming Doom,* both of which warn against allegiance to the DEVIL. One passage asserts that at the Last Judgment, the earth will be destroyed, "wrong will disappear forever," and truth will reign eternal. Another quote cautions the faithful not to "yield your souls to SHEOL," the murky underworld of Hebrew texts. For in the end, a second rebellion will break out, but this time it will be against Belial rather than Yahweh. Justice will be swift and harsh for those who have pledged their loyalty to the dark lord.

Hell is mentioned is other parts of the Dead Sea Scrolls as well. The story of the fallen angels and the creation of the underworld is recounted in the *Epochs of Time.* This scroll has not been completely translated, but scholars have deciphered phrases about "eternal shame and contempt" and "punishment" that never ends. Passages from the *Book of Hymns* ask God for help in avoiding the "pangs of Hell" and the "raging blaze" of the underworld. One prayer begs the Creator, "Deliver me from the pit and the slough," where the "floods of Belial burst forth unto Hell itself."

Scholars continue to disagree on the historical validity of these texts. Whether the Dead Sea Scrolls are authentic writs of ancient times or clever forgeries from a more recent era, one fact is clear: The authors were deeply concerned with the terrors of the underworld.

DEBUSSY, CLAUDE The French musical genius Claude Debussy (1862–1918) dedicated the major part of his career to creating "infernal" images and "chilling" atmosphere through music. Debussy has been called the "father of the Impressionist movement of musical compositions," although he himself detested this label. His goal was simply to stir the soul with dark emotions and abysmal visions in much the same way many traditional composers have attempted to engender feelings of piety and religious reverence with music. Debussy applied his considerable artistic talents to invoking images of hell rather than heaven.

Debussy's supernatural masterpiece is *The Sunken Cathedral.* This work for piano brings to life a medieval fortress of the damned that rises from the mists at night and sinks back into the sea at dawn. The sounds of ringing bells, chanting monks, and wailing GHOULS mingle with his macabre melodies for a truly diabolical effect. It is an apparition reminiscent of specters from Christian VISION LITERATURE.

At the time of his death, Debussy was putting horror master Edgar Allan Poe's "The Fall of the House of Usher" to music. He died before its completion, and only fragments of several movements survive. Debussy's legacy continues, however, as he influenced many modern composers, including BÉLA BARTÓK.

DEMONS Demons, or unearthly evil spirits, are found in almost every belief system throughout the world. The word originates from the Greek *daimon,* meaning a deified spirit with supernatural qualities. As early as 270 B.C., the Septuagint, the first Greek translation of the Hebrew Old Testament, began using the term, referring exclusively to wicked specters. It has since become synonymous with evil.

Belief in the existence of demons is global. In African countries, these fiends are thought to be the souls of dead ancestors who become hostile if not honored with adequate sacrifice or homage. ASURAS, Hindu spirits, are associated with drought, death, and disaster. In Islamic belief, djinni are monstrous demons fathered by IBLIS, the equivalent of the Christian SATAN.

Judeo-Christian tradition identifies many demons: BELIAL, BEELZEBUB, SATAN, TARTARUCHUS, LUCIFER, (the DEVIL), INCUBUS, and SUCCUBUS. According to religious doctrines, the demons' mission is to tempt humankind into sin, facilitate damnation, then punish souls in hell. Some demons, such as Belial and Tartaruchus, have specific duties and are assigned roles in hell's hierarchy. Others, such as the incubus and succubus, are nameless generic fiends who terrorize the living and assist in the expansion of the infernal kingdom.

In the mid-tenth century, philosopher Michael Psellos defined six separate and distinct types of demons, each occupying a different space in the metaphysical universe. The lowest of these, the misophaes (haters of light), dwell in the deepest pit of hell. Psellos's theories were eventually dismissed by critics who found them absurd and baseless, but fascination with the nature of demons persists.

Today, demons are found in countless films, plays, operas, songs, poems, works of CHILDREN'S LITERATURE, novels, and other creative endeavors. They are a favorite image for TATTOOS and have been embraced by BIKERS and HEAVY METAL MUSIC enthusiasts. In popular culture, the underworld spirits adorn GIFT NOVELTIES, T-SHIRTS, and even FOOD NOVELTIES. And they remain a fixture in many religious cautionary tales.

DESCENT INTO LIMBO Artist Benvenuto di Giovanni illustrates the HARROWING OF HELL in his *Descent into LIMBO,* part of a series of works illustrating *The Passion of Our Lord.* The *Descent into Limbo* shows a triumphant Christ wrapped in a dazzling white shroud breaking down the gates of hell to free the souls of the patriarchs. He is standing before the entrance of the cavernous underworld atop broken pieces of the inferno's door, some of which crush SATAN, who is splayed defeated at Christ's feet.

From inside the jammed cave, the anguished faces of hell's inhabitants look hopefully to their redeemer. Their expressions show a mix of astonishment, relief, and joy. The various clothing styles and headdresses symbolize people of different ages and stations in life, depicting the cultures of the Old Testament. Adam and Eve appear draped in simple skins, while King David is in full royal regalia. Christ extends his arms to all, leading them out of hell and to their heavenly reward.

Giovanni's work does not depict any physical tortures of the underworld. However, he does convey the realm's dismal agony. Souls in hell are packed in so tightly that there is not an inch of space between them. Rows and rows of sorrowful inhabitants mourn their fate and await salvation, their suffering apparent from their baleful expressions. Even at the sight of Christ the souls in limbo are hesitant to rejoice, afraid of bitter disappointment and slow to comprehend what is happening. Only the dark DEVIL, lying smashed beneath the gates of hell, fully realizes that the underworld is being raided and that nothing can stop Christ's holy conquest.

DEVIL Devil is a generic term that applies to any of a number of supernatural creatures who dwell in the underworld. It can refer to a specific inhabitant of hell, such as the Christian LUCIFER or SATAN or the Islamic IBLIS, to a fallen angel, or to a DEMON who tortures the souls of the damned. The name sometimes is used to refer to wicked men who oppose the will of God. It originates from the Greek *diabolos* and the Latin *diabolus,* meaning "to throw across," a term associated with the fall of Lucifer, a blasphemous angel who is thrown out of heaven and into the abyss of hell.

Devils can take many different shapes, but the traditional image is that of a spiritual predator. Poets and painters have used dogs, snakes, goats, lions, and wolves to portray these infernal creatures. Numerous religions teach that devils are mutant creatures with a variety of animal characteristics, embodying the horror that results from rejecting the will of God. They are frequently shown as having horns, pointy tales, and razor-sharp teeth.

Countless texts attribute devils with the power to change their form in hopes of tempting humans. These crafty shape-shifters could appear as kindly scholars, beautiful women, or even holy clerics. In the New Testament, Satan takes appealing form to try to tempt Christ in the desert without realizing that he is dealing with the son of God. Stravinsky's opera *L'HISTOIRE D'UN SOLDAT* (A Soldier's Story) depicts the devil as a seemingly harmless elderly man prowling the byways for naive travelers. And in the made-for-television movie *INVITATION TO HELL,* the lord of the damned is played by voluptuous soap opera vixen Susan Lucci. In each instance, the devil carefully conceals his true identity—and appearance—until completing his diabolical mission.

Devils are featured in innumerable myths, plays, songs, artworks, ANIMATED CARTOONS, COMIC BOOKS, and feature films.

DEVIL AND BILLY MARKHAM, THE Shel Silverstein's offbeat one-act drama *The Devil and Billy Markham* is an odd mix of rhyme, music, and pop theology. The drama goes to hell to redeem the soul of a wayward loser, with lots of rich infernal atmosphere to set the mood.

In this classic update of the FAUST deal with the DEVIL theme, Markham is an aspiring musician who decides that hell can be no worse than his current existence. And its inhabitants are undoubtedly more companionable than the hustlers, managers, and music publishers who, Markham claims, have ruined his chances for success. He begins playing dice with a DEMON but soon ends up fighting for his soul. The battle goes back and forth, with each trying to outsmart (or simply outmaneuver) the other.

The underworld of *The Devil and Billy Markham* is a place of unpleasant characters rather than of FIRE AND BRIMSTONE. Markham represents the typical infernal resident: a shallow, crude scoundrel who trivializes woman, distrusts everyone, and condemns all who do not agree with his opinions. Those in hell are allowed to interact with the saved in heaven, but what sets them apart is their attitudes. Damnation exists in miring oneself in petty selfishness, a notion popularized by the philosophies of WILLIAM BLAKE and EMANUEL SWEDENBORG.

"DEVIL AND DANIEL WEBSTER, THE" Stephen Vincent Benét's 1936 short story "The Devil and Daniel Webster" updates and embellishes the FAUST legend. The tale, set in rural New Hampshire in the late 1800s, combines folklore, historical figures, and religious beliefs of the era. And this distinctly American version adds an imaginative twist: After selling his soul to the DEVIL, the repentant bargainer enlists the services of a lawyer to try to undo the deal.

In "The Devil and Daniel Webster," impoverished farmer Jabez Stone surrenders his soul to hell in exchange for seven years of good fortune and prosperity. At first he is delighted with his pact, but as the day of reckoning approaches, he becomes increasingly fearful of what lies ahead. When the devil comes to claim him, Stone hires famous attorney Daniel Webster to find an escape clause.

Mr. Scratch, the representative of hell, agrees to review the case in court, but on one condition: He must be allowed to select the jury. The grim DEMON searches the bowels of hell to find the underworld's most vile murderers, thieves, and cads to serve at trial. Satisfied that this collection of criminals will bring in a verdict against the farmer, Mr. Scratch gives a scathing speech describing Stone's infernal bargain, asserting that the devil kept his end and now the farmer must do the same. But through Webster's brilliant oratory, the jurors not only nullify the contract but also begin to have remorse for their own sins. Mr. Scratch, fearful that Webster's skills could empty the underworld of the damned, flees back to his abyss—without Jabez Stone.

"The Devil and Daniel Webster" has become a classic of American literature and has served as the inspiration for countless plays, operas, movies, and even ANIMATED CARTOON satires.

DEVIL AND MAX DEVLIN, THE Disney Studios explores the infernal terrain in the 1981 comedy *The Devil and Max Devlin,* a contemporary version of the FAUST story. When a callous slumlord is run over by a bus and sent to hell, he is offered a way out: He must recruit three innocent souls for the DEVIL in exchange for his own. If Devlin can bring about their ruin, he will be released from the underworld and restored to life. Otherwise, he is doomed to spend eternity broiling in the great inferno.

The film stars Elliott Gould as the corrupt Devlin and Bill Cosby as an amusingly menacing SATAN. Cosby, ruler of the misty hell of Disney imagination, gives Gould two months to find the three replacements. But the sleazy Gould begins to have second thoughts about working in league with the powers of darkness. He refuses to betray the young souls, and this act of decency ultimately saves him from eternal damnation.

Disney, at the time still committed to "family" entertainment, gingerly depicts hell as a steaming pit at the bottom of a long escalator. Butane and plaster replace FIRE AND BRIMSTONE; filming the underworld scene consumed 150 gallons of lighter fluid and an enormous amount of plaster for stalagmites and stalactites. The illusion of suffering is created through the distant sound of voices shrieking in agony. And the devil is not a horribly disfigured DEMON but rather a fast-talking, wisecracking prankster more interested in making snappy jokes than in inflicting pain.

Disney has also produced numerous depictions of hell in ANIMATED CARTOONS, including scenes from the 1940 classic *FANTASIA,* the 1996 *Hunchback of Notre Dame,* and the 1997 update of the *HERCULES* legend.

DEVIL'S DAUGHTER The 1991 German film *Devil's Daughter* puts the entrance to hell in the basement of a Rhineland tenement. Far below the cellar of this house is a deep sewer that Herbert Lom, playing head Satanist Moebius Kelly, declares is a doorway to the underworld of "he who has no name." Worshipers of this nameless beast are gathering at the portal for a dark ritual that will lead to the birth of SATAN's child.

Devil's Daughter offers only brief glimpses into the underworld, instead spending most of its 112 minutes depicting human sacrifices, brutal dismemberments, and grisly slashings. The worst of these is a graphic sequence in which a live victim has her entire face torn off by a series of carefully placed hooks. Lom then sews the detached skin over his own face, a rite that restores his life force. Viewers are also subjected to repeated scenes of birds ripping into the flesh of the movie's heroine—filmed in close-up. In one such episode a score of worms crawl out of the fresh wound.

What *is* seen of the subterranean inferno is murky: The sewer opens into a pit of blue-gray muck where the damned float in agonized anticipation of the birth of Satan's offspring. The intimation is that the horrors perpetrated by the Satanists are a pale preview of the gory tortures that await below.

DEVIL'S EYE, THE This 1960 Swedish film directed by Ingmar Bergman is based on the Danish radio drama *DON JUAN Returns.* Taking a playful look at virtue in the modern world, the premise is that the beautiful daughter of a conservative minister (played by Bibi Andersson) is giving SATAN a sty by refusing to part with her virginity before marriage. Her chastity becomes intolerable, and the DEVIL decides he must do something to rectify the situation.

Satan searches hell for a someone wicked enough to tempt the lovely Andersson into sin. Ultimately, he devises a plan to send legendary ladies' man Don Juan back to earth to corrupt the young maiden. But the Don discovers, to his sorrow, that his wiles have become outdated and even comical to the women of the twentieth century. Andersson finds his romantic overtures laughable, making the great lover wish he had never left hell in the first place. Her rejection is worse than any torment of the underworld and destroys his last remaining comfort: self-delusion.

DEVIL'S MESSENGER, THE

Three episodes of a 1961 failed television series were combined and released as a movie under the title *The Devil's Messenger.* Originally packaged as *#13 DEMON Street,* this Swedish production was marked by poor production values, deplorable acting (even by its marquee star Lon Chaney), and a predictable plotline. The movie suffers not only from these flaws but also from continuity problems resulting from the cutting and splicing necessary to consolidate the three shows into a seventy-two-minute film.

The Devil's Messenger follows the exploits of sexy demon (played by Karen Kadler) as she attempts to recruit souls for SATAN. Chaney, as the conniving fiend, plans to use Kadler to implement his elaborate, and somewhat nonsensical, plot to take over the world so he can leave hell and rule on earth. But the plan fails, and Chaney must remain in exile in his smoky abyss. The underworld of this odd production is a murky realm of dark corridors and confusing angles, borrowing images from the Greek HADES and CHRISTIAN HELL.

DEVIL'S RAIN, THE The 1975 film *The Devil's Rain* presents a cult of SATAN worshipers who suffer a peculiar damnation. They are condemned to wander the harsh desert of the Old West until they find the portal to hell, located somewhere in the arid region. Their fate is further complicated by the theft of a sacred Satanic book that lists the names of all the avowed disciples. Until this text is returned to the DEVIL, his followers must "suffer the devil's rain," a raging tempest of the damned. The precipitation of the title is a constant deluge that transforms the lost souls into vacant-eyed blobs of melted flesh.

Satanists who have signed over their spirits to the fiend are held in a sort of suspended existence while the devil searches for the book. When the descendant of one of Satan's disciples (played by William Shatner) finds the mysterious text, he goes to the desert to investigate. He is immediately stalked by the army of GHOULS (including John Travolta in his cinematic debut) and ultimately dragged into the underworld. The film ends with an eerie glimpse of hell, seen through an ominous hourglass that reveals a legion of souls writhing in agony.

The Devil's Rain is distinct from other "portal to hell" movies in that the makers used actual Satanists in developing the plotline and staging certain diabolic scenes. Anton Szandor Lavey, Elder of the Church of Satan, served as the project's "technical adviser" and helped ensure that the film was not just gory but spiritually disturbing as well.

DEVIL'S SON-IN-LAW, THE

Hell is a hazy pit of orange smoke where the DEVIL plots against humanity according to this bizarre 1977 comedy. An urban tale with elements of the FAUST drama, *The Devil's Son-in-Law* follows the exploits of Petey Wheatstraw (played by comic Rudy Ray Moore), an aspiring nightclub performer who is continually harassed by rival comedians. The film portrays LUCIFER as a refined black gentleman dwelling in a hell that looks suspiciously like a darkened basement with bad wallpaper.

After being continually thwarted in his attempts to find work, Moore agrees to marry the devil's daughter in exchange for success and power. Lucifer, who watches earth from hell through a crystal ball and communicates with the living via a Princess telephone, sends Moore a magic cane that enables him to sabotage the performances of rival acts. With the aid of this diabolical wand he quickly becomes the most successful comedian in town. But when the time comes for Moore to take his bride—a hideous, charred shrew—he decides to flee rather than submit.

Lucifer sends the "chosen of hell," a squad of horned, foul-smelling demons, to capture Moore and drag him to the underworld for the nuptials. Meanwhile, plans for the ceremony continue in the netherworld; the bride selects a gown of black satin, with matching ebony veil to hide her grotesque face. The captured Moore, recoiling in horror, finally succumbs and marries the beast. The film ends as the defeated comic and his new bride are borne away in a limousine to the honeymoon where Moore must make good on the second part of the agreement: to father a child with Lucifer's daughter.

DIARY OF A COUNTRY PRIEST, THE French writer Georges Bernanos's 1937 novel *The Diary of a Country Priest* details a young cleric's struggle to gain acceptance in his new community while facing criticism from his supervisors, small-town gossip, and piercing self-doubts. One of the priest's greatest challenges is addressing the nature of hell in order to save the soul of a despairing parishioner.

Trying to convince a grieving mother to set aside her anger and resentment over the death of her infant son and return to the sacraments, the young cleric reminds the woman of the grim alternative. He warns her that if she continues to hate God for what has happened, she will lose the boy not only in this life but for all eternity. Hell, he admonishes, means "not to love anymore." When she replies that God would not punish her this way, he tells her that she is still thinking in human terms: "The error common to us all is to invest these damned souls with something still inherently alive, something of our own mobility, whereas in truth time and movement have ceased for them; they are fixed for ever. Alas, if God's own hand were to lead us to one of these unhappy things, even if it once had been the dearest of our friends, what could we say to it? . . . The sorrow, the unutterable loss of those charred stones which once were men, is that they have nothing more to be shared."

The priest also criticizes what he calls the "layman's" concept of hell: a "kind of penal servitude for eternity, on the lines of your convict prisons on earth." This interpretation is fundamentally flawed, he asserts, because it is from the perspective of this world, and hell is not of this world. This trivializes the true horror of damnation, that is, the loss of God, who "is love itself."

DIS Dis is the Roman equivalent of the Greek god HADES, the lord of the underworld. The land of Dis has been called "the eternal house" and death "eternal sleep," although the Romans clearly believe that the soul lives on after death. Ancient tombs and MEMORIALS have been found bearing the inscription NF F NS NC, or *"Non fui fui non sum non curo,"* meaning "I was not, I was, I am not, I care not." This indicates that souls in the kingdom of Dis are pale shadows of themselves, oblivious to their former existence on earth.

The concept of Dis as a place of sorrow and agony for the dead was eventually incorporated into Greek myth as well. Dis became a realm in the land of Hades. It is reserved for those who are unworthy of paradise but not evil enough to be banished to TARTARUS, a pit of torture for the wicked.

Dis also appears in Dante's *DIVINE COMEDY: THE INFERNO*, as the walled city in the depths of hell where some of the worst sinners are tortured, and in Virgil's *AENEID* as a prison for the dead.

DIVES In some translations of the Christian Bible, Dives (Latin for "wealthy") is the rich man damned to hell for his callousness toward the poor. According to the parable of LAZARUS in St. Luke, Dives enjoys a life of parties and excess while the beggar Lazarus starves outside his gates. Eventually the two men die, and Lazarus is taken to paradise in "the bosom of Abraham." Dives, however, is condemned to the fires of hell. He sees the poor man in heaven and calls out to Abraham, asking him to send Lazarus to bring him relief.

Abraham refuses, telling Dives that there is an "impassable chasm" between the two realms so that one cannot pass from heaven to hell or from hell to heaven. Dives then pleads with Abraham to send Lazarus back to earth to warn his brothers to amend their lives, as they, too, are self-indulgent and at great risk of damnation. But the prophet refuses this request as well. He reminds Dives that they have Moses and the prophets, and if they ignore their words then even seeing a man rise from the dead will not melt their hardened hearts. (This was an allusion to the sacrifice of Christ, as those who have rejected Jesus' teachings likewise deny his miraculous resurrection.)

DIVINE COMEDY: THE INFERNO, THE The most extensive and imaginative fictional description of the afterlife ever written is *The Divine Comedy* by Dante Alighieri. Dante composed this poetic masterpiece during the early 1300s while living in exile from his beloved hometown of Florence, Italy. The work incorporates his religious beliefs about sin, salvation, and justice with his political troubles, social background, and educational experiences. The result is a masterpiece of literature as well as an insightful and historic account of the times.

The Divine Comedy is divided into three separate books corresponding to the three possible destinations of the human soul: *The Paradiso* (heaven), *The Purgatario* (purgatory), and *The Inferno* (hell). Each offers a vivid description of the sights, sounds, scents, and sensations encountered in the afterlife. *The Inferno* contains some of the most graphic and poignant depictions of hell found anywhere in world literature.

Dante wrote his trilogy in narrative style, sounding eerily like a firsthand account of supernatural travels. *The Inferno,* which outlines the infernal depths, opens on the eve of Good Friday in the year 1300. Dante's guide for this journey is the poet Virgil, author of the *AENEID,* who set his own epic in the underworld centuries earlier. Together the pair enters the dark abyss and visits its nine progressively horrific realms, each dedicated to punishing a specific type of sin.

Over the gateway to Hell is a grim inscription: "Abandon hope, all ye who enter here." Dante remarks that this is the reality of the underworld, that the living always have hope of salvation, but for the damned there is only despair. It is the agony of the heart. The realization that their predicament is eternal adds to the suffering of those in hell, for they have nothing to look forward to except continued pain.

After passing through the gate, the two immediately come upon a vestibule of wailing spirits. Virgil explains that these are people who would commit to neither good nor evil in life, deciding instead to serve their own self-interests. Since they did not choose evil, they do not deserve hell. But neither did they opt for goodness, so they do not merit heaven. Refusing to ally themselves with any cause, they are thus condemned to wander aimlessly in this no-man's-land between agony and ecstasy, eternally chasing a waving blank banner that symbolizes nothing. Should

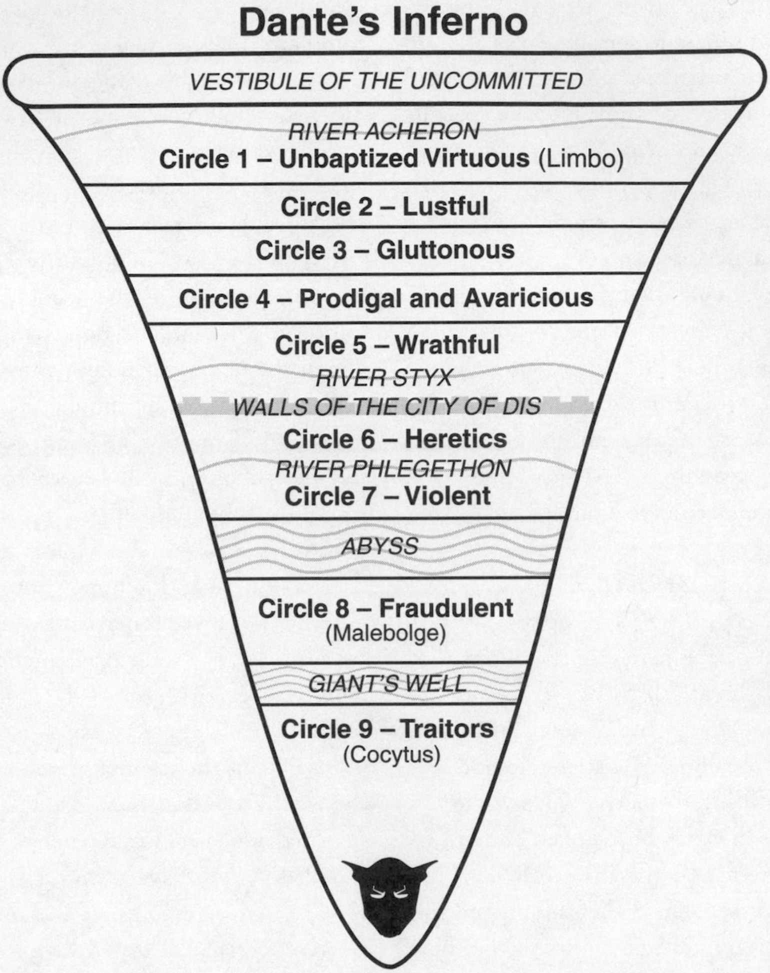

Dante's Inferno

VESTIBULE OF THE UNCOMMITTED
RIVER ACHERON
Circle 1 – Unbaptized Virtuous (Limbo)
Circle 2 – Lustful
Circle 3 – Gluttonous
Circle 4 – Prodigal and Avaricious
Circle 5 – Wrathful
RIVER STYX
WALLS OF THE CITY OF DIS
Circle 6 – Heretics
RIVER PHLEGETHON
Circle 7 – Violent
ABYSS
Circle 8 – Fraudulent
(Malebolge)
GIANT'S WELL
Circle 9 – Traitors
(Cocytus)

The underworld according to Dante's *Inferno.*

they fall to the ground during this pointless race, they are devoured by worms. In addition to the souls of accursed men, herein are the angels who stayed neutral when LUCIFER led a celestial rebellion against God.

Virgil then leads Dante to an outer realm of the underworld called LIMBO. It is a peaceful place for "virtuous pagans" and for those who died unbaptized, since only those who have accepted Jesus Christ as the Messiah can attain heaven. (Dante firmly believed that no one, no matter how virtuous, could save himself or herself. Salvation could be accomplished only through the merits and mercy of Christ.) The poet Virgil tells Dante that this is where his own soul spends eternity, his only sorrow being that he can never look upon the face of God. Here, Dante greets a number of pre-Christian philosophers and scholars, including PLATO, Aristotle, Homer, and Cicero. He pities their plight but is reassured that this is how they envisioned paradise: a congregation of great thinkers able to contemplate the mysteries of the universe for all eternity.

Next, the pair comes to "Hell Proper," the true beginning of the dark abyss. It is ruled by King MINOS, a legendary prince of Crete famous for his cruelty. Minos judges the damned and decides to which realm of suffering each will be sent. A constant flow of condemned souls pours before him awaiting a ruling.

In this first circle of hell, the sound of fearsome cries is deafening as spirits sweep by in an unending whirlwind. These are souls who succumbed to lust. Since they spent their lives being blown about by their passions, they are damned to spend eternity being tossed in this infernal tempest. (Artist WILLIAM BLAKE offers an interpretation of this first level in his *Circle of the Lustful.*) This first circle of "Incontinence" is followed by realms for gluttons, for the greedy and wasteful, and for the wrathful. In each, the punishment meted out likewise corresponds to the sin.

Hell's fifth circle is reserved for heretics. It lies beyond the walls of the city of DIS and glows from the burning of the underworld's unquenchable fire. The Furies (ERINYES) wait here to torture the damned. Inside the city walls, Dante sees an ocean of crypts burning with red flames. These are the tombs of those who rejected the teachings of Christ and preached their own gospel instead. They are damned to burn forever with the fire of truth.

Still descending, Virgil and Dante come upon a place of punishment for the violent. This seventh realm houses murderers, robbers, suicides, and other assailants who spent their lives inflicting physical injury to themselves and others. The blasphemers are the lowest among the violent, for their words and actions constitute violence against God himself. Punishments at this level include spending eternity as a tree in the "Wood of Suicides," suffering rain of fire, and being horribly disfigured by unrelenting heat.

A huge, black chasm separates this level from Malebolge, the next circle of hell. This eighth realm is for torturing the fraudulent, including (in order of evil, beginning with the most benign) seducers, flatterers, simoniacs (those who exchange forgiveness or church office for fees), fortune-tellers, grafters/extortionists (those who unscrupulously use their power or position for profit), hypocrites, thieves, evil counselors, sowers of discord, and falsifiers. Agonies of this realm range from being whipped by demons to being submerged to the neck in human feces. Fortune-tellers have their heads twisted backward for pretending that they could "see" the future, which is known only to God. Hypocrites are weighted down by garish robes that appear beautiful but are actually unbearably heavy garments of torture. Dante is especially critical of those who used their church office for personal gain. He tells one damned cleric, who is buried headfirst in a deep hole with only his blazing feet showing, that this is indeed his just deserts.

Finally, the duo reaches Cocytus, the ninth and lowest circle of the inferno. It is a frozen pit of indescribable terror. In the thick darkness, Dante thinks he sees the spires of huge buildings encircling the place, but these are in fact the figures of gigantic monsters sunk to their waists in the depths of hell. The floor of this realm is a lake of ice in which the damned are frozen up to their necks. The protruding heads mock and insult one another and gnaw one another's skulls.

This ninth circle is reserved for betrayers, the worst sinners in Dante's scenario. They are eternally damned to the icy abyss for forsaking the trust of those who loved them. At the center of this horrific chamber is SATAN, lord of the dark underworld. He has three faces: one black, one red, and one yellow. Each face is lined with a set of wings—their continuous flapping causes a frigid wind that keeps this circle forever frozen. The mouth of the red face chews steadily on Judas, while Brutus is gnawed in the black mouth and Cassius (who murdered mentor Julius Caesar) in the yellow. Virgil and Dante must climb down the back of this grotesque beast in order to escape hell and return to the surface. After emerging from this horrible place, Dante collapses in exhausted relief before continuing on to purgatory.

Dante uses numerous examples of infernal IMAGERY in his vision of hell, such as perilous chasms, treacherous rivers, and demonic beasts. Figures from myth, religion, and even his own life experience appear in the story. Mythic icons include the dog CERBERUS, guardian of the gates of hell; the infernal city of Dis; the river STYX; ferryman CHARON; and even the beautiful Helen of Troy, whose kidnapping led to the Trojan War.

As a devout Roman Catholic, Dante also incorporates Christian images and biblical references into his description of hell. The underworld is ruled by Satan, the sworn nemesis of Christ. The beast is eternally gnawing Christianity's worst sinner, Judas Iscariot, who betrayed Jesus by handing him over to be crucified. *The Inferno* also offers Virgil's account of the HARROWING OF HELL, when Jesus came to claim the souls of the patriarchs after his death. And the two poets hold several discussions regarding the LAST JUDGMENT when all souls will be called forth to face their ultimate fate.

The author vents his wrath on his contemporary enemies by naming several clerics as inhabitants of hell. For although he had a lifelong respect and admiration for the papacy and the church, Dante often found himself in bitter disputes with Catholic authorities, usually over matters of politics. Dante damns both Pope Celestine V and Pope Boniface VIII—Celestine for his weakness at resigning as pope and clearing the way for the corrupt Boniface, and Boniface for plotting to seize Italian lands for his own profit. Dante felt that these two brought great harm and disrespect to the papal office and the Catholic church, which he dearly loved. He repaid them by including them among the damned in his classic work and making their names synonymous with evil.

Throughout *The Inferno,* Dante vividly describes the various sensual terrors of hell. He uses noise—screeching, wailing, moaning—as a component of suffering in the underworld rather than a result of it. Many passages detail the putrid smells of the abyss, while the feel of hell, unbearably hot in some circles and fiercely cold in others, is also illuminated. To Dante, damnation involves an assault on all the senses as well as on the mind and soul.

Dante's purpose in writing *The Inferno* is to remind us that hell is a choice made by humanity, not a punishment imposed by God. The poet emphasizes that every person must take the decision to ally himself or herself with either the forces of heaven or hell and must then accept the profound results of that choice. Free will is so important to his concept of the afterlife that Dante sentences those who refuse to make a selection—the uncommitted—to hell, since their refusal to commit is in itself a coward's decision. Dante wrote his trilogy as a warning to all that how and where they spend eternity is entirely up to each individual.

Since its publication in the 1300s, Dante's *Inferno* has never been out of print. Over the centuries, the work has inspired thousands of paintings, dramas, SHORT STORIES, songs, films and other works of art. Among the best known are Rodin's sculpture *GATES OF HELL,* paintings by William Blake, and etchings by GUSTAVE DORÉ.

DOCTOR FAUSTUS During the 1500s, the legend of FAUST and his contract with the DEVIL enjoyed unbridled popularity. This real-life figure inspired a number of books, plays, poems, and artworks detailing the scholar's demonic activities. Among these is Christopher Marlowe's play *Doctor Faustus,* written around 1592. It follows the story contained in *The Faustbook,* published several years earlier, although it offers a more specific vision of hell. Marlowe patterned his Renaissance drama after the format of traditional MORALITY PLAYS.

According to Marlowe's account, Faust enters into a deal with the devil to attain forbidden knowledge but soon degenerates into an immature nihilist obsessed with physical pleasures. The DEMON MEPHISTOPHELES, a brooding, introspective devil, serves as Faust's attendant and answers his inquiries about the underworld. The fiend tells Faust: "Where we are is Hell, and where Hell is there we must ever be. . . . All places shall be Hell that are not Heaven." When Faust persists, Mephistopheles takes the doctor to hell to give him a firsthand account of the place of the damned. Faust meets GHOULS and demons, witnesses orgies, and talks with the damned. He returns to earth more morose than ever and resumes his empty life of hedonism. After several years of this indulgence, Faust dies and is dragged back into the inferno for all eternity.

Marlowe's *Doctor Faustus* differs from other adaptations of the Faustian story by subtly showing that Mephistopheles did not cause Faust's damnation; the scholar brought that on himself. The drama depicts a man who betrays his lofty quest for knowledge in favor of indulging his carnal whims. Mephistopheles, the demonic aide, is an almost sympathetic character who is merely the tool used as the means to Faust's inevitable end.

This account inspired an opera, *Doktor Faust,* composed by Ferruccio Busoni in 1925. The scholar in *Doktor Faust* is reluctant to enter into a pact with hell but is convinced to sell his soul after the devil points out that the doctor is deep in debt, sought by the angry brother of a woman he seduced, and has no other hope of relief. Faust grudgingly agrees to become the demon's servant in exchange for genius, power, and wealth.

After the contract is signed, Faust commits a number of atrocities. He indulges in sacrilege, murder, and adultery—seducing a lovely duchess on her wedding day and then abandoning her to her heartbroken husband. When, a year later, she presents the doctor with the corpse of their dead infant, Faust regrets his evil and begs for another chance to redeem himself. Hell rebukes this prayer with a number of horrific visions.

Faust imagines that he sees the duchess (who has committed suicide) and their dead child everywhere. He tries to pray before a crucifix. However, he envisions the body on the cross not as Christ's but as that of a beautiful woman with the duchess's face. As the devil comes to claim him, Faust wills his soul into the body of his dead child (which has reappeared), then dies in a scream of agony and remorse.

These opera and dramatic versions of Faust differ from other accounts, in which the doctor is eventually saved. The "ultimate" Faustian story is Johann Wolfgang von Goethe's *Faust: A Tragedy,* which ends with the man's redemption through the intercession of the VIRGIN MARY.

DON GIOVANNI

Wolfgang Amadeus Mozart's opera *Don Giovanni* has been called the artist's consummate masterpiece; many music authorities have gone so far as to declare it "the greatest opera ever written." The 1787 work is based on the legend of DON JUAN, a notorious womanizer who ultimately faces justice at the hands of an angry father.

In the opera, the suave Don Giovanni prides himself on his sexual prowess. He keeps a list of the many women he has bedded as a testament to his bravado, showing no concern for his lovers or for their pain at being used and abandoned. The Don travels the country seducing new conquests, but when he returns to his hometown of Seville, Spain, he finds that his sex appeal is waning.

Back home, Giovanni sets his sights on Donna Anna, a beautiful young maiden who has caught his eye. She wants nothing to do with him and flatly rebuffs his advances. Frustrated and insulted, a masked Don Giovanni breaks into Anna's bedchamber, determined to seduce her. The terrified girl sees him and screams for help. Her father, the Commendatore Don Pedro, rushes in and confronts the veiled intruder. Don Giovanni challenges the old man to a duel and ultimately slays him before fleeing into the night.

Since no one can identify Don Giovanni as the murderer, his crime goes unpunished. He and his lecherous companion, Leporello, laugh about the matter, confident that the Don has escaped justice. But when Don Giovanni runs into Anna at a party, she recognizes his voice and begins planning her revenge. Anna vows she will not rest until Don Giovanni has paid for his wickedness.

Don Giovanni, unaware that he has been identified as her father's killer, continues to joke with Leporello about his feats. The two visit the cemetery where the commendatore is buried and stop to mock a statue of the dead man. Suddenly, the marble image comes to life and confronts Don Giovanni. Still defiant, the evil Don invites the statue to a dinner party at his castle to prove that he remains unafraid of retribution.

To the horror of Don Giovanni's guests, the statue does indeed arrive at the villa as promised. The commendatore tells Don Giovanni that this is his last chance for repentance, but Don Giovanni feels no remorse for his crimes. At this, the earth opens up (through use of a trapdoor), and flames spew out from the depths of hell. The statue grabs Don Giovanni and drags him into the inferno as demons howl and claw at their new companion.

Mozart's operatic masterpiece is extolled in George Bernard Shaw's 1901 drama *MAN AND SUPERMAN*. In this play, Shaw revisits Don Juan in hell and suggests that perhaps his damnation is unjust.

DON JUAN Don Juan is a figure of medieval Spanish legend attributed with phenomenal powers over women. The story of Don Juan's amorous adventures has been the source for hundreds of works, including poems, plays, stories, paintings, and films. Among these is Wolfgang Amadeus Mozart's classic opera *DON GIOVANNI* and George Bernard Shaw's drama *MAN AND SUPERMAN*.

According to the legend, Don Juan is able easily to seduce any woman he wants. He finds ladies of honor and nobility especially appealing and delights in fouling their virtue. After bedding one such maiden, the girl's father challenges the cad to a duel. Don Juan kills the old gentleman, then laughingly moves on to his next object of prey.

As the cruel Don plots the seduction of another young lady, he notices a statue erected to the memory of the man he slew. Don Juan mockingly invites the dead man to dinner to witness his prowess with women. But justice is served when the slain father arrives at the banquet and drags Don

Juan, screaming in agony, into the depths of hell.

The legend of Don Juan has been used as a source for works as diverse as a satire by the French author Molière, a musical composition by Richard Strauss, and an epic poem by Lord Byron. Byron's work differs from most treatments, however, as the irreverent poet sees the Don as a hero rather than a villain. His poem about the saucy lover was left unfinished at the time of the poet's death, but it was to include a scene depicting Don Juan in hell. The literary master did not live long enough to complete the infernal passage.

DONNE, JOHN John Donne (1572–1631), one of England's greatest metaphysical poets, earned a reputation for his moving sermons about heaven and hell. His work is marked by complex themes of startling metaphors, delicate argumentation, and a dazzling mix of wit and wisdom. His published works include *Divine Poems, Elegies,* and *Satires.* Twentieth-century literary genius T. S. Eliot called Donne a master at "unification of sensibility."

During his career as an Anglican priest, Donne wrote more than 160 sermons. They offer imaginative explanations of complicated biblical themes and provide touching illustrations of God's love and mercy. Among his more compassionate works are a number of lectures regarding the nature of hell. Unlike most preachers, Donne poked fun at the inferno below, hoping gently to remind his followers of the possibility of damnation without frightening or alienating them.

A harsh critic of the Catholic church, Donne penned a satirical sermon about the founder of the Jesuit order of priests, St. Ignatius of Loyola. Donne sends the saint to the underworld, where Ignatius manages to infuriate the DEVIL himself. After disrupting the land of the damned and angering SATAN, the priest is sent to colonize the moon, where the devil is sure he will be less dangerous. By using such comic allegories, Donne brings the agonies of hell alive without using graphic descriptions of pain and torture. He uses this tactic for talks about the LAST JUDGMENT as well.

Donne also originated such common literary phrases as "no man is an island" and "never send to know for whom the bell tolls; it tolls for thee." These images are from one of Donne's greatest sermons, given in 1624.

DORÉ, GUSTAVE French artist Gustave Doré (1832–1883) was the most prolific and popular book illustrator of his time. His woodcuts decorated the pages of almost one hundred texts, including the Bible, collections of poetry, and ancient literary classics. Doré's specialty was creating grotesque portraits of supernatural themes. He had a particular flair for portraying haunting scenes of the realm of the damned.

Among Doré's works are illustrations of hell for Dante's *DIVINE COMEDY: THE INFERNO* and Milton's *PARADISE LOST.* His pictures feature frightening DEMONS, pitiful sinners, and seemingly impassable obstacles that the characters must conquer on their metaphysical journeys. His "Wood of Suicides" from the *Inferno* shows a sad forest of human trees, their arms elongated into branches, their faces masks of sorrow. And the "Slough of Despair" of *Paradise Lost* depicts a harsh, forbidding chasm brimming with sorrow.

Doré's compositions remain among the most hauntingly beautiful and compelling illustrations of English literature. His magnificent pictures are still included in modern reprints of these centuries-old stories.

DOS SANTOS, LUCIA At age eleven, Lucia dos Santos was the oldest of three children who claimed to have had supernatural visions during 1916–1917, including a horrible glimpse of hell. She and her cousins, Francisco (age eight) and Jacinta (six) Marto, were poor, illiterate shepherds tending their parents' flocks in Aljustrel, Portugal, when they were visited by an "angel of light." He asked them to pray with him and encouraged them to attend daily mass and offer sacrifices to atone for humanity's sins. After several meetings, the children were also greeted by a "woman clothed with the sun" at Cova da Iria at Fátima, Portugal.

In her written account, dos Santos describes the lady as "dressed in white, more brilliant than the sun." The woman said she was from heaven and promised the children that they would all be there with her one day, Francisco and Jacinta quite soon. She also answered their questions about the fate of family and friends who had recently died. The children agreed to come to the same spot on the thirteenth day of every month to pray with the beautiful lady.

When word of their visions spread, the three were ridiculed, beaten, and eventually jailed by civic authorities who thought they were perpetrating a hoax. The local pastor called their mystic experiences "a trick of the DEVIL." However, not one of the three would recant the story, even under threat of being put to death. Only one family member, Francisco and Jacinta's father, Ti Marto, believed the children unconditionally. He supported them and made sure that they kept their word by visiting Cova every month on the thirteenth.

The children told the lady of these repercussions, and she sadly replied that they would suffer much in this world. Dos Santos confided that she had been having nightmares about being pulled into hell by a clawing demon, but the woman reassured Lucia that her soul would find eternal peace in paradise. The lady taught the trio a prayer for avoiding suffering in the afterlife: "Oh my Jesus, save us from the fires of Hell. Lead all souls to Heaven, especially those most in need of thy mercy." "She then gave them a frightening vision of what awaits unrepentant sinners in the next world. Dos Santos later recorded the details of this awful specter. She recalls seeing: ". . . a huge number of devils and lost souls in a fiery ocean. The devils resemble black animals, hideous and unknown,

Salvador Dalí's *A Vision of Hell* was inspired by dos Santos's supernatural apparition.
PHOTO COURTESY OF THE BLUE ARMY OF OUR LADY OF FÁTIMA, USA, INC.

each filling the air with despairing shrieks. The lost souls were in their human bodies and seemed brown in color, tumbling about constantly in the flames and screaming with terror. All were on fire . . . with never an instant's peace or freedom from pain." After this vision, the lady told them, "You have seen hell." Though the apparition lasted only an instant, the children said that it was so horrible that they would have died if they had watched the spectacle an instant longer.

This apparition was also dismissed as a hallucination, or perhaps even an outright fabrication. However, many critics were quieted in October of 1917 after the "Miracle of the Sun." Dos Santos had told the townspeople that the lady promised to perform a tremendous feat on the thirteenth of that month to prove herself to skeptics. The thousands who gathered at Cova that afternoon witnessed an incredible sight: The sun seemed to spin wildly in the sky and then fall to the earth before rocketing back to its normal position. This miracle gave credibility to the children's' story and to their claim of having seen a vision of the underworld.

Authorities of the Roman Catholic church investigated the episode at length and decreed the apparitions "worthy of credence." They also proclaimed that the "woman clothed with the sun" was the VIRGIN MARY, the mother of Jesus Christ, who is believed to have the power to save souls from hell. In 1962, famed surrealist Salvador Dalí painted *THE VISION OF HELL* based on Dos Santos's apparition of the fiery abyss that includes the comforting image of the Virgin Mary. Today, a shrine at the site in Fátima, Portugal, draws hundreds of thousands of visitors annually from all over the globe.

DREAM MODEL Throughout history, numerous scholars and philosophers from various faiths have envisioned hell as an everlasting nightmare. According to the theory, death is simply a perpetual sleep state colored by the memories accumulated during a lifetime. In this dream model, souls in the afterlife constantly relive their life's actions, and their vile deeds carry repulsive memories. Thus it is not a wicked judge or cruel overlord who punishes souls in the next world; evildoers are tormented by the recollections of their own ghastly atrocities.

The ancient BARDO THODOL (Tibetan Book of the Dead) asserts that there is no supreme being who sentences souls to hell in the afterlife. Each departed spirit must look into the "mirror of truth," and for the iniquitous, the reflection itself is damnation. Defiled souls will sink and suffer under the weight of their own detestable acts.

Roman Catholic bishop and doctor of the church ST. AUGUSTINE postulated a similar concept as early as the sixth century A.D. He suggested that unrepentant sinners would never find rest in the afterlife since the ugliness of their own souls would be intolerable. These proud, self-obsessed spirits would be damned through their refusal to ask for mercy and their insistence at worshiping themselves rather than adoring the Almighty.

The modern philosopher H. H. Price taught that the afterlife is an indestructible state of consciousness in which "life memories" are continually revisited. The soul, free of its physical shell, spends eternity reflecting on the deeds of its earthly existence. The nature of these acts determines whether the afterlife will be a pleasant recollection of joy and happiness or a bitter prison of despicable images and cruel thoughts. For Price, inescapable guilt is the ultimate damnation. These memories are so real that they retain sensations from the body such as stench, bitter taste, ugliness, and intolerable screeching.

This theory has been explored in fiction works as well. A number of episodes from *THE TWILIGHT ZONE* depict evildoers forever trapped in horrors of their own creation. The films *TALES FROM THE CRYPT, VAULT OF HORROR,* and the urban *TALES FROM THE HOOD* offer a similar interpretation of the abyss. In these movies, characters are damned to spend eternity confessing their atrocities to one another in an endless nightmare of remorse, humiliation, and self-recrimination.

DREAM OF HELL Raoul de Houdenc formulated a unique picture of the underworld in his 1215 composition *Dream of Hell.* In this story, the main character, Journeyman, visits the land of the dead and is sickened by what he finds. In the underworld, he encounters a number of grisly sights and nauseating events. Pontius Pilate (who was responsible for Jesus' crucifixion) meets him at the Mountain of Despair where the two discuss Christ's trial and condemnation. The DEMON Beelzebub offers him a dinner of cooked human flesh while the two discuss witchcraft. Journeyman also speaks to a number of damned sinners whose worst suffering stems from regret and despair.

Although the work reads like VISION LITERATURE, *Dream of Hell* was clearly offered as fiction. It is a speculative account of the land of the damned, not a cautionary tale meant to be taken seriously.

DRITHELM Drithelm (Drycthelm, Drythelm), a North Umbrian landowner of the seventh century, was said to have died, lain dead for more than eight hours, and then been restored to life following an illness in 693. While "dead," his spirit visited heaven, hell, and purgatory under the guardianship of a mysterious angel, "a handsome man in a shining robe." His account has become a classic in VISION LITERATURE of underworld journeys.

After "dying," Drithelm claims that his soul left his body and was met by this supernatural guide. The angel escorted him to an endless abyss, "a very broad and deep valley of infinite length." On one side, flames burned into the night sky, while a fierce blizzard raged on the other. Anguished souls flailed in agony on either side, jumping from one bank to the other in search of elusive relief. The angel told Drithelm that this was not hell but a purging place where humanity's sins are burned away.

The guide pointed to a place farther away where the flames burned black, and every burst of smoke was filled with human souls. Drithelm saw there a foul pit where bodies are boiled, simultaneously screeching in pain and shrieking with hysteric laughter. DEMONS kept dumping new spirits into the chasm, some of whom Drithelm recognized. Several of them charged toward him, but the angel repelled the attack. Drithelm was terrified and asked the angel to deliver him from this horror.

Before returning Drithelm to his body, the angel explained to him that only the souls in the pit were irrevocably damned for their evil. They were beyond hope of salvation. The ones burning and freezing along the chasm would suffer only until the LAST JUDGMENT, at which time these spirits would advance to heaven, their sins finally purged.

The angel gave Drithelm a quick glimpse of paradise, then delivered his spirit back to his body. Upon awakening, he immediately sold all his property and declared that "hence forward, I must not live as I used to, and must adopt a very different way of life." Drithelm immediately entered the Melrose Monastery on the river Tweed and remained there for the rest of his life. Apparently the angel's warning worked: Drithelm lived an exemplary life and was eventually declared a saint in the early Christian church.

DRUGASKAN Drugaskan is the lowest realm of hell according to ZOROASTRIANISM, an ancient Persian religion. The region is so thick with darkness and gloom that all those dwelling in Drugaskan are blinded. It is named for the son of AHRIMAN, the Zoroastrian equivalent of the Christian SATAN.

DUAT Duat (Tuat) is the Egyptian "Valley in the Sky" where departed souls will find rest or retribution. It is a realm divided into twelve chambers representing the hours of night, each containing a variety of terrors. Steep mountains encircle Duat, cutting it off from the land of the living and from paradise. Spirits of the dead must overcome the horrors of Duat in order to survive in the afterlife. This could be done only by worthy souls who knew all the correct magic spells and incantations listed in the BOOK OF THE DEAD. The damned, unable to negotiate these perils, would be devoured by serpents, tortured by DEMONS, or forced to eat human excrement until they were eventually destroyed.

During the nighttime hours, the sun god Ra takes the form of Auf, the "dead sun," and travels the corridors of Duat. To the good, Ra offers encouragement and comfort. But for the wicked, Ra has only stern condemnations. The deity sees to it that no unworthy soul is able to overcome the horrors of Duat. Wicked spirits will eventually face ANNIHILATION in the bowels of one of Duat's toothy demons.

E

"ÉLOA, OU LA SOEUR DES ANGES" "Éloa, ou la soeur des anges," an 1826 poem by Alfred de Vigny, describes hell as a place for those who try to replace spiritual love with physical lust. In this work, SATAN becomes mesmerized with Éloa, a simple girl whose innocent beauty captivates him. But since he still refuses to repent his rebellion against God (the sin that brought about his damnation), Satan's power to love is tainted and warped. Thus his desire to stain and corrupt Éloa overpowers his fondness for her. Satan eventually seduces her, concealing his identity and telling her only that he is a misunderstood creature at odds with God.

Éloa tries to convince him to ask forgiveness, reminding him that God is infinitely merciful. Satan struggles to admit his wrong but simply cannot bring himself to do so; his pride is too intense. The relationship between the two breaks down when Éloa feels powerless to reach him, and Satan realizes he is utterly incapable of understanding the gentle girl. He explodes with frustration, infuriated that her love cannot save him. Satan's hatred of God and his destructive pride are far greater than his feelings for Éloa. Their failed affair only makes Satan loathe his Creator all the more.

Disgusted with himself but unwilling to repent of his sins, Satan drags Éloa down to hell with him. Even at this point, she still fails truly to recognize who he is. Her final agony comes when Satan reveals himself to her and then declares that she is doomed to spend eternity with him in the land of the damned. Éloa's bitterest misery comes from realizing that her love was not sufficient to save either of them.

ELUCIDARIUM The twelfth-century Christian author Honorious of Autun offers a breakdown of hell's geography in his *Elucidarium,* a textbook for composing HELLFIRE SERMONS.

According to his thesis, the underworld is divided into two distinct sections. There is an "upper" hell of earthly suffering for punishing minor offenses. It is a place of inconveniences and discomfort rather than torture, where the damned feel eternal hunger, thirst, sorrow, and other human pains but endure no excruciating agony. They also suffer estrangement from God, the source of true beauty and love.

"Lower" hell is reserved for the most egregious offenders of God's law. It is a ghastly chamber of horrors that consists of nine separate torments: fire, cold, stench, worms/serpents, demons, darkness, horrific apparitions, shame, and confinement in burning shackles. Sinners who have committed the seven deadly sins, ignored or rejected church teachings, or broken the Ten Commandments are eternally tortured in this odious abyss. The punishment meted out to each damned soul directly corresponds to the spirit's sins.

The *Elucidarium* was a popular text among clerics of the day. Hundreds of priests and ministers relied on the author's descriptions of the underworld for inspiration when addressing their congregations about the afterlife. The work also furthered the evolution of CHRISTIAN HELL and shaped what are now common notions of hell and its horrors.

EMMA-O King Emma-O is the first father of humankind in Eastern religious tradition, the approximate equivalent of Christianity's Adam. Also the first man to die, Emma-O became the ruler of the dead and master of hell. He was eventually incorporated into the Japanese Buddhist pantheon and is considered the keeper of afterlife justice and retribution. He has been called the ruler of BUDDHIST HELL and is usually portrayed wearing a judge's robes.

According to the legends, death initiates the "journey of intermediate existence," a melancholy trip across a huge, deserted plain during which a person must confront his or her regrets and mistakes. While on this trek, evil souls are snatched by infernal guardians and borne away to the gates of the land of the dead.

At the entrance to the underworld is Shide-no-yama, the Mountain of Death. It is a steep cliff veiled in mist that the soul must claw its way up. After entering the gate, the soul then faces Mitsuss-kawa, the River of Three Passages. The first is a small stream for those who have committed only minor offenses in life. Over the second river is a bridge of precious metals that the saved pass on their way to paradise. The third is a gulf of monsters and fierce storms that must be forged by the worst sinners.

Once past the rivers, the soul comes to Sanzu-no-baba, the Old Woman of the River of Three Ways. The ugly crone strips souls and hangs their clothes from the limbs of a dead tree. Then the Gozu Mezu, a legion of guards with heads of oxen and bodies of stallions, seize the soul and present it to Emma-O. He holds a mirror and a staff to help him discern the truth and is aided by the Gushojin, two secretaries who keep records on everyone's

A thirteenth-century Japanese sculpture shows a chthonic judge sentencing souls.
WERNER FORMAN/ART RESOURCE, NY

deeds. (In some versions, the Gushojin are represented by two disembodied heads.) One sees all secret sins; the other smells evil in a person's soul. Some tales claim that Emma-O is also helped by the Juo, kings who each specialize in a specific type of sin.

Emma-O forces the spirit to look into his mirror, an enchanted glass that reflects the merits of each soul. After this, the underworld deity reflects on the soul's worth, then assigns it to one of the eight sections of hell to purge its evil. He could also assign the spirit a "destiny" as a phantom, an animal, a titan, or a god. Thus the soul would return to the course of transmigration.

Originally, Emma-O was an indifferent overseer who kept eternal watch over departed souls. This notion, however, was in conflict with the Buddhist belief in reincarnation, so Emma-O became a torturer who punishes souls before returning them to another incarnation. Over time, his realm became increasingly associated with pain, agony, and vicious torment. Emma-O evolved into a red-faced, angry overlord who delights in inflicting anguish upon his tenants. He took up residence in the lowest circle of hell and tortures the worst sinners. Agonies in his realm include bludgeoning the damned, forcing them to swallow hot coals, impaling them on spears, and hurling them into a lake of fire.

Emma-O is often associated with YAMA, another underworld deity of eastern legend. Depictions of both deities can be found in CHURCH ART AND ARCHITECTURE of the Far East.

ENKIDU The mythic figure Enkidu appears in the ancient Gilgamesh epic, a complex history of Mesopotamian legends that dates back at least four thousand years. In the poem, Enkidu gives an account of the underworld that paints a very grim picture of what awaits humankind in the afterlife.

At first, Enkidu and the epic's hero, Gilgamesh, are adversaries. Gilgamesh is the strongest and most powerful man in the world until the gods create Enkidu to be his rival. The only substantive difference between the two is that Gilgamesh is a man of civilization while Enkidu lives wild and naked among the animals. They eventually meet and duel. Enkidu emerges as the winner, but rather than reinforcing the rivalry, this event makes them great friends. Each is finally able to enjoy the company of a true equal.

Gilgamesh and Enkidu become bosom companions and share many adventures. But when the men offend the goddess Inanna by rebuffing her romantic overtures, she decrees that one of them must die for the offense. Enkidu soon becomes ill and dreams of the dull, dusty underworld ARALU, a place where soldiers and heroes lose their glory and become shadowy shells of their former selves. Enkidu dies soon after experiencing the grim vision.

Gilgamesh is fearful that he may face the same fate and becomes obsessed with discovering the truth about Enkidu's departure to the next world. He searches out Ziusudra, a mortal granted godlike powers, to ask for advice. With his aid, Gilgamesh makes a long and perilous journey through impermeable darkness and scorching deserts to the underworld abyss that lies beyond the "waters of death." There he finds his friend Enkidu among the dead.

Gilgamesh asks Enkidu what Aralu is like. Enkidu replies that it is too horrible for him to describe. The place is filled with rats that gnaw at the bodies of the dead. Spirits in the underworld are forced to eat dirt and filth. But that is not the worst torture: The real agony is the tedious, boring existence of the departed souls. Enkidu longs for the exciting days of battles, games, and quests. Gilgamesh cries out in terror upon seeing the intense suffering of his friend but is powerless to help him. Filled with sorrow, Gilgamesh returns to the earth determined to find a way to cheat death and thus avoid this horrible fate.

The Gilgamesh epic describes his attempts to become immortal. Ultimately, however, he must face the fact that death is the fate of all, and that one day he will join Enkidu in the land of gloom. It is a specter that will haunt him for the rest of his life.

ENLIL In Sumerian mythology, Enlil (Bel) is a powerful creator god who is exiled to the underworld for raping Ninlil, a young virgin. Enlil had been the lord of heaven and earth and was ruler of the seas, the winds, and all living creatures, but he had been tempted by a beautiful maiden bathing in the enchanted waters of a clear river. The girl's mother, the goddess Nunbarshegunu, had hoped Enlil would see the girl and want her for his bride. But when Enlil beholds the naked beauty, he is overcome with desire and seizes the girl. Ninlil begs him not to molest her, telling him she is a virgin. Enlil ignores her pleas and rapes her on the riverbank, impregnating her with his son.

Upon learning what has happened, the outraged Nunbarshegunu demands that her daughter's honor be avenged. She and the other deities force Enlil into the underworld as punishment for his cruelty. In some legends, Ninlil joins him in the abyss and gives birth to his child, Sin, god of the moon.

ENNUKI The Ennuki are the CHTHONIC deities of ancient Babylonian myth. These underworld gods are often described as judges who determine the supernatural fate of humanity. They are included in the epic tale of ERESHKIGAL, goddess of the underworld, and the infernal war she waged against her sister, the goddess Inanna.

EPISTOLA LUCIFERI Satirical literature lambasting hypocrisy and superficiality became very popular in the fourteenth century. A favorite form of this was communiqués from the underworld thanking clerics for their service to the cause of the DEVIL. An example of this is the 1351 publication *Epistola Luciferi.* This open letter to the Christian faithful from LUCIFER attacks the corruption of religious leaders and exposes the immorality of their congregations.

The writer (actual author unknown) claims that his letter originates in the bowels of hell, written "at the center of the earth in our shadowy kingdom, in the presence of hordes of DEMONS." The *Epistola* promises to send "nobles of Hell to counsel and aid you" in perpetrating evil, such as gossiping, judging others, and committing violence in the name of religion. It subtly attacks Christians and questions their sincerity, noting that they seem to have more in common with the devil than with the Supreme Being.

The text was widely distributed throughout Europe, especially among critics of Christian tradition. It became a classic piece of liturgical satire and greatly reduced the stature of contemporary clerics.

ERESHKIGAL Ereshkigal is the Sumerian mistress of death and ruler of ARALU, the "Land of No Return." An ancient poem, "Hymn to the Locust-tree," explains that "Ereshkigal had received the underworld as her share" of creation. It is a dry, dusty place beneath Abzu, the "sweet waters of the underground." Aralu is a dimension of eternal darkness, a huge communal grave where languishing spirits eat dust and moan in sorrow. Another description from Sumerian myth states:

The pure Ereshkigal seated herself upon her throne,
The Annunake, the seven judges, pronounced judgment before her,
They fastened their eyes upon her, the eyes of death.
At their word, the word which tortures the spirit . . .
The sick woman was turned into a corpse,
The corpse was hung from a stake.

One of the most complex ancient myths about the underworld involves the legend of Inanna (Ishtarin some translations), Ereshkigal's sister, who makes a disastrous trip to the place of the dead. The beautiful Inanna, determined to shame her sister, decides to travel to the underworld to mock Ereshkigal and her lowly status as ruler of the damned. She dons her most glamorous clothes and finest jewelry and sets out for Aralu. Word quickly spreads to Ereshkigal that her sister is coming, charming everyone in her path.

Ereshkigal becomes jealous and orders her guards to seize a garment from Inanna at each of the seven gates she must pass through on the way to the depths of hell. Inanna does so, arriving naked and enraged at her sister's throne. A heated argument erupts over the incident, and Ereshkigal has Inanna impaled on a hook, where her body quickly turns green and decays, much to Ereshkigal's delight. The CHTHONIC deity displays her sister's withered corpse as a trophy in the halls of Aralu.

Meanwhile, in the upper world, Inanna's handmaid, who knows of the sisters' feud, works for Inanna's release. After intervention from a number of Sumerian deities, Ereshkigal reluctantly agrees to give up her sister's corpse. The gods revive Inanna with water and the grass of life, but the judges of the dead will not let her leave the underworld until she finds a substitute to take her place in hell. Inanna agrees to send a replacement back to her sister's kingdom.

A ghastly demon escort sees Inanna back to the land of the living. Upon her return, she discovers that her husband, Dumuzi, rather than mourning her loss, has been celebrating her absence with wine, women, and song. She immediately selects him as her substitute and sends him to Aralu to suffer in her place. Inanna eventually pities Dumuzi's plight and works out an arrangement with Ereshkigal so that he has to stay in hell for only six months out of the year.

Another legend tells how Ereshkigal used her wiles to trick NERGAL, a vain and lecherous warrior god, into taking up residence in the land of the dead. When Nergal ventures to the underworld to meet this legendary queen, Ereshkigal charms him into sharing her bed, knowing that this will seal his doom. After the seduction, the gods refuse to allow him to return to the upper world, so Nergal weds Ereshkigal and becomes the king of the dead. Together the couple oversees the souls of those who have departed to Aralu.

ERINYES The Erinyes, or Furies, are spirits who torment the damned in HADES, the underworld of Greek mythology. Their name means "the angry ones," and they never tire of inflicting pain upon their charges. The Erinyes are hideous winged monsters with snakes for hair. They are Alecto (never-ending pursuit), Megaera (envious anger), and Tisiphone (voice of revenge). Each uses an assortment of torments to punish mortals, but their favorite is driving their victims mad. Their eternal mission is to "make men pay for their perjury in the world below."

The Erinyes dwell in TARTARUS, the lowest realm of the underworld. If a mortal's crime is severe enough, the pitiless fiends can also seek vengeance against a living person; however, Hades is their home.

The Erinyes are described in Virgil's *AENEID* as guarding the gates of hell and in Dante's *DIVINE COMEDY: THE INFERNO* as punishers of the damned. More recently, the witches are described in Stephen King's novel *ROSE MADDER,* the story of a victimized woman who gets vengeance on her abusive husband with a little help from the supernatural deities.

ERLIK Erlik is the DEVIL and ruler of the underworld of Siberian mythology. He is the equivalent of the Christian LUCIFER, a once-favored creature who evoked the wrath of the Supreme Being and was cast into a great abyss.

Erlik is the archenemy of Ulgan, the good and just creator God. In some legends, Erlik and Ulgan were friends before Erlik betrayed his ally. After turning on Ulgan and angering the gods with his boundless pride and evil tricks, Erlik is banished to the underworld. He immediately claims the land of the dead as his own, infuriating the gods anew by bragging that he has more men in his realm of the dead than are left to Ulgan among the living. Unable to deny this fact, Ulgan eventually has to concede.

Determined to thwart Ulgan's plans for a beautiful world, Erlik controls an army of DEMONS who seek the ruin of human souls. His devils scour the earth, ready to snatch up the spirits of those who have sinned. He torments these souls in the great abyss below the ground. But legend claims that Erlik's reign is temporary, as Ulgan will defeat and annihilate his nemesis at the end of the world, a thesis similar to the LAST JUDGMENT doctrines of Christianity and Islam.

ETRURIA Etruria is the Roman equivalent of the Greek CHARON, the ferryman who delivers souls to the underworld. But unlike his Greek counterpart, Etruria does not simply transport spirits to the land of the dead; he torments them as well. Ancient drawings show the grim god gleefully smashing souls over the head with a huge mallet as they depart their physical bodies. (He is sometimes linked to the mysterious ETRUSCAN CIVILIZATION. However, few of these texts have been satisfactorily translated.)

ETRUSCAN CIVILIZATION

The ancient Etruscan civilization is one of the most mysterious cultures ever studied by anthropologists. This largely unknown people predates the Roman Empire, existing from 800 to 200 B.C., covering an area in Italy from Naples in the south to the Po valley in the north. Details about the origins, language, and customs of the Etruscans continue to mystify historians. However, one fact is certain: They were obsessed with the afterlife and with concepts of hell and damnation.

Anthropologists remain uncertain of the civilization's beginnings, as their language seems unrelated to any other of the era. What little Etruscan text does survive (no literature has ever been recovered) is a collection of brief inscriptions related to funeral rites, magic, and religion. This Etruscan Book of Fate and Death reveals that the citizens believe that everything—from everyday life to political affairs—is predestined by the unseen forces of fate.

These scattered texts also allude to a civilization rich in rituals. Etruscans offered animal sacrifices to their gods both to appease them and to seek favors. In some cases, humans were sacrificed, although records show that only captives and prisoners were used for these offerings. Etruscans also enjoyed elaborate games, parades, music, and even prizefights. All of these events were steeped in ceremony and performed according to strict regulations.

The remains of most ancient Etruscan villages lie buried below modern cities, so few excavations have been done. However, many of the towns have on their outskirts a necropolis—a city of the dead that parallels the land of the living—carved out of rock. Some of these are quite elaborate and contain extensive illustrations of the afterlife. Most Etruscan tombs include detailed drawings of DEMONS tormenting the dead in a dark, ghastly underworld. There is little, however, to indicate what a person must do to avoid damnation and achieve paradise.

Also common in these pictures is the god Charun (possibly related to the Greek ferryman CHARON), depicted as a bloodthirsty fiend wielding a huge hammer, ready to smash people's souls. He is an especially important deity since he represents the link between the living and the dead. Records refer to another underworld god, Tuchulcha, a deformed monster with donkey ears and the beak of a vulture entwined in serpents who carries off the souls of the dead. This image occurs repeatedly on tombs and other MEMORIALS throughout the area.

The long journey the dead must make to the afterlife is another topic frequently depicted. Souls are shown making this passage by foot, on horseback, and sometimes by chariot.

EURYDICE Eurydice is the wife of ORPHEUS, a hero of Greek myth who travels to HADES to retrieve his beloved bride. Orpheus and Eurydice are madly in love when Eurydice is bitten by a poisonous snake as she flees a would-be rapist. The wound is fatal. When Orpheus learns of her death, he journeys to the underworld to beg King Hades and Queen PERSEPHONE, lords of the dead, to restore his treasured wife. Touched by his devotion, they agree to let Eurydice return on one condition: Orpheus must go ahead of her and not look back until the two reach the land of the living. Orpheus agrees and goes on ahead.

At first, Orpheus is filled with joy at the prospect of having his lover back and keeps his promise not to turn around. But he starts thinking that he has been tricked and that Eurydice is not really following him. He calls out her name, but the only reply is his own voice echoing through the night. Unable to withstand the suspense, he whirls back, only to see her fade into the mist. Orpheus's distrust has cost him his bride, and Eurydice is doomed to remain in Hades for eternity.

EURYNOMUS Eurynomus is a monster of HADES, mentioned in some tales of ancient Greek myth. The beast is depicted in a fifth-century B.C. painting by the artist Polygnotus as a blue-black DEMON baring his teeth in anticipation of his feast. He sits at the banks of the river STYX and awaits the newest arrivals, who are ferried to the underworld by the boatman CHARON. Eurynomus's job is to punish the worst sinners according to their crimes. Scholars believe that legends of this beast were absorbed into the mythic CERBERUS, the dog-headed monster who guards the gates of hell.

EVERYMAN *Everyman* is the most famous MORALITY PLAY ever written. The English drama, first performed around 1500, is derived from a Dutch production about the soul's judgment at the time of death. Its purpose is to make viewers pause and reflect on their own lives and amend their evil ways.

The play opens as Death calls Everyman—representing humankind—to the afterlife to explain his sins and convince God that he should not be sentenced to eternity in hell. Everyman immediately panics, for he has squandered his life on selfish pursuits and has largely ignored the lessons of the Bible. God enters and warns Everyman (and the audience) that those who live for their own pleasure shall suffer in the underworld, where "they will become much worse than beasts."

Terrified, Everyman prepares for his somber pilgrimage. He asks his friends Worldly Goods, Beauty, Fellowship, and other lifelong companions to accompany him, but they refuse. Throughout his time on earth they have shared one another's company, promising to stick together even to the gates of hell. But when the time comes for Everyman to face possible damnation, these shallow cohorts abandon him. Worldly Goods laughs at Everyman's predicament, reminding him that "my love is contrary to love everlasting" and his job is "man's soul to kill."

The only one who agrees to accompany Everyman to the afterlife is Good Deeds. But Good Deeds is weak and pale from years of neglect and is wasting away. Unable to make the journey, he asks his sister, Knowledge, to escort Everyman to his hearing. She agrees on one condition: The traveler must stop in the House of Salvation and bathe in the river Confession. Feeling his first glimmer of hope, Everyman happily submits. After purging himself in the pure waters, Everyman discovers that Good Deeds has revived and will in fact join him.

Full of remorse, Everyman arrives for judgment. Seeing the error of his ways and admitting that his soul should surely face damnation, he begs for mercy. Everyman asks God to save him from the "day of doom" when he will be tossed into the depths of the underworld abyss. Good Deeds tells Everyman that he will testify on his behalf, then Everyman descends into the grave as the stage lights dim. An angel appears to inform the audience that Everyman will be spared from hell because of his "singular virtue," but he warns that all will not be so lucky. Patrons are left with the admonition, "Remember: beauty, wits, strength and discretion: they all at the last Everyman forsake."

Everyman continues to be performed in theaters throughout the world. An updated version, *Jedermann,* penned in 1911 by Austrian playwright Hugo von Hofmannsthal, also enjoys critical acclaim and commercial success on the modern stage.

EXPLOITS OF HERCULES

Mosaics, an ancient art form of creating pictures by arranging tiny bits of tile or glass in mortar, were once very common in palaces throughout Europe and North Africa. One excavation, at Piazza Armerina in Sicily, revealed a wealth of such compositions dating to approximately 400 B.C. These mosaics lined the floors of a ruined villa, depict the labors of HERCULES, son of Greek god Zeus, whose heroic adventures are among the most famous legends of all time.

The *Exploits of Hercules* illustrates many of the champion's successful quests, including his fearless storming of the underworld. According to the myth, Hercules is challenged by the gods to perform twelve labors in order to ingratiate himself to the powerful pantheon. The twelfth of these is to visit the Kingdom of HADES and retrieve CERBERUS, the three-headed monster who guards the gates of the underworld. (While in the land of the dead, Hercules also rescues his friend THESEUS, who is being held prisoner for trying to bring Hades' wife PERSEPHONE back to the upperworld.) In addition to performing this feat, Hercules defeats the Hydra, a water monster, and slays a cannibalistic rival king.

The mosaics of the *Exploits of Hercules* offer an odd assortment of grisly underworld images set against a white background. One depicts a writhing serpent with a human head and hair of vipers. Nearby, a fierce bull (the animal often associated with the evil King MINOS) lowers its head and rears menacingly. Another especially gory picture shows a naked warrior straddling a fallen horse, the beast's blood pouring forth from a vicious wound.

F

FAIRIELAND Fairieland is a vast mythic otherworld of trolls, goblins, brownies, FAIRIES, and other spirit beings. Belief in Fairieland originated from the "cult of the dead," a form of medieval witchcraft prevalent in the British Isles and in Western Europe. The realm has been linked with the DEVIL, hell, and the damned as well as with the dark arts of the occult. Self-proclaimed sixteenth-century Satanist ISOBEL GOWDIE refers to fairies as the infernal "hosts of Hell" in a lengthy confession of demonic activities. There are also many legends about humans serving as slaves in this mystic world of treacherous spirits.

One of the first literary references identifying Fairieland as hell is in the poem "Sir Orfeo," written during the late 1200s. It recounts the tale of ORPHEUS, the Greek musician who travels to the underworld to retrieve the soul of his deceased wife, EURYDICE. The text of "Sir Orfeo" renames the kingdom of the damned the "land of the Fairies." The inhabitants of this world are described as mutilated, insane, and tortured souls of the dead. During the same era, Fairieland was frequently used as the setting of MYSTERY PLAYS, either as a beautiful wonderland of magic or a grim prison for lost souls.

The ultimate story of this infernal world is Edmund Spenser's mid-1500s romance *The Faerie Queene.* A politically charged account of the court happenings of Queen Elizabeth I (renamed Gloriana), the text attempts to justify Elizabeth's persecution of Catholics and religious intolerance for any who refuse allegiance to the Church of England. The allegory attacks Catholics as agents of the devil while proclaiming the virtues of Henry VIII's heretical Protestant sect. Within the lengthy diatribe, *Faerie Queene* offers references to the river STYX, the underworld guard dog CERBERUS, King HADES, and the portal to hell, LAKE AVERNUS. It also features scenes of the damned being punished according to the depravity of their sins.

FAIRIES Fairies are an assortment of spirit beings who inhabit hell, or, in some versions, LIMBO. From the Latin *fata,* meaning "fate," fairies are found in cultures and civilizations from across the globe. The spirits are known by a variety of names—elves, brownies, leprechauns, trolls, nymphs, sprites, goblins—and can be either benevolent or malevolent. Wicked fairies are commonly associated with DEMONS, the DEVIL, and witchcraft. They share physical similarities with underworld dwellers, such as hooked ears, pointy features, and scowling faces.

Legends about the origin of fairies abound. In some tales from Christian cultures, the fairies are rebel angels who fought with LUCIFER against God and were cast from heaven. Other explanations offer the spirits as souls of pagans who are not evil and therefore do not deserved to be tortured in hell. Numerous African, Asian, and Indian myths describe fairies as being "children of the Earth Mother," nature spirits who inhabit the air and water and can interact with humans.

In Europe and its colonies, fairies eventually became inextricably equated with devil worship and witchcraft. Many accused witches were said to have communed with fairies and learned "unnatural" skills from these demonic spirits. Confessed Satanist ISOBEL GOWDIE enthusiastically described extensive dealings with fairies in a detailed confession. Gowdie called them the "hosts of Hell" and claimed they had escorted her to the realm of the damned on many occasions. Medieval texts routinely referred to the underworld as FAIRIELAND.

In the British Isles, fairies are closely linked to the ancient pagan winter festival SAMHAIN. According to the Celtic calendar, the winter season begins on November 1. Since a day runs from sunset to sunset, Samhain is celebrated beginning at dusk on October 31. During the dark hours of Samhain, fairies, demons, GHOULS, and souls of the dead are believed to walk the earth and warm themselves by fires in preparation for the long icy winter ahead. Bonfires are offered to appease the evil spirits, and when the last ashes are scattered revelers run away from the site screaming "may the devil take the hindmost!" This is done as a sort of mock offering to the dark gods. Masks are worn to confuse the fairies as to who is still living and who is a visitor from the other world. These traditions were eventually diluted into modern Halloween customs, a day of costumes and treats for children.

Today, fairies are usually depicted as lovable sprites or harmless tricksters. Classic stories like *Cinderella, Pinocchio,* and *The Elves and the Shoemaker,* films such as *Darby O'Gill and the Little People,* and even ADVERTISING icon Lucky Charms Leprechaun have greatly supplanted images of fairies as denizens of hell.

FALLEN ANGELS ENTERING PANDEMONIUM, THE John Martin's 1840 painting, *The Fallen Angels Entering Pandemonium,* is a vivid portrayal of LUCIFER's expulsion from heaven and damnation to hell. The work depicts in flaming reds and blazing oranges the dark angel's rebellion against God and the descent of his DEMON army into a wretched abyss below.

At the center of the painting is the guilded city of heaven, a beautiful fortress of crystal domes and golden spires. The spirit of God glows in a burst of silver above the enchanted paradise. The turquoise sky—Martin's only use of blue in the painting—is disturbed by a single bolt of lightning as scarlet clouds churn with the disturbance of the rebelling angels.

This achingly beautiful city is bounded by a river of raging fire. On the opposite bank is a harsh landscape of jutting rocks and broken cliffs, as if a tremendous earthquake has ripped the two regions apart. Unlike the gleaming metropolis of heaven, this cursed hell has no lights, no towers, no great buildings of polished marble. It is dark and desolate, illuminated only by the red glow of the molten river.

Scattered about the rocky cliffs are a myriad of fallen angels. Some shake their fists defiantly at the army of heaven that has vanquished them. Others cower on the ground, weeping at their wretched fate. A few line the edge of the chasm, thrusting their spears upward. The majority, however, are amassed at the center of the abyss, cursing one another and dejectedly beating their fists against the unyielding rock.

Martin's depiction of the war in heaven is drawn from the Bible's REVELATION. In this text, St. John vividly describes the damnation of Lucifer and the creation of hell.

"FALL OF HYPERION" John Keats's "Fall of Hyperion" is a recent literary foray into underworld mythology. Written in 1819, the poem offers a journey to TARTARUS, the lowest chamber of HADES, in the style of Dante's *DIVINE COMEDY: THE INFERNO.* Keats describes his pit of hell as a torturous realm of icy cold similar to the abyss in Dante's classic. The hero is called upon to endure the torments of the underworld in order to be reborn as the new god of poetry and lyric.

"Fall of Hyperion" mingles elements of the poet's own artistic suffering with fragments of Greek myth, such as the voyage of HERCULES to the land of the damned and the supernatural travels described in the *AENEID* and the *ODYSSEY*. The work was left unfinished at the time of Keats's death in 1821.

FALL OF THE DAMNED, THE Flemish master Peter Paul Rubens created a stunning vision of hell in his composition *The Fall of the Damned.* The work, painted from 1614 to 1618, depicts a fiery tempest of souls swirling in an eternal storm. It is a tumultuous vision of pandemonium, where the souls of wretched people and the figures of frightening fiends are mingled in a striking sea of suffering. Rubens displays his trademark technique of using visual spirals that draw the viewer's attention into the painting to create an unsettling whirlwind of torment. Also characteristic of Flemish works, there is no SATAN or overlord of hell, but instead a vast army of angry DEMONS who torture the damned.

The Fall of the Damned shows condemned spirits tumbling into a vast orange abyss of horror. Lining this hell are multiheaded serpents, moldering gargoyles, and fierce beasts that defy description. Some of the damned are being gnawed on by dark, toothy demons, while others are attacked by dragons of fire. Each face bears an expression of excruciating pain and utter terror. There is no discernible terrain in hell, but this suspended displacement adds to the sense of chaos. These dark souls have no place of rest; they are forever spinning in a pool of fierce affliction and unbearable anguish.

Rubens spent years studying the Renaissance masters MICHELANGELO, Rafael, and Titan to develop his style. The result is a highly energetic flair rich in sensual detail. One critic notes that Rubens paints with "fury." This is evident in his *Fall of the Damned,* as his condemned spirits seem truly vibrant even in the throes of their agony.

FALL OF THE REBEL ANGELS, THE Pieter BRUEGHEL, patriarch of the famous family of painters, depicts the rebellion against God in his *Fall of the Rebel Angels.* Done in yellows, earth tones, and copper, the mid-sixteenth-century composition shows beautiful creatures of light transforming into hideous mutants as they plummet into hell. The work is based on the description of the war in heaven described in REVELATION.

At the top portion of the picture is the glowing presence of the Supreme Being. He is surrounded by his heavenly army, magnificent winged warriors who defend their Creator. The figures at the center are engaged in a fierce battle: lovely seraphs locked in combat with horrible monsters. Ugly fiends line the bottom of the work: bloated toads with bursting stomachs, pigs, wolves, lizards with insect wings. The vile beasts scream in agony, unable to believe their metamorphoses. Several grope blindly for help as they descend into the abyss. The scene is permeated with anger, disbelief, and despair. Brueghel creates DEMONS who are as despicable in appearance as they are in substance.

FANTASIA Disney's 1940 classic film *Fantasia* is brilliant animation mated to great works of classical music. The movie features the compositions of such masters as Bach, Beethoven, Schubert, and Tchaikovsky. *Fantasia*'s final segment, set to the tune of Moussorgsky's *Night on Bald Mountain,* depicts a grim underworld scene where the damned rise and dance before their winged master Chernobog.

The *Night on Bald Mountain* sequence shows Chernobog, a fierce DEVIL, awakening at dusk from his hilltop perch. As he comes alive, ancient graves at the foot of the mount open, and the spirits of the dead slowly rise. They dance a macabre ballet as the fiend watches from above. Souls are ravaged by flames as an explosion of DEMONS erupts from a fiery pit. The spectacle continues until dawn, when Chernobog and his minions must return to their dark slumber.

Disney Studios revisits the theme of hell in a number of recent ANIMATED CARTOONS. In the 1996 *Hunchback of Notre Dame,* the corrupt judge Frollo sings "Hellfire," a song about his carnal obsession with the beautiful gypsy Esmerelda, against a background of towering flames. The 1997

HERCULES depicts a showdown between the legendary hero and nemesis HADES, lord of the dead, that climaxes with a journey to the depths of the underworld.

FANTASY ART Over the past several decades, fantasy art has become increasingly popular. The term refers to a contemporary style of illustration that incorporates images of hell, DEMONS, FAIRIES, angels, medieval heroes, science fiction, battlegrounds, and surreal backgrounds into themed works. These compositions can be purchased in the form of posters, limited-edition lithographs, calendars, or even TRADING CARDS. They appeal primarily to young adult males, as favorite subjects include scantily clad women being menaced, muscle-bound conquerors, and fiery scenes of mass destruction. Hell is a favorite backdrop for all these icons.

Fantasy art is also used extensively for commercial purposes, such as on movie posters, book jackets, and magazine covers. Horror and fantasy magazines from *Fangoria* to *TWILIGHT ZONE MAGAZINE* routinely highlight macabre artworks and feature interviews with their imaginative creators.

Artists typically draw inspiration from myth, legend, and fiction, with the underworld as a source of limitless possibilities. An example is Ken Kelly's *Dante's Inferno,* which offers a chilling portrait of the gates of hell as found in

Satanic rituals are popular themes for fantasy art.
PAGNEA CORPORATION—JOHN SCHULTE, JOHN BESMEHN, CHERLY ANN WONG

the classic *DIVINE COMEDY: THE INFERNO.* The painting shows a forbidding guard and three vicious dogs (reminiscent of the three-headed monster CERBERUS) barring the entrance to a broken world of fire and steam. Similarly, Jeffrey Jones's *At Night* depicts a decomposing corpse grinning as it rises from the smoky mists of a forlorn wasteland. And the horror novel *The Book of Skulls* has on its cover a piece by Jim Burns, showing an ancient demon brooding over his collection of damned souls.

In the other extreme, fiction borrows ideas from fantasy art. The director of the European horror film *The Church* patterned a supernatural scene after the fantasy piece *VAMPIRE's Kiss* by artist Boris Vallejo. The original work presents a winged, snake-tailed fiend embracing a voluptuous brunette in an ominous, misty realm. She is trapped in his evil talons, awaiting her doom.

The interest in fantasy art has become so widespread that this work is now exhibited at galleries across the country. Illustrations of the land of the damned are among the most popular—and best selling—compositions. And in the computer age, demonic fantasy art can be viewed on-line via a variety of Web sites, marketplaces, and electronic galleries.

FAUST The story of the infamous Faust and his legendary deal with the DEVIL has become the basis for many classics of world literature. The dark tale has also spawned thousands of artworks, plays, poems, and stories from across the globe.

The Faustian legend is loosely based on the real-life exploits of a controversial philosophy scholar, Johann Faust, who billed himself as a magician, psychic, and fortune-teller. This original Faust was a charlatan who performed feats of black magic and boasted about his demonic ties as a means of generating publicity for his act. Contemporaries claimed he was ultimately strangled by the devil, but it is more likely that he died at the hands of a swindled client. Faust's story was then intermingled with tales of the notorious THEOPHILUS, a sixth-century bishop who sells his soul to SATAN and later repents. The result is the Faust of modern legend.

Accounts of the life of Dr. Faust first appeared around 1507, although these early records included no mention of a pact with Satan. They were, however, rife with criticism from peers about Faust's odd lifestyle and questionable dabblings with the supernatural. The allegation of a deal with the devil first appears in 1587 in the *Volksbuch* (Folkbook), a mix of legend, fact, and folklore, by Johann Spiess. It was widely distributed throughout Europe.

This initial book tells of an impatient, vain intellectual who decides he would rather seek enlightenment through magic than through tedious and difficult study. Faust declares that he does not need the grace of God to grow intellectually, for he can develop his self-proclaimed genius through his own means. He proves his prowess by using ancient spells and dark rituals to

Faust conjures the demon Mephistopheles. ART TODAY

conjure a demon, MEPHISTOPHELES. When the black angel of the abyss appears, Faust proclaims his contempt for God again and swears allegiance to the forces of the occult.

Faust is fascinated with his own diabolical power and with the tales Mephistopheles tells him. The demon explains that hell is a kingdom in five realms, with LUCIFER as the emperor over all. Mephistopheles entices Faust with promises of even greater powers if only the scholar will renounce Christianity altogether and vow to subvert Christ's church by any means possible. Faust agrees, and their deal is sealed in blood. According to the terms, the doctor will receive twenty-four years of supernatural indulgence, after which he will remand his soul to hell.

At first he is delighted with his newfound strengths and enjoys exercising his evil skills. But as the deadline for this pact draws nearer, Faust begins to wonder if he has made a terrible mistake. He asks Mephistopheles exactly what awaits him in the underworld. The smiling DEMON answers by taking him on a tour of hell. There, Faust meets hordes of demons and deformed monstrosities among the damned. He finds hell a deplorable sewer of gray mist that stinks of sulfur and decay. Faust is horrified and wants to back out of the contract, but Mephistopheles tells him that it is too late. The doctor despairs but stubbornly refuses to ask for God's forgiveness. He decides that he would rather suffer eternal damnation than admit he has sinned through his immense pride.

After this final rejection of his Christianity, Faust resolves to make the most of his remaining years on earth. He spends this time reveling in lust, cruelty, drunken orgies, and humiliations of his enemies. When at last the time for his damnation arrives, he gathers a group of students around him and warns them not to fall into the same trap he has. Lucifer than drags him down into hell, leaving behind only a charred, mutilated corpse.

The *Volksbuch* also incorporates biblical lessons and Christian beliefs of its era into the legend of the accursed scholar. The text mirrors the story of the fall of Adam, as Faust's pride leads to his eventual undoing. Yet unlike his forebear, Faust is happily rid of God and does not want to be saved if it means admitting his own inferiority. The work reflects many contemporary concepts: anti-intellectualism, anti-scholarship, and fear of the occult. This early version of *Faust* also contains subtle intimations of the frenzied witch hunts to come.

This first book was followed by many others featuring Faust as the central character, including Christopher Marlowe's 1588 play *DOCTOR FAUSTUS.* Several centuries later, Johann Wolfgang von Goethe offered his interpretation in *Faust: A Tragedy,* which has been called the "Faustian masterpiece." Goethe worked on his epic for more than sixty years, during which time he went through many changes in religious beliefs. Before publishing *Faust* in the 1830s, Goethe had been an alchemist, a deist, and a mystic and had tried his hand at dozens of professions. These transitions are reflected in the complexity of his characters and the depth of their development.

Goethe's version opens as God proudly recognizes Doctor Faust as a shining example of faith and piety. Mephistopheles scoffs that he can easily turn anyone, including the admirable Faust, against God. The two wager over whether the pious doctor will succumb to temptation. God then allows the demon to tempt him but stipulates that the wager will end at Faust's death. Mephistopheles shall have no power over the man's immortal soul.

Mephistopheles quickly finds Faust's weakness: The doctor is despairing because his extensive studies have not unveiled the secrets of the universe. Faust considers experimenting with the occult despite the warnings of angels who tell him to reject this dangerous methodology. Mephistopheles appears to him then, first in the form of a black dog and, then as a scholar and a nobleman. Astonished by this apparition, Faust agrees to become Mephistopheles' servant in the next world if the demon will serve him in this life. The two sign a vague, ambiguous pact to that effect.

Having no intention of giving Faust the knowledge he seeks, Mephistopheles distracts him with a beautiful maiden named Gretchen. Faust uses her sexually, then abandons her when she becomes pregnant with his illegitimate child. Brokenhearted, Gretchen goes insane and drowns the infant. She is arrested for the crime and is sentenced to death. At this, Faust is finally moved to pity by her plight and begins caring for her, but it is too late. She is executed, and Mephistopheles gives Faust a vision of her soul wandering lost and forsaken through the netherworld.

Unlike the original Faust story, Goethe's version ends with the doctor's redemption. The VIRGIN MARY takes pity on Gretchen and brings her to heaven, and angels carry Faust to paradise as well. He has truly learned to love, God decides, and that is the essence of human salvation.

Over the centuries, the Faustian legend has been transformed into literally hundreds of operas, novels, artworks, and even puppet plays. Innumerable updates have been penned by various eras, such as the American classic "THE DEVIL AND DANIEL WEBSTER," the French "VATHEK," and even a made-for-television film entitled *INVITATION TO HELL*.

FAVOLA D'ORFEO, LA Claudio Monteverdi offers an operatic version of the famous Greek myth in his *La Favola d'Orfeo (The Fable of Orpheus)*. In this 1607 adaptation, ORPHEUS's wife, EURYDICE, dies after being bitten by a snake and descends to HADES, the land of the dead. Grief stricken, Orpheus vows to venture to the underworld to retrieve his bride, or die in the attempt.

On his journey to the afterlife, Orpheus encounters many obstacles. He must cross the river STYX and outwit the grim ferryman CHARON. Once arrived in the underworld, Orpheus charms Prosperine (PERSEPHONE), Queen of the Dead, who in turn begs King Pluto (Hades) to release the dead woman's spirit.

Pluto agrees to let her return on one condition: Orpheus must walk ahead of her, never looking back, until they have reached the living world. He agrees, and the two begin their ascent. But as Orpheus makes his way back home, he becomes convinced that his lover is not following but remains trapped in the kingdom of the dead. He gives in to his doubts and turns around, only to see her wither and collapse. An unseen force pulls Orpheus up and away from her, as a ghostly escort brings the girl back to the underworld. He has lost her forever.

At this point the opera departs from the legend. In Monteverdi's account, Apollo appears and, calling Orpheus "my son," offers to take the heartbroken mortal to the heavens, where he will be consoled by the beauty of the stars. Orpheus accepts and is taken bodily to paradise where his sorrow will be soothed. This last act "Christianizes" the ancient Greek tale, paralleling the legend of the HARROWING OF HELL, when Christ delivers languishing souls from SHEOL into heaven.

FEAR NO EVIL Director Frank Laloggia's 1981 debut film *Fear No Evil* brings visions recorded in the Bible's *REVELATION* to the big screen. The movie stars Stefan Arngrim as a modern incarnation of LUCIFER, depicted as a troubled teenage loner. Elizabeth Hoffman and Kathleen McAllen play a pair of present-day angels sent to return the fiend to hell. When Arngrim embarks on a spree of bloody violence and brutal mayhem, heaven's warriors must save humanity from his evil. The final apocalyptic battle takes place on the Isle of the Dead, where rising GHOULS and mangled DEMONS come to the aid of their infernal master.

FEW SIGHS FROM HELL, A *A Few Sighs from Hell: or The Groans of a Damned Soul* was written in 1658 by Puritan preacher John Bunyan, author of the Christian classic *THE PILGRIM'S PROGRESS*. Bunyan developed the idea from one of his HELLFIRE SERMONS and published his concepts in book form. *A Few Sighs from Hell* is the transcription of a horrific vision of the underworld "witnessed" by a dying sinner who was about to face divine justice. The text, which describes pits of flame, grisly tortures, and armies of cruel DEMONS, was designed to frighten parishioners into obeying the edicts of the Puritan faith.

The book was first published in 1658 and went through more than thirty editions by the year 1800. It became the author's second most popular text (following *Pilgrim's Progress*), and few Christian homes of the era were without a copy.

"FIN DE SATAN, LA" At the time of his death in 1885, Victor Hugo left unfinished a poem titled "La Fin de Satan" (The End of Satan). It describes SATAN's fall from heaven and his transformation from a beautiful angel of light into a grotesque winged DEMON mourning that "the angel in him died." It is loosely based on the writings of St. John in REVELATION.

Hell for this disgraced creature is the memory of what he has lost through pride. The last thing Satan sees as he falls from paradise is the dimming of the stars, until all but one are gone. He becomes obsessed with this final star, determined not to lose sight of it pinning his waning hope on that diminishing speck. Satan struggles for "ten thousand years" to fly toward the star "without finding a single place of rest" during the desperate quest. At times over the millennia, the star "seemed to darken and die" and the sight of this makes "the dark angel tremble." Finally, the star is extinguished, along with Satan's hope, and he finds himself in a desolate new realm: hell.

His misery in this unfamiliar abyss is the isolation from beauty and light, and rejection of the once-beloved angel by all that is good. He laments that God has "spat me out into the pit" where his soul hungers for "light and illumination" but finds none. Satan calls hell an "eternal absence" from the divine Creator, who the accursed fiend still loves despite his exile. This insatiable desire to be restored to paradise is "the flame" that burns the fallen angel, and will forever fuel his suffering.

In reply, God reminds Satan that he need only repent to be reunited to heaven, for God's mercy and forgiveness know no bounds. But Satan's pride is too strong, and he cannot admit his wrongdoing. This realization—that Satan himself is engineering and prolonging his damnation—only amplifies his agony.

FIRE AND BRIMSTONE Fire and brimstone is a common symbol of infernal IMAGERY used to denote hell. Brimstone (a now-obsolete synonym for sulfur) derives from the Old English word *brynstan,* meaning "to boil." It appears in REVELATION in reference to the place of the damned, describing both the pain of the underworld its putrid odor: "But the fearful, and unbelieving, and the abominable, and murderers, and whoremongers, and sorcerers, and idolaters, and all liars, shall have their part in the lake which burneth with fire and brimstone" (Rev. 21:8).

The concept of a fiery chasm emanating a nauseating stench derives from GEHENNA, an ancient site of human sacrifice. The place was eventually converted into a pit for burning trash and the prophets of the Old Testament likened the cursed valley to the underworld. Christian writers, such as St. John and St. Paul, picked up this image and used it repeatedly, referring to hell as a realm of fire and brimstone where the damned burn in eternal flames.

The term is often associated with HELLFIRE SERMONS, lectures about the underworld designed to terrify the faithful into behaving in accordance with church teachings. Fire and brimstone remains one of the most widely recognized metaphors for the underworld, appearing in everything from Hellish JOKES to infernal CLICHÉS.

FLATLINERS The 1990 dramatic film *Flatliners* takes a cynical look at NEAR-DEATH EXPERIENCES, especially those that are self-initiated. In the film, adventurous medical students (played by Kiefer Sutherland, Kevin Bacon, and Julia Roberts) experiment with the supernatural by using sophisticated medical equipment to bring about, and then reverse, clinical death. The young scholars pursue this dangerous course of action in an attempt to solve the mystery of death and answer the question of whether there is an afterlife. Instead, each finds a truly personal hell waiting on the "other side."

Sutherland, the leader of the group, is confronted in the next realm by the spirit of a young boy he tirelessly tormented when both were children. His teasing escalated from name calling to chasing to rock throwing, ultimately resulting in the boy's accidental death. In the afterlife, Sutherland becomes the prey, stalked by his former victim. His damnation is confronting his guilt over this event and reliving the dire consequences the incident had on his own life.

Roberts experiences another sort of agony when she ventures into the mystic world. She finds herself at the scene of her father's suicide. He had killed himself when she was just a child, and their reunion in the next life brings back years of repressed sorrow and desolation. She comes away from the experience haunted by the memory and by her own depression. Despite her warnings against this experiment, several other classmates make the ill-fated trip to the afterlife, all with similar unpleasant results.

Flatliners depicts a DREAM MODEL of hell, wherein the dead revisit the ugly actions of their lives. Unlike the physical tortures described in traditional concepts of the underworld, in this view, suffering consists of confronting one's own individual evil. The only way to avoid eternal agony is to make peace with these ghosts, preferably in this dimension.

FOLK PLAYS Folk plays are vernacular dramas presented by villagers (as opposed to professional thespians), usually to commemorate some cultural event. The first productions date back to ancient Greek and Egyptian times, when the stories of ORPHEUS and OSIRIS were the subject of frequent informal dramas. Other plays of the time emulated mysterious cult rituals and forbidden rites.

Folk plays reached the height of popularity during the Middle Ages in Europe, when virtually every planting and harvest festival was marked by a dramatic presentation. From Scotland to Bulgaria, folk dramas were a favorite part of such carnivals. Early free-form productions offered simple costumes and masks worn during the festival; later these were formalized into complex story lines and intricate plots. Many elements were combined in these works, from tales of St. George and medieval knights to the Egyptian lord of the dead Osiris himself. Elaborate sword dances and other performance art could also figure in the presentation. Scenes set in the underworld—by far the most popular sequences—were punctuated with fireworks, bursts of sulfur, and smoky explosions.

Unlike MORALITY PLAYS, folk plays were predominantly designed to entertain the masses rather than teach a moral lesson. Virtually all European folk plays treated themes of death and resurrection, sometimes alluding to the HARROWING OF HELL but often focusing more on magic and spells. Popular topics included harvesting, courtship and marriage (fertility), and other tenets of nature. They featured heroes and fools, providing audiences both action and comedy. As they developed over time, folk plays were often presented during wintertime to break the monotony and remind everyone of the impending spring.

Folk plays faded from the European scene after the Protestant Reformation, when Puritan leaders denounced all drama as sinful and the work of SATAN. The strict elders were especially angered by the comic treatment of hell and the DEVIL. This coincided with the rise of professional theater in England and surrounding areas, which was much beloved by the royalty and nobles of the era. Thus folk plays became less common in cities, although they continued to be popular in rural areas. It is believed that William Shakespeare saw many of these folk plays during his youth and incorporated some of their elements into his own literary masterpieces.

FOMORII According to ancient Irish myth, the Fomorii are a monstrous race of creatures who dwell far below the sea (similar in some aspects to the ancient LEVIATHAN) and are ruled by the god of the dead. The inhabitants of this gloomy underworld are horribly misshapen and deformed. Their overlord is Balor, the violent and angry god of death. Balor has a horrible temper and often strikes out against his subjects without provocation. Legends vary, but most agree that the Fomorii's evil caused their deformities and that Balor's wrath is punishment for the sins of their past.

Artwork for Southwest Specialty's infernal foods includes images of hell and the devil himself.
PHOTO COURTESY OF SOUTHWEST SPECIALTY FOOD, INC.

FOOD NOVELTIES Americans can feast on a number of food novelties that sport hellish names or infernal packaging. These include Old Nick's (a traditional English name for SATAN) beer, Underwood deviled meats, and Trappey's Red DEVIL hot sauce. The truly courageous can consume an entire line of foods "from Hell" distributed by Southwest Specialty Foods, such as salsa, chili, and mustard hot enough to be associated with the infernal region. And for those who wish to create their own diabolical dishes, there is the *Hotter than Hell* cookbook.

The packaging of these items usually includes illustrations of the nether region or its creatures. Cans of Underwood luncheon meat feature a red, pitchfork-wielding DEMON on the label. Old Nick's Beer takes the depiction a step farther, showing the lord of hell standing in the midst of a raging inferno. Going for an even more dramatic effect, Southwest Specialty packages its hellish delights in jars that not only have labels displaying the devil against a flaming background but also seem to bubble over with some seething subterranean substance. Each item also comes with cooking tips and menu suggestions from the great inferno.

Candy novelties of the underworld become commonplace every October, when Halloween treats picturing devils, demons, witches, and GHOULS fill store shelves. They are lingering remnants of the Celtic SAMHAIN, the festival of the dead in which offerings of food are left for malevolent spirits. These slightly scary confections remind us that the fascination with sampling foods from the dark below often begins in early childhood and becomes bolder with age.

FOURTH MAN, THE The 1983 Dutch film *The Fourth Man* features some of the most disturbing and grotesque visions of hell found in modern cinema. It stars Jeroen Krabbe as an alcoholic, bisexual writer who abandons the practice of his Catholic faith, only to long for its spiritual comfort and reassurance. During a gradual breakdown, Krabbe has repeated visions of himself in the ghastly realm of the dead.

As the story opens, Krabbe finds himself becoming infatuated with Christine (played by Renee Soutendijk), an androgynous young widow who owns a beauty salon. All three of the woman's previous husbands have died under mysterious circumstances, and Krabbe worries that he might be her "fourth man" to destroy. He is not sure what to believe about her, as she seems to enjoy, even perpetuate, his suspicions. The two begin an intensely sexual relationship in which Krabbe pretends she is a "beautiful boy" during intercourse. To complicate matters, Krabbe develops an obsession with Soutendijk's boyfriend and vows to live out his homoerotic fantasies with the handsome young man.

But as Krabbe embarks on his lust orgy with Soutendijk and her lover, he experiences a number of frightening visions. In one, Soutendijk cuts off his penis with a pair of beautician's shears. Another dream finds him in a crypt where three slaughtered bulls, representing the woman's three dead husbands, hang bleeding from steel hooks. And in a descent into the underworld, Krabbe envisions himself as a spider caught in the widow's web, trapped for all eternity among the damned in a murky hell of lecherous fiends and sensual tortures. For he knows that it is not simply his life Soutendijk wants; she is also determined to steal his soul.

Krabbe's waking hours are likewise filled with images of death and damnation. While walking the beach at Soutendijk's estate, he sees the corpse of a drowned man being pulled from the water. On a romantic drive with his new lover, the grisly carnage of a fatal auto accident captivates his attention. And disembarking from a train, he comes upon a coffin that seems to bear his name. When the hearse driver asks Krabbe if he ever thinks about death, he somberly whispers, "Constantly."

The line between reality and hallucination blurs as Krabbe struggles to determine whether Soutendijk killed her previous three husbands, or if his suspicion is merely an outgrowth of his intoxication and insecurity. As the plot unfolds, he becomes increasingly overwhelmed by a sense of impending doom, finally realizing that there is little distinction between his dark visions of hell and his empty existence as the diabolical widow's plaything. Ultimately, Krabbe consigns himself to the protection of the VIRGIN MARY, legendary mediator on behalf of doomed souls. Only after this metaphysical surrender does Krabbe begin to believe that his body—and spirit—are safe from damnation.

FROGS, THE *The Frogs,* written by Greek playwright Aristophanes in 405 B.C., introduces the idea of a MERRY HELL to the stage. The satire replaces the DEMONS and monsters of the underworld with a chorus of singing frogs who playfully greet the dead. This spoof of the journey of the hero HERCULES to HADES, land of the dead in Greek myth, offers a jovial realm populated by colorful characters who enjoy a good laugh.

In his drama, Aristophanes sends Dionysus to the underworld to bring back a tragedian, since Athens has found no one to replace the recently deceased Sophocles. Dionysus finds two writers of tragedy, Aeschylus and Euripides, quarreling with each other over who is the better author. Dionysus considers the works of both men, then declares Aeschylus superior and frees him from Hades to return to earth so he can write for the Athens stage.

Aristophanes wrote this play in response to what he considered the obsessive and oppressive Establishment teachings regarding the afterlife. He felt that the myths of Hercules, Hades, and other figures were becoming bland and stern, thus losing all their appeal. *The Frogs* brought a bit of whimsy to the concept of the underworld, while flouting the mores of Aristophanes' contemporaries. The play was immediately denounced by critics, but its popularity with the people made it impossible to suppress. Centuries later, writers of FOLK PLAYS borrowed this premise and depicted hell as a bawdy clubhouse for naughty but lovable pranksters. Productions of *The Frogs* continue on stages throughout the Western world.

FURSEUS Furseus, a seventh-century Irish missionary, had experienced many visions during his lifetime, beginning when he was just a boy. Some were beautiful encounters with the divine; others were prophetic glimpses of future events. And one was a terrifying apparition of hell.

The legend of Furseus's vision of hell was passed down by word of mouth to the Christian faithful for decades until an English monk, BEDE, recorded it in *The Ecclesiastical History of the English Nation* in 731. The vision reportedly occurred around 630 and may have been embellished over the years; however, the basic storyline is believed to be intact.

The story contends that under the protection of benevolent angels, Furseus was flown to an abyss where four pillars of fire burned with the souls of the damned. Sinners were separated according to their offenses and were continually tortured by DEMONS. The angels told Furseus not to pity these men, for they were receiving their just punishment. As he watched, the four columns of fire suddenly melded together and shot into the sky. The force of their mingling wielded the burning soul of an evil man whom Furseus had known into his face. The collision left a permanent scar, a black scorch mark, on Furseus's chin and shoulder.

According to Bede's account, Furseus suffered from the memory of that experience for the rest of his life. The scar left by the charred soul burned without ceasing. A fellow monk reported that he had seen Furseus sweating profusely even in the dead of winter, baking from the heat of the hell wound. Furseus's story became a staple of VISION LITERATURE and was often referred to as "proof" of what awaits the damned in eternity.

G

GA-GORIB According to the myth of the Khoikhoi of South Africa, Ga-gorib is a fearsome monster who tricks the living into falling into his bottomless pit. Ga-gorib perches on the edge of this chasm and taunts passers into challenging him. He offers them a stone to throw at him, to try to topple him into the pit. But the rocks always rebound and kill the thrower instead. Their bodies fall into the depths, much to Ga-gorib's delight. He has been compared to the Christian SATAN, who likewise tries to cause people to become ensnared in his spiritual traps.

Ga-gorib is eventually bested by Heitsi-Eibib, a brave and wise warrior who outsmarts the fiend and forces him into the underworld forever. After defeating Ga-gorib, Heitsi-Eibib is granted the power to return from the grave.

This story is likened to the Christian tale of the battle between Christ and Satan. Satan, like Ga-gorib, lures humans into sin and thus into his kingdom of everlasting torment. But Christ eventually defeats the DEMON and then rises from the dead.

GAMES Many games, both ancient and modern, have been connected to the underworld. The earliest American example of these is the Ouija (or Witchboard) patented in 1892. The Ouija is a printed board that shows the alphabet and the words *yes* and *no*. To play, at least two participants must guide a pointed "needle" to spell out answers to a player's questions. Originally designed as a toy to be used in parlor games, self-proclaimed psychics began claiming that it was in fact a tool for contacting the dead. The idea took hold, and Ouija boards have since been used to seek all sorts of information from the dead, including the secrets of the damned.

One of the most popular netherworld games of recent times is the role-playing game Dungeons and Dragons (also known as D & D). D & D was copyrighted in 1974 by its creators Gary Gygaz and Dave Arneson. It was sold in the form of a bare-bones instruction booklet listing basic rules of play. From this early, unpolished version, D & D went through many revisions and clarifications on its way to becoming a nationwide craze. It defined the concept of the role-playing game, where each player assumes the identity of a specific character for the contest's duration. Each player's strengths, abilities, and weaknesses in negotiating the match are determined by his or her assigned role. Movement through the dungeon—a hellish underground maze infested with demonic creatures—is accomplished through miniature figures of the different entities, which include DEMONS, wizards, and witches. Players can move between the "upper" and "lower" worlds of mortals and spirits.

D & D became phenomenally popular during the 1970s, especially among college students. The fad generated several magazines dedicated entirely to the rules, history, and champions of the fantasy game. But D & D had a dark side, too. It was condemned by many clergy members for its "diabolic" nature, "glorification" of the underworld, and "endorsement of witchcraft." D & D was even linked to a grisly murder in the early 1980s. The killers admitted to using the game as a pattern for their CRIME. This bad press, and the inevitable loss of its novelty, began the slow decline of what had been called "the ultimate in role-playing competitions."

A similar game, this one based on classic horror writer H. P. Lovecraft's SHORT STORY "Call of Cthulhu," gained popularity during the early 1980s. Its advertisements promised "unearthly effects from other dimensions" that could "drive anyone stark raving mad." Players were invited to "tread dark trails in search of eldritch horrors." Accessories were also available, such as "scratch'n'sniff" monster identification kits and the Cthulhu Monster Flash Cards.

Following the story's basic premise, the game sends players down "dark, foul-smelling holes" to battle "Minions of the Old Ones" and "eldritch horrors." Their only protection is holy water and "incantations for the Banishment of the Burrowers Beneath." These odd passageways are actually gateways to infernal regions of mutant monsters and bloodthirsty fiends. Characters such as GHOULS, serpent men, and "nightgaunts" attack and obstruct the players' progress. The object of the game is to conquer these demons and escape unharmed.

Hell has also made its way into one of the biggest trends of the early 1990s: POGs. These small cardboard circles are used in a competition similar to marbles, with the winner of each match collecting the pieces he or she has conquered. The paper game tokens are decorated with a variety of images, including symbols of the underworld. One POG shows a flame-enveloped DEVIL below the caption, "He loves you not!" Another offers a stylized CHARON ferrying skeletons to HADES, the underworld of Greek myth. And skulls, bones, pitchforks, and other infernal IMAGERY adorn scores of the cardboard chips.

The underworld is also the setting for a vast variety of COMPUTER GAMES. These sojourns to hell offer players the opportunity to take the ultimate risk and flirt with damnation via sophisticated electronics.

GARDEN OF EARTHLY DELIGHTS, THE

Artist HIERONYMUS BOSCH startled both art critics and religious leaders with *The Garden of Earthly Delights,* painted in the early 1500s. Unlike traditional interpretations of Christian themes, Bosch's composition mingles surreal images, striking colors, and innovative images into his interpretation of humanity's evil. It remains one of the most imaginative portrayals of hell in Western art.

The work is done in three separate panels: the first showing the Garden of Eden, the second depicting the corruption of humanity, and the last denoting the horrors of hell. *The Garden of Earthly Delights* illustrates the progression from innocence to damnation. It is exceptional in its nightmarish concepts of sin and anguish. Bosch uses a style of artistry—similar to modern surrealism—that is centuries ahead of its time. The result is a surprising and unsettling composition that stirs the soul as well as the senses.

Bosch's work shows that trouble is brewing even in Eden. The first panel depicts God presenting the innocent Eve to her husband, yet the unsettling image of a sinister cat gnawing on a dead mouse indicates that darkness and death are lurking close by, waiting to strike. In the center panel, every transgression from adultery to murder is graphically portrayed in an explosion of odd scenes. Naked soldiers ride bulls, savage fish devour humans, and huge winged rats prey on fallen women.

The depiction of hell is equally surreal. Unlike the first two panels, which are rich with bright colors, the illustration of the underworld is set against a black background. SATAN, at the center, is a sad-faced giant with an eggshell body and tree trunks for legs. Across a glowing river of molten pitch is a city in flames. A dark DEMON beats a screaming man with a chessboard while a huge rabbit chews on the feet of a faceless woman. In the foreground, Bosch offers a huge pair of human ears guiding an enormous knife on an underworld attack. Throughout hell, blades, swords, and hooks are used to antagonize the damned. These figures are interspersed with amorous pigs, ravenous beetles, and birds that eat (and defecate) sinners.

The Garden of Earthly Delights is a masterpiece of confusion and terror, showing incredible imagination and creativity in portraying the agonies of CHRISTIAN HELL. Bosch's work is a stunning accomplishment in supernatural interpretation.

GARM Garm is the guardian of the underworld according to Norse mythology. He is similar to the Greek CERBERUS, a vicious beast who protects the entrance to HADES. Garm is described in the ancient epic *Prose Edda* as a fierce beast who will be loosed at the end of the world. He is also likened to the Hebrew LEVIATHAN, a monster set upon devouring humans.

GATE, THE Curious children accidentally open the door to the underworld in the 1987 film *The Gate.* Looking for something to do while their parents are away, the restless boys find a mysterious rock with a crystal at its center in the backyard. They immediately begin digging deeper in search of more "jewels" but instead dislodge a boulder that covers a subterranean chamber teeming with fire and smoke. A flood of angry DEMONS and fiends spews up from the opening. The children must find a way to block the portal before they are pulled down into the depths of hell. With the help of ancient spells and rituals, they manage to do so just as the damned are about to attack.

GATES OF HELL (FILM) In the 1983 film *Gates of Hell,* set in dreary Dunwich, Massachusetts, the portal to the netherworld is inadvertently opened by a despondent priest's suicide. When the cleric commits the ultimate sin against hope by taking his own life, he releases a powerful evil from the underworld. The DEVIL promptly begins sending his legions to New England to spread corruption and violence throughout the world.

But the damned are interested in only one thing: devouring the villagers. Hell's flesh-eating fiends descend upon the living in droves. (The authors of *Cult Flicks and Trash Picks* call these graphic mutilations "gritty, blatantly gratuitous splatter.") Only a fiery purging can close the door to the underworld and return the wicked to the depths of hell.

Other cinematic productions about passageways between hell and earth include *DEVIL'S RAIN, GHOST TOWN,* and *THE GATE.*

GATES OF HELL, THE (SCULPTURE) AUGUSTE RODIN, considered by many to be the greatest sculptor since MICHELANGELO, was commissioned by the French government in 1880 to create an ornate set of brass doors for the Museum of Decorative Arts in Paris. Sculpting this composition, *The Gates of Hell* (the title was criticized by many at the time as being too self-important), became an obsession for Rodin for the remainder of his life. The artist spent several decades perfecting his masterpiece, which was still unfinished at the time of his death.

The images depicted in *The Gates of Hell* were initially inspired by Dante's *DIVINE COMEDY: THE INFERNO.* But as the work progressed, the artist began including touches reminiscent of Michelangelo's *LAST JUDGMENT* and Peter Paul Rubens's *THE FALL OF THE DAMNED.* Rodin also relied on his extensive knowledge of anatomy, Scripture, and literature to give life to the piece.

The unfinished work includes many illustrations taken directly from the work of Dante as well as more general and traditional examples of CHRISTIAN HELL. Rodin depicts bodies twisted and contorted into odd positions to show the agonies of the damned. It also includes the famous *Thinker,* a seated man resting his head on his hand as he contemplates his fate. Erupting flames line the sides of the archway, creating a feeling of envelopment by scorching terror.

The Gates of Hell, dubbed the "most ambitious" artistic undertaking of the twentieth century, remains a poignant interpretation of the horrors of the damned.

GAWAMA Gawama (Gauna, Gaunab) is one of the few lords of the underworld recorded in African tales. Most African myths offer only rest, paradise, or reincarnation as options for the dead, but the San of South Africa believe in the harsh deity Gawama. He is the leader of the spirits of the dead, often referred to as the DEVIL.

Gawama collects the souls of the dead and then uses them to harass the living, who greatly fear these ghosts. The San try to prevent the GHOULS from returning to earth by placing huge boulders over their graves. There are also a number of spells and rituals that can save the living from these menacing phantasms.

Most often, the spirits of the dead appear in the form of snakes. They can attack both people and crops and are considered quite cunning and manipulative. Gawama and his armies are blamed for famine, disease, and death. His ability to haunt and harm the living makes him an especially terrifying god and his underworld home a frightening realm of utter agony.

GEHENNA Gehenna is the land of the dead recorded in ancient Hebrew texts. The word is derived from the Valley of Hinnom, a canyon just south of Jerusalem. It had been consecrated to the ancient Ammonite god Molech and was used for pagan rituals, including human sacrifice. Some legends claim that the Ammonites used to burn children alive in Gehenna. It was declared accursed by the Old Testament prophet Jeremiah and was thereafter associated with hideous death and torture.

After the Hebrews took control of Jerusalem, they converted the valley into a communal trash pit. Garbage fires raged constantly, giving off a bitter stench. The image of FIRE AND BRIMSTONE, which would later be applied to the underworld, originated here. Prophets used Gehenna as a metaphor to warn against the horrors of the afterlife, and thus the name Gehenna eventually became synonymous with hell. Patriarchs Enoch, Daniel, Ezekiel, and Isaiah all mention the place by name in their texts.

Originally, Hebrews believed that the most despicable sinners would burn for eternity in Gehenna, whereas moderately evil souls would suffer for one year and then face ANNIHILATION. Early teachings described three entrances to the underworld of Gehenna: one in the wilderness, one below the sea, and one in Jerusalem. This last entrance is located alongside the gates of paradise, so that the damned have their agony increased by seeing the pleasures of heaven. The ocean portal is often associated with LEVIATHAN, a horrible sea monster later equated with the Christian SATAN.

Gehenna appears in New Testament teachings as well. Christ uses the image of Gehenna when describing the horrors of the damned. He warns his disciples: "If thy right hand offend thee, cut it off: for it is better to enter the kingdom of Heaven maimed than to be cast whole into Gehenna with its unquenchable fire" (Mark 9:43).

Early Christian leaders expanded Gehenna to a realm with seven sections, all seething with fire yet pitch-dark. Tortures are meted out depending on the soul's sins, with hanging, roasting, and choking on the "black smoke of death" the most common. Gehenna is filled with the "Angels of Punishment" who carry out the afterlife sentences. The suffering of the damned in Gehenna is amplified by their awareness of the joys of paradise, which, as in Hebrew tradition, is located close by.

JAHANNAM, Islamic hell, is also a derivative of the valley of Gehenna.

"GENESIS B" "Genesis B" is an adaptation of an ancient Saxon poem about the creation of hell. According to the poem, the angels were the first of God's creations. One proud angel, LUCIFER, decides he wants to be equal to God and sets up a throne for himself in the northwest corner of heaven. (North became associated with cold and desolation; west with sunset and death). He convinces a number of his fellow angels to renounce God and worship him instead. When the Supreme Being sees this he rebukes Lucifer and his followers and tells them to stop this mutiny. But the vain creatures refuse to obey.

God then casts Lucifer and the rebellious angels out of heaven. They fall for three days and nights, their angelic power and brilliance stripped away as they descend. The rebels (mutated into despicable DEMONS) land in a place of utter darkness and despair, which came to be known as hell.

Lucifer, refusing to admit that he has sinned against God, denounces the Creator as petty and unjust. He further mocks God for planning to allow humans—crude creatures of clay and mud—into heaven. He vows to turn humans into slaves of hell instead.

Lucifer sends one of the fallen angels to Eden to tempt Adam and Eve into sinning against God. The demon craftily convinces them to disobey the Almighty, then gleefully returns to hell and brags of his accomplishment. Lucifer celebrates this victory, but his jubilation is short-lived. For God promises to send a savior to redeem humanity's souls from eternal damnation, allowing entrance into heaven.

"Genesis B," and its Saxon poetic origin, drew inspiration and images from REVELATION. This biblical text describes the war in heaven, the fall of Lucifer, and the LAST JUDGMENT, at which time all will be assumed into heaven or damned to the pits of hell.

GHEDE Haiti is rich with dark myths and voodoo legends, including many frightening tales about the evil Ghede. This lord of death is a tall man who wears a long black coat, black top hat, and dark glasses. He is considered a powerful DEVIL who constantly seeks the ruin of souls.

Ghede stands at the eternal crossroads through which all souls must pass upon death. He has the power to resurrect the dead and to animate zombies. One of his most frightening attributes is his ability eternally to torment the souls of corpses stolen by sorcerers. Haitians believe that only prayer and holy ritual can save them from the clutches of Ghede.

GHOST One of the biggest screen successes of 1990 was *Ghost,* a love story about the afterlife. The film offers an intriguing blend of romance, suspense, and supernatural fantasy. It explores the power of the human soul to love from beyond the grave and examines the dark fate of those who choose evil over good.

Ghost stars Patrick Swayze as Sam, a young banker who is killed in an apparent mugging. When his spirit refuses to leave the side of his beloved Molly (played by Demi Moore), Swayze discovers that his murder was no random event but part of a plot to steal his bank's security codes. One of his coworkers, and a trusted friend, has engineered a complex money-laundering scheme and needs the codes to complete his illegal transfers. When the killer fails to retrieve the correct numbers, Moore becomes the hit man's next target.

Ghost offers a fascinating interpretation of the mechanics of salvation and damnation. Good souls are absorbed into a brilliant light, but the spirits of evil people are left among the shadows to be overtaken by darkness. Visually, this is accomplished by animating oil stains, blotches, and other gloomy black spots into living DEMONS that drag the soul, screaming in agony, into hell. (Movie critic Roger Ebert calls this effect "a particularly ridiculous visitation from the demons of hell.") Swayze tells Moore that the saved take love with them to heaven. The condemned, however, will spend eternity mired in their cruelty and hatred.

GHOST TOWN The 1988 horror film *Ghost Town* puts the underworld in the American West (as do the movies *DEVIL'S RAIN* and *HIGHWAY TO HELL*). However, in this western—nicknamed by critics "The Good, The Bad and The Satanic"—hell can be harrowed by a modern sheriff (played by Franc Luz) willing to take on a long-dead gunslinger to avenge the honor of the lawman's badge. Should he defeat the outlaw, the town will be rid of its curse. But if Luz is killed, he will join his fallen comrades as a zombie in the throes of "eternal pain."

The film begins as a mysterious woman disappears into a sandstorm, and Luz, concerned about her safety, follows her into the tempest. When the dust settles, Luz discovers that he has unwittingly entered Ghost Town, a chamber of hell populated by decaying corpses and mangled souls. Luz soon learns that he has been "chosen" to vanquish the evil by dueling his adversaries in Old West style. The restless spirit of a murdered lawman, gunned down a century ago, begs Luz to avenge him and end the curse that holds tortured souls in this dimension. Luz reluctantly agrees and forces the fiends into the depths of hell through use of his wits, virtue, and shooting skills.

GHOULS Ghouls are the children of IBLIS, the Islamic SATAN, according to Middle Eastern legend. They are fierce DEMONS who journey from hell back to earth in order to feed on human corpses. Ghouls have also been said to prey on the living if no cadavers are available. Their existence is debated by scholars, since some records indicate that Muhammad, the founder of the Muslim faith, said that these monsters are not real.

The term has been integrated into the vernacular to refer to loathsome creatures, living or deceased.

GIFT NOVELTIES Symbols of hell have made their way onto all sorts of gift novelties, ranging from refrigerator magnets to pen holders and just about everything in between. Shoppers

Satan, demons, and
the Grim Reaper Ankou
adorn a variety of figurines and trinkets.

can purchase sticky notes showing a DEMON engulfed in flames under the heading "Memo from Hell," kitchen thermometers decorated with FIRE AND BRIMSTONE asking "Hot Enough for Ya?" and ashtrays dotted with DEVILS proclaiming "Go Ahead—We Don't Mind the Smoke." Also available are a variety of red-robed SATAN dolls complete with horns, pointed tails, and pitchforks.

Other fads have introduced underworld novelties to American culture. The Dungeons and Dragons GAMES craze of the early 1980s left in its wake a myriad of demonic trinkets and toys. Novelty shops still offer statues of repulsive GHOULS, models of flame-enveloped castles, and full-color posters showing the world separated into mystic layers of wizards, witches, FAIRIES, and demons. Racks of stickers show an assortment of hellish scenes and diabolical creatures. These same illustrations adorn everything from book covers to coffee mugs. There is also a lucrative market in temporary TATTOOS of the damned: scary (but removable) body art for those unwilling to make the depth of commitment.

Images from ancient legends are another source of infernal wares. Pewter statuettes of CHARON, the ferryman of Greek myth who carries souls to HADES, CERBERUS, Hades' ferocious guard dog, and the underworld fortress itself can be found at gift shops. Serpents, scorpions, and horned demons of infernal IMAGERY have been transformed into masks, key chains, and model kits. Candy dispensers in the shape of the Grim Reaper, Satan, and other figures of the underworld are also prevalent, especially around Halloween.

The October holiday also brings an annual parade of diabolical trinkets. Perennial favorites include cardboard cutouts of underworld scenes, demonic costumes, and ceramic fortresses of the damned. Cinematic monsters likewise have inspired a deluge of MOVIE MERCHANDISING novelties, such as Freddy Kruger makeup kits and *BEETLEJUICE* coloring books.

GIMOKODAN Gimokodan is the underworld of the Bagobo people of the Philippines. It lies below the earth in two sections—one reserved for warriors who die in battle, the other for everyone else. Gimokodan is not a place of suffering or punishment but is a dull, somber realm that offers little comfort. It is insufferably boring compared to the constant challenges and rewards of life. A giantess suckles the spirits of dead infants, but there is no solace for others.

On their way to Gimokodan, the dead bathe in a magic river (similar to the Greek LETHE) that washes away most memories of earthly life. This helps spirits accept the sorrow of departing the world and leaving loved ones behind. In Gimokodan, souls turn to dew during the day, then revert to astral form when darkness falls. They suffer only an eternal aching for their former, and vastly more enriching, earthly lives.

The Bagobo believe that the dead can interfere with affairs of the living and offer gifts to dead relatives to extract favors or garner protection from evil. Such offerings are thought to distract the departed from their miserable existence in Gimokodan and thus keep them from haunting those still alive. Over time, spirits in the underworld will completely forget about the living and remember only time spent in the murky land of the dead.

GISLEBERTUS The TYMPANUM RELIEF, carved above the doorway to the Cathedral in France was produced under the leadership of French sculptor Gislebertus from 1130 to 1135. It shows the *LAST JUDGMENT,* the event prophesied in the Christian Bible when all will be consigned to heaven or hell. Carved portrayals on this theme became a component of almost every

Gothic cathedral erected in Europe during the Middle Ages. The compositions were usually situated over the church entrances so the images of salvation and damnation could serve as a constant reminder to the faithful about their ultimate fate.

Gislebertus uses images from the Bible, Christian tradition, and ancient myth to create specific portraits of the underworld and its agonies. His *Last Judgment* relief shows huge snakes and dragonlike fiends snatching evil souls and thrusting them into a gaping HELLMOUTH. At Christ's left hand, DEMONS weigh the fate of souls on a scale similar to the one described in the Egyptian BOOK OF THE DEAD. Bloodthirsty DEVILS try to tip the balance in favor of evil. The faces of the damned are contorted with pain, their arms outstretched in vain supplication for comfort that will never come.

This work is significant not only in that it draws images from a number of distinct sources, but also because it is one of the first artworks of the Middle Ages that can be positively attributed to their creators. The artist, whose style is denoted by abnormally elongated human bodies and the extensive use of ruffled textures to create depth, signed his composition. Gislebertus's work is therefore important to the study of advancements in art as well as in the evolution of underworld beliefs.

GNIPAHELLI Gnipahelli is the cave entrance to NIFLHEIM, the underworld of Germanic myth. It is a dark, foul-smelling opening that leads to the kingdom of HEL, goddess of the damned. Gnipahelli is guarded by the fierce dog GARM (a beast similar to the Greek CERBERUS). The ferocious monster is ever watching for Hermodr, the dark ferryman who brings the dead to the underworld. Garm also prevents spirits from escaping Niflheim.

GNOSTIC HELL The Gnostics (a term meaning "those who know") are members of an early Christian cult that rejected many of Christ's teachings, especially regarding the nature of matter. They believe that material creations are inherently evil and that existence on earth is equivalent to damnation in hell. Humanity therefore dwells in a state of damnation during life and can reach paradise only by ridding itself of all association with matter.

Gnosticism teaches that God is a distant being who has little contact with humankind. He did not make the world: This was done by the child of the fallen angel Sophia (meaning knowledge). Her son was a lower god who created the realm of human existence. People are thus flawed, and their good comes only from Sophia and her attempts at atoning for her sins. She is destined to be continually reborn, as Helen of Troy, Mary Magdalene, and other prominent women, until the end of time.

According to Gnostic belief, Jesus' incarnation was actually a descent into the underworld. He routs the lower god's kingdom, bringing its subjects secret knowledge, or gnosis. This enables people to attain paradise. Hell is thus the denial of union with the higher God, not a place of corporal punishment. Since on earth we are separated from God, this life is no different from existence in hell. And because the material universe (including human life) was created by a fallen god, it too is evil. Therefore everyone must pass through the "inferno" before being saved.

A manuscript from the third century, the PISTIS-SOPHIA, describes the Gnostic nature of hell. In the text, Jesus tells Mary Magdalene that the underworld is a "huge dragon" that completely surrounds the world. Inside the dragon are "twelve dungeons of horrible torment," each containing its own overlord, a brutal DEMON who administers torture.

Christian leaders immediately condemned this teaching on several grounds. First, they rejected the concept of God as cold and aloof rather than as a loving father. Second, the hypothesis that some "lower god" had so much power over humans and their fate was illogical and baseless. Most important, Gnostic faith rendered the crucifixion and resurrection of Christ irrelevant, since his very incarnation released souls from hell.

GODKIN, GEORGE *On the Other Side,* an analysis of out-of-body experiences written by Marvin Ford, includes the incredible story of George Godkin, a farmer from Alberta, Canada. While suffering from a series of health problems in the mid-1940s, Godkin "died" and had a frightening vision of hell. The Godkin case is unique since it predates most modern accounts of NEAR-DEATH EXPERIENCES and does not involve artificial resuscitation of a "clinically dead" patient. Godkin's vision and revival occurred without the intervention of medical techniques, drugs, or other outside stimuli.

Godkin's health had been rapidly deteriorating, when one night he awoke to find himself in hell. He was immediately struck by a "darkness so intense that it seemed to have a pressure per square inch." His soul was overcome with a sickening feeling of loneliness and despair. And the heat was unbearable: "Your eyeballs are so dry they feel like red hot coals in their sockets. Your tongue and lips are parched and cracked with the intense heat. . . . The interior of your body has a sensation of scorching hot air being forced through it."

When the farmer revived, he had difficulty overcoming the shock and horror of his vision. Though he was able to offer a brief description of the realm's horrors, he stressed that it would be impossible to recount adequately what he had experienced, since "the agony and loneliness of Hell cannot be expressed." Attempts to discredit or debunk his story were unsuccessful: Godkin steadfastly stood by his account and remained unfazed by skeptics. Years later, renowned cardiologist MAURICE RAWLINGS would include Godkin's case in *To Hell and Back,* an updated investigation of negative near-death experiences.

GORA-DAILENG The underworld is a dreadful place of agony according to myths of the Caroline Islanders of Micronesia. Gora-Daileng is the lord of the dead who punishes depraved souls for the wickedness of their lives. His tortures include eternally roasting spirits in an unbearably hot furnace and casting them into an endless river from which none return. He is considered so frightening to the islanders that they do not speak his name aloud, lest he think he is being summoned.

GORGIAS Fourth-century B.C. Greek philosopher PLATO offers his view of the afterlife in his drama *Gorgias*. In the play, Plato describes the underworld as a sort of supernatural bureaucracy where souls are evaluated and assigned according to their merits. He names the judges of the underworld: Aeacus, Rhadamanthus, and MINOS. Each has specific duties, and each man's decisions could be appealed to a higher court. The job of these arbitrators is to review the lives of recently departed spirits and decide whether to send the souls to bliss in Elysium (paradise), to LIMBO for uncommitted spirits, or to punishment in TARTARUS, the lowest realm of the underworld of King HADES.

Plato patterns this afterlife cataloging system after his own judicial ideal exhibited in the courts of ancient Greece. His work is quite similar to Socrates' *PHAEDO,* sharing the same ideas about underworld magistrates, sentencing, and punishment.

GOSPEL OF BARTHOLOMEW One of the earliest accounts of Christ's HARROWING OF HELL is found in the Gospel of Bartholomew, written during the first century after Jesus' death. The work is an apocrypha and was immediately rejected by Christian leaders who did not consider it to be a product of divine inspiration. But the Gospel of Bartholomew became popular among early followers of Christ since it offers details on his raid on the underworld and other subjects not covered in the four Gospels sanctioned by the church.

The Gospel of Bartholomew explains that SATAN and his rebel angels have become ugly fiends who torture souls in the underworld. They inflict pain but are themselves suffering from their disunion with God. When Christ descends into hell after his death on Good Friday, the DEMONS are infuriated that some souls are being redeemed while they are left to writhe in despair. Satan shouts that the harrowing is unfair, but Christ rebukes him. The dusty underworld is emptied of the saved, and the dark angels are left seething in anger, cursing their fate, and envying the lowly creatures who have been taken up to paradise.

This account was eventually supplanted by the GOSPEL OF NICODEMUS, a later apocrypha that provides much more lavish details on hell and the release of the patriarchs.

GOSPEL OF NICODEMUS The Christian apocrypha Gospel of Nicodemus includes a lengthy description of Christ's trial before Pontius Pilate, death on the cross, and HARROWING OF HELL. Records of the first printed copy date to the sixth century; however, the Gospel of Nicodemus had been circulated orally for decades—perhaps even centuries—by the first Christians. The text (supposedly dictated by two deceased sons of Simeon who witnessed the underworld events) is not considered "the divinely inspired word of God" by church authorities and has thus been excluded from the Bible and from Christian teaching.

In the Gospel of Nicodemus, the underworld is a subterranean prison of sorrow but without corporal punishment. After his crucifixion, Christ storms the gates of hell in order to redeem the souls of the just, shouting the battle cry, "Hell, I am your sting!" SATAN, ruler of the underworld, plots to seize and enslave Christ in the inferno, believing that he has already conquered God's son by having had him tortured and crucified. Christ bursts through in an explosion of light, shouting, "Let the King of Glory in!" He wrestles Satan into submission, binds him in fiery chains, then shepherds the saved to heaven. The deceased "authors" of the Gospel of Nicodemus describe their experience being delivered from SHEOL (the underworld of Hebrew texts): "We were holden in Hell in darkness and the shadow of death; suddenly there shone upon us a great light, and Hell did tremble and the gates of death."

The Gospel of Nicodemus also foretells an apocalyptic battle between Christ and Satan that will take place at the end of the world. Christ promises to force the fiend into "eternal darkness" after the LAST JUDGMENT and chain him in hell where he will be unable to harm others. This is the essence of Satan's final agony: He was first banished to hell because of his pride, wanting to be as powerful and as important as God. But the DEVIL will ultimately be reduced to an insignificant prisoner immobilized at the bottom of the underworld.

Greek mythological King HADES is also mentioned in this mysterious text. He is the personification of death and shares rule of the underworld with Satan. But Christ defeats him, too, symbolizing the fact that humanity need no longer fear death, for there is life eternal in Christ.

GOTTSCHALK Gottschalk, a simple German peasant, claimed to have seen a vision of hell in 1189. After suffering from fever and sickness, Gottschalk went into a coma that lasted for five days. When he awakened, he told of a ghastly visit to the underworld.

According to his story, Gottschalk was greeted by angels who led him to a huge tree covered with shoes. Beyond the tree was a thorny desert, but only those who had been kind and pure during their lives were allowed to take a pair of shoes from the tree. The rest had to cross the field of thorns barefoot, their flesh tearing and bleeding with every step.

After crossing this treacherous bramble, the dead must navigate a river filled with razor-sharp blades. The angels told Gottschalk that this gory gauntlet continued on for miles into the horizon. Souls of evildoers were then set upon a road that led nowhere, lined with an endless array of torturous obstacles. The damned spend eternity in this horrid maze.

Gottschalk awakened and recounted his tale to the awestruck villagers, who agreed that this vision was a divine warning about their wickedness. Many who heard the story promised to show charity to others and to spread the word of Gottschalk's strange journey.

GOWDIE, ISOBEL Isobel Gowdie (c. 1610–1665) was a beautiful, witty, and intelligent Scottish farm wife who created quite a controversy with her unprompted confessions of demonic activities. Bored with her monotonous life on the farm, she went into town one sunny spring day and announced that she had been practicing witchcraft for more than a decade. Gowdie further shocked the townspeople with her graphic descriptions of perverse sexual encounters with the DEVIL, claiming to have enjoyed frequent intercourse with the fiend despite great pain caused by his icy, gigantic phallus.

But Gowdie's contact with SATAN was not limited to intimate coven rituals. The self-proclaimed witch also bragged that she had visited hell as the devil's guest. During April and May of 1662, Gowdie repeated her incredible story on four separate occasions without once contradicting herself. Officials

Gowdie described numerous Satanic rituals, including a ceremony in which she was baptized in her own blood. ART TODAY

had little choice but to accept her story as genuine.

According to her account, Gowdie was approached by Satan and invited to participate in a local coven of witches. She accepted, proving her allegiance to him by renouncing her Christian name in a black baptism and taking Janet as her coven name. She began practicing witchcraft in secret, participating in a variety of Satanic activities such as orgies, ritual slayings, shape-shifting, and black masses. Gowdie eventually consummated her union with Satan in a violent sexual encounter performed before the coven faithful.

Satisfied with her loyalty, the devil then took her to the underworld to show her his legions. She referred to this realm as the "Land of FAIRIES" and the infernal tribes as "hosts of Hell." Gowdie described hell as a dark region located below the surface of the earth. She was flown there by an enchanted horse that breathed fire and reeked with the stench of the grave. According to Gowdie: "The hills opened up . . . there were elf-bulls routing and skoyling up and down there, and it affrighted me. . . . They were making elf-bolts. . . . The devil sharps them with his own hand."

Satan reassured her that she would not be harmed as long as she stayed by his side. An elf-bull handed her a cache of the demonic weapons he had been forging, and Satan showed her how to shoot them using her thumb as a bow. Gowdie and Satan then went "hunting," killing Christians on the rural hillsides before the horse brought her back to her farm.

Gowdie's confession of Satanism was remarkably extensive. She offered numerous accounts of other evil activities, even naming fellow townspeople as members of the coven. Her case was unique, since unlike most "witches," Gowdie did not confess under torture but came forward of her own accord. Her story was neither corroborated nor dispelled by any of the alleged witches she named as coven members, since none of those she fingered shared her desire to espouse such shocking escapades.

Some historians believe that Gowdie was chosen by the coven to serve as a human sacrifice, since her confession would almost certainly result in a bloody execution. Others argue that Gowdie had simply tired of her dim-witted husband and the boredom of country life and was seeking attention and amusement. Some contend that her dreary lifestyle had driven her mad. In any case, there are no records of what happened to Gowdie after her startling admissions. It is assumed that she was executed for her blasphemous activities.

GREAT DIVORCE, THE Author C. S. Lewis, one of the most brilliant Christian intellectuals of the twentieth century, offers an imaginative and compelling account of the afterlife in his *The Great Divorce.* A professor of medieval and Renaissance literature at

Cambridge University, Lewis has addressed the question of the nature of heaven and hell in a number of fiction and nonfiction works, including the novel THE *SCREWTAPE LETTERS* and the treatise *The Problem of Pain.* He is also the author of the classic series *The Chronicles of Narnia* and the *Space Trilogy.*

Lewis's central theme in *The Great Divorce* is that how and where a person spends eternity is entirely up to him or her. He calls this an "either-or" choice of two very different options. Those who choose hell can never have heaven. And those who select heaven must cast away "even the smallest and most intimate souvenirs of hell." *The Great Divorce* illustrates examples of both alternatives.

The Great Divorce was written as a refutation of WILLIAM BLAKE's *The Marriage of Heaven and Hell.* Lewis considers Blake's thesis—that good and evil are temporary states rather than qualities of the soul—to be "a disastrous error." For Lewis, evil can never develop into good; it can be eradicated only by finding the error and taking specific, targeted actions to correct it. Thus heaven and hell are irreconcilably separated realms.

The Great Divorce begins at an eternal "bus stop" in a gray, rainy town of perpetual dusk. The village is lined with dreary shops, decrepit apartments, and bleak warehouses. There are no people visible anywhere in the area except in the bus line. As they wait, the prospective riders quarrel among themselves over their places in line, how many people can fit on the bus, even whether they want to make the trip at all. By the time the vehicle arrives, many have either left or been forced out of the line. The rest board the bus, which has plenty of room to spare.

During the ride, the narrator learns much about his fellow passengers. One, declaring himself a "genius" unappreciated by his contemporaries, has committed suicide after failing to gain the reputation as a great poet he felt he richly deserved. Another claims that the "gray town" is in fact a "nursery" for cultivating creativity now that material things are gone, rather than a desolate place of perpetual gloom. Throughout the ride, those on the bus erupt into knife- and gunfights, yet no one is injured. They continually bicker over opening windows, talking too loudly, and a host of other petty grievances.

The narrator notices that the bus is not moving forward, but *upward.* It glides smoothly hundreds of miles above the misty town of endless rain. Seeing the place from above, the narrator cannot believe how large it is. He is promptly informed that the reason for the town's gargantuan size and its seeming lack of inhabitants is that the residents of the gray town cannot get along and are forever moving farther out to get away from one another. (Simply imagining a house makes the structure appear, although it is in fact a mere illusion of a house. The strongest roofs and thickest walls provide no protection from the rain.)

Since the townspeople have no real "needs," they do not have to interact and so choose to withdraw from one another. "Gray town" is now a million miles across, with most of its streets empty as inhabitants are continually quarreling, moving away, and then quarreling with the new neighbors in an ongoing cycle of petulance.

When the bus arrives at its destination, a beautiful land of green mountains, blue rivers, and mountains of pearl, the narrator notices that the bus riders—including himself—are no more than opaque shadows. They are "man-shaped stains on the brightness of the air." Several of his fellow passengers immediately return to the bus, deciding that they want nothing to do with this realm. Others ask the driver when they must return to the gray town, and he replies they may stay as long as they like; the choice is theirs to make.

Suddenly a great crowd of "solid people" approaches, each drawn to a specific new arrival. There are many scenes of greetings and reunions of friends and family members and even of offenders coming to seek forgiveness from those they have injured in life. The welcoming party, all residents of heaven, explains that each has been sent as a guide to bring one passenger across the fields to the mountains of paradise. It would be a long, difficult journey, but once arrived the former inhabitants of hell would become substantive and would join the community of paradise. All that is required is that the newcomers agree to make the trip.

However, many of the gray town visitors find this offer unacceptable. One refuses to go with his appointed guardian, angry that his former employee has been enjoying heaven while he, a "decent man," has been dwelling in hell for so many years. The rider declares, "I'd rather be damned than go along with you!" Another reluctant visitor rejects the idea that he has been in hell and that this is heaven, clinging to his "intellectual" convictions rather than accepting "superstitious" beliefs about sin and retribution. When the citizen of heaven asks, incredulous, if his friend does he not realize he has *been* in hell, the apostate laughs, "My dear boy, that is *so* like you." Unwilling to repent his "sins of the intellect," the damned man cheerfully tells his guide that a superior mind must forever be open to new concepts, theories, and interpretations. Thus he chooses to return to the gray town where he can bask in his own cerebral eminence rather than remain in a paradise where he must submit to God's rules.

The narrator encounters a number of similar situations. He sees a mother who had spent years begrudging the death of her young son refuse to enter heaven because she does not want to dwell with a God who would "steal" her child. A man who still clings to a score of petty complaints against his gentle wife is devoured by the personification of his own cruelty. And a manipulative women demands that if she remain in this bright land she be given "a free hand" to whip her husband—now enjoying the delights of heaven—into shape. When this request is denied, the wife's rage literally explodes, and her ghost disappears.

In addition to these failures, there are souls who put aside their anger, pride, or whatever sin has kept them suffering in the underworld and choose to remain in paradise. The difference between these spirits and their return-trip counterparts is the willingness to surrender the self in order to find complete fulfillment. This is the irony of the afterlife: Those who empty themselves shall be filled, while those who hold fast to their selfishness will have no room in their souls for eternal joy.

This is the main point of Lewis's *The Great Divorce:* Salvation can occur only when each person acknowledges the errors of his or her life, admits that he or she has been wrong, and asks for forgiveness. Those who refuse are condemned to return to the gray town, hell, and steep in their pride and shallowness. Thus damnation is not a sentence imposed by God but a free choice made by horribly misguided humans.

GREETING CARDS The abode of the damned has made its way onto greeting cards celebrating a variety of occasions. These include cards about growing older, taking a new job, moving, getting married, and having children. One greeting for the bride- or groom-to-be reads, "Marriage is out of this world," and offers a full-color illustration of hell—complete with fire, torture devices, and a grinning DEVIL—on the inside. Another infernal take on married life claims, "Hell hath no fury . . . like a woman who gets a vacuum cleaner for her anniversary."

Greeting and novelty giant Hallmark produces many products with hellish allusions. An especially intriguing card with broad appeal for graduating seniors, newlyweds, and aging baby boomers states simply, "You are now entering the TWILIGHT ZONE," printed above the classic television series's logo and graphics. Hallmark also distributes a variety of notepads, stickers, and other GIFT NOVELTIES displaying playful DEMONS, smirking devils, and other underworld IMAGERY.

There are also numerous "from hell" cards featuring everything from birthdays to neighbors to pets from the infernal region. A feline, poised above a city in flames, accompanies the legend, "Happy Birthday from Me . . . and the Cat from Hell." Another, spoofing the pursuits of retirees, shows the "Winnebego from Hell" spewing smoke and sporting BUMPER STICKERS from "World's Largest Ball of Wax" and "Slippery Sludge Beach." New parents might receive the "Baby from Hell" card, warning Mom and Dad to be careful, that new little critter "leaks noxious fluids from both ends."

A 1911 greeting card depicts Satan tossing souls into hellfire. ART TODAY

The Athena International company offers an entire line of cards inspired by hell entitled "Little Devils." Each features a smiling, red-suited demon with horns and pointed tail along with an inscription appropriate for the occasion. One has the little fiend set against a murky orange background of dark cliffs saying, "I'm no angel . . . but I miss you like the devil." Another boasts, "I may be a devil . . . but I thank Heaven for you," as the trademark demon stands amid the flames of hell.

GREGORY I Pope Gregory I (c. 540–604), also known as Gregory the Great, wrote extensively on the nature of SATAN and the underworld. He believed (as did ST. AUGUSTINE) that the ultimate suffering of hell is disunion with God and the aching to be in his magnificent presence. Those in the underworld—the fallen angels and souls of the damned—are mired in misery from being forever blinded to the goodness of God.

The first monk to become a pope of the Roman Catholic church, Gregory was well respected for his knowledge and wisdom, eventually earning the title doctor of the church. In his four-volume *Dialogues*, written around 590, Gregory recounts a number of visions of hell experienced by various monks, nobles, and townspeople. The work offers details on both the geography of the underworld and its grotesque facilities.

One account features the supernatural experience of a local soldier. As the man slipped in and out of consciousness, he suddenly found himself on the bank of a fetid river of excrement, which gave off an "intolerable stench." A narrow bridge spanned the river, but only the just and pure could cross to the other side. On the opposite bank were sparkling mansions and pristine knolls. The damned longed to reach them, but

DEMONS emerged from the river of pitch to seize any sinner who presumed to make the passage.

The soldier, unable to resist the distant beauty, started across the bridge but immediately slipped and was grabbed by grisly monsters. Just before he sank, a contingent of angels lifted him up, restoring him to life and reviving his body.

Another story in *Dialogues* tells of a corrupt monk who was damned for breaking his vows and abusing his position. Sent to hell for his sins, he wandered the vast expanse of the barren wasteland, unable to find rest. He was terrified to see several of his fellow monks writhing in everlasting torment and begged for another chance to redeem himself. An angel heard his prayer, took pity on him, and returned him to the land of the living on the condition that he change his ways.

There are numerous examples of infernal IMAGERY contained in Gregory's works. All the underworld stories recounted in *Dialogues* include fire and perilous bridges and most feature treacherous creatures, tortures, despair, and a putrid stench. Gregory suggests that this type of VISION LITERATURE serves as an important reminder to the faithful about the reality of hell and as a powerful warning against provoking the wrath of God.

GREGORY OF TOURS Gregory of Tours (539–594), a colleague and contemporary of Gregory I, also wrote several texts of VISION LITERATURE. His works include histories of the lives of the early saints and of their supernatural powers. But the most powerful of Gregory's works is his *History of the Franks,* which features a grisly description of what hell has in store for immoral clerics.

In the *History of the Franks,* Gregory of Tours recounts a vision of hell related to him by SUNNIULF, a monk of Randau. The abbot described seeing a riverside jammed with people waiting to cross an impossibly narrow bridge. Flames leaped from the foul-smelling river at the throng of souls huddling by the bank. Sunniulf witnesses what happens to clerics in the afterlife: The just cross without difficulty to the paradise on the other side, but those who were lax or corrupt in their duties sink in the black ooze. The depth to which they descend corresponds to their degree of evil: Some are in up to their waists, others up to their necks. Horrified, Sunniulf is restored to life after promising to live a devout life. (Scholars believe this story is likewise recounted in *Dialogues,* a book of mysticism authored by GREGORY I.)

Among the poems of Gregory of Tours is an Easter composition written for Gregory I. In this celebration of the Resurrection, the author joyfully recalls Jesus' HARROWING OF HELL, when Christ descends to the underworld to redeem the souls of the patriarchs.

GWYNN Gwynn is one of the Celtic gods of the underworld. He is a hunter who preys on souls, claiming them for ANWNN, a dark hell. Gwynn is also associated with FAIRIES, called the "hosts of hell" in Celtic literature.

H

HADES Hades is the Greek god of the underworld, which is called the Kingdom of Hades. He and two brothers defeated their father, Cronus, and divided up the world into three sections: Zeus rules the earth, Poseidon the seas, and Hades the land of the dead. Hades' kingdom is separated into many realms, including TARTARUS, a place of unceasing torture for the evil dead. Over time, Hades eventually became synonymous with the dreary realm of the dead. It is used in Greek translations of the Christian Bible to refer to hell.

Departed souls in the underworld of Hades are known as SHADES, mere shadows of their former selves. Although his realm is a grim, murky place, Hades himself is not evil or unjust. He does not torment souls; that is the job of the ERINYES (Furies). They mete out punishment according to a person's sins. Homer describes the Erinyes as fiends who "make men pay for perjury in the world below." The witches are also mentioned in the AENEID as the guardians of the gates of Tartarus.

Hades is separated from the land of the living by a series of rivers: Acheron (pain), Cocytus (groaning), STYX (abomination), LETHE (forget), and Phlegethon (river of fire). When a person dies, the soul passes through a mysterious dark mist called the Erebus before arriving on the banks of the underworld rivers. (Over time, Greeks came to believe that the one true entrance to Hades is at LAKE AVERNUS, a black pool outside Naples, Italy.)

The spirit is then ferried across the water by CHARON, a skeletal boatman who delivers the soul to the "mouth of hell" or entrance to Hades. Those who do not have the coins to pay for the ride are condemned to spend eternity wandering the banks of the Acheron without ever finding peace. (This is also the fate of the unburied dead.) In the epic poem the *Aeneid,* the hero comes across such pitiful spirits and tries to intervene with the gods to grant them rest.

The gates of Hades are guarded by CERBERUS, a three-headed dog, who keeps the dead in and the living out. He is often depicted as having a serpent's tail or being entwined with snakes. Only two mortals, HERCULES and ORPHEUS, were ever able to defeat the beast. Hercules wrestled him into submission through his legendary strength; Orpheus subdued the monster by lulling him to sleep with his enchanted music.

In Hades, souls endure a lethargic, empty existence, but few are tortured physically. Only the most wicked and vile offenders are subjected to pain in the underworld. Legends recount specific agonies inflicted on the worst sinners in Tartarus. For these spirits, the punishment is commensurate with their crimes. Anyone who angers or outwits the gods can also be made to suffer in Tartarus.

Over the years, many came to

believe that the kingdom of Hades consists of two completely distinct realms. The Greeks gradually developed the idea of a divergent road in the underworld of Hades. One path leads to Elysium, an earthly paradise. The other runs to the city of DIS, the hellish realm of agony and retribution. Dis itself is further divided into increasingly horrific layers, with Tartarus being the lowest chasm for the most abominable sinners.

An ancient legend tells how THESEUS and Pirithoüs raided the underworld to reclaim PERSEPHONE, the daughter of goddess Demeter who was kidnapped by Hades and forced to become queen of the dead. The two mortals are caught by Hades and chained to a rock in the depths of the abyss. Hercules rescues Theseus during his journey to the underworld but is unable to release Pirithoüs, who must remain in Tartarus, suffering unending torture for his crime against the ruler of the underworld.

The Greek Hades has been the setting for hundreds of novels, operas, and plays and has inspired as many paintings and other works of art. Dante's *DIVINE COMEDY: THE INFERNO* uses many components of this mythic underworld in the fictitious account of a tour of hell. Its images appear in Offenbach's opera *ORPHEUS IN THE UNDERWORLD* and in the modern film *HIGHWAY TO HELL*.

HAHGWEHDAETGAH A North American myth of the Iroquois describes Hahgwehdaetgah, the creator of evil and ruler of the underworld. The Iroquois believe that the kingdom of Hahgwehdaetgah lies at the bottom of an abyss below the earth. It is filled with the broken bodies of enemy warriors slain in battle. The realm is one of despair, regret, and an overwhelming sense of failure, but not of physical suffering.

Hahgwehdaetgah and his twin brother Hahgwehdiyu, a good god, were born of the creator goddess. Hahgwehdaetgah killed his mother during childbirth and then went on to create all things vile: horrible monsters, fierce beasts, and all manner of plagues and disasters. He was despised by all other creatures and by his virtuous twin.

Eventually the two brothers fought a battle to determine who would rule the earth. Hahgwehdaetgah tried to use trickery, but the good god knew his brother's evil ways and was able to defeat him with an enchanted arrow. Hahgwehdiyu exiled his brother to the underworld, where he oversaw a kingdom of half-man, half-monster spirits. They are shape-shifters who can return to earth to terrorize the living. Hahgwehdaetgah also became overlord of the dead.

HAIZMANN, CHRISTOPHER
Christopher Haizmann (c. 1645–1700), a Bavarian artist, kept a detailed diary of a FAUST-like bargain he struck with the DEVIL. This account includes elaborate illustrations of his pact with SATAN and his visions of hell. However, records indicate that Haizmann even-

tually regrets his bitter bargain and seeks protection from the fiend from both church and civic authorities.

According to his story, Haizmann was approached by a kindly nobleman who promised to help the struggling painter find success. If Haizmann would surrender his soul and ally himself with the Prince of Darkness, he would receive in exchange nine years of joy and prosperity. After this time, he must forfeit his soul to Satan and take his place among the damned. Haizmann agreed and signed the contract in his own blood.

But his happiness was interrupted continuously during the following nine years by a variety of horrible visions. The devil often came to Haizmann in the form of a beast to check on his charge. In pictures found in the diary, the artist shows the fiend with a human torso, horns and a tail, full female breasts, and bird claws. Haizmann also had recurring apparitions of the underworld, a nauseating realm of fire in which the damned shriek in perpetual agony. He reported seeing a DEMON perched atop the rim of a caldron of souls, pouring "flaming resin, sulfur, and pitch" on them as they begged for mercy. The underworld was also permeated by a stench so foul it made Haizmann ill.

As the date of recompense drew closer, the artist became obsessed with finding release from his pact. He fled to a shrine at Mariazell and subjected himself to numerous exorcisms in hopes of ridding himself of the infernal burden. One cleric summoned the VIRGIN MARY, who was able to retrieve and destroy the original contract (he describes witnessing the Mother of Christ "triumph over the devil"), although this did not put an end to the disturbing visions. Even after Haizmann secluded himself in a rural monastery the diabolical images continued. He died on March 14, 1700, still plagued with frightening hallucinations and dread over the fate of his soul.

HARROWING OF HELL During the three days between the time of Christ's death on Good Friday and his resurrection on Easter Sunday, Christians believe that Jesus descended into hell and freed the souls of the just who had died prior to his crucifixion. Until the redeemer's sacrifice and death, no one could enter heaven because of Adam's sin. This event, called the harrowing of hell, is not included in the Bible, but it has been taught by religious scholars from the earliest days of Christianity. The harrowing is mentioned in the Apostles' Creed: "He descended into Hell; on the third day he rose again from the dead." The doctrine has since been embraced by most Christian denominations.

Some accounts of the harrowing include a trial held in the underworld to determine whether Christ's action is just. LUCIFER, lord of hell, appoints the silver-tongued BELIAL as his attorney and charges that Jesus has no right to take souls from hell, since Lucifer was given reign over human souls after Adam and Eve sinned in Eden. Different versions list a number of advocates for humanity, including the VIRGIN MARY, Solomon, and Christ himself. Belial cleverly quotes Scripture and presents a compelling case in favor of Lucifer.

But God decrees that Christ has paid sufficient ransom for humanity and that mercy is more powerful than justice. Belial appeals this decision, and the two sides eventually settle with a concession that Lucifer shall be allowed to keep the souls of the truly evil and that he may continue to tempt future generations into sin and damnation. His activities, however, will end with the LAST JUDGMENT, when the DEMON will be confined to hell for all eternity.

Harrowing of hell illustration from a thirteenth-century French manuscript. ART TODAY

Other versions of the story pose the problem of specifically *who* was saved: everyone in the underworld or just the souls of the Hebrew patriarchs? Many philosophers, including Origen and AUGUSTINE, postulated that when Christ descended into hell he preached his truth to the pagans. Those who had been virtuous in life accepted his word, converted to Christianity, and were redeemed. Thus all had the opportunity to enter heaven with Christ.

The harrowing of hell is a favorite subject for illustrations in BOOKS OF HOURS and in Christian CHURCH ART AND ARCHITECTURE.

SATAN's defeat is depicted in a number of ways. One of the most prevalent is portraying the DEVIL lying crushed and broken at Christ's feet beneath the smashed gates of hell. In many such compositions, the destroyed doors have isolated Satan, leaving him alone in a tiny makeshift prison while the souls of the dead happily escape under the redeemer's leadership. Locks, hasps, and bolts are often included to convey the concept that Christ has now confined Satan to the depths of the abyss.

In these artworks, hell is typically depicted as a cave or a gaping HELLMOUTH. The interior is crammed with souls awaiting the Messiah. Some compositions include demons in the depths of hell. They are shown cringing from Christ as he storms their fortress. Other works simply feature Satan as the sole fiend of the underworld.

The harrowing of hell also is the subject of many MORALITY PLAYS. It is also described in Dante's *DIVINE COMEDY: THE INFERNO*. And an ancient Jewish text, *Testament of the Twelve Patriarchs*, describes a Messiah who will travel to the underworld to free his allies from the Satan's grasp. Similar "mystic rescue missions" are contained in other religions and myths from around the globe.

HAUNTING OF HILL HOUSE, THE Shirley Jackson earned a place among America's preeminent horror writers with her ghostly novel *The Haunting of Hill House*. The chilling tale explores the notion that places on earth can be so inherently evil that they are virtual extensions of hell. Hill House itself is more a character in the story than a mere object. It is alive with evil, "holding darkness within."

In Jackson's novel, biblical quotations about hell decorate the manor's rooms, especially the nursery, which is the site of several mysterious deaths. A homemade book describes the inferno at length and includes numerous illustrations of snake pits, torture chambers, roasting corpses, and mutilated sinners. The volume was created by a zealous father as a gift for his young daughter, designed to frighten her into leading a life of virtue. His inscription lamented that he could not show the girl hell itself, for if her "eyes could be seared" by the macabre specter, she would surely avoid putting her soul in jeopardy. He likens the fires of the underworld to a candle burning a sheet of paper, noting that the flames of the abyss are "a thousandfold more keen" and are "everlasting." The fanatic signs the book in his own blood.

Haunting blends traditional concepts of evil with the anxiety of sinking into madness. For the novel's main character, spinster Eleanor Vance, dreary life with her overbearing sister and brother-in-law in their cramped apartment is a truly hellish existence. When she flees to become part of an expedition studying the supposedly haunted Hill House, she finds the prospect of being swallowed up by the mansion and its ghosts to be an appealing alternative to her former life. After all, she muses, she has spent her whole life waiting for something to happen, for some place to "belong," and this might be it.

Eleanor's sanity rapidly deteriorates, and she becomes convinced that the house does in fact "want" her. When its phantasms—or those in her imagination—attempt to take her life, she willingly surrenders. Yet Eleanor's death leaves her more isolated than ever. For the author declares that those damned to dwell in the evil mansion "walk alone." This reflects the prevalent concept of hell as a place of cruel irony: where the one thing a person longs for (in Eleanor's case companionship and acceptance) is forever denied.

HAUNTINGS People of many different belief systems believe that restless souls are unable to enjoy a peaceful afterlife, so they remain in this world in astral form. Spirits who are not able to separate completely from this life and progress to the next dimension are said to cause hauntings, harassing people and places important to them in life. These disoriented, often angry, souls must endure the agony of residing between two worlds, one material and one spiritual. It is a form of living damnation, often called "living hell" or "hell on earth."

Hauntings have been linked to the DREAM MODEL of hell, in which evildoers must eternally revisit their vile deeds. This sometimes means returning to the scene of their nefarious acts, either to remember what transpired or to make amends. Souls trapped in between the two realms are usually condemned to perform impossible tasks, such as making ropes out of sand or moving unbearably heavy stones back and forth. For these accursed spirits, no rest is possible.

Other punishments are tied directly to the person's transgressions. A common legend claims that women who have abortions will spend eternity trying to wash bloodstains out of linen that never comes clean. Another tale describes a man who hangs himself in his attic to spite his wife who he believes is cheating on him. He immediately regrets his decision but dies before he can free himself. His spirit is damned to pass the aeons in the dusty attic, repeating the hanging over and over again.

Hauntings can also be tied to a specific place. A wicked soul might be linked to the site of its death, the place of its sin, or the location of some important event. Those who have been left unburied or who have not been interred with the prescribed rituals are particularly likely to haunt the living. This belief originates from the legends of restless souls wandering the banks of the river STYX, as in the account from Virgil's *AENEID* and Homer's *ODYSSEY.*

HEAVY METAL The 1981 animated feature film *Heavy Metal* is a collection of episodes covering a variety of odd themes. It is a sort of updated *FANTASIA,* combining cartoon drawings with popular music of the day. The sci-fi, surreal (and rather confusing) plots are reminiscent of the stories in many modern COMIC BOOKS and images from FANTASY ART about the supernatural. This includes stylized visions of a grisly hell.

One sequence in *Heavy Metal* features a plane crash on a mysterious island. The harsh terrain is marked by rocky landscapes and overgrown weeds. When the lone survivor emerges from the wreck, he is in for a horrible shock. As he tries to assess his situation, he is overtaken by an army of the damned. The GHOULS descend, welcoming their new companion to hell. The recently restored supernatural sequence "Neverwhere Land" likewise depicts a bleak realm of infernal terrors.

HEAVY METAL MUSIC The genre of modern music most closely associated with hell is Heavy Metal, an ear-splitting mix of loudness, rude (often unintelligible) lyrics, and screeching guitars. Distinguishing characteristics of performers include extensive TATTOOS, long hair, and multiple body piercings. Often dismissed as a fad gone awry, Heavy Metal continues to be one of the most popular forms of American music, even being named as its own category of the music industry's Grammy Awards. Best-selling artists include Kiss, Guns 'n' Roses, Alice Cooper, and Motley Crue.

Heavy Metal proudly embraces the underworld, DEMONS, and all things damned. Heavy Metal's catalog, a text listing its five hundred best-selling albums, is appropriately titled *Stairway to Hell.* The violent lyrics of some songs have been blamed for teen suicides, SATAN worship, and other nefarious CRIMES, causing many religious leaders and politicians to condemn the maniacal melodies. Thus, metal became "the DEVIL's" music.

Some of metal's biggest artists have equally hellish names. These include Black Sabbath, Judas Priest, Megadeath, and Slayer. The groups routinely use underworld IMAGERY—skulls, devils, horns, inverted crosses, and SWASTIKAS—as their symbols. Many songs are deliberately infernal, such as AC/DC's "Highway to Hell" and KMFD's "Go to Hell" (theme song from the film *HIDEAWAY,* an adaptation of Dean Koontz's tale of the damned). Blue Oyster Cult became a favorite among professed Satanists as hits "Don't Fear the Reaper," "Specters," and "Burning for You" all use demonic images in their lyrics. The group also features occult symbols as ALBUM COVER ART on virtually every release.

But the infernal connections go far beyond diabolical song texts and demonic pictures on record covers; underworld ties extend to the concert performances as well. The extensive use of pyrotechnics—fiery explosions and bursts of flame—help create the onstage illusion of the great inferno. Many performers also use elaborate props, such as oversized demon heads or menacing HELLMOUTHS, to entertain their live audiences. These can be punctuated with extensive light shows to enhance the hellish effect.

English group Iron Maiden has been called the "master" of spectacular stage shows that involve fiendish icons. The British musicians—who refer to their fans as "Hell Rats"—create "concept concerts" that incorporate songs, sets, props, and special effects into their presentations. For the *Number of the Beast* tour, Iron Maiden boomed a passage from REVELATION about Satan through scores of speakers before bursting into song. Several years later, they revisited the land of the damned with the *No Prayer for the Dying* promotion. (The band can also be heard in the film *NIGHTMARE ON ELM STREET* performing its brutally energetic "Bring Your Daughter to the Slaughter.")

One of the most infamous demonic groups is W.A.S.P. (fans claim that the name is an acronym for "we are sexual perverts"), led by singer Blackie Lawless. Known for its grisly depictions of bloody bodies and extensive use of pyrotechnics, W.A.S.P. became especially notorious after declaring to its fans, "The gods you worship are steel, at the altar of rock and roll you kneel." During stage shows, Lawless would drink blood from a skull and simulate slashing the throat of a naked woman strapped into a medieval torture device. The allusion to a ritual Satanic offering provoked a public outcry, eventually prompting Lawless to revise his act.

A similar controversy surrounds the song "Sacrifice" by the Heavy Metal group Venom. The ditty graphically describes the ritual slaying of a virgin to "LUCIFER, my master." The performers describe the entire procedure, detailing the setting of the dark altar and the specifics of the black mass. Demands that this song be stricken from Venom's catalog failed. Supporters cite the group's First Amendment right to freedom of expression, no matter how depraved or tasteless that expression might be.

Such grisly antics have made Heavy Metal music a target of many parent organizations seeking to put legal limits on what can be sold to (and performed before) minors. The closest brush Heavy Metal has had with legal intervention occurred in the 1980's when future-vice president Al Gore's wife, Tipper, organized the Parents' Music Resource Center (PMRC) to try to censor albums and regulate sales. She resoundingly condemned Heavy Metal during congressional hearings into the issue, calling the music "dangerous to the children of America" due to its violent and demonic content. Lawmakers seemed ready to impose severe restrictions on the art form.

In response, the music industry offered to "self-regulate" by putting stickers on its most graphic releases to warn parents about "explicit lyrics."

Since the nature of Heavy Metal music makes it difficult to dance to, most fans simply listen while violently bobbing their heads to the frenzied beat. For this reason (and the allusions to danger), Heavy Metal fans have been dubbed "headbangers." When video versions of these songs developed, Music Television (MTV) dedicated an entire show to these clips called the *Headbangers' Ball.* With this national exposure, many MUSIC VIDEOS of such groups as Iron Maiden, Dio, Ozzy Osbourne, and Motley Crue made it to the mainstream charts, rivaling contemporary Top 40 songs in popularity.

To headbangers, only the most raunchy and ribald groups are truly worthy of the title Heavy Metal. They consider artists such as Poison, Faster Pussycat, and Skid Row to be "posers": mainstream bands that pretend to be demonic through the use of makeup, leather attire, and stage gimmicks simply to gain notoriety and increase sales. On the other end of the spectrum are Thrash Metal bands, such as Motorhead, Every Mother's Nightmare, and Anthrax, whose songs are too rife with obscenities and gory lyrics to be played over public airwaves.

The connection between Heavy Metal music and hell has been the subject of several films and documentaries. *TRICK OR TREAT, BLACK ROSES,* and the satirical *This Is Spinal Tap* focus on infernal bands and their cultlike followings. The comedy *BILL & TED'S BOGUS JOURNEY* also jokingly explores the underworld's ominous musical allegiance.

HECATE Hecate is the Greek goddess of black magic and the keeper of the keys to the underworld. Often called the goddess of SHADES (ghosts), Hecate appears entwined with snakes and is associated with pain and suffering. In some representations, Hecate has three heads and can look in all directions at the same time. She is feared not only for her powers as a witch but also because she could cause sickness, infertility, and insanity. A minor goddess, Hecate has been called the mistress of "everything dark and uncanny."

At night, especially during the new moon, Hecate leaves the infernal regions and roams the earth with an army of dead souls and a pack of hounds of hell. The sound of howling dogs is a warning to villagers that Hecate is nearby. Believers, fearing her anger, often sacrificed small animals and young children (usually females) to the dark goddess. During the daylight hours and when the moon is full, Hecate is confined to the depths of the underworld, where she plans her future exploits.

Hecate appears in Virgil's epic poem the *AENEID*. The hero must seek the grim goddess's permission to enter the underworld as he searches out his dead father's spirit. Hecate's coming is heralded by howling wolves and a rumbling earthquake. She is also the subject of a painting by artist WILLIAM BLAKE, in which she is surrounded by such odd creatures as a brooding owl, a lizard-faced DEMON, and a rapacious beast.

HEL Hel is the Germanic goddess of the dead and ruler of NIFLHEIM, a brutal underworld. She is the daughter of the trickster god LOKI and is depicted as half human and half rotting corpse. Hel's palace is called Sleetcold, and her kingdom is an icy, barren wasteland. Some legends claim that in the underworld, Hel feasts on human flesh.

Hel's kingdom is surrounded by steep walls that are impassable to the living. (The word Hel means "concealed.") It is entered through GNIPAHELLI, a dank, foul-smelling cave. The fortress of Sleetcold lies on the other side of Echoing Bridge, a treacherous passageway to the land of spirits. Souls are challenged and assaulted as they try to cross. The gates of Hel's realm are guarded by GARM, a fierce dog who devours trespassers.

Some spirits of the dead are ferried to Hel by the messenger Hermodr. At the lowest level of her kingdom lives a monster named Nidhoggr (corpse tearer). He punishes the wicked by eternally gnawing on their broken bodies. In some tales, the damned are boiled in huge caldrons before being fed to the beast.

"HELL IN TEXAS" "Hell in Texas," a poem by author unknown, offers a unique perspective on how the

Lone Star State was formed. According to the narrative, the DEVIL runs out of room for the damned in hell and asks God for some additional land to extend the underworld's boundaries. God sympathizes, but all he has to offer is some acreage along the Rio Grande, which even the fiend does not want because it is so dry and inhospitable. God, desperate to get the tract off his hands, promises to wet it down enough to meet the devil's standards:

For he had some water, or rather some dregs,
A regular cathartic that smelt like bad eggs.
Hence a deal was closed and the deed was given,
And the Lord went back to His place in Heaven.
And the devil said "I have all that is needed
To make a good Hell," and thus he succeeded.
He began to put thorns on all the trees,
And he mixed the sand with millions of fleas,
He scattered tarantulas along all the roads,
Put thorns on the cacti and horns on the toads. . . .

This explains, according to the anonymous writer, why Texas is filled with mosquitoes, scorpions, rattlesnakes, sand burrs, and all manner of unpleasant creatures. Furthermore, those who are not protected by the "devil's own brand" will be covered with "the marks of scratches and bites by the score." The poet sums up SATAN's annex by noting that "it's a Hell of a place he has for a Hell."

HELLFIRE CLUB During the mid 1700s, a group of English intellectuals formed a society dedicated to ridiculing Christianity and mocking its sacred rituals. They dubbed their new fraternity the Hellfire Club, embracing SATAN as their master and anticipating their damnation to his abyss. The group members were rich, educated men who had a great deal of political and social power. They considered themselves above the "superstitions" of conventional religion and preferred instead to worship the DEVIL in exchange for temporal rewards. Whether they truly believed their own manifesto is unclear; however, they most certainly reveled in a number of dark ceremonies, including black masses, Satanic baptisms, and drunken orgies.

London hosted a number of Hellfire Clubs during the early eighteenth century, but by far the most notorious was a troupe that met at a ruined monastery near Buckinghamshire. The men held their annual meetings (which lasted for two weeks) at Medmenham Abbey, a rustic site on the banks of the Thames. In an attempt to capture the atmosphere of hell, the group met in dimly lit rooms or caves, surrounding themselves with mementos of death and decay. A blasphemous altar served as the heart of the clubhouse, complete with pornographic parodies of religious paintings, inverted crucifixes, and satirical versions of sacred prayers.

The Medmenham brothers called their sect "the Superior Order." It consisted of twelve members in a mockery of Christ's twelve apostles. When not indulging in drunkenness, eroticism, or Satanic practices, the club members played tricks on one another to test their fortitude. It was not uncommon for a member of the Superior Order to find a snake in his bed or a human skull staring in at him from an open window. One particularly resourceful man dressed an ape in a dark cape, pointed tail, and horns and covertly released it on his brethren. When the beast mauled one of his brethren, the perpetrator quipped that the victim should get used to being attacked by DEMONs, since they would all surely encounter worse torments in hell.

Hellfire Clubs faded out of existence as members became too old for such antics, quarreled among themselves, and eventually died. Polite society, even in the Enlightened Age, frowned on such sacrilegious practices, and the ranks of the clubs were not replenished. By the turn of the century, Hellfire Clubs—and their deviant practices—were a thing of the past.

HELLFIRE SERMONS From the earliest days of the Christian church, ministers have used vivid images of the torments awaiting the damned to convince followers to lead virtuous lives. St. Jerome, who lived just a century after Christ, was among the first to preach a scorching inferno of sensual tortures. His grim views of the underworld, enumerated by ST. AUGUSTINE three centuries later, were eventually sanctioned by the church's Synod of Constantinople in 543. Thus, hellfire sermons became a liturgical mainstay.

Hellfire sermons reached the height of popularity during the Middle Ages, tailored specifically to an illiterate congregation of common folk. The graphic descriptions of eternal agony were much more easily understood by the uneducated than were the complex doctrines and dogmas of the Christian faith. Many of these homilies were based on VISION LITERATURE, stories from people who claimed to have seen hell firsthand.

Writer and preacher John Bunyan adapted his *A FEW SIGHS FROM HELL*, a terrifying treatise on damnation, from one of his own hellfire sermons. It describes a torture-steeped underworld with an extensive catalog of ghastly terrors. The book was first published in 1658 and went through dozens of editions over the next century and a half. No Puritan home was without a copy. It became the author's second most popular book, outsold only by *THE PILGRIM'S PROGRESS*.

Catholic priests of the Jesuit and Redemptionist orders from the seventeenth through twentieth centuries were famous for their frightening depictions of the horrors of hell. A typical lecture about the afterlife contained a litany of punishments, each devised for a specific type of sin. Author James Joyce bases the grim description of the underworld in his novel *A PORTRAIT OF THE ARTIST AS A YOUNG MAN* on a Jesuit sermon he heard as a boy in Ireland.

Jonathan Edwards's "Sinners in the Hands of an Angry God" is perhaps the best-known American hellfire sermon. In the oratory, Edwards rejects the notion of ANNIHILATION, declaring that the suffering in hell is permanent and unrelenting. He describes the agonies of the damned down to the writhing of their fingertips, eyes, tongues, and bowels. The eighteenth-century preacher claims that souls in the underworld "shall be in extreme pain . . . every joint, every nerve" for all eternity. He adds that the suffering of hell is seen by the saved, making paradise more enjoyable.

Today, hellfire sermons have become virtually obsolete. Modern Christian clerics prefer to entice followers with glorious images of heaven rather than frighten them with horrific visions of hell.

HELLMOUTH One of the most pervasive symbols of the underworld is the hellmouth. It is found in diverse myths, religions, legends, and even as a metaphor in CHILDREN'S LITERATURE. The hellmouth is one example of infernal IMAGERY that transcends time and culture, appearing in illustrations of the afterlife from all corners of the globe. It is personified in Egyptian mythology as AMMUT, the eater of the dead. In Canaanite lore, the hellmouth is linked to the undersea demon LEVIATHAN. Virgil's *AENEID* includes the hellmouth metaphorically as the "jaws of a lake," the "yawning pit" of TARTARUS, and the Hydra, a ferocious water GHOUL.

Centuries later, the Christian poet Dante revisits the image in his *DIVINE COMEDY: THE INFERNO.* Western artists associated the hellmouth with the practice of throwing Christians to the lions. And an illustration from *Das Buch Belial* (*The Book of BELIAL*), a fifteenth-century German text, shows the underworld as the gaping mouth of a dragon spilling forth with flames and screeching DEMONS.

Most depictions of the hellmouth are just that: a huge jaw, wrenched open and lined with rows of sharp teeth, waiting to devour the damned. This picture often represents the gates of hell, replacing a traditional doorway to the underworld. One of the implied agonies of damnation is being digested in the bowels of the underworld for all eternity. (Some artists go so far as to show sinners being excreted from SATAN's rectum.) In many illustrations

The Jaws of Hell,
from a 1568 French manuscript. ART TODAY

of the HARROWING OF HELL, Christ is shown leading the faithful out of the gaping maw of a gigantic, wretched demon.

The concept of the hellmouth most probably originates from legends about huge sea monsters that had the power to destroy ships and swallow entire armies. These mythic beasts derived in part from tales about sailors mistaking whales for islands and hooking their anchors to them during storms. When the whale swam away, it dragged the tethered ship and its helpless crew to the ocean depths. Storytellers claimed that this was done on purpose by the evil and cunning "water demons" who kept the lost sailors in a dismal kingdom at the bottom of the sea. Thus the open mouth of the whale quickly became synonymous with the gates of hell.

Since few artists had ever seen a whale, they portrayed the unknown ocean creature as a dragon or a huge fish with razor-sharp teeth. Its enormous mouth represented horrible death and unspeakable agony. This conceptualized underworld appears in illustrations from both Eastern and Western cultures, although the idea of the hellmouth became especially popular in Western belief systems.

The Old Testament story of Jonah, a reluctant prophet who is swallowed by a whale and then expelled after agreeing to obey God's orders, reinforced the view of the hellmouth as a diabolical means of punishment. Later, Christians equated Jonah's three days in the belly of the whale with Christ's three days in the tomb between his crucifixion and resurrection, and the redemption of Jonah with the harrowing of hell. Tales of the impending apocalypse include a "Great Beast" who rises from the sea to terrorize humankind. This solidified the place of the infernal maw in Christian tradition.

During the Middle Ages, the hellmouth became an important part of MORALITY PLAYS and MYSTERY PLAYS. These dramas, designed to teach moral lessons and offer harsh warnings about the agonies of the underworld, used it to represent damnation. In the plays, which focused on such biblical themes as the harrowing of hell and the LAST JUDGMENT, the hellmouth was an important piece of scenery. The most elaborate of these were actual hinged doors decorated with painted (or even sculpted) jaws that could open and close according to the action of the play. Sinners were cast into it; the saved were yanked out. Lavish productions included smoke, stench, and shrieks that spewed forth from the hellmouth to heighten the excitement. Eventually, scenes involving the gaping grimace became the most popular part of the dramatic presentations, an early form of theatrical special effects.

The hellmouth is also commonplace in Christian art, becoming a popular characteristic of Christian CHURCH ART AND ARCHITECTURE. Versions of the enduring symbol appear in paintings and sculptures throughout Christendom and adorn the pages of numerous BOOKS OF HOURS.

HELLRAISER CLIVE BARKER's 1987 film *Hellraiser,* based on his novella *The Hellbound Heart,* explores the nightmarish world of the damned, offering a host of innovative infernal creatures. And unlike other contemporary films about portals to hell—such as *THE GATE* and *THE SENTINEL*—the passageway to the underworld is not a fixed location but a portable doorway that can be accessed anywhere. It also differs in that it is a two-way conduit: DEMONS can use it to enter the land of the living, and humans can travel to the abyss via the strange talisman.

The plot traces the misadventures of a nihilistic rogue played by Sean Chapman. Chapman is constantly searching for new sensual pleasures and depraved practices to satisfy his rapacious appetite. He happens upon a mysterious puzzle box that promises the ultimate in physical gratification. But when Chapman opens the box, he finds instead the doorway to hell. A contingent of mangled GHOULS arrives to take him to the underworld, where his flesh will be subject to every type of dark torture.

These fiends, called Cenobites, are under the leadership of Pinhead, a pale fiend whose face is a patchwork of protruding needles. Pinhead and the other members of the demonic troupe are maimed villains with open, oozing wounds. They salivate at the prospect of mauling Chapman. He is bound in chains lined with hooks that literally rip his body apart before his soul is dragged into the dimension of the damned.

Barker's Cenobites have since been incorporated into COMIC BOOKS, MOVIE MERCHANDISING, and COMPUTER GAMES. There have also been numerous sequels to his *Hellraiser,* although to date none has been written or directed by Barker. The British horror maven has, however, worked on a host of other supernatural films, including *Candyman, Lord of Illusions,* and *Nightbreed.*

HERCULES Hercules is a mortal possessed of extraordinary strength, according to ancient Greek myth. He is the son of the god Zeus and of a mortal woman. One of Hercules's legendary feats is performing the twelve labors, a series of seemingly impossible tasks that require superhuman abilities. The last of these labors is to descend to HADES and retrieve the monster CERBERUS, the three-headed guardian dog of the underworld.

Hercules journeys to the land of the dead and wrestles the fierce beast into submission. He is one of only two mortals ever able to best the monster. (The other is ORPHEUS, who lulls Cerberus to sleep with his magical music.) While in the underworld, Hercules rescues his friend THESEUS from Hades's prison. Theseus had tried to rescue PERSEPHONE (kidnapped by Hades and made Queen of the Underworld) from the abyss, but was captured and chained to a rock in the pits of the inferno. Hercules manages to free him and return him to the land of the living.

According to Homer's epic poem the *Iliad,* Hercules shoots Hades with an arrow and leaves him writhing in agony at the gates of hell as punishment for the underworld king's cruelty to his comrades.

The mythic hero has inspired hundreds of songs, stories, artworks, television programs, and movies. These include an entire series of films from the early 1960s. (*Hercules in the Haunted World* sends the muscleman to hell to find a cure for a doomed princess) and the 1997 ANIMATED CARTOON *Hercules* from Disney Studios. This latest epic features King HADES himself as the archvillain of a musical underworld who vows to defeat the mighty Hercules.

HEROES IN HELL Author Janet Morris created a unique underworld saga with her 1984 book *Heroes in Hell,* a witty novel that declares, "Nobody who is anybody went to Heaven." The collection of infernal vignettes features everyone from the legendary hero GILGAMESH to actor James Dean in the great below, with the likes of Caesar and Mao Zedong thrown in for color. Trapped in the abyss of fire, the villains continue vying for power and position in the underworld to the delight of SATAN, their new overseer. *Heroes* was published with a companion novel, *Gates of Hell.*

Heroes was followed by a series of similar works, including *Rebels in Hell* and *Crusaders in Hell.* Each book is a collection of SHORT STORIES linked through the common thread of damnation. Innovative and clever, the *Damned Saga* weaves myth, legend, fact, and fantasy into a fascinating tapestry of underworld lore. The *Heroes* series also testifies to the immense popularity hell enjoys even in this modern age of literature.

HEROINE OF HELL The 1995 independent film *Heroine of Hell* skillfully blends medieval concepts of the underworld with modern New Age psychic episodes in a fascinating depiction of divine reckoning. It features extensive use of hellish IMAGERY, employing such familiar icons of the netherworld as DEVILS, DEMONS, flames, pitchforks, and gory tortures of the damned. Yet the movie asks more questions than it answers, straddling the line between faith and superstition. At its heart is the eternal question of whether hell even exists: Is there a fearsome realm of terror for unrepentant sinners, or, as one character quips, is it true that "hell is a wish" for justice for those who go unpunished in this world and nothing more?

The enigma is explored by Magda (played by Catherine Keener), a struggling young artist who works as a hotel chambermaid. After experiencing a cryptic vision of a man being burned alive in a car while a second car speeds away, Keener finds that she is unable to think of anything else. The horrible apparition quickly overtakes her life, becoming inextricably mingled with notions of hell and supernatural recompense. Despite being "not at all" religious, the girl begins reading the *Vision of TUNDAL,* a grisly portrayal of the underworld from the Middle Ages, and incorporating the infernal descriptions into her paintings. This sudden preoccupation with damnation disturbs her friends, who fear that Keener is losing her sanity.

But the obsession escalates when Keener reads a newspaper account of a fatal accident that mirrors her ominous vision. She locates the widow (played by Wendy Phillips) and begins leaving gruesome passages from *Tundal* about the punishments for evildoers on Phillips's answering machine. Eventually the two women meet and forge an odd friendship while confronting the truth behind the mysterious car crash.

Heroine of Hell is unique, since despite its focus on the underworld, it is neither a horror film (such as *HELLRAISER* or *DARK ANGEL: THE ASCENT*) nor a cinematic interpretation of the afterlife based on religious texts (*RAPTURE*). Instead, it is a thought-provoking piece on how age-old beliefs factor into contemporary notions of the supernatural and on the enduring power fear of hell has in shaping our actions.

HETGWAUGE Hetgwauge is the Haida underworld for wicked souls. It is a dusty, dark wasteland ruled by Hetgwaulana, lord of the dead. In Hetgwauge, spirits of evildoers are eternally tortured for their sins.

HIDEAWAY Dean Koontz's 1992 novel *Hideaway* offers readers two hells: one, the final abode of the damned; the second, a man-made inferno that takes on a terrifying new dimension when it becomes the hideout of a vicious killer.

The story follows the supernatural experience of Lindsay and Hatch Harrison, a middle-aged couple who lost their only child, a five-year-old son, to cancer. Unable to have more children, the two are rebuilding their lives and trying to cope with the pervasive loss when a terrible car accident leaves Hatch clinically dead for more than an hour. Heartbroken, Lindsay resigns herself to the fact that she is now alone in the world.

But doctors inform Lindsay that Hatch has been revived through a highly experimental medical technique. No one knows for sure what, if any, lingering problems this procedure may cause. At first Hatch seems to be suffering no side effects whatsoever; however, he soon begins having strange visions of brutal crimes being committed by some vile fiend. Doctors can find no medical or psychological reason for these apparitions and believe that Hatch may be going insane. What he is actually experiencing is a glimpse of hell through the eyes of one of its own.

Hatch's NEAR-DEATH EXPERIENCE has mystically linked him to Jeremy, a sadistic teen obsessed with Satanism. The brutal killer has committed a score of grisly murders before finally slaughtering his mother and sister. Longing to renounce his life and join his brethren in hell, Jeremy commits suicide. In the afterlife he is damned to a deep chasm lined with bones and crushed skulls. The sky is a pulsating mass of black DEMONS, and the darkness is so thick it seems alive. It is hell as he always pictured it in countless infernal fantasies.

Jeremy feels welcome here, having embraced death as the "gift of SATAN." But when he is resuscitated by the same technique that saves Hatch, he vows to make himself worthy to rejoin the DEVIL's horde. Feeling that his soul was unfairly snatched from the underworld, Jeremy determines to spend his days on earth desecrating and extinguishing life. He renames himself Vassago, a title from one of his Satanist books meaning "Prince of Hell." The revived teen's body still bears the marks of damnation: His eyes are impossibly, irreparably dilated from the utter blackness of the dark abyss.

Jeremy then creates a hell of his own in an abandoned amusement park. Deep in the park's bowels is a crumbling CARNIVAL ATTRACTION called Dante's Inferno, a subterranean house of horrors. The Inferno consists of an underground pit with a thirty-foot statue of Satan at its center. Vassago uses this as his altar, bringing the grim idol a series of human sacrifices. Here, beneath the figure of hell's ghastly lord, Vassago lingers in a macabre existence "between the world of the living and of dead."

In Tri-Star's film adaptation of *Hideaway,* hell is depicted as a huge mass of intertwined souls eternally mired in pain. Visually, this is displayed as a burning ball of damned spirits that surges and bubbles as aching spirits try—unsuccessfully—to escape the agony. This molten quasar of wicked souls erupts in a hundred places at once, revealing scores of contorted faces screaming in horror at their fate.

HIGHWAY TO HELL HBO Video's 1992 *Highway to Hell* offers a distinctly modern vision of the underworld. The film opens with young Charlie (played by Chad Lowe) playing an infernal COMPUTER GAME also called *Highway to Hell.* After combating the video DEMONS, Charlie and his lovely girlfriend, Rachel (played by Kristy Swanson), head to Las Vegas where they plan to marry. Trying to elude disapproving parents, the teens avoid the interstates and take only back roads on their trek to the altar. But when Lowe ignores the warning of a strange old man and takes a mysterious shortcut, the couple ends up on a detour through the great abyss.

Their trouble begins when Lowe is stopped for speeding by HellCop, a horribly disfigured lawman. He takes the virgin Swanson to Hell City, where she is to be given as an offering to SATAN. Her dismayed fiancé is told he has twenty-four hours to find and retrieve her or she will be imprisoned forever in the underworld.

The film's interpretation of hell includes a variety of clever fixtures. HellCop stops at Pluto's Donut Shop, a roadside café in which damned policemen eternally try to hail a waitress who never responds. The AAA of the underworld does not stand for American Automobile Association but rather for "Anarchy, Armageddon, ANNIHILATION." The top television program in the inferno is the insipid game show *Bowling for Leftovers*. Everyone in the abyss drives a Volkswagen Beetle, one hosting a BUMPER STICKER that reads "Pontius is my Co-Pilot." And the road to hell truly is paved by the Good Intentions Paving Company, an organization that grinds the bodies of fallen do-gooders into tar for the underworld's highways.

But *Highway to Hell*'s depiction of the accursed realm has a dark side, too. In an infernal nightclub the great monsters of history play (and cheat at) a game of cards. Hitler emerges the winner, being the most unscrupulous conniver at the table. The beautiful vixens of the underworld are in fact gruesome hags with sagging breasts and monster faces, their real appearances reflected in the mirror of truth. Social interaction in hell consists of beatings, rapes, gunfights, and a variety of other violent clashes.

Highway to Hell depicts numerous mythic images of the land of the dead. Lowe must negotiate his way through a number of traditional obstacles, including a bottomless pit of fire and a river of filth and pitch. The gates of Hell City are guarded by CERBERUS, the monstrous three-headed dog from Greek myth. And the hooded CHARON ferries the damned across the river STYX to HADES, a place of "infinite levels of hell."

Lowe and Swanson are given another challenge reminiscent of legendary heroes: They will be released from the kingdom of the damned if they can defeat the DEVIL in a contest of his design. This battle of skills takes the form of a drag race. Many traditional themes mark this competition: the devil's manipulation of humans for his amusement, exploitation of jealousy and competitiveness, and the reduction of the soul to a bargaining chip. But despite these doctrinal allusions, it is not Lowe's *faith* but his *love* that ultimately enables good to conquer evil.

HIISI Hiisi is the name of the DEVIL in Finnish literature. He is ruler of HITTOLA (PAHA VALTA in some tales), the "DEMON's domain." His kingdom is a place of scorched earth and perpetual despair. Hiisi also refers to the demons that exist in Hittola.

HILDEGARD OF BINGEN Born in medieval Germany, Hildegard of Bingen (1098–1179) was a quiet, intelligent girl who recognized at a very young age that she had a vocation to religious life. She entered the convent while still in her teens and quickly gained a reputation as a powerful mystic. Even in her youth, she experienced visions and offered prophesies of the future. This supernatural ability drew extensive notoriety, and she was often called the "Sibyl of the Rhine." She used these as inspiration for scores of poems, sermons, hymns, and a MORALITY PLAY.

In the convent, Hildegard spent the majority of her time in solitary prayer and mediation. It was during these prayer sessions that she saw troubling images of hell and of the punishments awaiting the damned. In her book *Nosce Vias Domini (Know the Ways of the Lord)*, or *Scivais,* she recounts twenty-six supernatural visions, among them a number of dismal glimpses into the underworld. Hildegard records seeing a ghastly darkness dotted with "eyes of fire" where bodies are perpetually tortured. Hildegard warned unrepentant souls that they faced boiling and fermenting for all eternity if they did not amend their lives. She urged sinners to admit their wrongdoing and accept Jesus' unconditional forgiveness in order to avoid the horrors of hell.

Because of her reputation as a mystic, Hildegard was constantly sought by popes, nobles, and kings to give advice on matters of religion, politics, and business. She traveled extensively throughout the Rhineland and founded several convents and abbeys. During these travels, Hildegard made many enemies by reprimanding corrupt clerics and unjust monarchs who were abusing the poor. She further upset church authorities by allowing a man who had been excommunicated to be buried on blessed ground. (Some texts indicate that the real source of friction between Hildegard and her critics was her prophecies of hell, which included some familiar faces among the damned.)

Although Hildegard was never officially declared a saint, she is still highly revered in areas along the Rhine. Pope John Paul II referred to her as an "outstanding saint," and recordings of her hymns and musical compositions continue to be popular throughout the world.

HINDU HELL Because Hinduism is based on the idea of perpetual reincarnation, Hindu hell is merely a stopping point where souls burn off evil before proceeding to the next life. The number of hells varies greatly, with some accounts listing as many as 136 separate underworld realms, each corresponding to a different sin. In these chambers of punishment, the spirit rids itself of bad KARMA (the sum of its evil acts). Tortures in the lower hells, the worst places of agony, include being burned alive, boiling in oil, and being eaten by ravenous birds.

HISTOIRE D'UN SOLDAT, L'

Igor Stravinsky's 1918 musical composition *L'Histoire d'un Soldat* (A Soldier's Story) does not fit into any identifiable category of performance. Technically speaking, it is not an opera, since there is no singing in the entire production. However, it is more than a symphony as it includes lengthy passages of spoken dialogue. But *L'Histoire* is not a mere stage play, either, since it relies heavily on the haunting music to advance the plotline. (For convenience, *L'Histoire* has been classified an opera, although it clearly has components of many forms of dramatic presentation.)

The composition tells the story of a war-weary soldier and his tragic encounter with the DEVIL. *L'Histoire* opens as the young man, on his way home from the battlefield, stops by the roadside to sift through his souvenirs. He comes to his favorite item: a worn violin from which he coaxes a lovely, simple melody. The devil, disguised as an old man, approaches and offers to trade the fiddle for a book that he promises will make the soldier rich beyond his dreams. The man agrees and surrenders the violin, even showing the devil how to play the delicate instrument.

The two continue down the road together, stopping to indulge in several days of debauchery. Eventually the soldier wearies of this hedonism and resumes his trip home, but when he arrives no one recognizes him. Even his mother refuses to believe he is her son, who she claims is no longer "among the living." They curse the "ghost" and send him away. The devil laughs, informing the soldier that it was not *days* that they spent reveling in wine, women, and song, but *years*. When the boy did not return home at the war's end, all assumed he was dead.

Heartbroken, the soldier decides to strike out on his own and earn his fortune through use of the enchanted book. He soon amasses great wealth but is increasingly unhappy as time passes. Only one thing, his old violin, appeals to him. But when he retrieves it from the devil, he learns that he has lost the ability to play it. More despondent than ever, the soldier loses his fortune and falls into despair.

He and the devil meet again, and the soldier begs to be released from their bargain. He will gladly return the sorcerer's book if only he can remember how to play the violin. The devil challenges him to a card game and tells the soldier if he wins, their union will be dissolved. The young man wins the contest and is overjoyed to discover that he can once again play his beloved violin.

The soldier's tune is so hauntingly beautiful that the music cures a sick princess who was thought to be dying. When the king learns that his daughter has been healed, he gives her hand to the soldier in marriage. But as the two set out for a honeymoon visit to the man's old hometown, the devil overtakes the couple and demands the soldier's soul. Deals with the dark angel cannot be dissolved, he declares, and carries the sorrowful gent off to hell. "The Triumphal March of the Devil" plays as the two disappear into the mists, and the house lights go dark.

Stravinsky uses extensive supernatural symbolism in his tale of damnation. The violin is in fact the soldier's soul, and once he has forsaken it his innocence is lost. He experiences a premonition of hell while living off the fortune earned through the infernal book, for although his material needs are met, he is spiritually dead. And his friends and family fail to recognize him because they are saved creatures, whereas he is a specter, the empty shell of a damned soul. At the opera's close, the soldier is borne off to the gloomy abyss, his agony amplified by the loss of his princess, who symbolizes the love of God. He has made his choice and now must accept its bitter, and eternal, consequences.

HITTOLA Hittola is the Finnish "DEMON's domain," a strange parallel of CHRISTIAN HELL. It is a dark, gloomy dimension of scorched mountains and barren fields that houses evil spirits. HIISI, also called Juutas, rules Hittola and commands its legions of cruel ghosts. He is the Finn counterpart of SATAN, lord of the damned.

HIYOYA Hiyoya is the Papuan underworld of the Wagawaga people. According to myth, the dead dwell in a prison located far below the ocean floor. Hiyoya is ruled by Tumudurere, a "fair-haired god" whose origin is unknown. Dead spirits cannot leave Hiyoya, although the living can visit the underworld if they take special precautions to guard themselves against starvation and suffocation. The Wagawaga claim that certain flowers originated in Hiyoya and were brought back to earth by travelers who had toured the undersea kingdom. These underworld plants have special magic powers and must therefore be handled very carefully.

HUNHAU The Maya, indigenous inhabitants of southern Mexico and Central America, were the first people of the North American continent to keep written historical records of their beliefs. Inscriptions on pottery, monuments, and murals date as far back as 50 B.C. No manuscripts of the ancient Maya culture survive, but most of the hieroglyphics and symbols found in ancient artwork have been deciphered. These records recount a rich collection of mythic heroes, gods, and goddesses. Among them is Au Puch, the Maya lord of Hunhau, the bitter land of the dead.

The Maya are a remarkably peace-loving people who believe that evildoers who have eluded justice during their lifetime will receive eternal punishment in Hunhau. Upon death, immoral souls are sentenced to different circles of the underworld in direct correspondence with their sins. Each layer in Hunhau is increasingly horrific, with the worst punishments melted out at the bottom of a deep chasm. Torments awaiting unclean spirits include being boiled, being sliced with razor-sharp stones, and being gnawed upon by ravenous beasts.

Au Puch (whose name means "spoil") presides over the ninth and lowest circle of Hanhua, an abominable pit of unspeakable anguish. He is likened to the Christian SATAN. Au Puch is a formidable figure portrayed as a skeleton or as a horribly bloated corpse with a haunting grin. His one true delight is tormenting souls of the dead, and he never tires of administering pain. Also referred to as Yum Cimil, the Lord of the Dead, Ah Puch could prowl the earth causing sickness, death, and war. He is ever watchful for vulnerable humans who could be tempted to commit evil at his command. Once Ah Puch puts his mark upon such a soul, there is no hope of redemption. That spirit is eternally damned to the horrors of Hunhau.

I

IBLIS Iblis is a powerful DEMON, the Islamic equivalent of the Christian SATAN. Stories vary on his origin. One legend says he was created out of fire;

another claims he was originally the beloved angel Azazil who fell from grace after offending the Almighty. Iblis's sin was mocking and taunting Allah's new creation (humans) and refusing to praise this fragile creature. For this he was thrust out of heaven and banished to the underworld, where he became the lord of JAHANNAM, the Arabic hell. There Iblis set up his own kingdom of evil and became father to the djinni, a race of demons.

According to the KORAN, the Muslim holy book, Allah has granted Iblis the power to tempt people and test their faithfulness to the divine will. But this shall continue only until the LAST JUDGMENT, at which time Iblis will be cast into the bottomless pit of Jahannam to suffer for all eternity along with his accursed followers.

Iblis appears as a central figure in William Beckford's dark tale "VATHEK," the story of a rich nobleman whose obsession with hell leads to child murder, molestation, and unspeakable acts of brutality.

IMAGERY Hell is symbolized in myth, religion, and literature with a number of images that recur from culture to culture. These include allusions to CHTHONIC deities and the infernal kingdoms under their rule.

Most ancient tales about the underworld include bridges, chasms, pits, rivers, boats or ferrymen, guardians (usually monsters), and gates that must be negotiated by spirits in the next world. Examples of these are found in myths regarding the Greek HADES, Persian CHINVAT BRIDGE, Germanic NIFLHEIM, Far Eastern EMMA-O, Babylonian ARALU, Egyptian DUAT, and Briton ANAON. Likewise, one or more of these features are described in such literary works as Virgil's *AENEID,* Dante's *DIVINE COMEDY: THE INFERNO,* Homer's *ODYSSEY,* and Milton's *PARADISE LOST* to signify damnation. And there are numerous allegorical and metaphorical uses of hell's images in CHILDREN'S LITERATURE.

In popular culture, the symbols of the underworld have concentrated on human mortality. Skulls, bones, graves, DEMONs, and GHOULS have become synonymous with a dark and unpleasant afterlife. Such Satanic icons as the inverted cross, pentagram, 666 (biblical "number of the beast"), and the Cross of Confusion (which

The Satanic Cross of Confusion combines an inverted cross with a question mark, mocking Christianity.

combines an inverted cross and a question mark) have also been connected to the infernal regions. These images are used extensively by today's HEAVY METAL music bands, BIKERS, and TATTOO artists to flout traditional religious values and to imply allegiance to hell.

Common religious images of hell include flames, desert wastelands, FIRE AND BRIMSTONE, and pitchforks. These derive from tales in the Christian Bible and Islamic KORAN about the sufferings of the damned.

INCUBUS An incubus, according to Judeo-Christian legend, is a masculine DEMON sent to bring the souls of young maidens to hell through sexual depravity. Medieval accounts of such diabolical couplings claim that intercourse with these fiends is usually painful and unpleasant, yet women often find incubi irresistibly seductive despite the physical agony. Elders warn against such blasphemous carnal unions, declaring that to have relations with an incubus is the "quickest path to hell."

Men are similarly admonished to avoid the SUCCUBUS, the female version of this notorious demon. They, too, have overwhelming sexual powers and could easily lead men to damnation.

INFERNO Artist Francesco Traini created a striking portrait of hell in his *Inferno.* The work is a blaze of vibrant, sensual reds and oranges, masterfully dotted with dark serpents and green GHOULS. Despite being partially destroyed, the picture creates a dynamic underworld swirling with DEMONS, condemned spirits, and SATAN himself. The *Inferno* stirs the imagination with graphic depictions of pain and torture against a background of utter, formidable chaos.

The painting shows a huge orange Satan with many mouths (representing the HELLMOUTH) all breathing fire

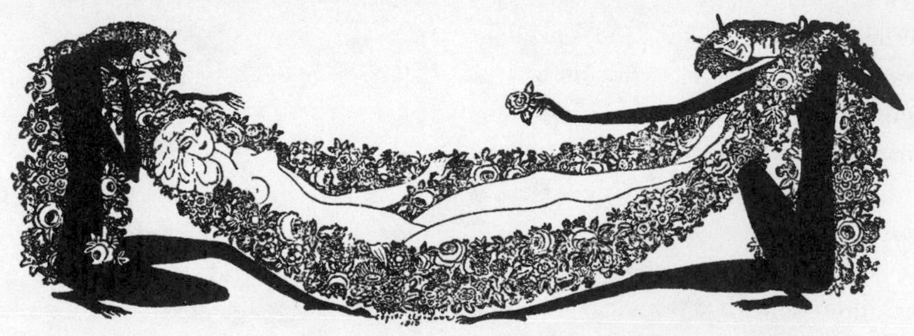

Incubi inducing sexual dreams in a sleeping virgin, Tschechonin, St. Petersburg 1913.
ART TODAY

through rows of piercing teeth. His blazing body is layered with gray-green scales, especially along his tentaclelike limbs. One arm snatches up a sinner, ready to drop it into the beast's gaping maw. All around the fiend, the damned are groped and molested by demons, burned in caverns of fire, and jabbed with smoking pitchforks. The entire underworld is riddled with snakes: They encircle the heads of the condemned and slither through the crevices of hell. Meanwhile, rat-faced demons prowl the abyss, searching for souls to torment.

INTERROGATION OF THE DEAD Though it is not an official doctrine, many Muslims believe in the interrogation of the dead. This is the Islamic time of judgment and sentencing in the afterlife.

According to tradition, after a person is buried and all the mourners have left the graveside, two angels—Munkar and Nakeer—come to examine the dead person's soul. They pose a series of questions to the departed, asking, "Who is God?" "What is his word?" and "Who is his prophet?" The righteous soul responds, "Allah is the Lord God, Islam is the true religion, and MUHAMMAD is God's true prophet." Upon hearing these answers, the angels open the gates of heaven and allow safe passage.

Infidels, however, are unable to respond correctly. They are deposited at the gates of hell, where the angels and all who are good and just abandon them. The heat and pestilence of the underworld come up to claim these souls, crushing them in their graves.

The interrogation of the dead is sometimes called heresy by Muslims, since the KORAN clearly states that all acts are accurately recorded in the Divine Scrolls. These are Allah's own records, which will be read at the time of judgment. Since such mystic accounts are kept, there is no need to rely on an interrogation to determine who is damned to hell.

INVITATION TO HELL The 1984 made-for-television movie *Invitation to Hell* offers a slick update of the FAUST legend. Directed by horror master Wes Craven (*NIGHTMARE ON ELM STREET*), the piece is a chilling tale of social climbing taken to its ultimate extreme.

The films stars Robert Urich as an upscale suburbanite whose promotion brings him to a highbrow neighborhood in California's Silicon Valley. The residents of this posh locale are obsessed with Steaming Springs, an exclusive country club where the "beautiful people" mix and mingle. The manager of Steaming Springs is played by soap opera star Susan Lucci, a seductive SATAN who recruits new prospects and sets membership criteria. Lucci tirelessly pursues Urich, vowing to entice him into joining her glamorous fraternity.

Urich is somewhat reluctant to sign up, but his wife and children are determined to become members. After just one visit to Steaming Springs, they become captivated by the club and hound Urich to join with them. When he finally succumbs, Urich discovers that the price of membership is high indeed: It will cost him his soul. Lucci leads her new victim to the entrance of hell, located in the basement of the luxurious clubhouse, where they seal the infernal bargain. This underworld of the modern media is a steamy swirl of pearly smoke emanating from some unseen chasm.

As soon as he makes the pact with Lucci, Urich is seized with regret. His life quickly deteriorates, and he discovers that his once-happy family has been horribly transformed into a clique of superficial zombies obsessed with self-aggrandizement. They are damned to a shallow existence as slaves to Lucci and her hordes. The family's only hope of release lies in renewing their commitment to each other, renouncing the enticements of the dazzling country club, and choosing substance over appearance. This ending is reminiscent of Goethe's version of the Faust story, in which love alone can save the condemned from hell.

IZANAGI The tale of Izanagi's journey to the underworld is one of the most elaborate underworld legends of East Asia. The story is found in the *Kojiki,* a centuries-old account of Japanese Shinto history. According to the tale, Izanagi and his wife, Izanami, created the Japanese islands and gave birth to many gods and goddesses. The couple lived happily under the blessing of heaven, until Izanami died while giving birth to the god of fire.

The *Kojiki* says that when Izanami dies, Izanagi travels to the Land of Darkness to retrieve her. When he arrives in the underworld, he discovers that she has built herself a castle there and is reluctant to see him. He begs her to return with him to earth, promising that a life of happiness and splendor awaits them in the land of the living. But Izanami refuses, saying it is too late. Her husband persists, unaware of the fact that she has eaten the food of the dead and has begun to decay. She hides in the shadows and keeps him at a distance, telling the grieving widower to go back without her.

But Izanagi is determined and pulls his bride out into the light. To his horror, he discovers that his once lovely wife is now a green, rotting, maggot-infested corpse giving off an unbearably foul stench. He screams, flings her aside, and flees. Humiliated by this insult, Izanami sends an army of 1,500 shikome (DEMONS) after her husband to punish him for disgracing her in the underworld.

As the shikome descend upon Izanagi, he throws off his headdress. It immediately turns into grapes, and the shikome stop to eat them. Next, he casts off his right comb, which becomes a patch of bamboo shoots. They devour these, and the pursuit continues. But before the shikome catch up with Izanagi, he is saved by the August Male, a kind protector. The August Male sympathizes with him and strikes down many of the shikome with an enormous sword.

Finally, Izanagi reaches the passageway between the Land of Darkness and the Land of Light. Here he finds three peaches and throws them at the last of his pursuers, demanding that they leave him and return to the underworld. He escapes into the land of the living and blocks the passage with a huge boulder.

Izanami shouts out to her husband from behind the stone. She vows to kill a thousand men every day until he returns to the Land of Darkness to appease her. Izanagi laughs, saying he will cause enough births to offset the deaths. Realizing at last that she is defeated, Izanami says good-bye to her love and they make a final break. Izanagi returns to the living while Izanami must forever remain in the Land of Darkness.

J

JAHANNAM Jahannam is the hell of the Islam religion. The name is the Arabic derivative of GEHENNA, an ancient valley in the Middle East once used for human sacrifices. The underworld of Islamic faith is a fiery pit enclosed by seven gates located far below the surface of the earth. Its features are similar to those of the Middle Eastern deserts: dry, hot, and desolate. In Jahannam, burning souls long for water but find no relief and suffer from various tortures inflicted on them by DEMONS. The KORAN (Islam's holy book) mentions seven regions of Jahannam: Jahannam proper, Latha (flaming inferno), Hutamah (destroying blaze), Sa'hir (blaze), Saqar (scorching fire), Gahim (fierce fire), and Haiyeh (great abyss).

According to Islamic teachings, when a person dies, he or she must face Allah directly. There is no intermediary to help weigh the factors of judgment in determining the soul's fate. Allah, being merciful and good, wants the soul to enjoy eternal paradise, but he is also just and must therefore hold each spirit accountable for its actions. Thus, all who have defied the will of Allah can blame only themselves for their damnation.

Hell itself is located underneath Al-Sirat, a narrow path that leads to paradise. Every spirit must cross over the bridge, and only the mercy of Allah can guarantee safe passage. Those who are unworthy will tumble into the seven-layered inferno below and suffer eternal damnation in the fiery chasm. According to the Koran, Jahannam is a horrific realm of retribution: "For the wrongdoers will be an everlasting place of final return: Hell! They will burn there . . . an evil bed to lie on indeed . . . a bed of fire, whose sheets encompass (the damned). If they should ask for relief, then water like molten copper shall be showered upon them to scald their faces. . . . They shall be lashed with rods of iron. Whenever, in their anguish, they try to escape from Hell, the angels will bring them back, saying 'Taste the torment of Hell-fire!' "

As the skin of the damned burns away, Allah regenerates it so sinners can suffer anew. But Allah is also merciful and can redeem souls from this punishment. A passage from the Koran states that the damned in hell "shall dwell there so long as there is a Heaven and an Earth, unless Allah wills it otherwise."

Muslims also believe in the LAST JUDGMENT (called the Day of Decision), a time at the end of the world when everyone, living and dead, will face final justice. Allah's faithful servants will be taken to paradise, while infidels shall be banished forever to Jahannam. Islam teaches that all Muslims will be saved on the Day of Decision, and Jahannam will be filled only with the souls of nonbelievers who refused to accept Allah as the one true God.

JAIN HELL Jainism, a 2,500-year-old outgrowth of Buddhism, teaches that the universe is divided into three parts: as a headless body with trunk, waist, and legs. Hell is located in the section corresponding to the right leg. It is a realm of 8.4 million torture chambers where a soul burns off bad KARMA, the spiritual residue of evil acts.

In each section of the underworld, souls are punished and purged of their evil before rejoining the reincarnation cycle. Every chamber has a specific DEMON who specializes in torturing damned spirits according to their particular sins. Torments include being torn apart by sharp hooks, clawed by fiends, and slashed with razor-sharp swords.

Once sufficient suffering has been inflicted, the soul moves on to another existence in the terrestrial world. Some followers believe that irretrievably evil spirits will burn in the lowest pit of the great abyss for all eternity. The rest will reenter the cycle of transmigration (symbolized by the SWASTIKA) and continue the quest for spiritual perfection.

JIGOKU Japanese Buddhist mythology describes Jigoku, a place of the dead located far below the earth. In Jigoku are eight "hot hells" and eight "cold hells" where souls are punished according to their sins. Damnation to Jigoku is not permanent; intercession, sacrifice, and prayers from living friends and relatives can redeem a soul sent to Jigoku, or at least reduce its punishment.

Jigoku is ruled by EMMA-O, a harsh judge of the dead. He is aided in his adjudication by two severed heads, Miru-me and Kagu-hana. Miru-me has the power to see a soul's most hidden sins, and Kagu-hana can detect even the faintest stench of small offenses. In Jigoku there is also an enchanted mirror that each departed spirit must stand before. Reflected in the mirror are all the sins committed during the soul's lifetime. After reviewing all this evidence, Emma-O sentences the spirit to the appropriate hell for divine punishment.

JOKES Despite its traditional reputation as a place of unending pain and despair, hell is the setting for hundreds of jokes. Early examples of this comedic interpretation of the underworld date back to around 400 B.C., when Greek playwright Aristophanes wrote *THE FROGS,* a satire of the infernal afterlife. His drama depicts HADES as a MERRY HELL where a chorus of singing amphibians replaces the dour dirges of traditional CHTHONIC works. *The Frogs* was denounced by contemporary authorities as "insulting to the gods," but the play was popular with audiences. Infernal jokes have thrived ever since.

In 1910, some two millennia after *The Frogs* first hit the stage, a new Off-Broadway theater opened in New York City with a similarly sacrilegious show. The now-defunct Folies-Bergères offered as its first production *Hell,* a "profane burlesque" hosted by "Mr. and Mrs. DEVIL." The program featured crude gags about drunks, old maids, sex-crazed sailors, and other damned souls. Like its ancient predecessor *The Frogs, Hell* was decried by the critics and hailed by the people. Thus underworld humor continues to thrive.

In the electronic age, television regularly brings infernal puns to the masses. The long-running variety show *LATE SHOW WITH DAVID LETTERMAN* has reaped big laughs over the years with numerous "Top Ten Lists" about the realm of the damned. These have speculated on everything from hell's headlines ("Ice Water Canceled—Again") to unpleasant underworld occupations (intestine adjuster). And Letterman frequently chides his viewers with remarks likening the show to the great abyss. On more than one occasion, he has greeted his studio audience with "welcome to hell, ladies and gentlemen."

Bill Maher's comedy talk show *Politically Incorrect* likewise reaches into the abyss for laughs. One episode, taped shortly after the controversial dignitary's death, posed the question, "Did Nixon go to heaven or hell?" Guest Martin Mull quipped, "I hope he brought his suntan oil," and noted that the ex-president "would go to whichever is closer to Yorba Linda." Other commentators were not so kind in guessing what his afterlife fate might be.

Radio, too, has provided a media for devilish humor. The Cutler Comedy Service, an agency specializing in comedic material for the airwaves, recently offered a "Sitcom Hell" sketch in which former *Mary Tyler Moore Show* characters Lou Grant and Ted Baxter vie for the affections of *BEETLEJUICE* star Winona Rider. The exercise presents an underworld of bad television reruns, similar to the inferno of the film *STAY TUNED.*

Even syndicated radio talk show host G. Gordon Liddy has probed the depths of hell for a laugh. The witty conservative has frequently remarked that he hopes "God is all-merciful," since that is his only hope of avoiding damnation after living such a colorful life. He explains that he is most certainly headed for hell if what he learned in parochial school is true. One sympathetic listener responded that at least in the great inferno Liddy will be among friends, whereas he would have "no one to talk to" in heaven.

And in an age where many people profess not to believe in eternal damnation, cocktail party jokes about the underworld remain popular. Among the most common: A man died and was sent to hell. When he arrived, the Devil greeted him and gave him a choice of three rooms in which to spend eternity. In the first, the man saw DEMONS beating the damned with whips and chains. The next was even worse: Here demons cooked and devoured condemned souls at a huge feast. In the third room, the damned sat in a waist-deep pool of human excrement, sipping tea. Repulsive as this was, the man decided it was preferable to the other two options. He joined the tea drinkers in the cesspool. But just as he sat down, a demon walked in and shouted, "Okay, everyone, break's over! Back on your heads!" The punch line of this joke can be heard in rock star Sting's 1993 recording "ST. AUGUSTINE in Hell."

The perennial popularity of jokes regarding the underworld is a testament to our enduring fascination with the land of the damned. Like COMIC BOOKS and ANIMATED CARTOONS about hell, such humorous outlets allow us an opportunity to laugh in the face of the ultimate—and eternal—peril.

JULIEN The 1913 French opera *Julien,* written by Gustave Charpentier, follows the life of a passionate poet completely devoted to his artistry. He places his work above all else, more important to him even than his beloved Louise. Betraying this dedication is the ultimate sin in Charpentier's work. And hell in *Julien* is the bitter punishment for abandoning dreams and forsaking beauty.

The opera opens as Julien visits the Temple of Beauty on the Holy Mount to consecrate himself to his art. He pledges to suffer for it, enduring humiliation, sacrifice, and ridicule to produce great works. His lover, Louise, realizes that she will never be as important to Julien as is his poetry, but she is content knowing that he is happy in his endeavors. But when the temple's high priest warns Julien that all his efforts will amount to nothing, that in the end his pride will be his undoing, Louise becomes concerned for the artist's soul.

After leaving the holy place, Julien comes to the Valley of the Accurst, a grim realm for damned poets who have betrayed their artistic vows. In this abyss, the sound of wailing and screaming drowns out all lyric of joy. The inhabitants of the Accurst Valley are forced to spend eternity lamenting their lost dreams and cursing their weak resolve. They call out to Julien, proclaiming that he will one day dwell among them.

Julien ignores this warning and begins pursuing his work, but he soon finds his vow to serve truth and beauty sorely tested. He does not find the inspiration he had hoped for but instead learns that the world is an ugly, cruel place where real beauty is rare. The only source of radiance in his life is Louise, and when she dies he is devastated. Julien decides that there is no appreciation for spiritual joys in a world obsessed with "animal pleasure," so he, too, will become a beast. Renouncing his vow, Julien willingly becomes one of the "animals" who have bitterly succumbed to despair.

In the closing scene, Julien has degenerated into a drunken vagrant rioting in the streets. He follows a mob into the Theatre of the Ideal, where the proprietor and attendants seem hauntingly familiar. Julien joins the revelers in vandalizing the theater before realizing that he is back at the foot of the Holy Mount. He recognizes the strangers as the maidens and priest of the Temple of Beauty, now mutated into terrible beasts. The horror of this revelation and the memory of his youthful aspirations seize Julien's soul. In his final moments Julien understands that he has lost everything: his innocence, his beloved Louise, and now his immortal soul. He dies at the feet of the DEMONS, ready to assume his place in the Accurst Valley with the rest of the damned.

K

KAKUREZATOR Kakurezator is a DEMON of hell according to ancient Japanese mythology. He carries the souls of the damned to the underworld. Kakurezator is blind but can smell sin and invades the homes of evil people as they are dying. Once the body has expired, he brings the defiled spirit to hell.

KALICHI Kalichi is the dreary hell of ancient India. When a person dies, he or she is judged by YAMA, lord of the dead. The god Chandragupta records and reads the sum of the soul's virtues and sins, then Yama can send it to Kalichi, to paradise, or to another existence on earth. In Kalichi, Yama administers divine justice in the form of sadistic torments. He is often shown riding a buffalo and carrying a lasso to snag souls.

Evil spirits face a number of horrors in Kalichi. In this pit of gloom, sinners are punished according to their offenses. Those who marry outside their caste are forced to embrace molten human forms, the cruel are boiled in oil, animal tormentors are ripped apart, evil priests are tossed into a river of impurities and gnawed by water DEMONS.

Now absorbed into Indian religion (which teaches transmigration of souls), the suffering of Kalichi is believed to be temporary. Eventually, all souls are believed to be given another chance at salvation through reincarnation.

KANALOA Kanaloa is the Hawaiian squid god of death. He rules the gloomy underworld, located at the bottom of the sea, which is sometimes referred to as Po. Kanaloa gives off a putrid smell that reflects the odor of people's sins. He is heavily identified with despair and is also called the god of darkness.

Kanaloa is one of the few underworld gods included in Native American mythology, although little is known about the deity. One story suggests that Kanaloa was once a benevolent deity who betrayed his kind and assembled an army of rebellious spirits. For his transgression, Kanaloa was forced to the ocean depths to dwell eternally with unclean spirits. This legend parallels the Christian tale of LUCIFER's fall from heaven and may have been influenced by early missionaries.

KARMA Karma is a concept of many Eastern religions, including Buddhism, Hinduism, and Jainism, all of which date back centuries before the time of Christ. Karma refers to the sum of a person's actions during the phases of his or her life and the corresponding consequences. Bad karma results in damnation, although this state is temporary. Souls do not receive eternal punishment or reward but continue throughout time on an unending cycle of reincarnation, death, purging, and rebirth. There is no supreme god in Eastern religious teachings and likewise no ruler of hell. Each person's fate is determined solely by his or her karma.

The nature and number of hells where bad karma is burned away differs with each religion. In the BARDO THODOL (the Tibetan Book of the Dead), souls must face the "Mirror of Karma" in the afterlife. This enchanted looking glass reflects the truth about the spirit's good and evil and determines his or her supernatural destination. Other Eastern faiths feature JIGOKU, EMMA-O, and YAMA as components of retribution in the spiritual realm where karma is purged.

KASANAAN Kasanaan is the "village of grief and affliction" of the Tagalog people of the Philippines. This somber underworld is a place of sorrow more than pain, where souls exist in a lethargic state. Spirits in Kasanaan resemble the Greek SHADES, who likewise find the afterlife to be unbearably monotonous rather than fearsome. There is no torture in Kasanaan; the afterlife suffering is the loss of the excitement and energy of life on earth.

KIDS IN THE HALL Lorne Michaels, best known as producer of the long-running variety show *SATURDAY NIGHT LIVE*, is the creator of the Canadian comedy series *Kids in the Hall*. During the show's 1989–1994 run, hell serves as the backdrop for humor in a variety of sketches. Kevin McDonald plays the recurring character Simon McMillan, a dark figure who hosts a talk show broadcast from "the pit of ultimate darkness." McMillan describes himself as the "gatekeeper to the boys' club that is the underworld" and laments that man must "walk alone along the path of evil." McMillan's set consists of a red, fiery cave of wafting smoke and murky darkness.

McMillan is assisted by David Foley playing "manservant Hecubus," the very incarnation of iniquity. Hecubus often refers to his favorite underworld pastimes, such as attending "garage sales in hell" rife with infernal curiosities. He also delights in playing tricks on mortals, such as sprinkling women with "zombie dust" in order to seduce them and disclosing the final scenes of suspense movies.

Another sequence offers Mark McKinney in the role of a red-faced, horned SATAN. One sketch depicts the DEMON watching television from his infernal recreation room. He channel-surfs until lighting upon his favorite show: *The Golden Girls*.

McKinney's DEVIL shows up again in a rock and roll showdown with Bruce McCollough as Bobby, a rebellious and misunderstood Toronto teen. When McCollough retreats to the garage to escape his nagging parents, Satan challenges the boy to a guitar-playing contest. The demon uses all his tricks—including shape-shifting into a gorgeous pinup model and growing extra arms to play complicated riffs—to win the musical match. But McCollough has a trick of his own: an enchanted "wah-wah" pedal. With the aid of this innovation, the teen blasts Satan back into "rock and roll hell" in a fiery explosion.

In addition to these sketches, the *Kids in the Hall* features JOKES about the land of the damned. These routinely consist of mocking the devil, making light of hell, and depicting the underworld as far more interesting and colorful than paradise.

KITAMBA According to the Mbundu people of Angola, King Kitamba kia Xiba contacts the underworld in hopes of reclaiming his dead wife. Distraught at the sudden death of his lovely bride, Kitamba is so overcome with grief that he forces all his people into silent mourning. After months of this enforced sullenness, his subjects grow tired of mourning and want to return to their rich life of colorful ceremonies and shared joys. Kitamba refuses to repeal the edict, insisting that all share his sorrow. Desperate to end the grieving, the villagers decide to send a shaman to the underworld to try and retrieve Muhongo, Kitamba's deceased queen.

The doctor digs a tunnel to the underworld beneath his hut. He reaches the land of the dead and finds Muhongo, but she tells him she cannot return to life, that death of the body is final. The soul, she explains, lives on in a dull, dank realm where there is no sadness but no joy, either. She asks the doctor to return to Kitamba and let him know that although she is unable to leave, she is not in any pain. Muhongo gives the doctor the bracelet she was buried with and tells him to show it to Kitamba to prove that he has truly seen her. (In some versions, the medicine man meets Death personified, who promises that the royal couple will not be separated for long, since Kitamba has only a few more years to live.)

The shaman returns to the land of the living through the tunnel and presents the bracelet to Kitamba along with Muhongo's message. Kitamba recognizes the jewel and finally accepts her death and puts an end to the mourning. He spends the rest of his days anticipating his own death, when he and Muhongo will be reunited in the gloomy underworld.

KORAN The Koran (Qu'ran) is the holy book of Islam, comparable to the Christian Bible. In addition to explaining doctrines of the faith, the Koran also contains accounts of the supernatural travels in heaven and hell of MUHAMMAD, Islam's founder. The Koran offers detailed descriptions of the underworld and of the suffering that awaits infidels (nonbelievers), defilers, and sinners in JAHANNAM, Islamic hell. According to the sacred text, in Jahannam damned souls ". . . shall be lashed with rods of iron. Whenever, in their anguish, they try to escape form Hell, the angels will bring them back saying 'Taste the torment of Hellfire!' "

In some translations, the Koran refers to GEHENNA, the fiery pit of damnation of Judeo-Christian belief, where IBLIS (SATAN) shall torture souls for eternity. Allah (God) will tell wicked souls, "Said He, 'Depart!' Those of them that follow thee [Iblis]—surely Gehenna shall be your recompense! . . . Those who disbelieve, and cry lies to Our signs—they are the inhabitants of Hell." Another passage describes the fall of Iblis from heaven. The story bears similarities to the Christian legend of LUCIFER and his rebellion against God. According to the Koran, when Iblis is cast into hell, he vows to seek the ruin of human souls by making false promises and employing trickery: "Satan promises them [infidels] naught, except delusion."

The Koran also foretells a LAST JUDGMENT, when all human souls will be called before Allah to account for their lives. It is the wish of Allah, who is infinitely merciful, that all souls be united with him in paradise. However, since the deity is also infinitely just, he will not force salvation on anyone. Damnation, therefore, is not a divine sentence but a choice made freely by those who prefer serving themselves and refusing the truth and following "the detestable lies" of Iblis.

KOWALSKA, MARY FAUSTINA Helena Kowalska, a virtuous woman who experienced many supernatural encounters, including visions of hell, was born in Poland in 1905. She entered the convent at nineteen, taking the name Sister Mary Faustina as her religious title. Suffering from chronic ill health, Kowalska devoted herself to a quiet life of contemplating Christ's divine mercy. She kept a detailed diary of her daily prayers until she became too ill to continue writing.

That diary, published in the United States in 1987, contains numerous accounts of contact with the supernatural. Kowalska transcribes prayers dictated to her by Jesus and records seeing angels praising God. Among these mystical experiences, she also describes a place of sorrow and agony where souls languish in abject misery: "In a moment I was in a misty place full of fire in which there was a great crowd of suffering souls. . . . I asked these souls what their greatest suffering was. They answered me in one voice that their greatest torment was longing for God. . . . An interior voice said 'My mercy does not want this, but justice demands it.' "

Kowalska refers to this realm as a "prison of suffering," a PURGATORIAL HELL where souls expunge the evil residue of their sinful actions. She warns that hell holds more terrifying horror than this. In another account, she describes being led to the "chasms of Hell" by an angel. There she saw ". . . a place of great torture; how awesomely large and extensive it is. The kind of tortures I saw: . . . the loss of God . . . perpetual remorse of conscience . . . fire that will penetrate the soul without destroying it—a terrible suffering, as it is purely spiritual fire, lit by God's anger . . . continual darkness and a terrible suffocating smell . . . the constant company of SATAN . . . horrible despair, hatred of God, vile words, curses and blasphemies. These are the tortures suffered by all the damned together, but that is not the end of the sufferings. There are special tortures of the senses. Each soul undergoes terrible and indescribable sufferings, related to the manner in which it has sinned." This agony is magnified by the soul's realization that its fate will never change; this punishment will continue for eternity. Kowalska encourages devotion to Christ as a safeguard against this frightful damnation. Her diary contrasts these dark images with the indescribable joys of heaven and urges all to embrace Christ's divine mercy. She stresses the fact that God wants all souls to be united to him in paradise, but that he will not force salvation on the unwilling.

Kowalska died of tuberculosis in 1938 and is currently a candidate for sainthood in the Roman Catholic church.

L

LADDER OF JUDGMENT St. John of Climax created his vision of what happens to the soul upon death in the painting *Ladder of Judgment.* The work, which now adorns the Monastery of St. Catherine at Sinai, shows a diagonal ladder that reaches from earth to heaven. Deceased souls must ascend to paradise with the aid of angels sent to escort the saved. Evil souls, however, are shot with arrows by demons who dot the bottom of the painting. Others are impaled on pitchforks and pulled into hell. St. John's implication is that it is a person's own actions, and not a Supreme Judge, that determine whether each soul is ultimately saved or damned.

LAKE AVERNUS Lake Avernus is the entrance to the kingdom of HADES according to ancient Greek myth. A real lake, the dark pool is located near Naples, Italy. Its murky black waters and dense forest surroundings create an ominous feel of sorrow and doom, causing the lake to become associated with the gateway to

H. Winslow's depiction of Lake Avernus, c. 1800. ART TODAY

the underworld. Avernus is described in Virgil's epic poem the *AENEID* and in Dante's *DIVINE COMEDY: THE INFERNO* as the portal through which spirits enter the realm of the dead.

LAND OF NO RETURN Ancient Babylonian myth calls the underworld the Land of No Return. This place of the dead is described in the ancient Gilgamesh epic as the end of a road that leads only one way. The realm is surrounded by high, impenetrable walls and bound by seven locked gates. In the Land of No Return, the dead eat clay dust unless their families have made offerings of food for sustenance in the afterlife. Mythic figure ENKIDU offers a dour description of this desolate land in the story of *Gilgamesh*.

According to the myth, each new grave serves as a passage to the underworld, which is located deep within the earth. A bird-faced ferryman escorts the deceased from their tombs to the Land of No Return, where they must pass through the seven gates. Later myths incorporated these beliefs into the story of ERESHKIGAL, ruler of the dead in the abyss of ARALU.

LAND OF THE DEAD Land of the Dead is a generic term describing the unpleasant realm of departed souls. This term is found in a variety of myths and religions, ranging from Greek legends about the kingdom of HADES to the ancient biblical mentions of GEHENNA. The land of the Dead can be a dull place of monotony, such as the Mesopotamian ARALU, or a ghastly chamber of grisly tortures, as in the

East Asian TI YU. The phrase never connotes a paradise or heavenly eternal repose.

LAST JUDGMENT The concept of a Last Judgment—a time when all souls will be called to account for their acts and be given final justice—is a tenet of many religions and mythologies. The Papyrus of Ani, an ancient Egyptian artwork, shows souls being judged in the hall of OSIRIS, lord of the afterlife. In the BARDO THODOL (the Tibetan Book of the Dead), spirits must account for their deeds in the Hall of Two Truths before rejoining the cycle of reincarnation. This adjudication occurs shortly after physical death.

Jewish beliefs about the Last Judgment focus on retribution. This event is seen as a final purging, when all those who have exploited or oppressed the Jews throughout history will be punished for their evil. Some believe that at this time the Messiah (rather than Yahweh) will preside over the court of the divine reckoning.

Islamic tradition refers to this event as the Last Day. When this occurs, everyone who has ever lived will be resurrected in his or her human body before facing Allah. Thus righteous souls will enjoy physical delights in paradise while the wicked endure unending sensory agony in the underworld. Many believe that all Muslims will be saved at the Last Day (even those who had previously been damned to hell), for Allah's mercy outweighs his sense of justice. No infidel, however, can ever be admitted into the presence of the Almighty. Those who do not embrace Islam and its teachings will suffer the horrors of the underworld or face ANNIHILATION after the final accounting takes place.

According to the Christian religion, the Last Judgment will come at the end of the world, when the earth itself will be destroyed. This event is mentioned in the Apostles' Creed, when Christ "will come to judge the living and the dead." As in the Islamic faith, Christians believe that body and soul will be reunited at this time. After the fates of all spirits have been determined, SATAN and his minions will be confined to hell and no longer allowed to wander freely outside of the underworld. The evil and unjust will then be sentenced to spend eternity in the depths of hell, a realm that REVELATION describes as a "fiery pool of burning sulphur." And according to the Gospel of St. Matthew, at the Last Judgment the Lord will tell the condemned: "Depart from me, you accursed, and enter the fire prepared for the DEVIL and his angels; for I was hungry and you gave me no food, I was thirsty and you gave me no drink, I was a stranger and you did not welcome me, naked and you did not clothe me, sick and in prison and you did not visit me" (Matt. 25:41–43)

The theme of the Last Judgment is among the most popular topics for MORALITY PLAYS. These dramas take their themes from the Bible and from

Christian tradition, focusing primarily on the fall of LUCIFER, the HARROWING OF HELL, and the coming of the blasphemous Antichrist. Typical morality plays of the Last Judgment feature DEMONS delighted that hell will now be filled for eternity with the souls of the damned. After Jesus sorts the "lambs from the goats," a chorus of the condemned wails as it enters the underworld, then Christ locks the gates of hell for the last time.

Images of the Last Judgment also figure prominently in a vast array of artworks, most notably in CHURCH ART AND ARCHITECTURE.

LAST JUDGMENT (art) The theological concept of the LAST JUDGMENT, a final divine reckoning when souls will be judged and sentenced in the afterlife, is illuminated in artworks throughout the world, most commonly in Christendom. Christian portrayals often include elements from the Bible's REVELATION: SATAN, DEMONS, and tortures of the damned. The archangel Michael, who led the angels in defending heaven, is frequently pictured holding the scales that weigh people's souls to determine if they are saved or damned.

Hell is a brutal place of insufferable torment according to these works. At the Cathedral of Santa Maria Assunta in Torcello in Venice, a twelfth-century mosaic has toothy demons trying to pull down the scales of justice and drag souls to underworld. The Church of St. George in Veronet, Romania, hosts a fresco from around 1550 that completely covers the west wall. Christ is seated at the center of the painting and a river of fire pours forth from his throne. The current flows to the left and into hell, where it drowns the damned. The terrain of the inferno is a scorched landscape littered with the charred remains of the condemned.

The Last Judgment has long been a favorite topic for master painters and world renowned artists. Fra Angelico took up the subject in a work that presents souls being devoured by a grisly HELLMOUTH before being cooked in caldrons or chewed up by black, horned GHOULS. The work uses dark colors—browns, blacks, and burnt oranges—to create a somber mood of brooding despair. Winged demons poke at the damned with fiery spears and pour molten iron into their mouths. The bodies of those in hell are repeatedly raped, sliced, and torn to pieces. Snakes, DEVILS, and flames fill the background.

Leandro da Ponte da Bassano's *Last Judgment* offers further grisly torments of hell. God and Christ are shown at the top center of the painting bathed in brilliant white, while far below and to the left the condemned are carried off to the underworld by muscular fiends. In the inferno, the souls are jabbed with spikes, gnawed by demons, and menaced by serpents. One beast grasps a man's jaw firmly as he plunges a spear into the damned soul's eyes. Other accursed spirits look sorrowfully to heaven, their agony enhanced by seeing the splendor of paradise.

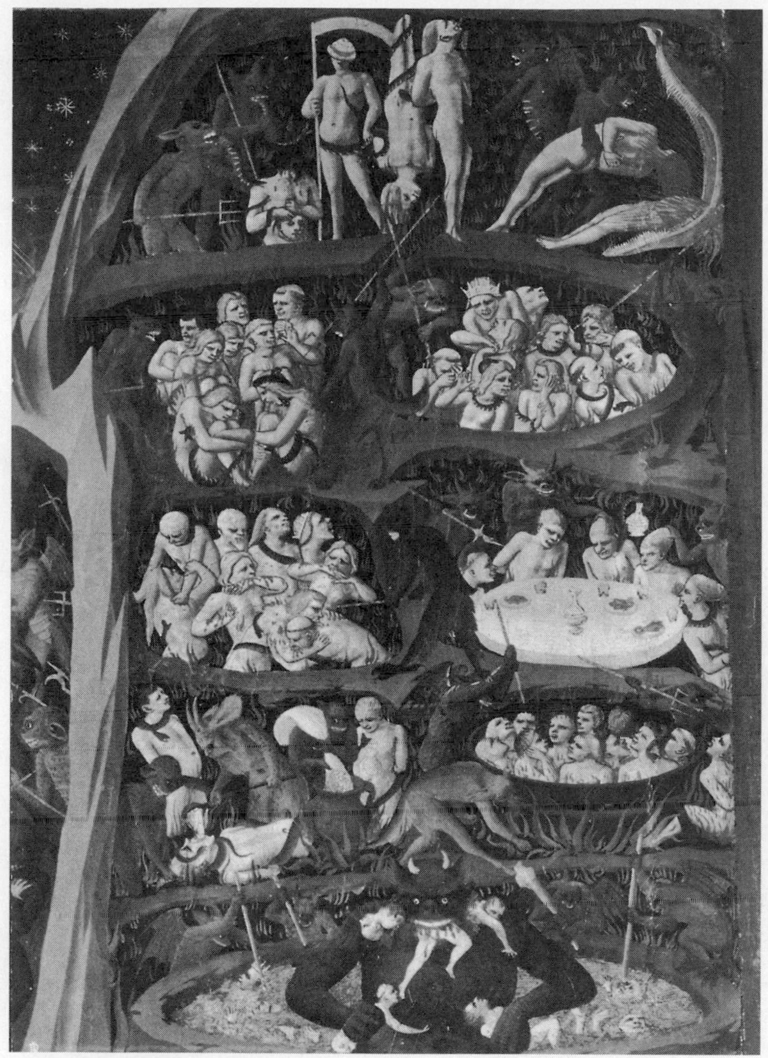

Detail of hell from the *Last Judgment,* Fra Angelico c. 1435.
ALINARI/ART RESOURCE

For his Last Judgment altarpiece, created around 1450, Rogier van der Weyden painted a series of panels to depict the earth, heaven, and hell. The underworld is to the left of God, a dark place of shadows and gloom. The damned are dragged by the hair to the rocky, flaming cliffs of the abyss. Despairing souls shriek in agony and claw at one another trying to free themselves from imprisonment in the inferno.

Unquestionably, the ultimate depiction of the Last Judgment in Christian art is MICHELANGELO's fresco in the Sistine Chapel in Rome. It shows the damned, naked and afraid, disembarking from a boat onto the shores of hell.

Infernal IMAGERY—fire, serpents, faces contorted in utter agony—fills the masterpiece. So frightening is Michelangelo's *Last Judgment* that when the finished work was unveiled, Pope Paul III fell to his knees and begged God to spare him from hell.

But the composition had many critics, too, who denounced it at the time as obscene, even blasphemous. This was mainly due to the fact that Michelangelo depicted souls as naked, stripped of all their earthly adornments. Many felt that nudity had no place at the altar, even in a religious artwork. Over the years, church officials have tried to amend or even destroy the work, going so far as to paint loincloths over the offending anatomies. Despite these attempts to modify the painting, Michelangelo's poignant vision endures.

The Last Judgment continues to fascinate artists even in modern times. Creative genius WILLIAM BLAKE offers his vision of the supernatural tribunal, using pale grays and whites rather than the traditional oranges, reds, and yellows used to depict fiery tortures. His work is filled with silvery ghosts and smoky spirits in a bleak, cavernous hell where those who have offended God must spend eternity in chains. Blake's interpretation, painted in the twentieth century, attests to the enduring interest in this prophesied phenomenon.

LATE SHOW WITH DAVID LETTERMAN Comedian David Letterman has used hell as a foil for JOKES in numerous episodes of his long-running variety show *Late Show with David Letterman.* His lighthearted "visions" of the underworld reflect beliefs from a variety of myths, religions, and legends of the infernal depths.

When introducing an agenda he finds less than thrilling, Letterman has often greeted his live audience with, "Welcome to hell, ladies and gentlemen." Should his witticisms fail to extract a positive reaction, he can be heard rhetorically asking, "So, what, am I going to hell now?" And over the years he has frequently noted, "Now I know what hell is like," in response to tawdry news items and abrasive guests' comments.

One of Letterman's trademark gags is the "Top Ten List," a humorous look at a category of his choosing. Lists have included the worst jobs in hell (intestine adjuster, staff psychologist for the Islamic jihad), the ways to know summer is over in hell (molten lava slide closed for the season, anguished cries for water replaced by anguished cries for doughnuts and hot cider), and the hottest mall shops in hell (Brown Julius, Jim Jones's Juice-a-teria).

Late Show has also offered a list of hell's best newspaper headlines. This collection includes "Ice Water Canceled—Again," "Most Residents Prefer Flame Broiling to Frying," and "Slumbering Carnivorous Worms Awaken in Very Bad Mood." Letterman's comic spins on the underworld have been immortalized in his *Book of Top Ten Lists* and *Altogether New Book of Top Ten Lists.*

LAZARUS The tale of Lazarus is found in the Bible, in St. Luke. In the account, Christ tells followers of a man named Lazarus, an invalid who sits at the gate of a rich man's estate begging for food. The man ignores Lazarus, leaving him hungry, cold, and humiliated while the wealthy man and his friends enjoy an orgy of excess. In time, Lazarus dies and is taken to his reward, to spend eternity "resting in the bosom of Abraham." Soon after, the rich man also dies but is not so fortunate. He is delivered to hell to writhe in agony. Looking up, the rich man sees Lazarus and cries: "Father Abraham, have mercy on me, and send Lazarus to dip his finger in water and bring it here to cool my tongue, for I am tormented in this flame" (Luke 16:24).

Abraham refuses this request, telling the man that he had received comfort in earthly life and now it is Lazarus's turn to be happy. He also points out that there exists "a great gulf between us which none can pass," referring to the chasm between heaven and hell. The rich man then asks Abraham to send Lazarus back to earth, for the wealthy man has five brothers who are headed for the same dire fate. Abraham refuses this, too, saying that if they would not heed the words of Moses and the prophets, then even seeing a man return from the dead will not move them to change their ways.

St. Luke uses this as an analogy to the resurrection of Christ. If people set their hearts against virtue, nothing can break them. Such wicked sinners will find ways to rationalize their actions and reject truth, going so far as to deny Jesus' rising from the dead. And those who choose this path will share the fate of the rich man, damned to pass eternity in "unquenchable fire."

Illustration of Lazarus languishing at the rich man's gate from an 1874 Bible.

LELWANIS An ancient Hittite myth refers to Lelwanis, a god whose sex is uncertain, as the ruler of the underworld. Lelwanis's realm includes not only the souls of the dead but also an older generation of defeated gods and other mysterious spirits. Unfortunately, the few remaining Hittite records are almost impossible to interpret, although historians believe that the legend of Lelwanis contains elements of myth borrowed from the Greeks and Sumerians. The texts that have been deciphered indicate that the damned face agony and torture in the kingdom of Lelwanis. One story tells of a defeated weather god whose eyes and heart are torn out by a dragon. Others describe an assortment of unpleasant fates, such as mutilations, burnings, and impalements. These bear similarities to accounts of TARTARUS, lowest realm of the Greek HADES, and of the Sumerian Land of the Dead ARALU.

LEOPARD In medieval Christian legend and art, the leopard is often used to symbolize hell and the DEVIL. Leopards are depicted in various works as gnawing on the damned in the underworld or being subdued by holy men. In Dante's *DIVINE COMEDY: THE INFERNO,* the narrator is challenged by a wild leopard as he tries to reach the "Summit of Enlightenment." The beast is eventually joined by a lion and then a she-wolf, and Dante is driven back into the dark valley. Scholars believe that these three animals represent the beasts described in the Bible in Jeremiah as preying on the souls of humankind.

LETHE Lethe is one of the mythical rivers that separate the Greek underworld HADES from the land of the living. According to the myth, the waters of Lethe have the power to make people forget their earthly lives. All newly deceased spirits drink from this stream as they enter the underworld to help ease the pain of leaving their loved ones behind.

Lethe appears in many works of Western literature. Thirteenth-century poet Dante describes the river in his *DIVINE COMEDY: THE INFERNO* as a cleansing drink that helps people forget their sins against God. In Virgil's *AENEID,* sipping from Lethe's waters is a prerequisite to reincarnation, as it enables souls to lose their former identities before returning fresh to the world of the living. The ancient waterway even appears in a modern novel by horror writer Stephen King. In his 1994 *ROSE MADDER,* King leads his heroine to the banks of a dangerous supernatural river with waters that cause a person to forget everything, "even your own name."

LEVIATHAN Leviathan (Lothan in Canaanite texts) is the monster found in ancient Hebrew records associated with the underworld. He is a giant, seven-headed serpent that inhabits the ocean depths. In the Book of Job, a sacred text of both Jews and Christians, Leviathan is described as a horrific beast that no human can conquer: "Can you draw out Leviathan with a hook? . . . Can you put a hook into his nose, or bore his jaw through with a thorn? . . . Behold, the hope of him is in vain: shall you not be cast down even at the sight of him? . . . Out of his mouth go burning lamps, and sparks of fire leap out. Out of his nostrils goes smoke as out of a seething cauldron. His breath kindles fiery coals, and a flame jumps from his mouth. . . . When he raises up, the mighty are afraid. . . . He is the king over all the children of pride" (Job 41:1, 2, 9, 19–21, 25, 34).

The beast is also mentioned in *REVELATION,* a text of the Christian Bible that describes the end of the world. Leviathan is the monster that rises from the sea to devour humankind: "And I stood upon the sand of the sea, and saw a beast rise up out of the sea, having seven heads and ten horns, and upon his horns ten crowns, and upon his heads the name of blasphemy. . . . And the dragon [SATAN] gave him his power and his great authority" (Rev. 13:1–2).

References to the beast Leviathan can likewise be found in the DEAD SEA SCROLLS, an ancient text describing supernatural events. According to the scrolls, the "Sons of Light" will one day defeat the evil "Sons of Darkness" and bring about Leviathan's ultimate destruction.

An illustration of Leviathan is contained in LES TRÈS RICHES HEURES DU DUC DE BERRY, a BOOK OF HOURS created around 1413. The picture shows a scaly DEMON lying on a furnace, simultaneously devouring and belching the souls of the damned. In this illustration, he is identified with Satan, overlord of hell and archenemy of Jesus Christ. He also appears in many works of Western literature, including Milton's *PARADISE LOST,* as the embodiment of supernatural evil.

Aquatic monsters similar to Leviathan exist in numerous mythology systems from around the world. Australian myth includes Bunyip, a ferocious water beast who dwells in the silt of lake bottoms, reaching up to drown mortals who come too close. Chilean Indians fear Camahueto, a sea monster notorious for attacking ships and dragging sailors to their deaths. Since the days of ancient Greek myth, seafarers have claimed to have spotted an enormous, hideous creature called the Kraken. This beast has the power to destroy entire ships with one blow or to wipe out seaside villages with a single swipe of his mighty arms. And KANALOA, squid god of the underworld from Hawaiian legends, bears striking similarity to the Judeo-Christian Leviathan.

LIFE OF GUTHLAC An eleventh-century text titled *Life of Guthlac* describes an incredible vision of the underworld. According to the account, the devout Guthlac is taken to hell by DEMONS who want to break his spirit. SATAN, insanely jealous of the man's fidelity to the Christian church, vows to tempt him away from God. When his "arrows of temptation" fail to shake Guthlac, Satan unleashes a legion of evil spirits who appear to him as grotesque deformities.

Screaming curses and shouting vile blasphemies, the fiends drag Guthlac through fields of thorns and into a swamp of putrid water. Finally, the GHOULS bring him to hell and force him to witness the tortures of the damned. There, Guthlac sees hollow-eyed souls writhing in agony and screeching for relief. Satan boasts that these damned attest to his great power. But his attempt to win Guthlac backfires: The vision of hell leaves the saint more determined than ever to serve

Christ and to prevent further souls from choosing the demon's dark bargain.

Guthlac's story became a popular text of medieval VISION LITERATURE.

LILITH Lilith is a female DEMON from Jewish, Christian, and Islamic folklore. In Muslim legend, she is the wife of the Islamic IBLIS, ruler of hell, and mother of all demons. In stories from Jewish and Christian tradition, Lilith is the first wife of Adam who rejects her husband and chooses to copulate with SATAN instead. Now a queen of evil and darkness, Lilith prowls the night searching for children to devour. She is described in Isaiah as a "screech owl" who incurs "the Lord's divine fury."

Lilith also seeks to bring souls to hell by seducing men as they sleep. She is a SUCCUBUS who is aided in her diabolical work by an army of female fiends. Men who fall to her charms face certain damnation unless they repent this sin and perform purifying rituals.

The film *NIGHT ANGEL* offers Lilith as a dark beauty risen from the underworld to seek the ruin of human souls. She takes one intended victim on a fascinating, yet grotesque, tour of hell in hopes of winning his allegiance.

LIMBO Limbo is a supernatural realm for spirits who are neither good nor evil. They have not been wicked enough to deserve hell, but neither have they merited heaven through their virtue. These are morally neutral spirits, such as babies who die in infancy, lunatics, or people whose lives have not been distinguished by either saintly or diabolical behavior. In Limbo, souls suffer no torments; however, they are unable to dwell in the presence of God. Their only pain is the loss of union with the divine.

The existence of limbo is held, either officially or as a plausibility, by a number of religions, including Catholicism, Judaism, and Islam (Islamic limbo is called AL AARAAF). Some believe that limbo will eventually be emptied and its souls redeemed, most likely at the LAST JUDGMENT. Until then, spirits in limbo will dwell in quiet tranquillity.

Another belief about limbo concerns the HARROWING OF HELL. Since most biblical scholars agree that damnation to hell is permanent, the underworld Jesus raised after his crucifixion must in fact be some other realm. The souls of the patriarchs and of those worthy of heaven but unable to enter until Christ's sacrifice are said to have been in limbo, awaiting their Redeemer. This would serve justice, since they would not have been forced to suffer the undeserved agonies of the damned while anticipating their redemption.

Limbo appears in a number of literary works. In Dante's *DIVINE COMEDY: THE INFERNO,* the souls of "virtuous pagans" (such as the poet Virgil and philosophers Plato, Aristotle, and Socrates) exist in limbo along with the spirits of unbaptized persons who led blameless lives. And Edgar Allan Poe's poem "Al Aaraaf" describes the place as a brilliant star circled by four radiant suns.

LIVING END, THE Stanley Elkin's 1977 novel *The Living End* derides afterlife notions from paradise to the underworld. Its hell is "the ultimate inner city," a stinking, perilous locale of violence, pain, and ugliness. Burning streets, covered in an odious mix of vomit, blood, and human feces, are lined with lost souls. These damned spirits try to be "sociable" to one another through "rapes, fights and muggings." Other than this rough contact, they cannot bear to speak to or even look at one other.

The agony of hell is magnified by a quick glimpse of heaven that the damned see on their way to the murky depths. This haunting memory "induced sadness, rage." As for their former lives, hell's inhabitants have long forgotten most of the details as "constant pain and perpetual despair" overwhelm all other thoughts. One character is described as "a vessel of nausea, a pail of pain." Conversations with God incite further fury, as most are not satisfied with his explanations of why they have been sent to the underworld.

Those who persist in annoying God with complaints could suffer a worse fate: ANNIHILATION. In *The Living End,* this consists of being hurled into a dark tunnel of nothingness so piercing that the damned "missed the pain" of hell. Annihilation is the equivalent of being interred in a coffin while still fully conscious, imprisoned in eternal isolation. The only sound in this bitter realm is the soft gnawing of worms eating away at the slowly decomposing flesh, until all that is left is an "ashen mess."

One character who is annihilated, Ladlehaus, discovers that he can communicate to some extent with Quiz, a living man. Quiz routinely takes his lunch break near Ladlehaus's grave, and the two exchange thoughts through the dimensions. For Ladlehaus, however, this leads only to increased suffering when Quiz decides to play a cruel joke on the dead man. He convinces Ladlehaus that a war has broken out in the world and refuses to talk about anything except the utter destruction. Ladlehaus longs to hear about everyday life—home-cooked food, pretty women, music—but Quiz only accelerates his taunting, offering Ladlehaus hope and then plunging him deeper into despair.

Elkin's novel portrays hell as a gulf of pain that penetrates the spirit as well as the body. His inferno is an endless, cruel wasteland of utter despair.

LOKI Loki is the trickster god of Norse myth, often identified with SATAN. He is a small, handsome, crafty fellow whose name appears more than any other deity's in Germanic/Nordic mythology. Loki is also included in other works, such as epic poem *Balder Dead* by Matthew Arnold and Wagner's opera *Die Walküre.* He is associated with fire and has a reputation as a malicious meddler who enjoys slandering and betraying others. His hobbies include lying, playing cruel

Sculpture of Loki by Scandinavian artist H. E. Freund. ART TODAY

tricks, and ridiculing his peers. Loki has no honor and shows no loyalty to anyone.

Loki is intimately connected with the infernal underworld. His daughter, goddess HEL, is the ruler of NIFLHEIM (Land of Mists) and overseer of the damned. Once an attractive figure who aided the gods, Loki is banished to the underworld after becoming increasingly hostile and deceitful. (This tale parallels the story of LUCIFER's fall from heaven.) He eventually kills a fellow deity, sealing his fate.

In the underworld, Loki prays for the prophesied "final catastrophe" in which the world will be laid to waste and the powers of evil released. Loki also enjoys advising Hel on how to inflict agony upon her subjects.

One underworld myth tells how Loki conspired to keep the beloved god Balder imprisoned in Niflheim. Balder had died and been handed over to Hel, but Balder's wife, Nanna, begged Hel to release her husband and return him to the living. Hel agreed on the condition that all creatures on earth mourn for the dead god. Loki, disguised as an old woman, refuses to shed a tear for the fallen hero. Because of this, Hel refuses to release Balder and instead sets him afire on the flaming ship of death along with the inconsolable Nanna. This trick was among Loki's favorites, and he often bragged about how he had vanquished the mighty Balder.

LUCIFER Lucifer (lover of light) is the rebellious angel of Christian doctrine who sinned against God by setting himself up as his creator's equal. After refusing to repent for his boundless pride, Lucifer is cast into hell where he now holds dominion. His subjects include the dark angels who joined him in his rebellion and the souls of the damned. After the fall, he is sometimes referred to as the DEVIL or as SATAN (although some religious scholars insist the two are separate and distinct DEMONS). In the Bible, the names are used to refer to the same fiend: "I beheld Satan as lightning fall from Heaven" (Luke 10:18).

Lucifer is described as the most beautiful of all angels, who has been given a place of honor in heaven. Yet he is not satisfied with this position and wants to overthrow God. This sin of pride brings about his banishment. After being damned to hell, Lucifer is transformed into a grotesque demon who is terrible to behold. Typical illustrations depict the fiend as a winged beast with cloven feet, horns, and a tail. He is associated with pride, vanity, and nihilism and is identified with the planet Venus (a pagan symbol), also known as the Morning Star.

Lucifer is named the king of the underworld in numerous literary and dramatic works, including *THE DIVINE COMEDY: INFERNO*, *THE PILGRIM'S PROGRESS*, and *PIERS PLOWMAN*. The fall of Lucifer and his damnation to hell are also popular themes for MORALITY PLAYS including the epic *LUCIFER* by Joost van den Vondel.

LUCIFER The drama *Lucifer*, written by Dutch playwright Joost van den Vondel in 1654, depicts the bitter consequences of placing pride above reverence to God. As the play opens, LUCIFER is a beautiful "angel of light" who enjoys a place of honor in heaven. But when he learns that God is creating a new being—humans—and will one day take human form himself, Lucifer becomes furious. He is jealous of the dignity this will confer upon humankind and disgusted that he, so splendid an angel, will have to pay homage to the Almighty incarnated as a lowly human being. Unwilling to accept the deity's plans, Lucifer plans to overthrow God and place himself on the throne of heaven.

Lucifer gathers an army of angels who share his repulsion at God's imminent incarnation, including the cunning and powerful BELIAL and Beelzebub. But before launching their rebellion, they travel to earth to tempt humans away from God in hopes of keeping the new creatures out of heaven forever. This part of the plan succeeds: Adam and Eve turn against the Father. God punishes them harshly, but not, as Lucifer expected, by barring them eternally from entering the kingdom of paradise. Lucifer is even more enraged at God's merciful treatment of these humans. He angrily unleashes his army in an assault on heaven.

A great battle ensues, but the forces of good are victorious. The defeated Lucifer declares that he would rather rule his own dark kingdom than serve in God's. Having made this choice, Lucifer is transformed into a hideous toad and cast out of heaven. He lands in a bleak abyss, devoid of the love of God and bound in unbreakable chains. The fallen angel curses his creator and his fate but refuses to repent. It is this defiance that keeps him imprisoned, for all eternity, in the pit of despair. The play concludes with the now-wretched Lucifer, despicable even to himself, sinking to the depths of his everlasting inferno.

M

MAGIC LANTERN SHOWS In the late 1800s—before the invention of motion pictures or slide presentations—people were fascinated by

Victorian era drawing of children enjoying a magic lantern show. ART TODAY

magic lantern shows. These were simply exhibitions of images projected onto walls by means of a simple light source. Showmen would illuminate painted glass panels, silhouettes, or shadow figures from behind, creating glowing pictures. In the hands of industrious ministers, this technology became a popular means of graphically illustrating HELLFIRE SERMONS.

The most effective method was to place two disks, each painted with splashy yellow and orange flames, together in the lantern. As the preacher spoke of FIRE AND BRIMSTONE, he slowly rotated the disks in opposite directions. This created a powerful and frightening image of a blazing inferno. The illusion was often enhanced by stenciling in the figure of a man. By gently shaking this disk, the image seemed to depict a condemned soul languishing in the raging fires of hell. After witnessing this disturbing vision, many hardened sinners were converted to Christianity.

Magic lantern shows, and their religious usage, died out around the turn of the century, when photography and then motion pictures captured society's collective imagination and rendered them obsolete.

MAGICIAN JAMES An illustration from an eleventh-century Anglo-Saxon manuscript titled *Magician James* depicts the grim underworld of medieval tradition. The picture shows the bodies of the damned smoldering as they burn with unquenchable fire. As they writhe in agony, snakes strike at their faces and coil around their bodies, crushing them. The DEVIL oversees this torture. He is portrayed as a humanlike creature with horribly bloated hands and long, sharp nails. His face is a grotesque mask of withered skin, piercing teeth, and haunted eyes.

The work represents the prevailing view of CHRISTIAN HELL during the Middle Ages: a horrific subterranean dungeon of brutal punishments and unrelenting agony. It also alludes to the coming rash of witch trials, which linked the magic arts to SATAN, FAIRIES, and hell.

MALIK Malik is the DEMON who rules JAHANNAM, Islamic hell. He is also responsible for bringing the souls of evil people to the underworld. The KORAN states that sinners often beg Malik to intercede for them; however, he offers no comfort. He will be silent until a millennium after the LAST JUDGMENT, at which time he will taunt sinners, declaring that their damnation is eternal.

MAMBRES The legend of Mambres dates back to the medieval days of Anglo-Saxon witchcraft. According to the tale, Mambres, grief-stricken over the death of his brother—who was reputed to be a dark wizard—uses a book of his brother's spells to try to contact the dead man's spirit. As he delivers the incantation, the jaws of hell open before him and Mambres's brother appears. But the creature Mambres sees is not the brother he remembers but rather a huge, hairy monster with his brother's face. The giant is feeding on the damned, chewing souls as they writhe in agony. Horrified, Mambres casts the spell book into hell and swears never to use magic again.

As he does this, the mouth of hell closes, and the grotesque mutation of his brother disappears. Mambres then runs off to the nearest church, where he vows upon his soul never again to dabble in the dark arts.

MAN AND SUPERMAN *Man and Superman,* written in 1905 by Irish dramatist George Bernard Shaw, offers an intriguing concept of hell, heaven, and the nature of suffering. In a dream interlude titled "DON JUAN in Hell," Shaw depicts an afterlife where salvation and damnation are simply a matter of perspective. This notion, explored in depth by WILLIAM BLAKE, suggests that some souls would find paradise insufferably dull and would welcome condemnation to the feisty inferno.

Often called "a play within a play," this portion of *Man and Superman* is frequently performed independently and has become a standard on the Broadway stage. But when "Don Juan in Hell" was first produced, many critics found Shaw's interpretation of the afterlife offensive, even blasphemous, prompting some proprietors to demand that the author include a "disclaimer" in the show's program. When London's Royal Court Theatre presented the drama in 1907, management required that Shaw justify his unconventional work. His explanation, which was distributed to all patrons, decries "legends" of hell as "a place of cruelty and punishment." To Shaw, the underworld is a realm "given wholly to pursuit of immediate individual pleasure" rather than a fiery torture chamber.

"Don Juan in Hell" has only four characters: legendary ladies' man Don Juan; Dona Ana, an object of his infatuation; Don Gonzalo of Ulloa, Commandant of Calatrava, Ana's father who was killed by Don Juan while defending his girl's honor; and LUCIFER, lord of hell. The play opens as Don Juan, long a resident of hell, welcomes the aged Dona Ana to the afterlife. Horrified at the thought that she has been damned, Ana insists that she has been unfairly condemned. The two then discuss heaven and hell, a debate eventually joined by her father (who is visiting from paradise) and Lucifer himself.

What follows is an intricate dialogue in which heaven is derided as "dull and uncomfortable" and hell extolled as "the home of honor, duty, justice and the rest of the seven deadly virtues." Don Juan notes that "all the wickedness on earth is done in their name." Even the commandant (who has taken the form of his memorial statue) declares of the underworld that "the best people are here!" whereas the citizens of paradise are the "dullest dogs" of honor, "not beautiful, but decorated." Before deciding to remain forever in hell's "palace of pleasure," the commandant admits that he fought for Ana not out of love or devotion but because it was his "duty," and he worried that refusing to do so would sully his reputation.

Don Juan, on the other hand, is revealed as a man so thoroughly committed to finding the deeper meaning in life that he could not be satisfied with human love. It was this hunger for purpose and not carnal lust that caused him to go from woman to woman in a futile search for fulfillment. In hell, his desire for infinite knowledge is further frustrated. The Don laments that although he suffers no physical agony, the underworld "bores me beyond description, beyond belief." In Shaw's estimation, hell is a place of gratification, whereas heaven is a realm of contemplation. Meditation before the Almighty, a fate the superficial commandant finds unbearably tedious, would be ultimate bliss for Don Juan.

A similar analogy appears in AUCASSIN AND NICOLETTE, a French drama in which the star-crossed lovers vow they would rather suffer together in the depths of hell with other "interesting" heroes than languish in a celibate heaven filled with "dull" saints.

MANALA According to the myths of Finland-Ugaria, souls of the dead travel to Manala, the "land beneath the earth." The passage to this underworld is at the mouth of a river that opens to an ocean of ice. Dead souls cross the river, then follow an enchanted bird to the gate of Manala. Unhappy spirits linger at the entrance, haunting rivers and lakes in protest of their fate.

Manala's ruler is Nga, an overseer who also controls the spirits that cause sickness and death.

Since Manala has no light of its own, the dead must take a spare sun or moon with them to the underworld. Those shapes are often engraved onto tombstones for the dead person's use in the afterlife. Physically, the underworld is thought to be quite similar to the terrestrial plain, sharing the same plant life and geological features.

The dead are buried with their own clan in family cemeteries in the belief that the departed dwell directly under their tombs and want to remain close to their loved ones. In their new existence, inhabitants of Manala are vaguely aware of what is going on above them but cannot interact with the living. They survive on offerings of fruit, bread, and other foods brought to their graves by relatives.

Death is considered a transference to another state rather than a time of judgment, and residence in Manala is temporary. After a brief time lingering in this realm, souls die a "second death" when family members stop bringing offerings of food to the grave site. Spirits eventually fade completely (a version of ANNIHILATION), though many believe that departed souls can be reincarnated in the bodies of grandchildren and future generations.

MARDUK Marduk is the ancient Mesopotamian god of the underworld. He is an abominable beast associated with plagues and horrible deaths. In addition to abusing damned souls, Marduk can attack the living. He is considered particularly evil and sadistic among the dark deities of CHTHONIC lore.

MATEXZUNGUA Mythology of the Sioux of North America includes Matexzungua, the lord of the dead. Matexzungua lives in the north, in a place of insufferable cold and perpetual blizzards. His task is to torture the souls of evil people in his PURGATORIAL HELL. Once they have been cleansed of their wickedness, these spirits are allowed to journey to a tropical paradise located in the south.

MEDIEVAL DRAMA European drama took a four-hundred-year hiatus between 533 A.D., the date of the last public performance in Rome, until the tenth century, when Roman Catholic church officials began producing dramatizations of religious doctrines. These first performances were crude retellings of supernatural events such as the expulsion of LUCIFER from heaven, the HARROWING OF HELL, and the LAST JUDGMENT. Each different setting—heaven, hell, the Garden of Eden—was represented by a wooden booth, with actors moving from one to the next as the plot unfolded. Early medieval plays were strictly overseen by church officials, but by the late 1300s, most public dramas were produced by craft guilds dedicated to theatrical arts.

Some of the most powerful scenes in these dramas invoked images of the underworld. In *Fall of Lucifer,* the DEVIL declares, "I make my way to Hell to be thrust into torment without end!" The villain of an early passion play introduces himself to the audience with, "I am your Lord Lucifer that came out of Hell! I am called SATAN!" Another play of the period shows Judas writhing in infernal torment for betraying Christ. Such graphic portrayals of the inferno became progressively more horrific and complex as audiences grew and staging techniques evolved.

As the plays became less a province of the church and more an entertainment form, texts strayed from literal biblical interpretations to more speculative treatments of the supernatural. Depictions of the Antichrist and of the horrors of hell became the biggest crowd pleasers. Innovative set designers constructed the theatrical HELL-MOUTH, a trapdoor that opened from below to spew fireworks, noxious fumes, and horrible sound effects, to further tantalize audiences and boost attendance.

The resurgence in popularity of public performances eventually branched off into several different areas. MYSTERY PLAYS treated aspects of the supernatural but with increasing emphasis on the occult, FAIRIES, and other subjects frowned on by church hierarchy. Christian authorities began funneling their efforts into MORALITY PLAYS, dramas that adhered strictly to the teachings and events of the Bible. FOLK PLAYS, a less polished version of theater, also became increasingly popular throughout Europe. These dramas could be satirical or even irreverent, as in the case of the comic *Mankind*. This late fifteenth-century tale told the story of a "sinner" using obscene JOKES, jabs at church doctrine, and interaction with audience members. Unlike morality plays, the point of these performances was to entertain rather than educate.

Medieval dramas also began the evolution of theater that resulted in the rise of such literary geniuses as William Shakespeare, Christopher Marlowe (author of a FAUST play), and a host of European dramatists.

MEFISTOFELE Arrigo Boito brought the FAUST legend to Milan's operator stage in 1868 with his flamboyant *Mefistofele.* Set in medieval times, the opera opens as the DEMON Mefistofele (MEPHISTOPHELES) brags that he can tempt any man away from God and that finding souls to add to the legions of hell is ridiculously simple. No sooner has he made this boast than the vain scholar Faust offers to surrender his soul to the netherworld in exchange for "enlightenment" about the mysteries of the universe. The DEVIL agrees and promises to show Faust the hidden truths of humanity.

The two embark on a journey toward the "Valley of Schirk" down a lonely road to the abode of SATAN. They arrive at the infernal fortress, a place of flames, tortures, and a thousand screaming voices, on Walpurgis Night, the witches' sabbath. Faust watches the dance of the wizards with an exhilarating mix of excitement and terror. A coven of warlocks invites Faust to stir the black caldron and join in the revelry.

Through the next three acts, Mefistofele shows Faust "the Real and the Ideal," satisfying his thirst for "human wisdom and knowing." In the process, Faust seduces and then betrays "love" in the form of a human woman and of a goddess. Eventually, he sees the sorrow of humankind and laments his role in perpetuating that sadness. At last, the "death trumpet" sounds, and it is time to deliver his soul to damnation. But Faust repents at last and begs for mercy. A fierce battle breaks out between the forces of good and evil, the prize being his soul. Good ultimately prevails, and as Faust is received into heaven, Mefistofele sinks into murky hell, vowing to renew his diabolical efforts to corrupt all humanity.

MEMNOCH THE DEVIL

Novelist Anne Rice, famed author of macabre books about VAMPIRES, takes on the ultimate supernatural plotlines in her 1995 best-seller, *Memnoch the Devil.* This fifth and last in the Vampire Lestat series sends the undead cad through space and time and ultimately to heaven and hell. Highlights of Lestat's epic trek include witnessing the Crucifixion, losing an eye in a brutal underworld accident, and enthusiastically drinking menstrual blood. Between these escapades, Rice devotes the majority of her text to convoluted (and sometimes incoherent) theories about the nature of God, the evils of organized religion, and the "ever unfolding" process of evolution.

Approached by SATAN as he stalks his latest victim, Lestat is told "I need you" to assist in the battle for humanity. Satan, who now refers to himself as Memnoch, then takes Lestat on a tour of history, stopping to watch the fall of the rebel angels, the expulsion of Adam and Eve from the Garden of Eden, and other historic events before taking him to the land of the dead. Afterward, he demands that Lestat make a choice: Will he serve God or the DEVIL?

The underworld of Rice's imagination is the grim, dusty, somber SHEOL of ancient Hebrew tradition. In Sheol, departed spirits endure a bleak and unrewarding existence in an "awful, gloom-filled place" but suffer no physical pain. Their only sorrow is loss of their sensual earthly life and separation from God. In *Memnoch,* the souls in Sheol are further tormented by the belief that their Creator has abandoned them and forgotten his precious children. They struggle to "forgive" God for his cold indifference, but their hearts ache with a bitter, forlorn sadness.

Memnoch, a stylized version of traditional Satan, is depicted as an angel who has sinned by refusing to accept God's new creation—the material world. In an attempt to understand its mysteries, he takes on flesh and visits the earth. Memnoch immediately succumbs to the sensual delights of his human body and begins indulging in sexual intercourse with the "Daughters of Men." God demands that Memnoch return to heaven and account for these offenses against the "Divine Plan."

But instead of apologizing and asking forgiveness, Memnoch rebukes God for abandoning humans to "corrupted ideas . . . and instinctive fear." Angered that Memnoch places allegiance to humans over obedience to the Almighty, God sentences him to become "the Beast of God" on earth. He is damned to rule in hell and to be hideous to the human beings he so dearly loves.

According to Rice's theological vision, Memnoch gladly accepts this new role, determined to use his powers to save souls rather than destroy them. He declares, "I will bring more souls through Sheol to Heaven than you will bring by your direct Gate." Thus the underworld becomes a sort of PURGATORIAL HELL where human spirits cleanse themselves of unworthiness before ascending to heaven. Memnoch transforms the murky land of SHADES into a battlefield of frightening images and grisly phantoms, where souls must learn to forgive themselves for the atrocities they once committed. After matriculating in this infernal "school," the damned graduate to paradise.

Rice's novel stirred considerable controversy at the time of its publication for what many considered to be blasphemous treatments of God, Jesus Christ, and many important events in Christian history. According to the book, it is Memnoch, not Christ, who is responsible for the HARROWING OF HELL and for the release of souls languishing in Sheol. Sending Jesus to earth as the divine incarnation is likewise done at Memnoch's prompting, since the DEMON suggests that this will help the Creator become more empathetic with humanity. *Memnoch* consistently portrays this fallen angel as a sympathetic, compassionate being while God comes across as an egotistical tyrant with no regard for the welfare of humankind. Rice's depiction of hell has also been rejected by various religious scholars as ridiculous, illogical, and theologically absurd.

MEMORIALS Images of the underworld have been found on memorials throughout the globe. These include sarcophagi, tombs, mosaics, and other tributes to the revered dead. The earliest examples date back centuries before Christ, when Egyptians, Greeks, and ETRUSCANS alike burned with incessant curiosity about the afterlife. An ocean away, ancient Peruvian Indians were likewise embroidering images of CHTHONIC GHOULS tormenting human souls on death shrouds and burial wraps.

Relics of ancient Greece, such as intricate vases, murals, and carvings on tombs, often depict HADES and PERSEPHONE, the king and queen of the underworld. Families of the departed would place such images near the dead to try to win favor with the deities. Many believed that by honoring Hades and Persephone in this way, their loved ones would elude the horrors of the underworld and enjoy a more restful afterlife. Such compositions might also include other icons of Greek chthonic myth, such as the ferryman CHARON, the river STYX, and the monstrous guard dog CERBERUS.

A tomb found in the ancient city of Thebes is similarly decorated with pictures of souls riding across the river of death to the underworld. Mingled with the pleasant symbols of paradise are horrific scenes of the damned suffering in unending agony. Similar illustrations adorn sarcophagi discovered in Bologna and Volterra. Etruscan mortuaries reflect that culture's obsession with death and the afterlife. Early tombs showed great feasts and celebrations, but these portraits later gave way to frightening depictions of underworld torture.

Detail of *Charon Ferrying Souls on the River Styx*, marble relief from a sarcophagus. ERICH LESSING/ART RESOURCE, NY

Ancient Egyptians decorated tombs with elaborate pictures of the afterlife, usually focusing on rich rewards in the next realm. Figures of Anubis and OSIRIS have been identified on numerous necropolises (cities intended for use by the dead). Many show the supernatural beast AMMUT waiting to devour the hearts of souls judged unworthy of paradise.

The spread of Judaism and Christianity largely ended the practice of using infernal images as ornamentation on memorials. Rituals designed to soothe and appease dark lords of the underworld were largely condemned as pagan magic by both Hebrew and Christian authorities. Clerics instead began stressing the ability of humanity to attain salvation by accepting the word of God, living a virtuous life, and asking for divine forgiveness. With this positive approach in mind, Christians and Jews began marking their graves with images of hope. Among followers of Christ, crosses (the symbol of redemption), Bible verses, and angelic figures became popular, while Jews routinely display the Star of David and comforting words of the Hebrew prophets.

MEPHISTOPHELES

Mephistopheles is one of the DEMONS of hell according to Christian literature and legend. He is mentioned in virtually every version of the FAUST story as the infernal agent who entices the scholar to sell his soul to the DEVIL. Mephistopheles is a shape-shifter who assumes many forms to tempt Faust and who can grant many supernatural powers. The fiend also takes Faust on a tour of hell to show the damned man what awaits him in the afterlife. In

Christopher Marlowe's version of the Faust tragedy, the demon goes even further, stating that he is the very embodiment of hell. When Faust asks how it is that the demon can leave the underworld, Mephistopheles responds, "Why, this *is* Hell, nor am I out of it."

Mephistopheles has since become synonymous with the devil. Popular music icon Sting mentions the demon in his 1983 hit "Wrapped Around Your Finger," likening the evil spirit to a beautiful—but forbidden—lover who can bring only sorrow and angst to her obsessed admirer. The host of hell has also inspired numerous plays, paintings, and works of music such as Arrigo Boito's 1868 opera *MEFISTOFELE*.

MERLIN Merlin, the mystic wizard of Arthurian legend, is in some accounts the child of the DEVIL and part of a plot formed in hell. According to the story, the minions of hell conspire to aid an evil king, Vortigern, in conquering his enemies. They believe that his temporal victories will result in the damnation of many souls, thus increasing their infernal kingdom. But in order to win this diabolical assistance, Vortigern's fortress must be fortified with the sacrifice of a fatherless child. So the DEMONS arrange to impregnate a virgin with SATAN's seed.

The girl succumbs to the seduction and becomes pregnant. Regretting her sin, she seeks the advice of the wise cleric, Blaise, who vows to help thwart the devil's plans. He hides the girl in a remote tower until she gives birth to a son. As soon as the child is born, Blaise baptizes him in the name of the Christian Trinity, calling the boy Merlin. Since he has been consecrated to Christ, he can no longer be used as a human sacrifice to the vile Satan. However, the boy has inherited tremendous mystic powers from his supernatural father. Much to the fury of the demons of hell, he uses these powers for good rather than evil.

Merlin is credited with many superhuman feats. Legend claims that at age five he successfully defended his mother in a notorious witch trial. He also had visions of otherworldly events that helped him give counsel to kings. The gifted sorcerer could shape-shift into many animal and human forms. Some accounts say that Merlin erected Stonehenge in a single night during the dark of the moon. His most famous role, however, is as adviser to the legendary King Arthur of the Round Table.

Legends also differ on how Merlin meets his demise. Some stories claim that he is tricked by the Lady of the Lake and damned to spend eternity in the trunk of an enchanted tree. Other versions state that he did not die, but lives on to this day in an underground library where he continues to study and philosophize. A particularly somber tale says that he accidentally sat in the Siege Perilous, the seat at the Round Table left empty to represent Judas and to warn against betrayal. When he sat down, a crack in the earth opened and Merlin was pulled down to the abyss. In any event, Merlin remains a perennial figure in the Arthurian legend cycle and tales of his extraordinary wisdom and powers persist.

MERRY HELL Though most interpretations of hell depict a horrid realm of misery, there is an opposite model of the underworld: a merry hell where those devoid of virtue experience an eternity of drinking, wantonness, and camaraderie. This glamorous inferno is presented as an attractive alternative to a "boring" heaven of stern do-gooders and sullen saints.

The play *THE FROGS,* written by Greek author Aristophanes in 405 B.C., first introduced the idea of a merry hell to the stage. In a parody of Greek tragedy, the underworld kingdom of HADES is portrayed as an ongoing party where singing amphibians, not fearsome monsters, stand guard. *The Frogs* was immensely popular with audiences who had grown weary of terrifying tales of a wretched afterlife awaiting them in the next realm.

This satirical treatment of the abyss evolved over the years, reaching its height in European MEDIEVAL DRAMA. Plays of this period featured fools costumed as DEMONS who ran out into the audience belching, shouting obscenities, and passing gas. They invited spectators to join them in the eternal "celebration" in the abyss. More elaborate productions included fireworks and small explosions to add glamour and excitement to the infernal foray.

MYSTERY PLAYS, dramas based on supernatural events of both pagan and Christian traditions, likewise depict the underworld as a magical place of merriment and feasting. *The Devil Is an Ass,* produced in 1616, shows SATAN as a comic buffoon attended by his minions, a colorful assortment of likable characters. And the early twentieth-century Off-Broadway production *Hell,* hosted by "Mr. and Mrs. DEVIL," was declared a "profane burlesque," raucous and rowdy in its irreverence. Similar depictions of a happy hell appear in *AUCASSIN AND NICOLETTE* and *MAN AND SUPERMAN.*

Today, the concept of a merry hell remains popular. Americans poke fun at the underworld through infernal JOKES, BUMPER STICKERS, CARTOONS, and T-SHIRTS. Performances involving a wickedly amusing inferno also abound. Modern examples of this hellish humor can be found on television programs *LATE SHOW WITH DAVID LETTERMAN, SATURDAY NIGHT LIVE,* and *KIDS IN THE HALL.*

MICHELANGELO Renaissance master Michelangelo Buonarroti (1475–1564), artist, sculptor, poet, and architect, is considered by many to be the greatest artist in history. Born and raised in Florence, Michelangelo produced great works of CHURCH ART AND ARCHITECTURE in his beloved homeland and in Rome. His 1496 *Pietà,* which depicts a grief-stricken VIRGIN MARY cradling the lifeless body of her crucified son, won him worldwide acclaim and launched a career that continued for seven decades.

The prolific artist drew much of his inspiration from religion (he was a devout Roman Catholic) and concentrated on producing works depicting religious heroes. During his lifetime, he composed statues, paintings, and frescoes of biblical figures such as Moses, David, Adam, angels, and even the Almighty himself. But his creations also reflect the sorrows of his life: political unrest in Italy, recurring clashes of will between the temperamental genius and his often equally stubborn clients, and anxiety about the afterlife.

Michelangelo's LAST JUDGMENT reflects his fascination with what awaits people on the other side of the grave. The massive work (considered the greatest interpretation of the subject ever painted) depicts stunned sinners disembarking from a somber boat ride into the land of the damned. Traditional IMAGERY of hell abounds: skeletons, snakes, and loathsome DEMONS. Jesus is depicted not as a gentle advocate but as a stern judge in the act of dispatching souls to unending torment. The mood of the painting is unsettling; the gallery of faces wrenched in agony conjures a sense of utter despair. So moving was his work that when Pope Paul III saw it for the first time, he fell to his knees and begged for divine mercy.

The artist includes some familiar faces among the damned. The likeness of papal master of ceremonies Biagio da Cesena, who upon seeing the *Last Judgment* before its completion denounced the work as "obscene," can be seen in the face of MINOS, prince of hell. But Michelangelo does not limit his speculation about destiny to others; he has painted himself in the inferno as a flailed skin.

As Michelangelo aged, it was not beauty but faith that increasingly fueled his creativity. His later works depict subjects as "real" rather than "ideal," recognizing the vulnerability of human souls. He continued to interpret religious themes while constantly speculating on his own ultimate fate. In his waning years, the artist referred to himself as having "a heart of flaming sulphur," an ancient biblical symbol of hell.

Michelangelo died at age eighty-nine while working on a revised statue of Old Testament hero King David. This version shows the man's human frailties rather than depicts him as the flawless ideal. The artist went to his death terrified of facing the infernal visions of his imagination yet hopeful that God's infinite mercy would spare him from the terrors of hell.

MICTLAN The Aztecs, indigenous to central Mexico, believe the dead depart to Mictlan, a place of malaise rather than terror, but certainly no paradise. Mictlan is an arid desert where spirits shift aimlessly about in eternal tedium. They are not tortured but must endure this unending monotony. In addition to housing the dead, Mictlan contains the bones of an earlier race.

Mictlantecutli, the lord of the sojourn of the dead, rules the underworld with his wife, Mictlantecihuatl. He is depicted as an open-mouthed monster waiting to devour souls or as an owl clutching a skull and crossbones. The trickster god is associated with the color red. When the Christian missionaries began evangelizing Mexico, Mictlan was equated with SATAN, vicious tormentor of the dead.

This mythological underworld and its grim ruler are embellished in the SHORT STORY "The Road to Mictlantecutli," written by Adobe James in 1965. In James's adaptation, Mictlan is a horrific hell where evil souls face retribution for their sins.

MIDER Mider is the god of the underworld according to ancient Gaelic myth. He is a just overlord who does not torture spirits in his kingdom. His realm is a place of tedium and sorrow rather than physical pain. Mider has a magic caldron capable of performing supernatural feats. However, his daughter betrays him and helps the hero Cuchulain steal it from the underworld.

MILITARY INSIGNIA
Throughout history, soldiers from around the world have incorporated infernal IMAGERY into their insignia. Examples of this date back centuries, to the first warriors who marched beneath flags emblazoned with such underworld images as DEMONS, DEVILS, flaming landscapes, tridents, pitchforks, and charred skeletal remains. The practice continues as modern elite troops both here and abroad proudly display logos featuring all manner of ghastly specters.

Contemporary examples of this abound: a French Special Forces patch depicts a green, horned devil toting menacing weaponry. Similar graphics adorn the uniforms of Italian Elite soldiers; these show a fierce SATAN wielding lightning bolts. American troops likewise borrow images from hell to strike terror into the hearts of their enemies. Popular infernal symbols include snakes, lizards, winged demons, flaming skulls, and vicious beasts analogous to the evil LEVIATHAN. The Grim Reaper (a derivative of Briton lord of hell ANKOU) makes an appearance on a U.S. Marines patch, straddling the word *Deathwatch*. Others simply include the word *hell* in their designs, conjuring fearsome images of the fiery underworld.

Easily the most recognizable use of afterlife imagery in military insignia is

U.S. Army's 2nd Armor Division emblem

the SWASTIKA, used by the Nazis in the early part of the century. The origin of the swastika remains unknown, but representations of the symbol have been found on ancient relics of many civilizations. It is a sacred symbol in religions that teach reincarnation, used to illustrate the possible fates of the human soul. Each of the four branches depicts a specific judgment: to be reborn as a human, to be confined to the body of an animal, to be elevated to union with the gods, or to be damned to hell.

Adolf Hitler was fascinated with ancient religions and saw the swastika as an emblem of sacred power. Using the basic design, his designers developed the *hakenkreuz* (hooked cross) to identify Hitler's faithful. It was adopted as the official Nazi insignia in 1935 and was added to all banners of the Third Reich. Deeply superstitious, the Führer sought to give his troops a supernatural edge over the enemy and believed that forces marching under the mystic symbol would be unstoppable.

MINOS Minos is a judge of the dead according to both Greek and Roman legend. The underworld lord is derived from tales of a vicious king infamous for his tyranny. King Minos forced captured warriors and other prisoners to fight bulls in his labyrinth, a maze on the isle of Crete, for his amusement. They were not expected to survive the ordeal but to provide a good show for the king as their bodies were torn to bloody ribbons by the beasts. According to the tales, the vile king is eventually killed by one of his prisoners and thus became an overlord in HADES.

Minos appears in a number of works of art and literature. He is named as one of the judges of the underworld in the ancient *GORGIAS* by Plato. In Dante's *DIVINE COMEDY: THE INFERNO,* he sits at the entrance of hell and determines to which circle of the abyss damned souls will be sent. Minos is similarly represented in the *ODYSSEY,* Homer's epic account of a supernatural journey, and in Virgil's *AENEID.* Art scholars identify Minos in RODIN's sculpture *GATES OF HELL* and in MICHELANGELO's *LAST JUDGMENT.*

Stephen King's 1994 novel *ROSE MADDER* alludes to the ancient Minos as a bloodthirsty bull at the center of a subterranean maze. The malicious beast displays a callous disregard for human feelings and a disturbing capacity for cruelty. In a climax reminiscent of Greek epic quests, King Minos is challenged by the story's heroine in a grisly confrontation of brute force and blind faith.

MORALITY PLAYS In the 1300s, church officials decided that MYSTERY PLAYS, dramas centering on Christian teachings about heaven, hell, and redemption, were becoming too secular. Religious leaders felt that the plays titillated rather than terrified audiences with lavish hell scenes, many of which depicted a MERRY HELL of eternal wantonness and carousing. Churches banned the offending productions and began offering morality plays. These productions adhered strictly to biblical text and official Christian doctrines. They often focused on the common person's fight against evil in everyday life (represented by the DEVIL incarnate).

Common themes for these dramas included the war in heaven, creation of the earth, the HARROWING OF HELL, the prophesied apocalypse, the LAST JUDGMENT, and sufferings of the damned. Abstractions such as Lust, Honor, Obedience, and Gluttony were often personified and became the heroes and villains of these cautionary tales. Theatrical sets included elaborate HELLMOUTHS featuring dazzling emissions of smoke, fumes, and shrieks designed graphically to depict the horrors of the damned.

The 1654 production *LUCIFER* contains extensive scenes set in the underworld. DEMONS, gleeful when they learn that Adam has sinned, conspire to cause the damnation of generations of humanity. As the play proceeds, the condemned begin filling hell, wailing and cursing their fate. But when Christ arrives to harrow hell, he binds Lucifer's hands and feet and takes the souls of the faithful with him to heaven. The savior then locks the doors of hell forever, leaving the demons in amplified agony. Such productions often used fireworks, explosions, and primitive pyrotechnic effects to create the great inferno.

The most famous morality play ever written is *EVERYMAN,* first performed around the year 1500. This English drama depicts the soul's journey to the afterlife. When a typical sinner is called before the throne of God to face possible damnation, he must enlist the aid of a variety of virtues, renounce many vices and learn true contrition.

Morality plays began losing their appeal around the seventeenth century, when drama became the province of professional writers and performers. Today, revivals of such productions as *Lucifer* and *Everyman* are lauded for their historic importance and artistic merit rather than their religious educational value.

MOT Mot is the ancient Canaanite god of death and the archenemy of the benevolent god Baal. The legend of their battle, which dates back more than four thousand years, describes how Baal banishes Mot from the earth and confines him to the underworld. Unwilling to admit defeat, Mot dares Baal to visit him to the dark, foul-smelling land of the dead. Baal accepts this challenge, with disastrous results.

When Baal arrives, Mot forces him to eat mud, the "food of the dead." This proves fatal, and Mot gloats that now Baal is in *his* kingdom and things are going to change. But Baal's wife, Anat, refuses to surrender her husband so easily. She lures Mot out of his murky realm, then murders him and grinds up his body. A truce is eventually struck, and Baal returns to the heavens while Mot is restored to the underworld, where he must confine his exploits to torturing the damned.

MOVIE MERCHANDISING

Infernal movie merchandising began as early as the 1960s with Aurora Plastics' "monster kits" costing about $1 each. These glow-in-the-dark models promised "supernatural realism" of such screen fiends as the Wolfman, the VAMPIRE Count Dracula, and the Frankenstein Monster. The eerie kits were an instant hit, especially among adolescent boys. (Comparable models by Monogram Luminator currently sell for around $15.) Homage was paid to these terrifying toys in Stephen King's *Salem's Lot,* a film about vampires overrunning a New England village.

From such humble beginnings, underworld movie merchandising has boomed into a multimillion-dollar industry. Over the past few decades, retailers have jammed store shelves with *NIGHTMARE ON ELM STREET* board games, *BILL & TED'S BOGUS JOURNEY* Grim Reaper dolls, and *HELLRAISER* Halloween masks. CHTHONIC movie villains can be found on watches, posters, makeup kits, COMIC BOOKS, action figures, stickers, and TRADING CARDS. Even "family-oriented entertainment" giant Disney Studios is getting into the act, peddling a vast array of trinkets depicting Greek lord of the dead HADES from its ANIMATED CARTOON adaptation of the HERCULES legend. These include water globes with revolving "scenes from the underworld" and a limited-edition wristwatch that "flames" at the press of a button.

Savvy promoters have taken hellish marketing a step further through tie-ins

An assortment of promotional items from films on the supernatural.

with other consumer outlets. Fast-food chain Burger King offered free *BEETLEJUICE* and *Ghostbusters* toys with its children's meals. Video renters were given the opportunity to collect actual scripts, press kits, and other memorabilia from Full Moon Entertainment's supernatural thrillers *DARK ANGEL: THE ASCENT, Lurking Fear,* and *Castle Freak.* Cereal manufacturers began distributing *Bill & Ted's Bogus Journey* cassette tape holders and *Addams Family* flashlights with every "specially marked box" sold.

Not surprisingly, the success of memorabilia adorned with movie scenes of hell has now spawned a cottage industry of secondary trade. Publications like the defunct *TWILIGHT ZONE MAGAZINE* and the current *Sci-Fi* are filled with advertisements offering promotional items from infernal films released years ago. A quick scan reveals enticements to purchase *Nightmare Before Christmas* stuffed dolls, *Outer Limits* collector cards, and Freddy Kruger "razor gloves." There is also a heavy exchange of "vintage" marketing memorabilia at trade shows and flea markets around the country. With interest—and profits—in such memorabilia running high, the trend in mass-marketing of CHTHONIC movie merchandise promises to continue with no end in sight. As long as big-budget films about hell continue to be popular, the deluge of promotional items will likewise flow.

MUHAMMAD Muhammad (570–632), the prophet of Islam, claimed to have visited heaven and hell as part of a holy pilgrimage that led him to the "truths of Islam." This supernatural journey is recorded in a first-person account similar to Dante's *DIVINE COMEDY: THE INFERNO.* In the narrative, Muhammad vividly describes the terrain and inhabitants of JAHANNAM (hell) and offers warnings on how to avoid damnation.

The prophet Muhammad, founder of Islam.
ART TODAY

According to his account, the angel Jibril (Gabriel) appears to Muhammad in 610 and reveals to him divine truth, which Muhammad transcribes. This text, known as the KORAN, is the holy book of Islam, their equivalent of the Christian Bible. Muhammad calls this writ the "word of Allah" (God). The Koran teaches that the soul is "prone to evil," but Allah is a loving and merciful deity who gives humankind the tools necessary to attain salvation.

IBLIS (SATAN), the archfiend who opposes Allah, furiously toils to steer souls away from the truth and cause them to spend eternity in unrelenting agony. He manifests himself to Muhammad in many forms: a dog, a goat, a black DEMON riding a dark stallion, and a blaspheming Allah. As part of the revelation the prophet tours Iblis's kingdom of hell, a place so thick with DEVILS that he cannot drop a pin without hitting one.

Muhammad also warns of the impending Last Day (sometimes called Day of Decision), a LAST JUDGMENT that will occur at the end of time. On the Last Day—a date known only to Allah—the soul of every person who has ever lived will be called before the Divine Throne to account for its life. Worthy souls will be allowed to enter paradise, but the spirits of the wicked will be damned to Jahannam, where they will eventually face ANNIHILATION.

Muhammad is held in great esteem by followers of Islam throughout the world. In 1988, Salman Rushdie angered millions of devout Muslims with his novel *THE SATANIC VERSES,* which describes a shallow and self-serving false prophet who is obviously patterned after Muhammad. The book was denounced in many countries, banned in others, and even resulted in a "death sentence" being placed on the author by some Muslim extremists.

MU-MONTO Mu-monto is a figure of Siberian mythology who visits the underworld and witnesses the rewards and punishments of the afterlife. Hoping to retrieve a stallion sacrificed to the memory of his father, Mumonto travels to the far north seeking the entrance to the place of the dead. After overcoming many obstacles, he comes upon an enchanted boulder that separates the underworld from the land of the living. When he lifts the massive rock, a black fox crawls out and offers to escort him to the underworld.

Mu-monto accompanies the fox to the afterlife and learns that in death, justice is meted out according to the type of life each person has lived. There is no barrier between souls receiving reward and those being punished; it is the *manner* in which a person spends eternity that determines whether he or she is in paradise or hell. Unfaithful wives are stripped naked and lashed to sharp briars, and gossips have their mouths sewn shut. But those who were poor in life enjoy great banquets and fine wines; the sick and weak are healthy and vibrant. Mumonto returns to his village with a warning to all that their actions in this life will indeed have dire consequences in the next.

MUSIC VIDEOS Ever since Elvis Presley scandalized millions with his onstage pelvic thrusts, rock and roll has been dubbed "the music of rebellion." In this art form-turned-industry, artists frequently express the restlessness of youth by challenging the older generation's traditions, and religion and morality are favorite targets. The more the Establishment protests, the more outrageous the spectacles become.

Rapid advances in technology brought performances into every

American household via television. By the 1960s, top-selling artists were seen regularly on a variety of national programs. These televised performances evolved into short cinematic productions—music videos—and quickly became as popular as the songs themselves. Music videos proliferated, and by the early 1980s they were as essential to the success of a musical release as the audio recording. Shrewd marketing agents discovered that atrocious images yield massive publicity—and correspondingly elevated sales—and soon artists were gleefully including hell, SATAN, DEMONS, and orgies of the damned in their music video clips.

Hell has both visual appeal and psychological attraction for many performers. It is a sensual, exhilarating realm populated with those who brazenly indulge their wanton, carnal desires, celebrating rather than condemning the sex, drugs, and rock and roll lifestyle. And perhaps even more significant, the inferno is despised and decried by the older generation as a forbidden zone to be shunned and avoided. Directors blend these concepts into a MERRY HELL inhabited by scantily clad, voluptuous beauties, tanned musclemen, and grinning fiends engaged in a perpetual party. The intended viewers—teens and young adults—can assert their independence, assail their parents' values, and flout societal mores simply by tuning in and singing along.

Of course, some infernal music videos are more playful than derisive. Bananarama's 1986 clip for "Venus" features a leggy brunette sporting a skin-tight red leather DEVIL outfit complete with horns and tail. As she dances through a rocky terrain licked with flames, charred hands grab at her from a steamy pit. While this teasing ritual plays out, the song's lyrics repeatedly probe "what's your desire?"

Other artists incorporate more frightening visuals of the underworld into their videos. 1980s superstar Billy Idol routinely romped with an array of accursed creatures while crooning his macabre melodies. His "White Wedding" hosts a chapelful of undead guests scowling and howling at the bride and groom. In "Dancing with Myself," Idol goes Hollywood, featuring among the "animated corpses" a hellion originally designed for and used in the horror film *POLTERGEIST.*

COUNTRY MUSIC, too, has prowled the depths of hell for interesting video footage. 4 Runner's hit "Cain's Blood" and Mark O'Connor's "The Devil Goes Back to Georgia" offer flashy images of CHRISTIAN HELL. Both songs weave passages from the Bible into the lyrics and offer cautionary tales about damnation. The accompanying visuals suggest a hell of leaping flames, smoldering landscapes, and flowing lava. And unlike its rock and roll counterparts, country music's inferno is a place of punishment and terror rather than an eternal festival of the flesh.

Even "neo-classical" music is getting into the infernal act. A visual adaptation of Andrew Lloyd Weber's title song from *Phantom of the Opera* contains symbols from ancient CHTHONIC myths. The promotional video shows a boat navigating the river STYX, silent ferryman CHARON, and the kingdom of HADES from the underworld of Greek legend.

The undisputed master of hell in modern music is HEAVY METAL MUSIC, and nowhere is that more evident than in music video clips. From the first airings of NBC's *Friday Night Videos* (a precursor to Music Television [MTV]) and other similar programs, a host of self-proclaimed Satanists and death-obsessed performers belted out their ballads before a burning, beastly backdrop. Fans of the genre, typically dressed all in black and sporting demonic TATTOOS, were mesmerized by the unorthodox visuals. Underworld scenery had found its viewing audience.

Dio's video for the 1984 hit "The Last in Line" blends images of courage, mythic quests, and divine retribution. The clip shows an odious fiend overseeing an assembly line of damned humans slaving in a steamy orange pit. Leather-clad lead singer Ronny James Dio moans, "We are after the witch, we may never, never, never return," as he wades through the murky mess in an attempt to free the lost souls. Dio's brash style and unflinching valor recall centuries-old MORALITY PLAYS, in which heroes face demons and imperil their lives in the name of honor.

By the dawn of the 1990s, hell had become equated in many artists' viewpoint with the specter of nuclear annihilation. This is reflected in several of British band Iron Maiden's videos in which warmongers are the demons who threaten humanity. In "Can I Play with Madness?" a schoolboy grows bored with the incessant droning of his uninspired teacher. He flees the classroom and discovers a passageway to the underworld. Crawling through, he finds a realm of violence, pain, and senseless destruction. The enraged professor follows the child, representing the inescapable reach of authority, both civic and divine.

One of the most popular Heavy Metal groups of the decade, Guns 'n' Roses, blurs the line between the agony of life and the horrors of damnation. The 1991 video for "Don't Cry" shows lead singer Axl Rose trapped in a dark grave. Another scene includes the ghost image of a newspaper bearing the headline "Hell Revisited." The shivering, naked Rose ultimately visits a gloomy morgue, where his dead body is being examined. His hell is the icy cold of isolation and alienation rather than a chaotic, blazing inferno.

At the height of their popularity, these and other Heavy Metal videos were showcased on MTV in a regular program called *Headbangers' Ball.* (The term refers to the typical "dance" associated with Metal music, in which listeners violently rock their heads back and forth along with the beat.) The show was hosted by "Metal enthusiast" Riki Rachtman, who had been a devotee of the genre long before Music Television hit the airwaves. Each hour-long episode was packed with images of the abyss, grotesque demons, and hellish artwork. *Headbangers' Ball* was canceled when "alternative" music began gaining in popularity, greatly diminishing the prominence of Heavy Metal and its filmed performances.

Today, hell still surfaces occasionally in a variety of videos for rap, urban contemporary, and "grunge" songs. The music of Generation X, and its visuals, are considered pessimistic and cynical, often depicting the world as a joyless realm that must be endured rather than celebrated. With this prevailing attitude, the prospect of damnation is a hollow threat that generates more snickers than shudders. Hell has lost its capacity to shock and horrify, perhaps from overexposure during the past decades.

MYSTERY PLAYS Mystery plays describe a diverse genre of drama. Productions range from ancient images handed down from the Egyptians to Christian performances about the nature of the afterlife. Pagan dramas usually focus on rituals and magic spells as preparation for death and avoidance of punishment in the afterlife. The most common of these were plays dedicated to OSIRIS, the ancient Egyptian lord of the netherworld. During the productions, men stood in pits representing the land of the dead while animals were offered as sacrifice. The blood of the beast was then used to bathe the body, purifying the spirit and protecting it from the terrors of the underworld.

Most Christian mystery plays developed as an outgrowth of HELLFIRE SERMONS. Originally written in Latin (the language of the Christian church), these dramas were designed to educate the peasantry about biblical events and persuade, perhaps even frighten, followers into obedience. Eventually, these dramas were performed in the audiences' native languages to increase their appeal to the masses. The vast majority were based on passages from the Bible and were presented by local churches, usually to commemorate some important event or feast day. Such topics as heaven and hell, the LAST JUDGMENT, and the HARROWING OF HELL were especially popular.

Hell was always a favorite setting

Drawing of a Baroque set for mystery plays c. 1550, with elaborate hellmouth at stage right. ART TODAY

among performers and audiences alike. The most sophisticated troupes had props that belched smoke and shot flames from trapdoors below the stage flooring to graphically represent the dark abyss. Many included mechanical monsters and explosions of sulfurous fumes. Townships began competing for bragging rights as to which had the most exciting hell scene, adding splashy color, imaginative creatures, and special effects to the play. (Such grisly and terrifying productions were the forerunner of today's monster movies and horror films.)

This emphasis on style over substance led to a change in the nature of hell in these mystery plays. Rather than a pit of pain and despair, the underworld slowly evolved as a place of magic, enchantment, and revelry. This popularized the concept of a MERRY HELL where the bold and glamorous partook of forbidden delights, often incorporating exotic ideas from ancient myths and legends. No longer defined by Christian tradition, hell became a home for FAIRIES, pagan heroes, and ruthless champions.

Due to this glamorization of hell and shift away from traditional Christian doctrines, mystery plays were criticized and eventually condemned by thirteenth-century church officials who declared them evil, vile, and dangerous to the soul. As the plays became less and less theological, they were supplanted by MORALITY PLAYS, tales designed to teach lessons about ethics and behavior. These dramas continued to be the province of the church and were strictly overseen by religious authorities.

N

NAKAA Islanders in Micronesia believe that Nakaa, the god of the harvest, punishes evil souls in the afterlife. Nakaa sits at the edge of the spirit world where all departing souls must pass after death. The spirits of those who have led good and decent lives are allowed to pass and enjoy paradise. But when Nakaa detects a wicked soul approaching, he throws an enchanted net over the spirit, trapping it forever. Rather than finding peace in death, such souls struggle for eternity in a vain attempt to free themselves.

NEAR-DEATH EXPERIENCES
In the age of technology, literally thousands of people have been declared clinically dead only to be revived, usually with the assistance of sophisticated medical equipment. Many of these "death survivors" report having what is now termed a near-death experience in which they witness some vision of the afterlife. Most describe these happenings as joyful episodes of peace, warmth, and light. However, a growing number of such resuscitated patients are coming forward with dark stories of horrifying hells.

The details vary from person to person, but all dark descents have one thing in common: They leave the revived patient frantic for a second chance at redemption. Specifics about the underworld cover a variety of tortures, ranging from intense loneliness to imprisonment in a molten cage. One woman recalls an overwhelming sense of "chaos, confusion," complete with shrieks and screams so loud she felt unbearably disoriented. Others echo the sense of anxiety that permeates the soul, followed by a crushing despair.

Recollections of journeys to the "other side" are not new to this age. Centuries ago, VISION LITERATURE abounded, with hundreds of people claiming to have visited heaven, hell, and purgatory, usually under the guidance of some astral mentor. But modern accounts differ in that many have been related by avowed atheists and skeptics who considered belief in God to be baseless superstition. Among these contemporary converts are Canadian farmer GEORGE GODKIN, renowned surgeon MAURICE RAWLINGS, and respected college professor HOWARD STORM. Before the terrifying episodes, none of these men would have called himself "religious."

Dr. John Weldon, author of more than forty books on comparative religion, suggests that virtually all near-death experiences originate with SATAN. He believes that beautiful afterlife "visions" lull people into the false belief that there is a "tunnel of light" waiting to transport deceased spirits to paradise for reunions with friends and family. Such reassurances give the impression that living a life of virtue and seeking divine forgiveness for sins are unnecessary. Hunt further objects to the Heavenly Father being reduced to an impersonal "white light" promising nondescript salvation.

Those who have come forward with stories of damnation to the underworld believe that their experiences are not uncommon. Because of the moral implications of being sent to hell, experts who specialize in studying near-death experiences agree that most people are unwilling to admit they have been condemned. Thus infernal sojourns are thought to be at least as prevalent, if not more so, as "positive" visions of salvation. Such tales seem rare only because the attached stigma shames many into keeping silent about what they have encountered in the next realm.

NERGAL Negral is an ancient Sumerian god whose lecherous appetites result in his eternal damnation. Tricked into trusting the underworld goddess ERESHKIGAL, Nergal reluctantly agrees to marry the fiend and take his place as king of the dead.

According to the legend, the cunning Ereshkigal becomes jealous when she discovers that the heavenly deities are enjoying a lavish gala and she has not been invited. The gods reply that it would be impossible for her to attend, since she cannot leave her underworld kingdom of ARALU, the Land of Darkness. Refusing to be ignored, Ereshkigal sends an ambassador to represent her and bring back a sampling of celestial delights.

When Nergal, the god of hunting and war, sees that Ereshkigal has never sent a lesser spirit on her behalf, he mocks them both. The enraged Ereshkigal demands that he come in person to the underworld to apologize for his rudeness. Nergal protests, but the rest of the gods insist that he do so in order to avoid bringing her wrath on all of them. They give him a stern warning: Do not accept *anything* offered in Aralu, or else he will become a prisoner of the land of the dead.

Nergal makes the journey and is steadfast in resisting the treats Ereshkigal offers him. He refuses the food, the wine, even the water. But when Ereshkigal offers her body to him, he succumbs. Nergal enjoys a week-long sexual escapade with Ereshkigal, then tells her he must return to the higher world. She laughs at this, informing Nergal that his seduction has made him her subject, and he must now remain in Aralu. His pleas for release are in vain; Ereshkigal is determined to keep Nergal as her prisoner.

Misrable in Aralu, Nergal tries to trick her into allowing him to return to the Great Above. He tells Ereshkigal that he has fallen in love with her and wants to be wed, and he begs her to let him share news of their engagement with the other gods. Obviously skeptical of his sincerity and commitment, she lets him go but warns that if he fails to return promptly she will seek vengeance.

Nergal hurries back to the palace of the gods and tries to disguise himself so Ereshkigal cannot find him. But when she threatens to "let loose the dead to devour the living," the gods pressure him to surrender. Pouting and outwitted, Nergal returns to the Land of Darkness to rule with Ereshkigal. His lordship is in title only, as Ereshkigal refuses to share power over the dead with him.

Another ancient tale recounts a nightmarish vision of Nergal in Aralu. According to the story, an Assyrian prince has a dream in which he visits Nergal in the underworld. Little is known of the details of his passage, but the prince's terrified bride reported that he woke up screaming and shaking uncontrollably. He refused to tell her what he had seen, but he spent the rest of his life in terror of the horrors awaiting him after death.

NIFLHEIM The Germanic underworld Niflheim is a cold realm of icy suffering. Souls of those who die by any means other than in battle (warrior heroes go to the paradise Valhalla) are sent to Niflheim, a name that means "Land of the Mists." It is a dreary, dark place of everlasting winter where a poisonous fountain spews rivers of ice. The entrance to Niflheim is GNIPAHELLI, a cavernous passage that leads to the underworld.

Niflheim is ruled by HEL, a hideous goddess who is half human and half green, rotting corpse. Her odor is almost as disgusting as her appearance. She is the daughter of the trickster god LOKI and an ogress. Hel's palace, Sleetcold, overlooks the vast wasteland of ice, where the damned cry out in eternal agony. She is aided by Hermodr, a messenger who carries the dead to the underworld. The souls of immoral people wash up on the haunted shore Nastrond and are then delivered to Hel for punishment. Wicked souls are tortured by Nidhoggr, a dragon who lives near the lowest circle of the underworld. The "corpse tearer" continually feeds on the spirits of evil people.

NIGHT ANGEL The 1990 horror film *Night Angel* depicts the modern escapades of LILITH, an ancient SUCCUBUS who destroys men through sexual domination. In the movie's most memorable sequence, the voluptuous DEMON takes her prey on a tour of hell to lure him into her nefarious scheme.

Night Angel opens as Lilith (played by Isa Anderson) claws her way up from the underworld, emerging from a cemetery in present-day California. As she rises, the shrieks of the damned can be heard emanating from the steamy chasm below her. Covered in maggots and mud, Anderson prowls the streets beneath the full moon, her very presence causing a rash of crib deaths, rapes, and murders. She disappears into the night, the sounds of screams echoing throughout the town.

Anderson takes a job on the staff of *Siren,* a trendy fashion magazine. She immediately begins seducing fellow employees one at a time. Each sexual encounter ends with a brutal murder in which Anderson mutilates her prey. "Lust," viewers learn, "is her life force." The surviving coworkers suffer increasingly disturbing nightmares but continue to be drawn to the alluring Anderson. Finally, the fiend attempts to win the allegiance of one particularly attractive colleague by taking him to an orgy in hell.

The infernal tour commences when a picture of Anderson wrapped in a snake comes alive in the back room of a cocktail bar. She then descends a winding staircase, past deviants having sex with dismembered body parts, men lashed to poles by barbed wire wrapped tightly around their heads, and revelers guzzling green, bubbling potions while feasting on human flesh. One scene shows an obese woman fondling her enormous bosom, rolling her breasts upward to reveal screaming faces where her nipples should be. The pit of hell resembles a medieval torture chamber replete with whips, chains, and leather-hooded GHOULS. (Credits for this underworld sequence list "people in bondage," "woman with faces under breasts," and "man being served on table.")

Night Angel's hell is a sensual, lewd underworld of sexual obsession, similar in many ways to the infernal realm of CLIVE BARKER's 1987 *HELLRAISER.* Both films focus on the dark dimension as a place of ultimate physical gratification, where carnal fulfillment is, in the end, horribly painful.

NIGHT GALLERY *Night Gallery,* a collection of supernatural stories, served as Rod Serling's follow-up to his phenomenally successful *THE TWILIGHT ZONE* television series. After *The Twilight Zone* was canceled in 1964, Serling worked on radio programs, wrote several anthologies, and adapted novels for the screen (including the 1967 *Planet of the Apes*), but he shied away from what he called "walking dead and maggots" shows about fiends, GHOULS, and DEMONS. But in 1969, a trio of Serling's terrifying tales were combined in a made-for-television movie entitled *Night Gallery.* These spooky stories bore strong resemblance to the macabre plots of classic *Twilight Zone* episodes. The show was the evening's highest-rated program, and its popularity prompted NBC to offer Serling a new series.

Rod Serling's Night Gallery premiered in 1970 and remained on the air for two years. Serling, still weary from five years of clashing with network executives during the *Twilight Zone* run, served as the show's host but had no real voice in making production decisions. He was thus frequently disappointed with the quality of the scripts and considered the series to be suspenseful and entertaining but totally lacking in artistic merit. *Night Gallery* did, however, make several attempts at delving into the great mysteries of life and death, most notably exploring the nature of hell.

From its debut, critics and viewers alike could not help but compare *Night Gallery* to its famous forerunner. The similarities were striking: Many of the new *Night Gallery* episodes were little more than revamped *Twilight Zone* scripts. Others were unique ideas depicting chilling situations and unsettling "otherworlds." As Serling said of his former series, some were "real turkeys," some great classics. The same was certainly true of *Night Gallery.*

"Escape Route," a segment from *Night Gallery*'s pilot, was hauntingly reminiscent of an episode about damnation from *The Twilight Zone* entitled "Deaths-Head Revisited." In both instances, the story line centers around a Nazi official who escapes conventional justice after slaughtering thousands of innocent Jews in the concentration camps. And for each character, hell consists of having to relive his vile atrocities from the victims' perspective. These scripts rely on the DREAM MODEL of the afterlife, a theory that in the next world humans are either rewarded with memories of their virtuous lives or else tormented by recollections of their evil.

This theme recurs in several episodes about damnation. In "Lone Survivor," a passing cruise ship picks up a lifeboat that seems to be carrying a shipwrecked woman. This survivor is, however, a man (played by John Cilicos) in female disguise. Cilicos remembers donning the dress and pushing other women and children aside as he deserted his post and fled the sinking *Titanic.* But the captain of the cruise ship says this cannot possibly be, since the *Titanic* sank three years ago, and no one could live adrift in a lifeboat for such a long time. The disoriented sailor is informed that the year is not 1912 but 1915, and he is now aboard the *Lusitania.* Before he can solve the mystery, the *Lusitania* is torpedoed by a German submarine and goes down. Cilicos is once again alone in a lifeboat, this time to be picked up by the *Andrea Doria.* He finally realizes that he has been damned to drift from one doomed boat to another as punishment for his cowardice and selfishness.

A differing interpretation of hell, titled "Pamela's Voice," aired in 1971. The episode features Phyllis Diller as a nagging wife whose shrill voice drives her husband, played by John Astin, to murder. After dispatching her, Astin gleefully celebrates with "wine, women, and song." But her ghost soon appears with bad news: Astin's excesses have brought about his own premature demise. Diller tells the horrified man that *she* has gone to heaven, where souls can spend eternity in any manner they wish. Being a "social being, an extrovert," she has chosen to engage in her favorite activity—talking incessantly to her bored husband. Astin protests that he has no desire to spend eternity listening to her, but she happily exclaims, "The organization *you've* been assigned to is not so accommodating." The defeated Astin wilts, resigned to his particular damnation, as Diller launches into an unending monologue on his inadequacies. Hell, according to the scenario, is a matter of perspective. "Pamela's Voice" has definite overtones of WILLIAM BLAKE's model of eternity, where heaven and hell are differentiated only by each individual's outlook.

Astin returns to this philosophical view of the afterlife in "Hell's Bells." In this segment, he plays a hippie who dies in a car accident and is damned to a parlor populated by chatty yokels listening to monotonous elevator music. When Astin tells the DEVIL that this is unendurably boring, the DEMON replies that an identical room exists "up there," and that what to him is torturous damnation is paradise to others. Before disappearing, the devil advises Astin to "think about it."

The series presents another modern inferno in "Flip Side of SATAN," in which a nasty disc jockey played by Arte Johnson learns that having the perfect job is not always a blessing. Serling opens the show by noting, "We refer to him by different names: LUCIFER, MEPHISTOPHELES, Beelzebub." The episode then depicts Johnson as an adulterous con artist who swindles his friends and drives his lover to suicide without the slightest pang of conscience. All Johnson cares about is making a good impression as the new DJ on KAPH radio, but all the station's records offer only disturbing funeral music. One, by the group the KARMAS, includes a booming voice inviting demons to partake of the "sacrifice," which is in "the crucible from which there is no escape." Terrified by the mysterious happenings, Johnson tries to flee but finds the door locked from the outside. When he tries to shut down the station's electric power, the lascivious DJ is ignited into a burnt offering fit for Satan's feast.

During its run, *Night Gallery* also brought a variety of classic hellish SHORT STORIES to the small screen. The finest of these is "Camera Obscura," which depicts the realm of the damned as a mirror world where humans assume physical bodies to match the state of their souls. A heartless money-lender, obsessed with shaking down his destitute clients, accidentally stumbles into hell and discovers that he cannot escape. A throng of worm-infested, rotting corpses welcomes the condemned banker to his new, and eternal, home.

As the series slumped in the ratings, Serling was continually frustrated by the scripts the producers chose for *Night Gallery.* The one-hour show was eventually cut to thirty minutes, and writers dropped afterlife plots in favor of explorations into paranormal and psychic activity. Despite his grievances, Serling stayed with the series until it was canceled in 1972. *Night Gallery* marks his last contribution to original television projects, as the creative genius died of heart failure three years later at age fifty.

NIGHTMARE CAFE In the mid-1980s, horror director Wes Craven created a short-lived television series about meting out afterlife justice titled *Nightmare Cafe.* The supernatural diner of the title is a sort of LIMBO, a realm "between life and death" where souls can make a last stand in determining their fate. Robert Englund, famous for his role as a sadist straight from hell in the *NIGHTMARE ON ELM STREET* movies, was cast as the mediator who judges souls "somewhere between time and eternity."

The show lasted fewer than a dozen episodes, and most involved the DREAM MODEL of final reckoning. This theory contends that after death, the soul is bound in never-ending memories of the deeds of its lifetime. Those who were kind and decent in life will enjoy reliving their days of virtue, whereas the evil will be trapped in an eternal recollection of vile acts and despicable crimes. For the characters in *Nightmare Cafe,* judgment in the afterlife amounts to being forced to face their failures and accept the dire consequences.

NIGHTMARE ON ELM STREET, A The phenomenally successful *Nightmare on Elm Street* series of films began with a simple premise: What would happen if the horrors of our nightmares suddenly came to life, complete with the ability to harm us physically? Filmmakers had explored this concept earlier in 1984 (the same year *Nightmare* was released) with *Dreamscape,* a convoluted sci-fi/political fantasy about experiments to invade people's dreams as a means of manipulating—or even murdering—them. *Dreamscape* was a box office flop, but writer-director Wes Craven's *Nightmare* spawned one of the most profitable horror films of the decade, perhaps because of the added element of raising dream villains from the depths of hell.

The original *Nightmare on Elm Street*—and its many sequels—features the afterlife exploits of child killer Freddy Kruger, played by Robert

Englund. Burned alive by the parents of his victims, Englund returns to his neighborhood in the form of a dream invader who gives the surviving children horrible nightmares. When the young residents compare stories and realize they are all suffering the same bad dream, Englund steps up his plan and begins murdering them as they sleep. The teens must then find a way to convince the adults of Elm Street—who refuse to acknowledge their role in Englund's murder—that he has returned and is planning to rid the street of all its children.

The dream sequences of the *Nightmare* films offer several grisly depictions of hell. One of the most horrible scenes shows souls trapped in Englund's terribly scarred body. He opens his shirt to reveal dozens of shrieking faces lining his chest like open sores. Sneering, he informs one of his intended victims that these are his prisoners, damned to spend eternity with the vile creature. In the third movie of the series, *Dream Warriors*, a hapless teen is suspended over a bottomless pit that belches flames and foul smoke, a more traditional portrait of the underworld. And throughout the series, there are numerous depictions of the boiler room where Englund had been burned alive, with obvious parallels to the flaming pits of hell.

Despite being soundly trounced by critics (a British reviewer for *Time Out* commented that the film's only appeal is "watching unpleasant American teenagers ripped to death"), the movie became a box office blockbuster. Fueled by this popularity, Craven's concept generated a deluge of MOVIE MERCHANDISING, ranging from Halloween costumes to action figure dolls to book covers. Freddy Kruger soon became the host-villain of a series of COMIC BOOKS and a short-lived macabre anthology television series, *Freddy's Nightmares*, in the tradition of the TWILIGHT ZONE. The vile fiend is even paid homage in the finale of another gory cinematic series, *Friday the 13th*. In the final installment entitled *Jason Goes to Hell*, Freddy Kruger's trademark razor-fingered glove reaches out of the abyss to pull Jason into the underworld.

Englund himself parlayed his status as a horror icon into a role as the proprietor of *NIGHTMARE CAFE*, an otherworldly restaurant "somewhere between heaven and hell." He has also reprised his portrayal of Freddy Kruger in the 1994 *Wes Craven's Final Nightmare*. In this film within a film, the fictional fiend returns to terrorize the real-life actors (including Englund) who appeared in the original *Elm Street* movies.

NIGHTMARE ON THE 13TH FLOOR This 1990 made-for-cable film places the kingdom of SATAN on the thirteenth floor of a Gothic Victorian hotel. Debonair devil James Brolin allows travel writer Michele Greene a quick peek at the rituals and relics, yet when she reports having witnessed horrific crimes in room 1313, no one takes her seriously. A seemingly endless parade of the hotel's owners, employees, and guests vehemently insist that there *is* no thirteenth floor and that she is either imagining things or deliberately lying to boost magazine sales. But persistent snoop Greene eventually discovers that the mysterious realm is home not only to a cult of DEVIL worshipers but also to a damned ax murderer. Hell, according to the producers, is a state of mind that can exist in any plane, even in the land of the living.

NIGHT TRAIN TO TERROR

Producers of the 1984 horror flop *Night Train to Terror* use the premise of a debate between God and SATAN to string together this disjointed series of supernatural stories. It is obvious to viewers that the anthology is simply a blend of footage shot for other unfinished films. However, the film poses interesting questions about modern criteria and attitudes regarding damnation, the nature of evil, and the possibility of divine mercy.

As the film opens, the two ancient adversaries sit in the dining car of *Satan's Cannonball* arguing over which of the passengers' souls will be delivered to hell when the train crashes at midnight. The setting then shifts to scenes about the people in question as a voice-over assures viewers that these heroes and villains really are on the train, even though we see them only in flashbacks at other settings. Richard Moll appears in two (as two different characters), being damned in both incarnations. Other glimpses into these ill-fated travelers' lives include footage of sadomasochistic torture, portrayals of the Nazi concentration camps, and graphic depictions of exploding heads. Between these episodes, the narrator insinuates that the most horrible agony on earth is preferable to what awaits beyond "the gates of hell."

The final entry in this muddled anthology offers a firsthand look at the infernal kingdom. Claire Hanson plays a doctor who is haunted by visions of hell and sees vicious DEMONS outside her window. Her terror mounts as a mysterious stranger declares that her husband is "on his way to hell," followed by an anonymous letter stating, "Out of the pits of hell, Satan has come for you!" When Hanson goes to the basement to investigate disturbing noises, the floor opens up to reveal the ghastly and repulsive underworld. Demons and mangled bodies of the damned reach up from the fiery orange pit to pull her into the abyss as the shrieks of tortured souls boom forth. She escapes but is given a frightening task: She must extract "the heart of Satan," or else an unspeakable evil will overtake the world.

Like the other segments, this plot goes nowhere, fizzling out completely as Satan escapes unharmed to continue his wicked schemes. The film concludes as the train crashes in a thunderous explosion. Before the unseen passengers perish, God tells Satan that the rich, powerful, and self-important will always belong to hell. But, he reminds the fiend, the poor, the weak, and children will forever be heaven-bound. In a final testament to the bizarre nature of this film, the end credits list Lu Sifer (a play on the name LUCIFER) in the role of Satan, while God appears "as Himself."

NISE-E Nise-e, "likeness paintings," are illustrations popularized during the Kamakura period (twelfth century) in Japan. Many of these scrolls were inspired by stories of the dark underworld and show the horrors of BUDDHIST HELL and its vicious DEMONS, including YAMA and EMMA-O. A typical infernal nise-e shows the damned suffering a variety of grisly tortures such as being beaten with clubs, raked over hot coals, or chased by ghastly beasts. Text describing the scene usually accompanied the hand scrolls, offering details about the picture. Many nise-e survive in Asian temples and provide examples of CHURCH ART AND ARCHITECTURE of the underworld.

NO EXIT French playwright Jean-Paul Sartre offers a distinctly modern interpretation of hell in his 1946 drama *No Exit.* The one-act play depicts the underworld as a shabby hotel where sinners spend eternity trapped with quarrelsome roommates, unresponsive valets, and constant violent eruptions. But the worst of the suffering comes from having to endure their own individual guilt.

The play opens as three characters assigned to the same room begin to protest their damnation. All assert that there must be some mistake: They don't believe they have done anything so bad in life as to merit damnation. But as they compare stories, the truth comes out. Inez, a meddling gossip, admits that she "can't get on without making people suffer." The adulterous Estelle coldly explains that she became pregnant by her lover, then killed the baby girl despite the father's pleas to let him raise the child. Upon hearing of his daughter's death, Estelle's lover commits suicide over his grief. And army deserter Garcin describes how he treated his devoted wife "abominably," cheating on her constantly and ridiculing her for pure spite.

As the play continues, the three argue continuously and take turns verbally attacking one another. They fight over who should sit on which couch, if they should stay silent or talk, whose fault it is that the valet never answers the call bell. At last, Garcin declares, "Anything would be better than this agony of mind."

There are no torture chambers or flaming pits in Sartre's play: Hell in his drama is in being condemned to an eternity of pettiness, self-righteousness, and loathing. Quite simply, he contends that "hell is other people," especially ones as miserable and vile as his pathetic trio.

NOMOU Micronesian belief describes Nomou, a fearsome monster who devours souls of the dead before they can reach Falraman (paradise). The dark god Lug catches human spirits during the full moon and feeds them to the beast.

NYIA Slavic myth features an underworld ruler called Nyia, dubbed the Polish Pluto. He is the overlord of the navs, spirits of people who die prematurely, especially virgins and victims of tragedy. These souls are thought to be jealous of the living and can return to haunt those who have had full, rich lives of diverse experiences. In the underworld, the navs suffer the aching for all the adventures and sensations they did not have the chance to enjoy during life. Nyia does not torture or punish the navs; he merely watches over them.

Many Slavs worry that the unhappy dead come back as VAMPIRES. Some burn the dead to protect themselves; others impale them on alder wood.

O

OBATALA Obatala is the judge of the dead according to the legends of Nigeria's Yoruba. He is the spirit aid of OLODUMARE, a CHTHONIC deity. Obatala's task is to determine whether human spirits should be damned to an eternity of torment in hell or allowed to enjoy a peaceful afterlife.

ODYSSEY Homer's Greek epic poem *Odyssey,* written more than two dozen centuries ago, remains one of the most studied works of Western literature. It recounts the grand voyage of the hero Odysseus after the devastating battle of Troy. The poem features dozens of adventures with gods, goddesses, giants, monsters, and enemy warriors. Throughout the work, Odysseus is compelled to perform fantastic feats in order to appease the gods and ensure his safe return to his homeland of Ithaca. Among these adventures is a chilling journey through the land of the dead.

Book 11 of the *Odyssey* tells of this mythic voyage to HADES, the Greek underworld. Homer places this realm in the far north, beyond "a great expanse of immortal sea." In order safely to enter the land of the dead, Odysseus must catch the "north winds" until he can go no farther, then prepare a blood sacrifice for "pale PERSEPHONE," wife of King Hades and queen of the underworld.

When Odysseus comes to the place where the Rivers of Fire and of Lamentation join the ACHERON (which flows directly to the underworld), he digs a hole and pours in the blood of a sheep. As he does so, he vows to honor the departed souls of those he meets here. From "the trench came a moaning that was horrible to hear." Slowly, the SHADES (listless spirits) of his dead friends and legendary heroes come forward to drink the blood, which gives them the power to speak with him.

Elpenor, a fellow soldier left unburied after the Trojan War, begs Odysseus, "Do not abandon me, unwept and unburied," since souls who do not receive proper burial can find no rest. When Odysseus promises to return to cremate and bury the ashes of the man's corpse, the spirit goes away comforted. Odysseus then greets his mother, who was alive when he left for the war. When he asks how she died, she replies, "My loneliness for you, Odysseus, for your kind heart and good counsel, took my life away." He tries several times to embrace her, but she slips through his arms like the mist.

Odysseus sees a number of other ghosts, grim "phantoms" mired in "western gloom." Among them are the heroes Achilles and Agamemnon, now pale shadows of their former selves. The great Achilles tells Odysseus he would rather be a slave among the living than the ruler of all the dead. He laments that "were I but whole again," his suffering would be ended. The soldiers ask Odysseus for news of the world, but he can give none as he had been marooned on a deserted island for the past several years. The shades go away more desolate than before.

Odysseus continues his journey and meets MINOS, former king of Crete. In Hades, Minos serves as a judge of the dead, "dealing out justice among ghostly pleaders arrayed about the broad doorways of Death." (Minos has a similar role in Dante's *DIVINE COMEDY: THE INFERNO.*)

Beyond this passage, Odysseus witnesses the sufferings of TARTARUS, the darkest pit of punishment in the underworld. Here, TITYUS is punished for raping Zeus's lover by having his liver continually gnawed upon by vultures. And TANTALUS is tormented with thirst and hunger as pure water and delicious fruit abound just beyond his reach as punishment for betraying the gods and revealing their secrets. The nefarious SISYPHUS must push a boulder up a hill every day, only to have it roll back down again. These three are the only people in Hades who have physical bodies, so as to aggravate their suffering.

As Odysseus is falling into pity and despair, he is approached by the hero HERCULES, son of Zeus. Hercules had been charged with performing a dozen magnificent feats, one of which is to steal the guard dog CERBERUS from the underworld. He reassures Odysseus that the goddess Athena, mistress of wisdom, will lead him out of this hell. Cheered by this, Odysseus peers into the dimness hoping to see THESEUS and Pirithoüs, mythic heroes Odysseus had long admired. But instead of being inspired, he is overwhelmed by "shades in thousands, rustling in a pandemonium of whispers . . . brought from darker Hell" rushing toward him. The terrified Odysseus returns to his ship and casts off, greatly relieved to be back among the living.

Homer's *Odyssey* continues to inspire artwork, films, plays, and interpretations, including the 1997 multimillion-dollar made-for-television epic from Hallmark Theater.

O LE NU'U-O-NONOA O le nu'u-o-nonoa is the underworld of Samoan belief. It is a region of Sa-lefe'e (Land of the Dead) reserved for the souls of the wicked. The name O le nu'u-o-nonoa means "land of the bound," since damned spirits are imprisoned in this subterranean hell. The vengeful god Ita-nga-ta takes great delight in torturing these souls in the dour abyss.

OLODUMARE Olodumare is the underworld deity of the Yoruba of Nigeria. He is overlord of deceased souls and ruler of the land of the dead. Spirits deemed evil are tortured in the next world by hideous beasts who taunt and torment the damned. For condemned souls, the torments are both physical and psychological.

Olodumare is aided in his supernatural tasks by OBATALA, who judges each soul at the time of death. Obatala has the power to damn a soul to hell or escort it to paradise.

ORCUS The ancient Romans were undisputedly great warriors, but as a culture they had little imagination. Their mythology is almost entirely composed of bits and pieces of legends absorbed from peoples they conquered. From Greek myth comes Orcus, the Roman counterpart of HADES, lord of the underworld. Orcus is a grim, cold god who collects dead souls and takes them to the underworld. He is a just overseer of the dead who is not evil or bloodthirsty. Orcus simply sees to it that spirits receive whatever punishment they have earned through their crimes. The myth of Orcus is not as complex as that of Hades, since Roman legends are more basic and rarely include colorful details.

In Virgil's *AENEID,* the story of a fantastic journey to the underworld, the hero Aeneas passes through the Gate of Orcus on his mythic voyage. In this realm are all types of hideous beasts and fearsome monsters. Other tales link Orcus to DIS, a cruel lord of the damned who tortures spirits in the afterlife.

ORPHÉE The 1949 French film *Orphée,* an adaptation of the legend of the Greek musician ORPHEUS, has been hailed by critics as a masterpiece of cinematic poetry. In this version, the princess of death is sent to claim the poet Orpheus but instead falls in love with him. Unable to do her duty, she agrees to help him travel to the underworld to find his deceased bride.

Director Jean Cocteau uses many imaginative camera tricks and poignant scenes to portray the land of the dead. The river STYX is replaced as the border to HADES by an enchanted mirror through which the pair enters hell. The abyss itself is depicted as a smoky, somewhat confusing realm of wispy spirits and mysterious passageways. But the region is one of sorrow rather than torture, conveying a dark desolation that is overwhelmingly piercing. Cocteau's underworld is a place of spiritual suffering where the soul finds no consolation and has no hope of better things to come.

ORPHEUS Orpheus's voyage to the underworld is among the best-known Greek myths. It describes the supernatural quest of hero Orpheus, a gifted poet and musician, who journeys to hell to save his beloved.

Heartbroken after the sudden

Orpheus before Pluto and Persephone by Francois Perrier. ERICH LESSING/ART RESOURCE, N.Y.

death of his young wife EURYDICE (she is bitten by a snake while fleeing a rapist), Orpheus ventures to the House of HADES, the bleak underworld of ancient myth, to reclaim her. On his quest, the brave mortal must cross the river STYX, charm CERBERUS, the three-headed monster who guards the land of the dead, and present his sad request to the lord of death.

Arriving at the throne of King Hades, Orpheus plays and sings a love song filled with sorrow and longing. The ballad is so lovely it gives the damned a brief moment of rest from their torment. PERSEPHONE, queen of the dead, begs her husband to allow the girl to return upon hearing the haunting melody. Moved to "iron tears" by the beautiful music, Hades agrees to release Eurydice on one condition: Orpheus must walk ahead of her back to the land of the living. She will follow, but he must not look back. If he turns around at any time before returning to the surface, Eurydice will be trapped forever in the underworld.

Orpheus agrees to the terms, but as he ambles out of the underworld he begins to doubt that she is really there. When he calls out to her, only an eerie echo returns. Finally, Orpheus cannot resist the temptation to see if Eurydice is behind him. He whirls around, only to see his beloved turn to mist and vanish on the wind. His screams and pleadings do no good—she is lost forever. Devastated, Orpheus returns to the land of the living, heartbroken and unable to love again.

The legend of Orpheus has inspired countless artworks, operas, poems, and performances, including BRUEGHEL's painting *ORPHEUS IN THE UNDERWORLD* and the foreign films *ORPHÉE* and *Black Orpheus.*

ORPHEUS IN THE UNDERWORLD Pieter BRUEGHEL the Younger of the famous Brueghel family of artists created the masterpiece *Orpheus in the Underworld* in the sixteenth century. The work shows Greek mythic hero ORPHEUS playing the harp for HADES and PERSEPHONE, rulers of the underworld, in an attempt to persuade them to allow his deceased bride to leave the underworld and return with him to the land of the living.

Beyond the regents of the abyss is a sea of bitter agony. The dead squirm in pain and throw wide their arms begging for relief, their faces disfigured by the intense suffering. Amid the fire and smoke, Brueghel includes spider monsters with eyes of fire and winged reptilian demons. The entire work is done primarily in blacks and browns and murky greens, creating an overwhelming sense of terror and ugliness. Orpheus, vibrant and alive, is a stark contrast to the murky deceased souls. His radiance underscores the dull gloom of hell, where souls languish in muted sorrow.

OSIRIS King Osiris is the Egyptian judge of the dead and ruler of the underworld. His realm is the infertile wasteland that exists beneath the earth beyond the distant horizon. All departed souls must appear before Osiris so their hearts can be weighed on a scale against the "feather of truth." His judgment determines what happens to the spirit after death, as he has the power to distribute both rewards and punishments in the next world.

Osiris is also the archetypal Egyptian mummy. According to the legend, Osiris's brother Seth grows jealous of him and he murders the king. After this fratricide, Seth cuts his brother's dead body into fourteen pieces. He then scatters the sections throughout the land. Osiris's wife (and sister) Isis gathers the pieces and reassembles his body, using strips of cloth to bind it together, thus creating the first mummified pharaoh. The gods offer to restore the beloved Osiris to life, but he chooses instead to become the ruler of the dead. Under his instruction, proper embalming and mummification became essential to pharaohs hoping to enjoy a pleasant afterlife.

According to Egyptian myth, when a person dies, the soul follows the "river of the sky" in the boat of Ra, the sun god. The boat must pass through seven gates, and the deceased must call each gatekeeper by name. (The names are listed in the BOOK OF THE DEAD, a text detailing what one must do to avoid the horrors of the afterlife.) Anubis, a supernatural guide, then escorts the spirit to the "Hall of Justice" for Osiris's ruling.

Here, Osiris weighs the soul's heart against the feather of truth. If the heart sinks under the burden of its sins, it will be devoured by the monster AMMUT. Even spirits who pass this test

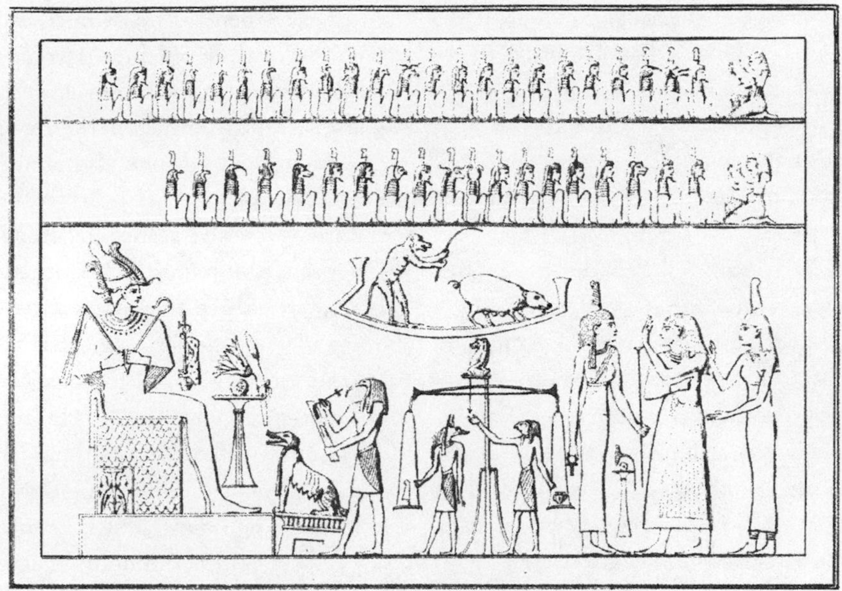

A drawing based on an Egyptian scroll shows Osiris judging souls in the afterlife.
ART TODAY

face a number of horrors in DUAT, the Egyptian underworld. These include ravenous serpents, flesh-eating locusts, and even second death.

Osiris appears in Milton's *PARADISE LOST* as a pagan agent of the DEVIL sent to divert humanity's attention from the true God. He is set up as a pagan deity, a mockery of the heavenly Father of the Christian faith. The ancient king and his death rituals have also been the topic of MYSTERY PLAYS.

P

PAHA VALTA Paha Valta is the Finnish underworld. It is a place of charred ruins and never-ending darkness. The abyss is ruled by Paha Miles, which means "evil man." Souls in Paha Valta face a dreary afterlife in the eternal pit of gloom.

PARADISE LOST Seventeenth-century English author John Milton wanted to write a Christian epic in the style of Homer's *Iliad* and Virgil's *AENEID.* After years of struggling with the concept, he wrote the allegorical *Paradise Lost,* a dramatic retelling of the war in heaven, the creation of hell, and the fall of Adam and Eve in the Garden of Eden. The book introduced an entirely new writing style, dubbed "grand style," to English literature and changed the way future books were written. This new format incorporated traditional verbiage with expressions, terms, and phrases from languages from across the globe.

Unlike the traditional Greek epics in which heroes eventually travel to the underworld, *Paradise Lost* opens with a scene set in hell. The reader is immediately thrust into the depths of the abyss, as SATAN, leader of the rebel angels, addresses his legions. They have just been cast into the underworld after defying God, and most of them are enraged, blaming Satan for leading the charge that resulted in their expulsion from heaven and for their horrific new existence in hell. The DEMON reassures his faithful that they are better off in this dark realm, since they are no longer required to pay homage to God. Satan explains that it is "better to reign in Hell than serve in Heaven." Most of the demons, still stunned and disoriented, are not ready to accept this philosophy.

A 1688 woodcut by John Baptist Medina depicts Lucifer torturing the damned in hell. ART TODAY

To raise their spirits, Satan tells the fiends about God's latest creation, Adam, a being far inferior to their magnificence and grandeur. He suggests that they corrupt the human and through his destruction enjoy a bit of revenge against God, since he seems to be especially partial to this creature. Satan rationalizes that if they cannot be rejoined to heaven, the next best option is to drag God's precious new creation into hell.

A great debate ensues over this proposal. Many of the demons want nothing more to do with God or any of his handiwork. Beelzebub, who is second only to Satan in hell's hierarchy, serves as his master's spokesman and convinces the rebel angels to try Satan's plan. He is aided in winning their allegiance by BELIAL, a crafty debater who promises all that damning humans will bring great satisfaction. Together, they organize a party of demons to build a bridge from hell to earth to bring sin, decay, and affliction to humankind.

Satan eventually succeeds in causing Adam and Eve to sin, but God is not ready to abandon his new creatures to the horrors of the underworld. The deity promises Adam that Jesus Christ, a being who is both human and divine, will come to reopen the gates of heaven to humankind. He further describes a LAST JUDGMENT, at which time hell will be forever sealed. Until then, the bridge will remain intact and people must use their faith, love, and wisdom to outwit the unrelenting forces of evil.

Paradise Lost features many images of the underworld from CHRISTIAN HELL, such as the sea demon LEVIATHAN and the proverbial snake in the Garden of Eden. But the book also includes numerous references to ancient pagan myths. The gate of the land of the damned is guarded by a hideous monster that invokes images of the Greek CERBERUS, the dog-headed beast at the gates of HADES. Hell proper is described as a region burning in eternal fire that gives off heat but no light. ARALU, the Sumerian underworld, is a place of similar darkness. Among the inhabitants of Milton's hell is the Egyptian pharaoh OSIRIS, lord of the dead. He admits that he is one of many pagan gods whose job it is to lure souls away from the one true God and from Christ the redeemer.

The writing of *Paradise Lost* took more than two decades to complete, as Milton went blind in the early 1650s and had to dictate his masterpiece to a scribe. The text was first published in 1667 and remains in print to this day. In 1671, Milton published *Paradise Found,* a detailed study of Christ's life and his defeat of Satan through his crucifixion and HARROWING OF HELL.

These works have inspired innumerable paintings, poems and artworks, including a rendering by WILLIAM BLAKE of *Satan Rousing the Rebel Angels.*

PATALA In Hindu belief, Patala is the name for the lowest realm of the underworld. Within Patala are numerous chambers, including Atala, Rastala, Tatala, Sutala, Vitala, Mahatala, and Patala Proper. Overall, Patala is a realm of ultimate physical gratification where the body is bombarded with carnal experiences. This sensory overload causes utter agony in the depths of HINDU HELL. However, in most versions, this damnation is only temporary. Eventually, evil souls will be purged of their wickedness and returned to the life cycle in a new incarnation.

PERSEPHONE According to ancient Greek myth, Persephone is the wife of HADES, ruler of the underworld. She is referred to as the queen of the dead. The two are often pictured together in their subterranean kingdom on ancient vases, tombs, and other MEMORIALS.

Persephone is the daughter of the powerful deity Demeter, goddess of the harvest. Hades becomes infatuated

An illustration of Persephone and Hades from a Greek relief. ART TODAY

with the young maiden and kidnaps Persephone and drags her to the underworld to be his bride. Enraged at this act, Demeter destroys the crops and renders the earth infertile. She vows to continue this condition until her child is returned to her, but Hades is determined to keep the lovely Persephone as his queen. A devastating famine results throughout the land.

Eventually, Zeus and the other gods intervene to settle the dispute. Because Persephone has eaten "the food of the dead," she is unable to return to the land of the living. When Demeter is informed of this, she and Hades strike a compromise: Persephone will spend half the year in the underworld the other half with her mother. This, according to Greek myth, is the reason for the winter season. It is the time when Persephone is with Hades, and Demeter is in mourning.

Persephone plays an important role in several underworld legends. When the musician ORPHEUS travels to Hades in search of his recently deceased wife, it is Persephone who convinces the king to restore the dead EURYDICE. Through Persephone's intervention, Hades agrees to let Eurydice return to the land of the living on one condition: Orpheus must promise not to look back until the two have reached the surface of the earth. At first Orpheus complies, but soon he becomes convinced that Hades has tricked him. Just before they emerge from the underworld, Orpheus turns around to make certain that his wife is following him. As he does so, the beautiful Eurydice disappears into the murky mist, lost to him forever.

In another famous story, the heroes THESEUS and Pirithoüs venture to the underworld to steal Persephone away from Hades and return her to her mother. They fail miserably and are damned to TARTARUS, the lowest realm of the dead. The two are mercilessly punished by the FURIES and even heckled by King Hades himself for their foolishness in trying to best the lord of hell. Theseus is later retrieved from this torment by the legendary hero HERCULES; however, Pirithoüs remains among the damned.

The beautiful Persephone also appears in such works as the opera *ORPHEUS IN THE UNDERWORLD* and the epic poem *ODYSSEY.*

PHAEDO Greek philosopher Plato offers his interpretations about the afterlife in *Phaedo,* written around 350 B.C. The work recounts the final day of Socrates, Plato's beloved mentor, and describes an underworld where souls are punished according to the sins of their lifetime.

Phaedo is written as a dialogue between Socrates and some of his students just before the philosopher is forced to drink hemlock. He explains that after death, evil spirits will be reincarnated in animal form as retribution for atrocities. The most reprehensible souls would be sent to TARTARUS, a gloomy pit of pain, for rehabilitation before reentering the life cycle. Plato also includes a true hell in his map of the underworld, called a place for souls "incurable" of their wicked ways. It is left to the judges described in *GORGIAS* to determine which souls are beyond hope and deserve this eternal damnation.

PIERS PLOWMAN William Langland's allegorical poem *The Vision of William concerning Piers the Plowman* (known simply as *Piers Plowman*) is a striking mix of religious teaching, social commentary, and supernatural fiction. Written in the 1300s (although not widely distributed until around 1550), *Piers Plowman* is as much a condemnation of the aristocracy and clergy of the Middle Ages as it is a religious treatise. The lengthy work, which has since become a classic of English literature, traces the creation of the world, the sin in the Garden of Eden, the life of Christ, and the HARROWING OF HELL. It also rebukes priests who charge a fee to forgive sins and denounces an upper class that dehumanizes and exploits the peasantry.

Piers Plowman is presented as a dream in which the author meets the title character, a representation of Jesus Christ, in the form of a simple farmer. He also encounters personifications of virtues and vices (symbolizing good and evil people in medieval society) and talks with the angels Gabriel and Michael. Piers Plowman (Christ) offers to guide them all to the beautiful yet elusive Tower of Truth (heaven), if they first help him plant and cultivate his fields. But to the Plowman's sorrow, most are unwilling to work for this goal and opt instead to serve their own shallow interests.

In the narrative, Langland describes a number of significant events, including the expulsion of LUCIFER from paradise. The author differentiates between SATAN and Lucifer, noting that the latter "was the loveliest light after our Lord till he broke obedience" and fell to the abyss. After his rebellion, he and his followers took on "loathy shapes," and Lucifer "lies lowest of them all." Satan, however, is the DEVIL, ruler of hell and punisher of damned souls. Both DEMONS have specific powers, as does the fiend BELIAL, a cunning trickster who preys on human weaknesses.

Langland describes, too, the harrowing of hell, when Christ descends to the abyss to free the souls of the patriarchs. Jesus, demanding that Lucifer yield to "the King of Glory," breaks down the gates of the inferno and calls forth his beloved. When the demon objects, Christ tells Lucifer that humans did not sin on their own but were tricked by the fiend's "trespass" in Eden. The Savior declares, "I did not hold out to them Hell here forever!" and explains that he has paid for their offenses with his own life. Jesus and the saved ascend to heaven, now a bitter memory for the fallen angels, who complain, "We've lost all our prey."

The story of *Piers Plowman* carries a strong directive: It challenges all people, from peasant to king, to dedicate their life to serving God and loving their neighbors. Only through this constant fidelity to the Divine can they hope to escape hell and enjoy eternity in Paradise.

PIETROS Hungarian legend holds that at the top of Pietros mountain is a castle owned by the DEVIL and is actually a portal to hell. The wicked proprietor lures people to his palace by hosting grand balls and lavish banquets, then invites guests to stay as permanent residents. Those who agree are cast into an eternal inferno as punishment for their self-indulgence.

According to one tale, an astute hunter named Iwanczuk discovers a magic salve that enables him to see the Pietros castle as it really is: a charred pile of rubble populated by damned souls. When the devil asks him to remain at Pietros, Iwanczuk calls out to heaven for strength, and the prayer forces the fiend to cringe and fall away. The huntsman flees the accursed site but is unable wash the balm out of his eyes. From that time on, Iwanczuk is able to see the forces of evil at work in the world. He spends the rest of his days trying to save others from damnation.

PILGRIM'S PROGRESS, THE
English preacher-turned-author John Bunyan wrote *The Pilgrim's Progress* in the mid-1600s, when his country was in the grip of religious intolerance and persecution. He himself spent twelve years in prison for the crime of unlicensed preaching of his faith. Under a law enacted by Queen Elizabeth I, citizens could follow no religion except the Church of England, which was founded by her infamous father, King Henry VIII. Those who refused were viciously persecuted. The experience of his incarceration, mingled with Bunyan's history of obsession with heaven and hell, resulted in the composition of *The Pilgrim's Progress,* a cautionary tale designed to fortify the spirituality of the common man and woman.

Bunyan had been having supernatural visions since early childhood. He reported seeing heaven, hell, angels, and DEMONS and even hearing the voice of God. In one poignant episode, the Heavenly Father asks him, "Wilt thou leave thy sins and go to Heaven, or have thy sins and to Hell?" This profound question followed Bunyan for the rest of his life, serving as the inspiration not only for *The Pilgrim's Progress* but also for a plethora of sermons, exempla, and essays, including *A FEW SIGHS FROM HELL* and *A Map of Salvation and Damnation.*

Bunyan was also heavily influenced by the teachings of John Calvin, a strict philosopher who taught that most people were destined to be damned, while only a select few had any hope of reaching heaven. This belief haunted Bunyan for years, until he finally came to believe that each person determines his or her own supernatural fate. But the graphic depictions of Calvin's horrific hell remained clear in his mind.

During Bunyan's prison term, these images mingled with the grotesque realities of his accommodations: a rodent-infested, overcrowded cell that carried the noxious stench of raw sewage. He saw hundreds of prisoners fall to fever, infection, and other gruesome afflictions. It was in this environment that he began writing *The Pilgrim's Progress,* from his own living hell.

The Pilgrim's Progress is a Puritan allegory that follows the story of Christian, a decent man who is sickened by the evil taking place all around him. He represents humanity, and his City stands for the world. When Christian learns that the City is about to be destroyed by the wrath of God, he picks up a heavy sack (sin) and sets off on a pilgrimage to the Celestial City (heaven), where he can dwell eternally with the Father. On this journey, Christian encounters a myriad of obstacles with such metaphorical names as the "Slough of Despond," "Doubting Castle," "Dark River," and "Difficulty Hill."

But the bleakest, most terrible part of his journey takes him through hell. Christian is terrified as he passes through the "Valley of the Shadow of Death," where he discovers the gates to the underworld. It is a desolate land of utter darkness inhabited by deformed monsters. The "Burning Pit" of hell creates such thick, putrid flames that Christian would have choked to death had he not shielded himself with "all-prayer," a sort of mystic cloak that wraps him in divine protection. Though the smoke is too dense for him to see much, Christian is chilled to his soul by the piercing screams of the damned and nauseated by the foul stench of evil. He is aware that demons swirl all around him, eager to snatch up his soul. Shaken to the core, he emerges from the depths with a renewed resolve to rid himself of any taint of sin.

Christian must also face APOLLYON, the dark angel described in the Bible as ruler of "the abyss." In *The Pilgrim's Progress,* Apollyon is a twisted creature covered with fish scales and dragon wings who belches smoke and stench through a gaping hole in his belly. The monster rules the "Valley of Humiliation" and refuses to let Christian pass. Apollyon showers him with flaming darts that pierce his skin and leave painful scars. But Christian, steadfast in his faith, wounds the demon with a sword so that the beast must retreat. Before fleeing, Apollyon vows to return again, as many times as necessary, to frustrate humanity's search for holiness.

Upon its publication in 1678, *The Pilgrim's Progress* was an immediate success. Written in a simple tone and style aimed at engaging the interest of the common reader, the book was far more enjoyable than typical literature of the day, which was developed for the intellectual elite. *The Pilgrim's Progress* was derided as trite and ridiculous by scholars of the day but accepted with great enthusiasm by the masses. Bunyan knew his audience: poor, humble, with little education, but eager for understanding. By putting complex religious ideas and philosophical concepts into an entertaining and easily grasped story, he captured the imagination of peasants of his native England and abroad.

Bunyan's work was so popular that within a few years of its publication, it had been widely translated and distributed throughout Europe. In response to the book's popularity and to many requests from readers, the author later wrote a sequel, *Part II,* which detailed the struggle of Christian's wife, Christianna, and their children to reach heaven despite the allure of evil. *The Pilgrim's Progress* has also had a great impact on Western literature and continues to be studied to this day.

PISTIS-SOPHIA

The Pistis-Sophia, a manuscript from around the third century, offers an interpretation of GNOSTIC HELL. In the text, Jesus describes hell to Mary Magdalene, calling it a "huge dragon" that encompasses the material world. This fierce beast has inside its body "twelve dungeons of horrible torment" where sinners are tortured by vicious DEMONS.

The Pistis-Sophia was denounced by early Christian leaders as blasphemous and ridiculed as nonsensical. A major point of contention was the manuscript's portrayal of God as an indifferent, almost cold, deity who had no compassion for his creatures. Theologians also decried the Pistis-Sophia's assertion that demons and "fates" could control people's lives and that free will and human responsible agency were almost meaningless.

But most offensive to church authorities, the Gnostic text declared Christ's crucifixion and HARROWING OF HELL unnecessary. Pistis-Sophia stated that material creations, inherently evil, were cleansed through Christ's incarnation. Therefore humanity (and all matter) had been "redeemed" when Christ assumed human form, and his death on the cross was inconsequential to the afterlife fate of humanity.

PLATO The ancient Greek philosopher Plato (c. 427–347 B.C.) offers several speculations about the afterlife through his literary works. In his *REPUBLIC,* an elderly man warns the young not to scoff at the idea of possible damnation. He reminds them that when one is young, death seems far off and unthreatening. But as people age, they must boldly face the fact that their days are numbered, and thoughts of hell become more terrifying. The sage explains that old men spend many restless nights lying awake in the darkness, tallying their sins and wondering what punishments might await in the next world.

The *Republic* also includes a grisly passage about TARTARUS, the darkest pit of the Greek underworld HADES. Plato describes a ghastly realm where DEMONS mercilessly beat and whip criminals before hurling them into the depths of Hades. He warns that even before death, evildoers are haunted by knowing that they face an eternity of suffering in the afterlife.

Plato offers further concepts of the underworld in *PHAEDO,* a drama about the death of Socrates, and in *GORGIAS,* a play that describes the system of judgment in the afterlife. All of his treatments hinge upon the idea of justice in the next world, where souls face reward or retribution for the actions of their lives.

PLUTON Pluton, often identified with the Greek HADES, is the hell of ancient Roman myth. The bleak underworld is ruled by King Pluto, a pitiless lord who metes out punishment to evil souls in the next world. In *Henry IV,* Shakespeare makes reference to "Pluto's damned lake . . . the infernal deep, with Erebus and tortures vile." Pluto is also mentioned as ruler of the dead in *LA FAVOLA D'ORFEO* and in *HIGHWAY TO HELL,* where Hell-Cop enjoys a snack at "Pluto's Donut Shop."

Illustration of an ancient statue of Pluto, ruler of Pluton. ART TODAY

POLTERGEIST *Poltergeist,* a modern ghost story rife with special effects and wry humor, became one of the biggest box offices successes of 1982. Steven Spielberg's supernatural thriller brings hell to the suburbs of California and has SATAN abducting souls through the television screen. And when a ruthless real estate developer builds homes over a cemetery without first relocating the corpses, the spirits of the dead come back for revenge.

Unbeknownst to homeowners Craig T. Nelson and JoBeth Williams, a passageway to hell evolves in their daughter's closet. It is a vile, putrid portal that resembles the inside of a cholesterol-jammed blood vein. From within, the steady drone of eerie noises resounds, and a noxious mix of smoke and pulsating fungus continuously wafts upward. Frantic mother Williams must enter this repulsive gateway in order to retrieve her child, with only a rope tied to her waist connecting her to the temporal plane. When she returns with the girl, both are covered with mucus and bloody afterbirth, as if they have been delivered from another realm.

The otherworldly villain of *Poltergeist* is an unseen Satan, called "the Evil One" by the psychic who arrives to advise the family on how to combat the siege of the damned. Viewers do, however, get a glimpse of what special effects whiz Craig Reardon calls his "animated zombies." These infernal creatures rise up from the underworld to terrorize the family. (One of these ambulatory corpses went on to star in MUSIC VIDEOS, appearing in Billy Idol's *Dancing with Myself* clip.)

Poltergeist is among a sad fraternity of films about the afterlife that have lost stars to untimely deaths. (Similar tragedies befell actors from *TWILIGHT ZONE—THE MOVIE, The Crow,* and *SCENES FROM THE CLASS STRUGGLE IN BEVERLY HILLS*). Less than a year after the film's release, seventeen-year-old costar Dominique Dunne was murdered by a crazed boyfriend. And Heather O'Rourke, who played the adorable cherub kidnapped into the afterlife, succumbed to a fatal stomach ailment before reaching her teens.

POLYGNOTUS In approximately 450 B.C., the artist Polygnotus painted the mural *Descent of Odysseus to HADES* at Delphi. His work illustrated Homer's epic journey the *ODYSSEY* but borrowed from other CHTHONIC legends as well. And though the work was destroyed centuries ago, descriptions of Polygnotus's illustrations survive and provide an early example of infernal CHURCH ART AND ARCHITECTURE.

Polygnotus's mural includes in the infernal kingdom of Hades the legendary ORPHEUS, an enchanted musician who follows his beloved wife to the underworld to try to restore her to life. The artist also shows the flesh-eating beast EURYNOMUS (precursor of the guard dog CERBERUS) devouring the dead in his gloomy lair. This bluish gray monster is depicted amid skeletons of his victims.

PORTRAIT OF THE ARTIST AS YOUNG MAN, A Irish author James Joyce offers a frightening depiction of hell in his semiautobiographical work *A Portrait of the Artist as a Young Man.* In his coming-of-age account of confusion and angst, Joyce incorporates passages from a HELLFIRE SERMON that terrified him as a child.

The novel's protagonist (Joyce's alter ego), Stephen Dedalus, recalls what his stern educators had said of the nether region: that the damned are abandoned in a mass grave permeated by darkness and the unbearable smell of decomposing flesh. It is a realm of "exterior darkness" since "the fire of Hell gives forth no light," only heat. This "never-ending storm of darkness" burns as black flames belch opaque smoke. Bodies smolder "heaped one upon another without even a glimpse of air." The horror is intensified by a putrid stench: "All the filth of the world, all the offal and scum of the world, we are told, shall run there as to a vast reeking sewer. . . . Imagine some foul and putrid corpse that has lain rotting and decomposing in the grave, a jelly-like mass of liquid corruption . . . giving off dense choking fumes of nauseous loathesome decomposition. And then imagine this sickening stench multiplied a millionfold and a millionfold again from the millions of fetid carcasses massed together in the reeking darkness, a huge and rotting human fungus."

Joyce's account claims that the air in hell is so "foul and unbreathable" that the fumes emanating from just one of the damned would be enough to contaminate the entire earth.

Critics believe that this description of the underworld was a common topic of sermons at the time when Joyce was attending regular church services as a young boy. The fear of hell instilled by such lectures stayed with him for decades, surfacing in his literary works years later.

PRINCE OF DARKNESS John Carpenter's 1987 film *Prince of Darkness* charts new depths in human agony. The convoluted movie depicts SATAN as an evil invader from outer space who has been imprisoned in a tank of fluorescent slime. The cursed container has somehow ended up in the basement of a California church, where a team of college students and a rogue priest stumble upon it. As they examine the canister and its accompanying texts, the group accidentally unleashes the extraterrestrial beast.

A scroll found with the tank describes a supernatural event in which the writer sees "a star fall from heaven into the bottomless pit" (an image taken from REVELATION). A horrible creature, the nefarious prince himself, rises from the pit, intent on destroying the earth. But before this is accomplished the DEMON is sealed in green glop by Jesus Christ, further identified as an "extraterrestrial" emissary from a humanoid race sent to warn earthlings about the brutal villain.

The horrors of hell, once relegated to the afterlife, now threaten to spill over into earthly existence. This infernal region is depicted as a liquid realm of black goo that can be accessed through a magic mirror. We see Satan's dad reach a monstrous black-clawed hand toward the human plain, although the demon's face is never shown.

The terror of the underworld menace is enhanced through numerous scenes of maggots eating human flesh and several disgusting depictions of zombies vomiting into the open mouths of hapless grad students. Demonic rape, an accelerated pregnancy, and bloody birth of the son of the antigod complete the abysmal atmosphere.

Prince of Darkness is littered with Satanic IMAGERY, most notably the Cross of Confusion, which combines an inverted cross with a question mark. This symbol appears on bruises of victims after demonic encounters. It indicates that for the unfortunate bearer, "living hell" has begun. Another scene shows a desecrated altar surrounded by defiled crucifixes. The allusion to traditional CHRISTIAN HELL is clear in this scene's heavy use of candles to create a "fiery" pit of depravity.

The film is little more than a thinly veiled attack on Christianity (described in the script as "a stupid lie") and specifically on Catholic clergy (self-serving "salesmen"). Hell, referred to as the "dark side," is no longer a place for evil souls but a sordid dimension populated by vicious monsters. *Prince of Darkness* vacillates between trying to instill holy fear for what awaits us in the afterlife and utter ridicule of the very notion of a world beyond. The result is a hollow hell that defies logic and mocks the concept of divine justice.

PURGATORIAL HELL Several religions teach that after death, the vast majority of human souls will go to a realm between heaven and hell to purge the evil of their lives. According to the theory, only the most pure ascend directly to paradise, and only the most vile are irrevocably damned. The rest—basically decent, moral people with an accumulation of minor offenses—must go to an intermediate place to rid themselves of the stain of sin. This afterlife waiting room is known as purgatory.

Religious scholars have debated the existence of purgatory for centuries. Accounts of the intermediate station from VISION LITERATURE (texts describing supernatural journeys to the afterlife) furthered the discussion during the early Middle Ages. The most spectacular of these is the *Vision of TUNDAL*, the tale of a twelfth-century playboy who goes on a mystic voyage to purgatory while touring the land of the dead. Belief in the transitional purging realm was officially accepted as Roman Catholic doctrine in 1253, but most Protestant Christian sects still doubt that purgatory exists.

In other faiths, such as Islam and ZOROASTRIANISM, hell itself is purgatorial. The realm of the damned will be destroyed along with the earth at the LAST JUDGMENT. Most condemned souls will be allowed to enter paradise, their metaphysical debt paid in full. Those beyond hope of salvation will face ANNIHILATION and be obliterated. Eastern faiths such as Buddhism, Hinduism, and Jainism likewise teach that souls remain temporarily in hell until they have rid themselves of evil and are ready to be reincarnated.

The philosopher Origen, whose ideas evolved into the concept of GNOSTIC HELL, taught that hell is indeed temporary and that even SATAN himself could be saved. Origen preached that souls could pass freely "from the highest good to the lowest evil," but these are only temporary states, not permanent judgments. In the end, all human spirits will find eternal rest in heaven.

Purgatorial hell has been popularized in fictional works of literature. The most famous example is found in Charles Dickens's *A Christmas Carol*. Greedy moneylender Jacob Marley, now deceased, appears wrapped in chains that represent the evil of his lifetime. He explains: "It is required of every man that the spirit within him should walk abroad among his fellowmen, and travel far and wide; and if that spirit goes not forth in life, it is condemned to do so after death. . . . In life, my spirit never roved beyond the narrow limits of our money-changing hole; and weary journeys lie before me!" Marley warns his former partner, Ebeneezer Scrooge, that a similar fate awaits him in the afterlife unless he changes his ways.

PYTHAGORAS Greek mathematician Pythagoras (c. 582–507 B.C.) gave Western civilization more than just his famous theorem for right triangles. In 530 B.C., he founded a philosophy school in Italy that taught the concept of transmigration of souls. He also claimed to have seen a vision of HADES, although this revelation remains suspicious, as the apparition focuses on seeing two of his old enemies squirming in eternal torment.

Pythagoras had long been critical of the works of early Greek writers Homer and Hesiod. He found their texts—especially Homer's *Iliad* and *ODYSSEY* and Hesiod's *Theogony: A History of the Gods*—to be filled with "lies about the gods." This blasphemy was, for Pythagoras, an unforgivable offense. After years of denouncing the pair, Pythagoras one day reported having a vision of the two scribes suffering with the damned. In his account, Hesiod was lashed to a blazing bronze column while Homer dangled from a tree encircled by serpents. Their pain, Pythagoras told his followers, was a just sentence for having angered the deities of Mount Olympus. He offered his vision as a warning to others who might have similar ideas.

Pythagoras is also responsible for pioneering one of the most pervasive symbols in supernatural IMAGERY. According to his system of numerology, the number 13 was synonymous with bad fortune. This has been absorbed into belief systems around the globe. In Christianity, there were thirteen men at the Last Supper, just before Jesus was handed over to be crucified. In Norse belief, there were a dozen gods in Valhalla until the evil LOKI arrived, only later to cause the death of the most beloved deity, Balder. A typical coven of witches has thirteen members. And in Tarot cards, believed by the superstitious to be capable of telling the future, the thirteenth card foretells imminent death.

Q

QASAVARA The people of Bangka Island in Melanesia have a rather distasteful view of the afterlife. Their belief is that damned souls end up as food for dragons, DEMONS, and ogres. The cruel cannibal spirit Qasavara gathers the dead and serves them to mythical monsters, and the condemned spend eternity in the bowels of the beasts.

QUETZALCOATL Quetzalcoatl is the ruler of the Toltec-Aztec underworld, a place known as the "land where only the feathered serpent knows no

Silver and abalone brooch depicting a ritual for Quetzalcoatl.

fear." The Aztecs (who inherited this CHTHONIC deity from the ancient Maya) had nine gods of the underworld, including the fearsome Quetzalcoatl, a winged snake who lurks in the dark places of the dead. He is the overlord of the gods as well as of all mortals, and his thirst for blood can be satisfied only with human sacrifices. His kingdom includes the World of Shadows, a murky realm of bitter gloom. He is associated with the number 7 and with the morning star (an affiliation that led Christian missionaries to connect Quetzalcoatl with LUCIFER, referred to in religious texts as "son of the morning star").

QUEVEDO, FRANCISCO GOMEZ DE Spanish baroque author Francisco Gomez de Quevedo y Villegas (1580–1645) spent the better part of his career composing satirical poems and novels denouncing the hypocrisy of Spain's "moralistic" society. His most stinging work, *Visions,* written in 1627, presents a variety of fantasies set in heaven and hell that expose the corruption of Spanish clergy, the cruelty of the aristocracy, and the indifference of the monarchy. Quevedo's motif of making salvation and damnation interchangeable in a self-absorbed culture bears similarities to George Bernard Shaw's play *MAN AND SUPERMAN,* which likewise calls into question the traditional criteria for afterlife judgment.

R

RADISH Radish is a hero of ancient Buddhist legend who travels to AVICI, the lowest circle of hell, to free the soul of his condemned mother. According to the tale, Radish learns of her damnation and vows to reclaim her spirit from this place of infernal torture. He journeys to the land of the dead with the help of incantations and magic spells but is unable to recognize his mother as she has been transformed into a dog. This is punishment for refusing food to a temple priest. When Radish realizes that his mother is now reduced to the shape of an animal, he begs the gods for mercy on her behalf.

His pleas touch the hearts of the deities, and they agree to allow her to return to the living world on one condition: She must dedicate her life to works of charity. Radish likewise must promise to strive for justice and compassion in order to end the curse. Both pledge themselves to this quest, and the two return to the upper world to fulfill their mission.

RAIKO Raiko is a legendary Japanese nobleman revered for his virtue and generosity. He is asked by the people of Kyoto to help rid the village of its DEMONS. Raiko agrees and is immediately stricken with fever and begins experiencing frightening visions of hell. The Kyoto demons, unwilling to be purged, taunt Raiko that they will one day have both his body and his soul.

The apparitions of the underworld grow increasingly horrific, and Raiko finds them so realistic that he starts believing that they are not hallucinations but actual experiences. In the most terrifying, Raiko is suspended on a huge web as a gigantic spider (representing evil) slowly moves toward him. As the spider draws closer, Raiko manages to seize his sword and cut himself free of the web. He then thrusts the blade into the creature, leaving it alive but severely wounded. The battle ended, Raiko collapses into a deep sleep that lasts for days.

Upon awakening, Raiko finds that his fever has lifted—and the demons that have been terrorizing Kyoto have mysteriously disappeared.

RAPTURE, THE Evangelical Christianity, the millennium, and concepts of CHRISTIAN HELL and salvation are probed in *The Rapture,* a 1991 supernatural drama. The film stars Mimi Rogers as a restless, world-weary woman who tries to escape the tedium of her life through wanton sexual escapades. This, too, soon becomes unsatisfying, and she moves on to a new obsession: charismatic Christianity. Rogers joins a congregation that believes the end of the world and the LAST JUDGMENT are imminent and that total surrender to God is necessary to avoid eternity in hell.

Rogers's character grows even more zealous when her husband is murdered in a senseless act of violence. Still in shock over his loss, she becomes convinced that God wants her to take her young daughter (played by Kimberly Cullum) with her to the desert to be assumed into heaven. She leaves her home and possessions behind and arrives penniless in the desert. But when the days pass and God has not delivered them, Rogers grows impatient and shoots her little girl, believing that the child will be better off in paradise. Fear of hell stops her from committing suicide, since she believes "you can't go to heaven if you kill yourself." Her faith turns to rage as she mourns her dead child.

While in the desert, Rogers meets a sheriff (played by Will Patton) who embodies the true spirit of Christ: He feeds the hungry, shelters the homeless, visits the imprisoned. He has no "religion" but displays a thirst for understanding and hope. The two engage in several discussions about philosophy and belief, but Rogers must ultimately admit, "I'm afraid of hell," and that is the basis for her religious adherence. When asked if she loves God, she must respond, "Not anymore. He has too many rules."

The night following Cullum's death, the Four Horsemen of the Apocalypse described in REVELATION arrive to signal the earth's destruction. Cullum appears to Rogers in her jail cell and quotes from the scripture of the "last days," declaring that the Last Judgment is about to take place. The girl urges Rogers to seek God's forgiveness, but her mother stubbornly insists that God must first explain himself and justify why there is "so much pain and suffering in the world" that he created. "Let me ask him *why,*" she demands, then perhaps she will repent.

For Patton, no explanation is necessary. His faith is simple and sincere. The film ends as he and Rogers stand on the brink of eternity, in a vast wasteland of darkness. "Is this Hell?" Patton asks as the two stand alone in the void. Cullum approaches and replies that they are on the banks of "the river that washes away all your sins." Heaven, she points out, is off in the distance. Patton, who is honestly able to profess his love for God, departs to paradise, but Rogers, bitter and resolute, refuses to go. She stands in the seamless gloom of hell, a chasm of nothingness, while her daughter's spirit joins the saved in heaven. Rogers must endure this cold damnation, without light, without love, without hope, "forever."

The Rapture makes a bold statement about devotion in the juxtaposition of Rogers and Patton. The former is an avowed "true believer" who attends services regularly and can quote Holy Scripture verbatim. Patton, on the other hand, is a kind-hearted gentleman who has had absolutely no formal religious training. Together, they represent the spectrum of human spiritual experience. The film likewise puts forth an interpretation of hell by defining its opposite. Damnation, in this view, is isolation from God, from loved ones, from beauty, and ultimately from love itself. *The Rapture* differentiates itself from other infernal films by asserting that the everlasting abyss is not reserved for murders, rapists, and pagans, but can be "chosen" by the pious as well.

RATI-MBATI-NDUA Rati-mbati-ndua has been called the SATAN of Fiji. He is a ravenous beast whose name means "one-toothed DEMON," and he delights in devouring the dead. When Rati-mbati-ndua flies through the night sky seeking victims, he leaves a burning meteor trail in his wake.

RAWLINGS, MAURICE
Renowned cardiologist Maurice Rawlings, M.D., explores negative NEAR-DEATH EXPERIENCES in his 1993 book *To Hell and Back.* Rawlings had often heard of such mystic voyages in the course of his work, but he routinely dismissed them as hallucinations. He believed that "patients who reported an after-death experience were a little crazy." A self-described cynic, Rawlings focused on the physical consequences of life-threatening episodes and left the spiritual implications to the clergy.

That attitude changed dramatically in 1977 while he was administering cardiopulmonary resuscitation to a man whose heart had stopped. As Rawlings worked, he was surprised when the frantic patient screamed, "For God's sake, don't stop! Every time you let go, I'm back in Hell!" Rawlings was accustomed to having recently revived patients yell at him to stop, declaring "you're breaking my ribs!" but he had never before been asked to continue. The man then asked Rawlings to pray with him, a request that left the cardiologist feeling "insulted." But he deferred to his patient's request, mumbling what he termed a "make-believe" prayer.

After the patient was revived, he told Rawlings a ghastly tale of being tortured among the damned. The doctor had heard many accounts of positive near-death and out-of-body experiences, but this was his first encounter with a negative one. Intrigued by the novelty of this story, Rawlings began interviewing emergency room personnel from across the country to see if similar incidents were occurring elsewhere. He kept of file of these reports, dubbing them "Hell cases."

Over the next decade and a half, Rawlings spoke with hundreds of patients who had been clinically dead and the doctors, nurses, and medical technicians who attended them. He compiled these accounts in *To Hell and Back*, the first book to focus on such repugnant near-death experiences. The work describes the specifics of trips to the underworld and explores the reasons why only happy, peaceful stories receive mass-media coverage.

The descriptions of the underworld recounted in *To Hell in Back* vary, but they are all distinctly unpleasant. One patient initially sees the proverbial "tunnel of light" but is horrified when it catches fire as he walks through it. The fiery passage burns "like an oil spill." Another account tells of a "conveyor belt" that spews huge, oddly colored puzzle pieces at the damned. The pieces "had to be fitted together rapidly under severe penalty from an unseen force." There is no heat or physical torture, but the pressure of working on this deranged assembly line is unbearable.

Equally terrifying is another woman's story of finding herself in a barren wasteland teeming with naked "zombie-like people standing elbow to elbow doing nothing but staring" at her. It is like being abandoned in the ward of an endless insane asylum. Many patients had their horrific experiences compounded by recognizing friends and family members among the tenants of hell.

To Hell and Back also poses some innovative theories about the connection between visions of hell and UFO abductions, which the author theorizes originate from the same diabolical source.

REPUBLIC Fourth-century B.C. Greek philosopher PLATO wrote many dialogues that speculated on the underworld, including the *Republic*. This treatise examines the concept of justice by describing a utopian society where everyone is treated fairly, the good are rewarded for their virtue, and evildoers receive just punishment. In contrast, he likens this world, the human plane, to a cave where humans are chained prisoners trying to interpret the shadows that surround them.

Plato describes in his *Republic* an elderly man who rebukes the youthful for dismissing the notion of a grim hell as nonsense. When a person is young, he tells them, he thinks himself immortal. The very thought of death, much less an afterlife, is inconceivable. But as years pass, the reality of the grave becomes undeniable and the possibility of damnation becomes increasingly frightening. The old man warns his young friends that they, too, will one day spend many restless hours pondering the world to come and fearing the torments that might await in that realm.

The *Republic* also features a passage regarding TARTARUS, the darkest pit of HADES reserved for the worst sinners. In the dialogue, Socrates tells the "Myth of Er," about a famous soldier who "dies," visits the underworld, then returns to tell his fellowmen about final justice. When Er falls on the battlefield, he is believed dead, and his SHADE (soul) joins a legion of departed spirits on a journey to the afterlife. In the next world, Er sees two chasms in the sky and two cutting into the earth. Between the chasms are judges who direct the souls into the appropriate chamber. Virtuous spirits are sent to the sky's upper right opening; damned souls are relegated to the earth's left chasm. Out of the other two channels, a steady stream of spirits is continually exiting.

Unlike the bright, joyful shades emerging form the sky, spirits leaving the earth are dirty, weary, and haunted. They tell of fierce DEMONS "of fiery aspect" who torture the damned without pity in a gloomy chamber where sinners are punished "tenfold" for their crimes. These vile fiends then hurl condemned spirits into the deepest pits of Tartarus, where they find no relief from their agony. Some souls are so steeped in their own corruption that they will never be released.

Er then travels with the purged spirits to the altar of the Fates, where souls are returned to the earth. Each one can choose what sort of life he will have in the next incarnation and inherently accepts the rewards and risks that accompany the selection. The Greek musician ORPHEUS asks to return as a swan; Odysseus, hero of the epic *ODYSSEY,* has had his fill of adventure and requests a simple, quiet life. Before embarking on the next destiny, each shade drinks from the river LETHE to forget his former existence. But Er is forbidden to do so, since he must remember and share his tale.

Plato's message in the *Republic* is that each person is responsible for his or her own actions and must be prepared to face the consequences. He reiterates this point by reminding readers that there is no escape from justice, since those who are evil in this life will be forced to pay for their sins in the next.

REVELATION The oldest depictions of CHRISTIAN HELL originate in Revelation. This book of the Bible was written by St. John the Evangelist while he was in exile for preaching Christianity and is based on visions he experienced during the first century A.D. In this extraordinary work, St. John describes a number of supernatural events, including the rebellion of LUCIFER, the creation of hell, and the impending LAST JUDGMENT. He offers this brief depiction of Lucifer's betrayal: ". . . there was a war in Heaven: Michael and his angels fought against the dragon [Lucifer]; and the dragon fought and his angels, and prevailed not; neither was their place found any more in heaven" (Rev. 12:7–8).

The greater part of Revelation is devoted to foretelling the cataclysmic events that will mark the destruction of the world. St. John describes an Antichrist who will try to corrupt humanity, numerous natural disasters that will claim millions of lives, and a horrible beast similar to LEVIATHAN, the oceanic monster of the Old Testament. He warns that when these things come to pass, all humans will be called upon to account for their lives before being damned to hell or welcomed into paradise: "And the sea gave up the dead which were in it; and death and HADES delivered up the dead who were in them. And they were judged, each one according to his works" (Rev. 20:13).

Revelation contains frequent references to SATAN and to the "Lake of Fire" that awaits the iniquitous in the world to come. The author calls damnation a "second death" that ravages the soul in the manner that physical demise destroys the body. This ultimate suffering is the loss of God and the everlasting separation from the Almighty's love, beauty, and joy.

A 1498 illustration by Albrecht Dürer of the Four Horsemen of the Apocalypse from Revelations: War, Hunger, Plague and Death. ART TODAY

RODIN, AUGUSTE French artist Auguste Rodin (1840–1917) has been called the best sculptor since MICHELANGELO by art scholars across the world. His 1877 sculpture *The Bronze Age* was so realistic that patrons believed that this was not a statue at all but a human being encased in metal. But Rodin's greatest creation is the *GATES OF HELL*, an elaborate set of brass doors for the Museum of Decorative Arts in Paris. Despite being left unfinished at the time of his death, the composition is a triumph in artistic accomplishment.

Gates of Hell is a massive sculpture illustrating the horrors of the underworld. Rodin uses images from Dante's *DIVINE COMEDY: THE INFERNO*, Peter Paul Rubens's *THE FALL OF THE DAMNED*, and Michelangelo's *LAST JUDGMENT* in creating a visual spectacle of CHRISTIAN HELL. Its single most famous component, *The Thinker*, depicts a condemned soul contemplating his fate at the doorway to damnation.

Rodin's work is significant in that it combines styles and symbols of classic art and literature into a contemporary depiction of the underworld. *Gates of Hell* is among the most complex and ornate compositions of the past centuries and serves as a testament of people's lingering preoccupation with the realm of the damned even in the Age of Enlightenment.

ROSE MADDER Stephen King's *Rose Madder*, a 1994 novel about a woman fleeing her abusive husband, includes allusions to HADES, the mythical underworld of ancient Greece. His tale of innocence, violation, and retribution includes images of the river LETHE, with waters that make mortals forget their lives, the ERINYES (Fates) who torment iniquitous souls, and the evil King MINOS, lord of hell featured in Dante's *DIVINE COMEDY: THE INFERNO* as judge of the damned.

The novel tells the story of Rosie McClelon, a battered wife who wants only to be rid of her vicious husband, Norman. But when she tries to escape, Norman tracks her across the country with murder on his mind. Rosie's only hope lies in a parallel world where a mysterious goddess offers ominous assistance, statues come alive, and wicked men are transformed into hideous beasts. It is a place of final reckoning, where justice is inescapable.

When Rosie and her boyfriend, Bill Steiner, enter the supernatural realm to battle the forces of evil, Bill asks, "Is this the afterlife?" But the response is deliberately vague, as King implies that rage itself is what truly damns us. This internal anger makes existence intolerable and threatens happiness in any plane.

S

SAINT PATRICK'S PURGATORY An Irish legend dating back to the mid-1100s includes a description of St. Patrick's purgatory, a place of great suffering for those who die without repenting their sins. Sir Owen, an adventurous knight, explores the region as part of his extensive travels.

Escorted by demons, Sir Owen visits the PURGATORIAL HELL, a putrid cavern located on a desolate island near County Donegal. Within its borders, souls are boiled in sulfur, thrown off cliffs, gnawed upon by monsters, and forced to endure bitter cold and excruciating heat. The region is permeated by a horrible stench of decay and burning flesh. Sir Owen must exit St. Patrick's purgatory by crossing a narrow bridge over a river of fire. Fearing for his safety, he kneels and begs for God's mercy and is mystically transported over the passage by divine intervention. The terrified knight then flees the accursed realm, vowing to live a virtuous life lest he be sent back to this hell after his death.

SAMHAIN Samhain (meaning "summer's end") is the ancient Celtic lord of the dead. Legends dating back to the days of the Druids explain how the worlds of the living and the dead come together at the feast of Samhain, a break in time between the end of autumn and the start of winter. As the Celts measure days from sundown to sundown, Samhain begins at dusk on October 31, the last day of fall. During this night and until dawn on November 1, damned spirits, DEMONS, and FAIRIES rise from the underworld to scour the earth, desperate to satisfy their bloodlust.

The Celts believed that the land of the dead exists directly below the hills of the Irish countryside and that certain spells and incantations could raise the spirits of the deceased. They lit bonfires and set out food for the ambulatory damned, hoping to appease them. Peasants wore masks resembling demons and GHOULS to make themselves blend in with the risen dead. On Samhain, no one went out alone.

One story tells that during Samhain, a witch summons from hell the soul of the Shadowman, an ominous spirit believed to have great supernatural powers. When the abyss is opened, the Shadowman steps forward amid an explosion of fire and sulfurous smoke. The enraged spirit demands that he be returned to the underworld, but the witch is unable to reverse the spell. In some versions of this tale, the Shadowman is left to wander the earth prowling for souls to steal. In others, he is destroyed by Irish folk hero Finn MacCumal.

Today, Samhain has been tamed into Halloween, a children's holiday celebrated with costumes, candy, and pranks. The modern custom of trick or treating originates from the ancient festival: Druids went door to door asking for wood to feed their sacrificial fires. If the residents refused to supply any, a curse was placed on the household. But those who gave scraps of timber were rewarded with protection from the marauding dead.

Carving pumpkins into Jack-o'-lanterns is likewise a remnant of Samhain. Many believed that souls of the dead could be confined in physical containers. Pumpkins, roughly the size of a human head, were hollowed out and decorated with faces to serve as receptacles for the raised spirits. The name derives from an Irish legend about a miser named Jack who plays practical jokes on the DEVIL. When he dies, neither heaven nor hell will accept his soul. He is condemned to wander the earth with his lantern until the LAST JUDGMENT, at which time God might show him mercy.

John Carpenter's classic 1978 horror film *Halloween* contains reference to Samhain and its rituals, bringing the age-old evil into the twentieth century via a diabolical villain who seems unstoppable. Like his ancient precursor, the fiend has a thirst for human sacrifice.

SATAN Satan is lord of DEMONS and ruler of hell in Christian and Jewish tradition (called IBLIS in Islamic texts). His name is the Hebrew term for "adversary," as Satan's mission is to frustrate the will of God. He is referred to in the Bible as "the liar," "angel of the bottomless pit," and "the enemy." Satan is sometimes identified as LUCIFER, the angel of light, although religious scholars insist that the two are separate beings. Confusion arises from passages in REVELATION: "There was a war in Heaven: Michael and his angels fought against the dragon and the dragon fought and his angels and prevailed not; neither was their place found anymore in Heaven. And the great dragon was cast out, that old serpent, called the Devil, and Satan, which deceiveth the whole world" (Rev. 12:7–9).

The name Satan is never applied to the angel while still in heaven, only after the fall, although Lucifer is used interchangeably. He is also known as the Prince of Darkness, the Beast, the DEVIL, Black Angel, and Lord of the Abyss.

One thing is clear: Satan, although God's adversary, is not his equal. The Bible states that Satan shall have power "in this age" but that he shall be vanquished in "the age to come." The DEMON has already suffered a painful defeat by Jesus Christ called the HARROWING OF HELL. According to Christian doctrine, after Christ's crucifixion, the redeemer raids the underworld and delivers the souls of the virtuous dead to heaven. A second victory over Satan is foretold at the LAST JUDGMENT, when the earth will be destroyed and the fiend will be bound for eternity in the pits of hell.

Satan is a key figure in hundreds of works of Western literature, most notably *PARADISE LOST, FAUST, DIVINE COMEDY: THE INFERNO,* and *PIERS PLOWMAN* (in which he is clearly identified as being distinct from Lucifer). The dark angel is also prevalent in MORALITY PLAYS, MEDIEVAL DRAMA, MYSTERY PLAYS, and artworks. In modern times, Satan is often a curiosity glamorized in HEAVY METAL MUSIC performances or satirized in sketches on *SATURDAY NIGHT LIVE, KIDS IN THE HALL,* films such as *STAY TUNED* and *BILL & TED'S BOGUS JOURNEY,* and in product ADVERTISING.

SATANIC VERSES, THE Author Salman Rushdie was catapulted to international fame in 1989 when Islamic leaders demanded that the writer be executed. The death sentence came in response to publication of Rushdie's *The Satanic Verses,* which irate Muslim clerics denounced as blasphemous and despicable. The book was banned throughout the Islamic world and even in India, Rushdie's native country, where authorities worried it would inflame tensions between warring religious groups.

Objection to the work stemmed from the fact that the main character, Mahound (an ancient name of the DEVIL), closely resembles the historic figure MUHAMMAD, founder of Islam. Mahound is depicted as a fanatic who claims to be receiving messages from an angel but is actually creating a religion according to his own whims. The faith he preaches is constantly "spouting rules, rules, rules . . . rules about every damn thing" that focus on mind control rather than spiritual development. And, as is often the case with

Muslim extremists, criticism is met with anger and condemnation. Mahound calls all dissent "devil's talk" and encourages followers to surrender their free will and "trust the Book."

The Satanic Verses opens with the explosion of a hijacked airline over the English Channel. Amid the debris, two passengers, a legendary Indian movie star named Gibreel Farishta and television voice-over specialist Saladin Chamcha, float gently to the earth, seemingly unharmed. But as they resume their lives, they begin to notice remarkable changes. Saladin's legs mutate into cloven hoofs, sharp horns grow from his temples, and he realizes that "some demonic and irreversible mutation is taking place in my inmost depth." Gibreel, too, finds that he has been changed. He now has a visible halo and radiates a "distinctly golden glow."

The book then launches into an allegory of the eternal battle between good and evil and the corresponding duality of humanity. As the characters soon learn, it is often difficult to tell who is angel and who is DEMON in this confusing realm. "Ghosts, Nazis and saints" dwell together, and salvation and damnation seem to be almost interchangeable. Even the two men, despite their new shapes, are uncertain about their own personal morality and their role in the grand scheme of destiny.

The Satanic Verses further illustrates the ongoing war by interweaving tales of Mahound and his unholy faith into the story of Gibreel and Saladin. Mahound calls himself the Prophet of Jahilia (City of Sand), a desolate place that resembles JAHANNAM, Islamic hell. At one point in the text, the dark angel Beelzebub and his demon legions take notice of the self-proclaimed holy man and ask, "Is he with us or not?" Even Mahound's scribe, who had given up everything to follow the prophet, begins to wonder if perhaps he has made a tragic mistake.

As Mahound's religion degenerates into a massive tangle of bureaucratic regulations, he keeps followers in line by reminding them of the dire consequences of disobedience. Those who scoff at "divine law" or refuse to obey will surely be cast into the raging inferno. Mahound teaches that this abyss is a PURGATORIAL HELL, a harsh realm where souls are purified of sin through various tortures and torments. "Even the most evil of doers would eventually be cleansed by hellfire," Mahound tells believers, albeit after much indescribable suffering.

Rushdie's massive work is also a study in the cyclical nature of life. Characters experience life, death, sin, forgiveness, adventure, homecoming, division, and resolution. The author accomplishes this by mingling religious concepts with fragments of Arabian folktales and other myths, creating rich stories within stories. His lesson is that hell, like heaven, is a state of being that can exist anywhere, even in the most unexpected places.

SATURDAY NIGHT LIVE Over its twenty-plus-year run, the comedy series *Saturday Night Live* has found numerous ways to lampoon hell. Segments poking fun at the underworld have included ADVERTISING spoofs, jabs at SATAN, song parodies, and even a lambasting of tabloid newspapers sensationalizing the everlasting inferno. Hell also arises frequently as the punchline of the show's infernal JOKES and ironic CLICHÉS.

In one 1983 sketch, a commercial for a tabloid offers to inform "inquiring minds" whether the recently deceased Gloria Swanson ascended to heaven or was damned to hell. The spot includes a look at the abyss, depicted as a flaming pit into which Swanson's photo is dropped. During the same season, cast member John Lovitz's SATAN was a recurring character, routinely popping up to antagonize guest stars and encourage DEVIL worship. His costume consists of a bright red satin suit with matching cape, black horns sprouting from his temples, a red tail, and a pitchfork. At the close of each such appearance, Lovitz would press his face against the camera and chant, "Worship me! I command you!" then erupt in maniacal laughter.

Another cast member, Christopher Guest, revived his role as guitarist for satirical HEAVY METAL group Spinal Tap for a demonic Christmas song. The holiday carol "Christmas with the Devil" describes what the yuletide season is like in hell. According to the lyrics, the "elves are dressed in leather," the "sugar plums are rancid," and the "stockings are in flames." During the performance, elfish DEMONS frolic wickedly as black snow blankets the stage. In a mock interview with the band, Guest quips, "A man's relationship with the devil is a very private thing."

Beer advertisements receive a grand bashing in a commercial spoof about what overachievers "deserve." Toasting one another with golden brew, the characters comment on how they have sold condominiums at five times their original value, climbed the corporate ladder at all costs, and shed the draining influences of family and friends. The tag line promises, "For all you do, you're gonna PAY!" as the "beautiful people" suddenly find themselves cast into the fiery bowels of hell. The now-screaming yuppies are tortured by demons as the narrator coos that this, quite simply, is justice.

Traditional religious depictions of the underworld have also been fair game. A 1994 sketch features guest host Patrick Stewart as a less than impressive Satan trying to discipline a band of wisecracking demons. Stewart, perched on a crimson throne in a smoky, cavernous kingdom dotted by leaping flames, showers his throng with bad jokes and ridiculous curses. When they mock him for his inane comments, he turns the fiends into "burning monkeys."

Comedian Jim Carey satirizes infernal clichés in the 1996 "See You In Hell" sketch. Carey plays an impetuous businessman who responds to virtually every comment with a hardy, "I'll see you in hell!" He writes the phrase on checks, uses it to greet his friends, drops it into party conversation. The segment ends with reunion in the underworld where Carey and his comrades do meet again amid the flames, smoke, and stench of the great inferno.

SCENES FROM THE CLASS STRUGGLE IN BEVERLY HILLS

In a dark parody of the shallow lifestyle of affluent 1980s Californians, *Scenes from the Class Struggle in Beverly Hills* features an amusing commentary on the nature of hell. Writer Bruce Wagner creates a scenario where servants and their wealthy employers live in the same locale but worlds apart, both in this life and the next.

The film follows the adventures of a self-absorbed widow (played by Jacqueline Bisset) who is routinely visited by the ghost of her equally vacuous, recently deceased husband (played by Paul Mazursky). Mazursky has accidentally killed himself in a mishap with autoeroticism and is now a resident of the smoky abyss. When asked why he keeps reappearing, the accursed man passionately exclaims about departed souls, "They live, they feel, they desire." His loneliness has driven him out of hell and back to Bisset's side.

Mazursky's ultimate goal is to convince her to join him in hell where they can resume their existence together. Trying to persuade her, he describes the realm of the damned as a close parallel to Beverly Hills, even noting he has a house "just like this one" picked out for them in the inferno. Mazursky assures his wife, "You'll love it in hell," and in fact will hardly notice the difference between the two worlds.

But even in death, the peasants and the privileged inhabit different realms. While Mazursky sketches a great below of lavish homes, expensive cars, and manicured lawns, the Chicana maid Rosa (played by Edith Diaz) conjures the primal, earthy underworld of ancient Aztec myth. Throughout the film, Diaz spouts dire warnings and pearls of wisdom from pagan Indian folklore. At the funeral of an obnoxious pet pooch, Diaz declares—with great drama—that the departed Bojangles is now "in the arms of QUETZALCOATL," a fierce winged serpent that dwells in the land of the dead. Her upper-crust employers, ignorant and oblivious, smile and nod through their tears. The last scene of the film shows the deceased dog nestled in Mazursky's arms as the two depart for the dark abyss.

Wagner uses the analogies to make a statement about superficiality, privilege, and the lack of human compassion. In one scene, a prominent "diet doctor" dismisses the controversy about his latest weight loss plan by casually commenting that when the wealthy become obsessed with becoming thin, "some of them are going to die." In a tragic irony of this life-is-cheap attitude, young costar Rebecca Schaeffer was murdered by a celebrity stalker not long after finishing *Scenes,* just as she was poised to begin a promising cinematic career.

SCREWTAPE LETTERS, THE

The Screwtape Letters is a masterpiece of infernal dialogue penned by the genius C. S. Lewis, author of THE GREAT DIVORCE. Originally written as an advice column in *The Guardian* newspaper during World War II, Lewis's letters are communiqués between Screwtape, a DEVIL and the "Undersecretary of the Department of Temptation," and his nephew Wormwood, a tempter in training. Through these dispatches, Screwtape gives the young fiend advice on how to corrupt souls to help SATAN reach his goal of "drawing all to himself" in the great below. Through this unusual medium, the author likewise instructs readers to guard against such diabolical tricks.

Lewis opens his book with a brief description of hell, a palce where each being "lives the deadly serious passions of envy, self-importance and resentment" for all eternity. It is a realm where there is no individuality, no dignity, for these things reflect God's goodness and have no place in the underworld. Hell is a bleak, ugly "Kingdom of Noise" where the dissonant sounds of wailing souls and tortured screams replace music and laughter. Human spirits serve as the "food" upon which DEMONS ravenously feast.

In his letters to Wormwood, Screwtape explains that Satan captures humans by lulling them into putting their own desires and interests ahead of God's divine plan. A devil's job is to cause people to "turn their gaze away from Him towards themselves." This, the dark angel declares, is the way to lead souls to hell, as there are relatively few murderers, rapists, and truly despicable people whose damnation is assured. For most, Screwtape tells Wormwood, "the safest road to hell is the gradual one—the gentle slope" unmarked by glaring atrocities. Humans who devote their lives to "causes," self-interest, pleasure—confident that they have done nothing vile enough to be condemned—will discover too late that they should have paid more attention to charity and the sacraments.

The Screwtape Letters concludes with an epilogue in hell, where Screwtape is offering a toast at the annual demon graduation dinner. The banquet's fare consists of the latest crop of human souls, served in such dishes as "Casserole of Adulterers" and "Municipal Authority with Graft Sauce" washed down with a vintage "Pharisee" wine. The devil complains that the quality of the food is not what it used to be—he reminisces on past delicacies of Hitler, Henry VIII, and Casanova—but at least the quantity of damned spirits is steadily increasing. Hell, he declares, has never had "more abundance."

In closing, Screwtape informs his fellow fiends that sinners are becoming "trash," scraps of sullied humanity that once would have been thrown to "CERBERUS and the Hellhounds" to gnaw and gobble. These modern souls are not truly evil, just lazy sloths who never bothered with salvation since it did not appease their immediate appetites. They are the children of democracy, wherein everything is a "choice" and no governing moral code is allowed. Such unfettered freedom, Screwtape declares, permits man to "enthrone at the center of his life a good solid, resounding lie." Modern man does not see his actions as sinful and therefore suffers no guilt, feels no remorse, and seeks no divine forgiveness. After a lifetime of these conscience-numbing decisions, these hollow souls simply trickle, without fanfare, into the pit of hell.

Lewis published his dark satire as a cautionary tale during the late 1950s, when "goodliness" was replacing "Godliness" as a prime objective of humanity. He urges a return to traditional devotion to the Heavenly Father and warns against intellectualism that puts humans at the center of the universe. *The Screwtape Letters* further suggests that the two most dangerous errors humans make regarding demons is to believe they do not exist, or to become fascinated with them. Falling into either trap, Lewis asserts, will surely take one down the path to hell.

SEASON IN HELL, A Arthur Rimbaud's autobiographical poetic allegory *Une Saison en enfer (A Season in Hell)* is among the most fascinating works of literature ever produced. Influenced by images of CHRISTIAN HELL (many works refer to SATAN, Beelzebub, and the sea monster LEVIATHAN), the poems convey a sense of restlessness turned to despair. Rimbaud's book is odd not only in its content but also in the bizarre story that surrounds its publication. For the young French poet, his short life, marred by scandal and tragedy, was indeed reminiscent of the sufferings of the damned.

In one passage titled "Night in Hell," Rimbaud likens his wretched life on earth to existence in the netherworld. This image comforts rather than horrifies him, as he feels more companionship with lost souls than with his living contemporaries. He goes so far as to declare that the "delights of the damned" will be far greater when his spirit descends "into the void" where he will finally dwell among peers and escape the harsh critics and stifling restrictions of the human plane. Thus it is not the thought of damnation that tortures Rimbaud, but the insufferable years of life that lead to it.

The author offers a considerably more grisly interpretation of what awaits the condemned in his "Dance of the Hanged Man." Here, Rimbaud describes the DEMON Beelzebub as a puppeteer who treats humans as toys, "slapping at their heads" to make them "dance, dance" for his pleasure. However these souls are being punished for their inhumanity and cruelty; whereas the author envisions himself as damned for his thoughts rather than his acts. Rimbaud anticipates no such physical torments for intellectual sinners.

Early in life, Rimbaud declared that his only ambition was to write poetry. His disapproving mother, however, tried to force her son into a more "respectable" line of work by forbidding him to read or write any poems and even banned from her house works of the French genius Victor Hugo. But her strategy backfired: Rimbaud ran away to Paris while still in his teens and began a homosexual affair with fellow author Paul Verlaine. Verlaine was both excited and disturbed by the boy's shocking, vulgar behavior, and at one point he truly believed Rimbaud to be a werewolf. This only added to the poet's appeal and to his enduring legend.

Rimbaud wrote *A Season in Hell* between the ages of sixteen and nineteen, then published the work in 1873 at his own expense. The collection laments his status as an outcast who is surely damned and contains haunting images of both the young writer's troubled past and his grim future in the underworld. Within the composition, Rimbaud speculates that true agony—in this life as well as in the next—is the torment of feeling lonely, isolated, and abandoned. Despondent and brooding, the author distributed several printed copies to friends in Paris, then burned the manuscript and swore never to compose another poem. Rimbaud soon departed to Africa, where he worked as a tradesman until a tumor necessitated the amputation of his leg. He returned to Marseilles, where died in 1891 at age thirty-seven.

Despite this austere start, Rimbaud has since been declared one of the great modern poets and *A Season in Hell* a masterpiece. He has been elevated to the status of cultural icon in France. In 1991, a gala event was held in Paris to mark the centennial anniversary of the author's death. The festival included games, banquets, and a nationwide contest for budding poets. To commemorate Rimbaud's life and his *Season in Hell,* the French Ministry of Culture even requested that the International Astronomical Union name a star in his honor.

SENTINEL, THE People have been fascinated with the prospect of a passage between earth and hell for millennia. According to Jeffrey Konvitz's 1974 novel *The Sentinel,* that gateway exists in a fashionable New York City brownstone. The contemporary fiction explores how this supernatural bridge would be received in the modern climate of disbelief in the great inferno.

Protagonist Allison Parker, a young model grappling with her father's death and her own failed suicide attempts, finds the apartment of her dreams in a quiet neighborhood on the Upper West Side. But after moving in, Allison begins to have doubts. She is unnerved by an odd assortment of neighbors, including a blind priest who sits day and night staring out the upstairs window, a pair of caustic lesbians, and a senile old woman who seems hauntingly familiar. Hoping to allay her fears, Allison's coldly "irreligious" boyfriend, Michael, does some investigating, only to find himself drawn further and further into a bizarre supernatural plot.

Michael informs Allison that the brownstone is actually "the bridge over Chaos," the "connection between the

Gates of Hell and the boundaries of earth." He tells the disbelieving woman that ever since Adam and Eve sinned in the Garden of Eden, a guardian has been posted at this site to "sit and watch for the legions of Hell," to prevent SATAN from releasing the damned to devour the living. She has been chosen as the next sentinel. When Allison rejects this preposterous theory, Michael erupts, revealing that he knows this because he himself is dead. He has been killed by those trying to protect Allison, and declares, "I've been damned to eternal Hell for my sins! *I am one of the legion!*"

Allison then must decide whether she will surrender herself to this new role, or take her own life. As the sentinel, she would be stripped of her senses, transformed into a hideous hag, and confined to a dark room for the rest of her life, but she would be promised salvation. Should she commit suicide, she would take her place among the condemned souls in eternal torment. The denizens of hell assail her, encouraging Allison to join them in "this infernal pit. Abominable, accurst, the house of woe, and Dungeon of our Tyrant!"

Konvitz's novel was made into a film in 1976 and joined numerous similar movies describing a mystic portal to the underworld, including *THE BEYOND, DEVIL'S DAUGHTER,* and *THE GATE.* But speculation about physical connections to hell go back centuries, to Greek myths about LAKE AVERNUS, early Christian folktales of ST. BRENDAN and the CAVE OF CRUACHAN, and African legends of KITAMBA and UNCAMA.

SERAPIS Serapis offers a rare link between Greek and Egyptian myth. This god of the underworld shows up in CHTHONIC legends from both civilizations. Serapis, who had power over fate and could reward or punish souls of the dead, is often depicted with a dog at his feet. He watches over the dead in a dark land of eternal night.

SHADES According to ancient Greek myth, departed human souls become listless, lethargic spirits called shades. In this faded form, shades journey to the kingdom of HADES, the Greek underworld, where they will spend eternity. There, most suffer no physical punishment but are deprived of the carnal joys of human existence. Human spirits dwelling in the Hebrew SHEOL were thought to be similar murky beings.

Shades describe their shadowy existence in a number of epics, including the *AENEID* and the *ODYSSEY,* and appear in such classic works of Western literature as *DIVINE COMEDY: THE INFERNO* and the recent novel *MEMNOCH THE DEVIL.* The 1962 cult classic film *CARNIVAL OF SOULS* likewise depicts spirits as vacuous and robotic, eternally going through the motions of some meaningless dance.

SHEOL Sheol is the underworld of ancient Semitic belief. It is a bleak place of unending monotony where existence continues at a low ebb. Souls in Sheol cannot interact with the gods, nor can they communicate with the liv-

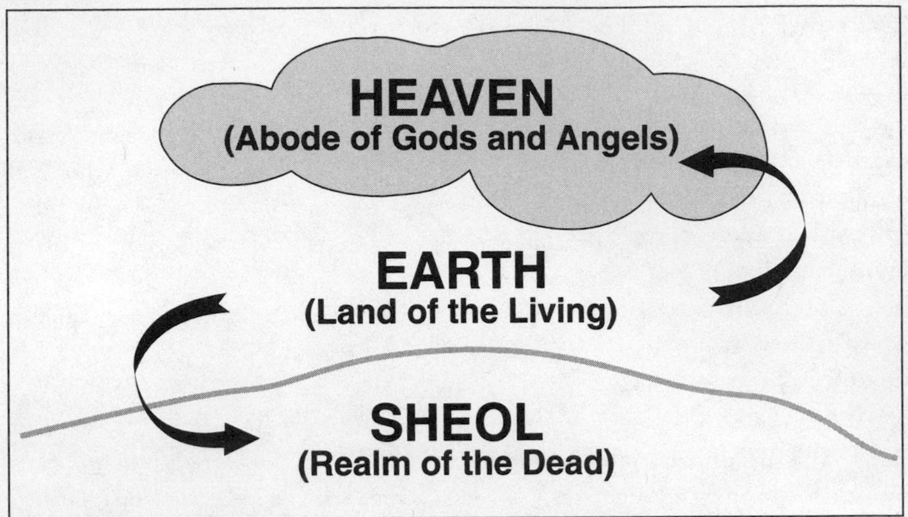

The living have awareness of heaven and Sheol; the dead are cut off from both upper realms.

ing and have little awareness of events outside the forlorn chamber's borders. Like the Greek underworld of HADES, Sheol is the repository of all departed souls, good and evil.

Early Jewish prophets absorbed the pagan image of Sheol and used it when referring to the afterlife. Hebrew tradition divided the realm into two sections: one for the wicked who have sinned against God; the second for virtuous spirits who have lived pious and reverent lives. Souls of the just suffer no torments in Sheol, but evil spirits are severely punished. Toward the end of the Hebrew Scriptures, there are hints of escape from the somber realm and restoration to a joyful existence, where the dead receive glory and relief from the hand of God.

The first writings about the realm, dating back to around 700 B.C., refer to the murky underworld as a "land of gloom and deep darkness." In the Old Testament, Enoch has a vision of Sheol that he declares "chaotic, horrible." These depictions of the underworld as a crowded, cavernous chasm have derived from pits used as mass graves during this time. Almost everyone, except members of the royal houses, was buried in large communal plots with no individual MEMORIALS, and so it was logical to believe that the next life would be similarly pedestrian.

The ancient concept of Sheol as a tedious prison for damned souls has been largely displaced by modern theories. Many now believe that evil souls will face ANNIHILATION and will be eradicated in the afterlife. Others envision the underworld approximating traditional CHRISTIAN HELL, a place of sheer torment for the wicked. This interpretation evolved in part from Isaiah's description of Sheol as having "levels," suggesting that a variety of punishments exist in hell. The prophet warns sinners: "Yet you shall be brought down to Sheol, to the lowest depths of the Pit" (Isa. 14:15).

Particularly wicked souls are thus cast deep into the murky abyss, a place of ultimate agony. This image was embellished and eventually developed into the concept of GEHENNA, a horrible subterranean torture chamber where wicked souls are mercilessly tortured for all eternity.

The ancient hell of Sheol is depicted in numerous works of art and literature, both ancient and contemporary. One of the most recent examples is Anne Rice's 1995 novel *MEMNOCH THE DEVIL,* which describes the dreary underworld of Sheol.

SHORT STORIES The nature of the afterlife has long captivated the imagination of writers, with hell being depicted as far more glamorous and fascinating than heaven. Such famous modern authors as Stephen King, Joyce Carol Oates, and CLIVE BARKER have penned short stories speculating on the realm of the damned. Forays into the inferno have been fodder for horror anthologies, articles in issues of *Alfred Hitchcock Magazine, TWILIGHT ZONE MAGAZINE,* and a host of infernal COMIC BOOKS. Adaptations of CHTHONIC short stories have been televised as episodes of *NIGHT GALLERY, TWILIGHT ZONE,* and *WAY OUT,* and have even inspired an assortment of ANIMATED CARTOONS.

Robert Bloch, author of the horror classic *Psycho,* offers his take on the great below in "That Hell-Bound Train," a short story written in 1958. The tale follows the misadventures of young Martin, a cynical man who decides that his best chance for happiness in life is in striking a bargain with the DEVIL. In this FAUST update, Martin agrees to ride the express to the underworld after his death in exchange for a chance to stop time at the moment of his greatest happiness. He believes this will actually allow him to cheat the devil, since he will be frozen in time and therefore be protected from death.

But Martin never finds that perfect moment; he keeps thinking that something better is on its way. Finally, he dies without ever having taken his opportunity. He boards the train and joins the damned, all of whom are enjoying one last party before arriving at "the Depot Way Down Yonder," where their eternity of agony will begin. Suddenly Martin realizes that *this* is as happy as he has ever been, and he demands that he be allowed to remain on the locomotive forever. The devil reluctantly agrees, and Martin becomes "the new brakeman on that Hell-Bound Train."

Basil Cooper describes a DREAM MODEL of hell wherein the evil dead must relive the ugliness of their sins in his 1965 "Camera Obscura." As the tale opens, Mr. Sharsted, a heartless moneylender who puts profit before compassion, goes to the home of Mr. Gingold to demand repayment of a debt. But the mysterious old man keeps changing the subject and eventually brings Sharsted to a dark study to show him his "Victorian toy," a camera obscura that "gathers a panorama of the town below and transmits it here onto the viewing table." The camera flashes a full-scale reflection of the town into view, and Gingold starts pointing out homes and businesses that Sharsted brought to ruin with his ruthless foreclosures. Gingold asks the banker if he will not reconsider his "unnecessary and somewhat inhuman" practices. Irritated with this conversation, Sharsted tells the man to mind his own business.

Gingold sighs and tells Sharsted "so be it," then shows the moneylender out through a door at the back of the house. Sharsted is happy to be away from the enigmatic old gentleman and looks forward to returning with an eviction notice. As he makes his way through town, Sharsted begins to notice that things are not quite right: Buildings that were demolished decades ago are now standing; once-familiar streets become confusing and lead him in circles; and long-dead associates stroll through the village, their rotted faces rimming with maggots. Cooper concludes his story by noting that the camera obscura shows the town "as through the eye of God" and that Sharsted and his ilk are "trapped for eternity, stumbling, weeping, swearing" in their own "private Hell." This chilling story was later adapted into a screenplay for the television series *Night Gallery*.

Ancient mythical descriptions of the netherworld have likewise made their way into contemporary short stories. Adobe James's "The Road to Mictlantecutli," also written in the early 1960s, conjures images of MICTLAN, the underworld of Aztec legend. When Morgan, the story's cop-killing villain, wrecks his car in the Mexican desert, he is approached by two very different figures. The first is a quiet priest who finds Morgan at the scene of the accident and offers to see him to safety. As they make their way through the night, a beautiful woman on a sleek stallion rides up and invites Morgan to accompany her to "Mictlantecutli's ranch," just down the road. The cleric begs Morgan to remain with him, declaring that "she is evil. Evil personified." Morgan, hoping that the brazen girl might offer more than just a horseback ride, considers this a "recommendation." He rides off with her, ignoring the priest's warning that "I am your last chance."

On the way to the ranch, the pair stops for a violent sexual encounter beneath the stars. Afterward, the girl tells Morgan she wants to show him something before they reach Mictlantecutli's. They ride back to the site of the accident, and Morgan is horrified to see his lacerated corpse—half devoured by vultures—behind the wheel. There on the roadside is the priest. "Help me!" Morgan shouts. But the cleric replies he cannot. "You have embraced evil; you have made your last earthly choice." Laughing, the beautiful girl transforms into a rotting cadaver as she takes Morgan to meet Mictlantecutli, also known as "Diablo, SATAN, DEVIL, LUCIFER, MEPHISTOPHELES."

The most commercially successful

modern writer of the genre, Stephen King, has offered several shorts dealing with the topic of afterlife agony. In "You Know They Got a Hell of a Band," a young couple takes a wrong turn and winds up in a supernatural village where they become eternal captives at a rock and roll concert that never ends. His "Mrs. Todd's Shortcut" sends characters down a road that leads to a woods where animated trees grab at passersby and monstrous creatures "not of this world" make frightening roadkill.

Contemporary short story writers continue to draw inspiration from the ominous underworld. Even in the modern world of religious cynicism, hell continues to fire the human imagination.

SHOBARI WAKA Shobari Waka is the hell of the Yanomamo Indians of Brazil and Venezuela. In this pit, the damned burn for all eternity. Wadawadariwa, a wise spirit, questions souls on their afterlife journey to determine whether they should be sent to Shobari Waka or to paradise. Those who reveal themselves as greedy, petty, or cruel are damned to the bitter underworld for everlasting punishment.

SHOCK 'EM DEAD 1990 horror film *Shock 'Em Dead* blends the FAUST legend with rumors about SATAN worship in HEAVY METAL MUSIC. Aldo Ray stars as the desperate musician who sells his soul in exchange for superstar status in the world of rock and roll. He consummates the bargain by touring hell and seeing the "delights" of the damned. In one particularly frightening scene, Ray is given three voluptuous lovers to satisfy him sexually, but when he looks into the mirror he sees reflected a trio of decaying hags. Other unpleasant surprises include discovering that food has become inedible and that he now must sustain on a diet of human flesh.

The hell of *Shock 'Em Dead* is an orgy of carnal excesses that ultimately delivers far more pain than pleasure. Similar cinematic depictions of the underworld include *HELLRAISER, HIGHWAY TO HELL,* and *NIGHT ANGEL.*

SIGNORELLI, LUCA Tuscan artist Luca Signorelli (c. 1441–1523) drew inspiration from the images of CHRISTIAN HELL for his creative works. He frequently depicts the underworld as the place of unrelenting torture and unspeakable suffering described in the Bible. But Signorelli's interpretations of the dark abyss differ greatly from those of his contemporaries and show particular genius and innovation. Unlike other masters, he shows a hell devoid of flames, fire, or any harsh landscape. His DEMONS differ, too, in that they are almost beautiful—created with exquisite muscle tone and brilliant color. Thus his underworld vision introduces the concept of spiritual and psychological agony to the medium.

Signorelli's portrayal incorporates the belief that these fiends of hell were once angels of God, lovely and alluring, before their rebellion and fall from

Drawing of Signorelli's vision of the creation of hell. ART TODAY

grace. The reality of having to accept their new status as beasts of the pit adds a psychological dimension to the horrors of hell. His *THE DAMNED CONSIGNED TO HELL* shows naked sinners being led away in chains by grinning winged monsters. The bodies of the damned are corralled into an impossibly crowded chasm to be heaped upon one another in a grisly landfill of human remains. A horde of orange and green demons is shown gleefully strangling, biting, and clawing, these condemned souls.

Signorelli's creations were a departure from traditional depictions of hell as a fiery pit of flames and beastlike fiends. By showing the fallen angels as beautiful, he stirs an element of sorrow at the unutterable loss of divine splendor, which renders the sufferings of hell more poignant and chilling. The artist's contributions to CHURCH ART AND ARCHITECTURE also include a LAST JUDGMENT scene featuring the Antichrist as well as hell, purgatory, and heaven. His visions are adapted from REVELATION, which foretells a fearsome apocalypse that will one day befall humankind.

SIN EATER In seventeenth-century Britain, the rich hired a sin eater to save the souls of their departed loved ones from hell. When a person died, a loaf of bread or pitcher of milk or wine was placed over the heart of the corpse to "absorb" the body's evil. The sin eater then consumed the tainted food or drink, thus accepting the guilt and punishment that were consequences of those sins. Ritual completed, the departed soul supposedly proceeded to the afterlife without fear of damnation.

Most villages had a designated sin eater, usually an old man with no other means of support. Others believed that the sin eater must be a total stranger with no ties to the deceased or his kin. During the height of this custom, nefarious cads would trick others into ingesting sins by giving contaminated bread or wine to beggars or passersby without revealing that it had been used to absorb a dead person's iniquity. This covert proffer was also used to exact revenge on enemies, since those who participated in this ritual truly believed that those who ingested sullied food would have to atone for another's wickedness.

The practice of hiring a sin eater was condemned by the Christian church and eventually lost popularity. Within a few decades, the very idea of hell and damnation was being called "ridiculous" and "superstitious" by religious scholars and secular philosophers, making the practice obsolete.

SIRAT Muslim legend tells of the great Sirat (Islamic for "road"), a path that serves as a bridge over hell. The supernatural pathway is "finer than a hair and sharper than a sword," and departed spirits must navigate the narrow road in order to reach paradise. Faithful souls will reach the other side safely, but infidels will fall into JAHANNAM (hell) below. Sirat is frequently associated with CHINVAT BRIDGE, a similar passageway described in ancient Persian folklore.

SISYPHUS Sisyphus, King of Corinth, is among the damned who suffer in TARTARUS, the lowest realm of the Greek mythic underworld HADES. He earned this punishment by trying to outsmart death and trying to blackmail Zeus, head of the Greek pantheon.

Sisyphus witnesses Zeus raping the nymph Aegina, daughter of Asopus, and threatens to tell the young maiden's father about the crime. Enraged, Zeus sends Thanatos (Death) to silence Sisyphus by taking him to the underworld, but the clever king ambushes Thanatos and binds him in heavy chains. Zeus dispatches Ares, god of war, to free Thanatos. However, by this time Sisyphus has devised another plan for evading his fate. He instructs his wife that if he should die, she must not offer the customary funeral sacrifices. Thanatos slays Sisyphus, and, as instructed, Sisyphus's wife buries him without conducting the proper rites.

When Sisyphus comes to the underworld, King Hades and Queen PERSEPHONE refuse him entrance, since he has not offered them traditional tribute. Sisyphus convinces the deities to let him ascend to the upperworld to take care of the matter himself. They agree and release Sisyphus, who has no intention of returning to Hades. He manages to elude both

Thanatos and Zeus for many decades before dying a second time.

This time, when Sisyphus arrives in the underworld, Zeus is ready. He devises a cruel punishment for the king: He damns Sisyphus to push a huge bolder up a hill only to have it immediately roll back down again. Sisyphus will be granted no rest in the afterlife until this impossible feat is accomplished.

The legend of Sisyphus inspired poems and plays and was immortalized on canvas by Venetian master Titian.

SIZE OF HELL Philosophers have been speculating about the size of hell for centuries. Using passages from the Bible, ancient legends, and simple guesswork, scholars have sought to determine the exact dimensions of the realm of the damned.

In "CHRIST AND SATAN," a Christian poem dating back to the 1100s, determining the area of hell is a major plot point. After Satan fails to tempt Christ in the desert, the DEVIL is ordered to measure his kingdom. The Savior demands that Satan go back to the underworld and crawl hell's length and breadth on his hands and knees through the foul-smelling darkness, then report on its size. Satan does so and declares that the underworld extends for 100,000 miles. Though an imaginative piece of prose, the measurement from "Christ and Satan" has been universally dismissed as a "colorful" but baseless concept. But the work attests to humanity's fascination with the subject of hell's perimeters.

Defining the scope of hell has received serious treatment from noteworthy Christian intellectuals as well. The most prominent preacher of the fourteenth century, Berthold of Regensburg, claimed that only one person in 100,000 would be saved. The rest would bake in an unquenchable fire for all eternity. This assertion has been largely condemned, however, not only for its pessimism but because it would necessitate an enormous place for the damned to reside.

Influenced by both the frivolous and somber estimations of the devil's kingdom, sixteenth-century scientist Galileo took up the concept during his early studies. He used specifications from Dante's *DIVINE COMEDY: THE INFERNO* to calculate the distance between earth, heaven, and hell as well as the dimensions of the underworld itself. And though his treatise was simply musing, his theories about mortality, the afterlife, and humanity's place in the universe are believed to have influenced numerous artists, including Milton (author of *PARADISE LOST*) who visited Galileo in Italy before writing his masterpiece.

Today, most people consider determining the exact size of hell a moot issue. Since hell is a spiritual dimension, physical measurements are meaningless and do nothing to amplify or ease the suffering of the damned.

SOVI Sovi, hero of folktales from the Baltic regions, is said to have seen firsthand the grisly terrors of the underworld. After hearing his tale, many villagers insisted on cremating their dead in hopes of escaping the spectacle he describes.

According to the story, Sovi kills a wild pig and eats the boar's nine spleens. After ingesting this feast, Sovi and his sons descend into hell and witness its many horrors. The men report seeing "worms and reptiles eat" the flesh of the damned. Swarms of "bees and mosquitoes sting" the souls who scurry about, unable to find cover from the piercing pests. When he returns to the land of the living, Sovi declares that only destruction of the corpse could ensure peace after death. Many superstitious clerics agreed, saying they could "see" the soul rise and ride off on a horse as the funeral pyre burned.

STORM, HOWARD Howard Storm is among the estimated eleven million people who have had a NEAR-DEATH EXPERIENCE, a term commonly applied to supernatural encounters of patients who survive clinical death and retain memories of their "otherworld" adventures. Unlike most reported incidents, however, Storm's experience was not a joyous trek through a tunnel of "bright light" to a place of incredible peace; it was a horrifying descent into hell.

Storm reports that before the incident, he was enjoying a comfortable life as a respected college professor. He did not take religion seriously and scoffed at the notion of eternal damnation. But after a near-fatal heart attack, Storm experienced clinical death and found himself cast into the underworld—a horrid, dark place of sheer terror. He repeatedly pleaded, "Jesus, save me!" and was soon revived by physicians.

The memory of that terrifying realm haunted him constantly. Unable to cope with the images of that horror, Storm began studying Christianity. As his knowledge increased, he saw the need to make radical changes in his lifestyle. Storm completed his theological studies and became an ordained minister. He now devotes his life to preaching the message of spiritualism and acceptance of Christ to avoid damnation. Part of his ministry is retelling his story and warning others of the reality of hell.

Rev. Storm also believes that there are thousands of people who have had similar infernal experiences—"dying" and finding themselves in hell—but seldom share them because of the negative implications. He suggests that there are many more of these than there are positive near-death experiences. The message in all this, he says, is to prepare for the day of final judgment. Hell is real, he warns, and most people who end up there will not get the chance to come back and repent.

Storm's incredible story has been recounted in numerous magazine articles, books, and on television talk shows. His supernatural journey was also profiled on a 1996 episode of *Unsolved Mysteries*.

STAY TUNED Hell is an endless lineup of awful television programs according to the 1992 film *Stay Tuned*. The comedy stars John Ritter and Pam Dawber as a suburban couple who buy a big-screen TV and satellite dish from a fast-talking salesman for Hellvision. But when couch potato Ritter tunes in, he discovers that the new set receives only bizarre shows he has never heard of, such as *I Love LUCIFER, Golden Ghouls, My Three Sons of Bitches, Duane's Underworld,* and *Beverly Hills 90666*. The set also receives infernal MUSIC VIDEOS too atrocious for Music Television. When Ritter investigates the mysterious satellite, he is pulled into the underworld of abysmal TV.

Dawber unwittingly joins her husband in the inferno, and the two are told by SATAN (played by Jeffrey Jones) that there is only one way to escape eternal damnation. They must survive in this electronic hell for twenty-four hours, after which time they will be restored to life. During their stay in the broadcast inferno, they will be hunted and assailed by villains from a variety of hell's television shows. If they are killed in any of the programs, their souls will be "canceled" and their fate sealed. Jones will observe their progress from his high-tech studio in hell proper, where the touch of a button on the diabolical remote control sends spirits into ever-evolving horrors.

STYX The river Styx separates the realms of the living and the dead according to ancient Greek myth. When a person dies, his or her SHADE (spirit) drifts to the riverbank and awaits CHARON, a ghostly ferryman who will transport the souls to the underworld kingdom of HADES.

The Styx is an actual river in Greece, believed to have metaphysical implications because its waters disappear underground. Scholars eventually revised their theories and came to believe that the entrance to the underworld is actually at LAKE AVERNUS in northern Italy. But the river Styx remains a mysterious and enduring symbol of the mythical underworld.

The Styx has been included in such literary works as the *AENEID,* the *ODYSSEY,* and Dante's *DIVINE COMEDY: THE INFERNO.* It has been further immortalized in a number of other works, including poems, paintings, operas, and films.

SUCCUBUS The succubus is the female DEMON of Jewish, Christian, and Islamic folklore who seeks to destroy human souls by tempting them with sexual images while they sleep. Some succubi could actually engage in intercourse with their sleeping prey. The succubus is the counterpart of the male INCUBUS, a fiend who preys upon women. Once a man succumbs to the "dream seduction," his damnation to hell is believed to be sealed.

The 1990 film *NIGHT ANGEL* features the modern adventures of the succubus LILITH. Lilith is a mythic DEMON who had been created to be mother of the human race but who chose to copulate with the DEVIL instead. After this lurid union, Lilith joined the minions of hell in vowing to corrupt mankind through sexual lust.

SUNNIULF OF RANDAU One of the most intriguing examples of VISION LITERATURE is the account of Sunniulf of Randau's visit to hell. Sunniulf's version of this journey was recorded by Bishop Gregory of Tours in his *History of the Franks*. According to the story, Sunniulf, a sixth-century monk and abbot of Randau, was reminded of what happens to immoral clerics through a terrifying underworld adventure.

The abbot, failing in his faith and doubting the goodness of God, falls into a deep trance, and his spirit is taken to the edge of a fermenting river. The riverbank is crammed with thousands of people, all trying to cross a narrow bridge that leads to a gleaming city of light. Sunniulf is warned that only clerics who have lived lives of virtue can pass. Others will fall into the muck and sink according to the depravity of their sins. Sunniulf watches as several souls try to make it across the bridge, only to slip into the filth. The worst among them sinks up to his neck in the foul bilge. Sunniulf worries that he might slide even deeper and is seized with indescribable terror.

But before Sunniulf can attempt to cross, he is delivered back to his body. When he awakes he asks for a confessor, shares his vision, and renews his vow to live a holy life. Skeptics discounted his story as the ravings of a very sick man, but countless others found inspiration in his tale—and in his candor at admitting his sins. Sunniulf's account was especially compelling, since, as a priest, most believers assumed he would be assured of salvation. If even a man of God could face damnation, then they, too, should take heed and amend their lives.

SWAHILI HELL According to African Swahili belief, hell is a deep abyss below the surface of the earth into which the damned are cast. It is the seventh thing God created and

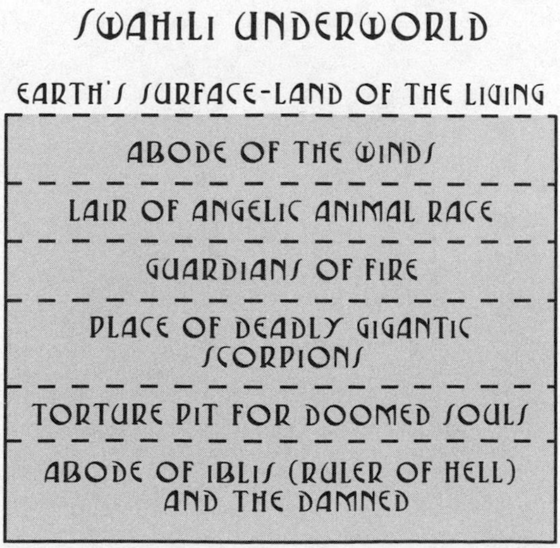

SWAHILI UNDERWORLD

EARTH'S SURFACE-LAND OF THE LIVING

ABODE OF THE WINDS

LAIR OF ANGELIC ANIMAL RACE

GUARDIANS OF FIRE

PLACE OF DEADLY GIGANTIC SCORPIONS

TORTURE PIT FOR DOOMED SOULS

ABODE OF IBLIS (RULER OF HELL) AND THE DAMNED

Universe of Swahili myth.

accordingly has seven descending levels. The worst sinners, those believed beyond hope of salvation, occupy the lowest realm, which is an icy place of unendurable cold. (Departed souls of moderately evil people could be sent to the sixth circle below the earth for punishment. These spirits had some hope of eventual salvation.)

The influence of eighth-century Arab traders is evident in the depiction of Swahili hell. As in the Islam faith, the deepest pit of the underworld is ruled by IBLIS (a harsh DEMON), who metes out punishment to his accursed subjects. Traveling merchants from Muslim countries also brought notions of JAHANNAM, the hell of Muslim belief. Their images of a horrible underworld of torment became mingled with indigenous concepts of afterlife justice. The result is a dark realm that features components of both faiths.

SWASTIKA Long before the Nazis appropriated this mythical symbol, the swastika had been a powerful icon representing the perpetual life cycle. Sometimes referred to as the "sun wheel," swastikas have been found in cultures throughout the world dating as far back as the eighth century B.C. From the societies of ancient Greece to Native Americans, this mysterious image has been respected, revered, and even feared.

In the Jain religion, an Asian religion that includes doctrines of a treacherous underworld, the swastika is among the most hallowed symbols. (The word *swastika* is derived from the Sanskrit *svasti* meaning "fortune, luck, well-being.") Its central point stands for life, and the four branches represent the possible fates of a departed soul: It could be condemned to hell, be elevated to the status of a god, be reincarnated in human form, or be reborn as an animal. Taken as a whole, the swastika forms a wheel that depicts perfect being (siddha), from which no rebirth is necessary.

According to the teachings of Jainism, damned souls must endure a myriad of tortures in hell. These include impalement, mutilation, and dismemberment meted out in direct relation to the spirit's offenses. Grisly as the inferno is, condemned souls could take solace in the fact that damnation is only temporary, since after all sins are purged through pain, the soul is reborn and resumes the life cycle. Thus the swastika, the wheel of being, continues in motion.

It is this ominous mystic power that intrigued Adolf Hitler. Being highly superstitious, he equated the swastika with immortality and developed the *hakenkreuz,* meaning "hooked cross," as the icon for his troops. The symbol was officially adopted by the Nazi party in 1935 and emblazoned upon Nazi flags, armbands, and banners. Hitler believed that troops marching under the swastika would be unstoppable and that his "perfect society" would endure forever.

Today, the swastika has come to be

identified with Nazism, anti-Semitism, and white supremacist agendas. It is commonly found on the propaganda and MILITARY INSIGNIA of such groups. Because of this irreverent and emotionally charged connotation, the swastika also has become an icon of HEAVY METAL MUSIC groups wanting to advertise their contempt of traditional mores.

SWEDENBORG, EMANUEL

Emanuel Swedenborg (1688–1772), a self-proclaimed "seer" and philosopher, wrote *Heaven and Hell* in the late 1750s. In it he describes his "experiences" with heaven, hell, angels, and DEMONS. Born to Swedish nobility, this son of a prominent Protestant bishop reported having supernatural visions beginning around 1744. Troubled by these sometimes disturbing images, Swedenborg began reading the Bible for insight in interpreting the otherworldly information.

According to Swedenborg's divination, the Christian messiah Jesus never actually became a man. He only disguised his divinity in human form to help the "fallen sons of Adam" find their way back to God. The sin in the Garden of Eden signaled man's desire to put himself before the Almighty, and Christ's mission was to return focus to the Father. His role was not to "redeem" humankind but to identify a system whereby each person could save himself or herself. Having accomplished this, Jesus shows that all humans can one day be "glorified" as he is, provided they climb the "staircase" to heaven rather than descend to hell by rejecting God's love.

During his career, Swedenborg wrote sixteen extensive tomes about his visions. In these, he claims to have visited heaven, hell, and even other planets. His *Concerning the Earths in Our Solar System* offers detailed descriptions of humanlike creatures on the moon, Venus, and Mars. His most complex work recounts an actual tour (in the tradition of Dante's *DIVINE COMEDY: THE INFERNO*) of paradise and the abyss, which he reaches via a brass elevator. After Swedenborg's death, these texts became the basis for the Church of the New Jerusalem, which claims to "complete" rather than contradict other Christian doctrines.

According to Swedenborg's theories, when a person dies, the soul enters a "spirit world" where it continues to eat, drink, sleep, interact with loved ones, and perform other human functions. Most of the newly deceased do not even realize that they are dead. This intermediate realm becomes a place of learning where spirits develop and grow—with the assistance of angels—before ascending to paradise.

Those unwilling to progress receive no such angelic guidance and become confused and lost. Stubborn and uncooperative, they find only paths to hell as they flee God and try to distance themselves from the Almighty. (Swedenborg stresses that souls are not condemned by a celestial judge but choose damnation through their refusal to improve themselves.) Spirits who have chosen this fate suffer mental and emotional pain rather than physical agony. They become trapped in their own limited, flawed, unfulfilled existence where damned souls prey upon one another in the most vile ways. He describes a typical scene in the abyss: "In the streets and lanes are committed robberies and depredations. In some hells are brothels disgusting to behold, being filled with all sorts of filth and excrement."

Swedenborg's teachings influenced the works of many modern artists, including the Irish poet WILLIAM BUTLER YEATS and the philosopher WILLIAM BLAKE. Despite his widespread popularity, Swedenborg also received a great deal of criticism from those who considered his "visions" to be hallucinations or even outright fabrications. His response to these detractors was simply, "I care not, since I have seen, lived and felt" these incredible experiences.

T

T-SHIRTS One of the most popular GIFT NOVELTIES depicting scenes of the underworld is the printed T-shirt. Examples of the informal attire include JOKES and COMICS about hell, reprints of infernal paintings and sculptures, and images of DEMONS and DEVILS. HEAVY METAL MUSIC bands such as Iron Maiden, Judas Priest, and Black Sabbath also routinely use hell and its IMAGERY in promotional apparel sold at their concerts. Shirts parodying the afterlife are also common items of MOVIE MERCHANDISING.

Many flout the traditional notions of hell as a place of horrible torment, opting instead to make light of SATAN's domain. Common epigraphs are, "Heaven doesn't want me and Hell is afraid I'll take over" or "My wife put me through Hell and all I got was this lousy T-shirt," the latter complete with simulated singe marks. Another spoofs Christian HELLFIRE SERMONS, showing a black and white spotted dog pounding the pulpit amid raging flames. The text reads, "Hellfire & Dalmatians."

Such comic representations comprise the majority of infernal T-shirts. A screened illustration of "Fisherman's Hell" shows the devil standing beside two tables, one laden with beer, the other with bait. The fiend laughingly tells the sportsman, "Choose only one." A 1988 episode of the new *TWILIGHT ZONE* television series features Ron Glass as an emissary of the "stygian depths" who appears in a variety of hellish T-shirts, including "Let's Do Damnation," "GEHENNA—More than a place: a way of life," and "Hell is a city much like Newark."

Reproductions of hellish FANTASY ART are also popular T-shirt decoration. These depict fierce demons, smoldering landscapes, and mutilated bodies of the damned. Such grisly garb is frequently worn by BIKERS, who sport the darkest fiends of the abyss on shirts and other apparel.

TAENARUS According to ancient Greek myth, the Path of Taenarus leads to the underworld of King HADES. It is a dark cavern that ends at the banks of the river STYX. Here the ferryman CHARON waits to take deceased souls across to the realm of the dead.

One story claims that the legendary hero HERCULES takes the Path of Taenarus to Hades and seizes the three-headed guard dog CERBERUS. Another recounts the famed mortal's venture to the underworld to free Alcestis, who is killed while trying to save her doomed husband. In both stories, Hercules must travel the dark, treacherous pathway that serves as a portal between the land of the living and the realm of the damned.

TALES FROM THE CRYPT The 1972 British film *Tales from the Crypt* presents the misadventures of five tourists visiting the catacombs. A mysterious tour guide shows each character a "vision" of the future, which includes a variety of nefarious crimes that the visitors are destined to commit. Their imminent atrocities include deceit, adultery, and murder. After the final revelation, the guide reveals his identity: He is actually SATAN, and the evil acts he described have already occurred. The five are not visitors but newly dead souls arriving in hell to be punished for their sins.

Tales from the Crypt depicts the realm of the damned as an underground maze of caves enveloped in fire. A skeleton-faced DEMON is charged with their torment. However, part of their suffering lies in being forced to face their own reprehensible acts. The agony of reliving despicable memories reflects the DREAM MODEL of hell, an eternal nightmare of the damned's own making.

Each story in the film was inspired by tales of the macabre in E.C. COMIC BOOKS of the 1950s. *Tales from the Crypt* was followed by *VAULT OF HORROR* and the urban update *TALES FROM THE HOOD,* which offer similar interpretations of hell.

TALES FROM THE HOOD *Tales from the Hood,* a 1995 update inspired by the 1972 British *TALES FROM THE CRYPT,* brings hell to the violent streets of the inner city. The movie is patterned closely after the original, consisting of separate episodes linked by a common theme: retribution.

The film unfolds as three black gang members enter a funeral parlor in search of stolen drugs. What they find instead is an eerie mortician (played by Clarence Williams III) who insists on showing them a variety of corpses being readied for burial. With each cadaver Williams relates a frightening story about the deceased's life, death, and damnation. By the end of the tour, the teens suspect that they, too, are prisoners of the eternal abyss.

Hell's agony has a mental as well as physical dimension in *Tales from the Hood.* The damned are psychologically tortured while their bodies burn in a raging fire. Writers Rusty Cundieff and Darin Scott equate this inner horror with the violence that infests modern society. Among the infernal characters are racist policemen, gang bangers whose only allegiance is to the almighty dollar, adults who brutalize children, and politicians who place power over principle. *Tales from the Hood* also makes a powerful statement against black-on-black violence, which is as odious and repulsive as any torment devised in hell.

Physically, the underworld of *Tales from the Hood* is a flaming pit where the damned burn for eternity. Ruled by a fearsome SATAN, the film has elements of CHRISTIAN HELL as well as allusions to the DREAM MODEL of the afterlife. In this theory, human spirits pass the aeons recalling the actions of their earthly lives, and evil acts carry abhorrent memories that sting the soul.

TANTALUS Tantalus is one of the sinners of Greek myth damned to TARTARUS, the lowest realm of the underworld HADES. He had once been a beloved mortal who was frequently invited to join the gods in their celebrations. Then Tantalus devises a cruel test for the deities: He cooks and serves his son Pelops at an astral banquet to see if the gods can discern that they are eating human flesh. The horrified deities restore the boy to life and damn the cruel Tantalus to the depths of hell.

In Tartarus, Tantalus suffers extreme hunger and thirst while delicious food and wine are just out of reach. (The word *tantalize* derives from this myth.) According to the *ODYSSEY*, Tantalus is one of only three men who have bodies in the underworld (along with SISYPHUS and TITYUS), since his suffering is physical as well as spiritual. All others exist in death as SHADES, murky residues of their former selves.

TARTARUS Tartarus is the lowest and most gruesome realm of HADES, the underworld of ancient Greek myth. It is reserved for the souls of evil people and for those who have angered the gods. Tartarus is surrounded by a bronze shield that keeps the damned from escaping. It is bordered on the west by the river STYX and marked on the north by a forest of black poplar trees. Said to lie far below the surface of the earth, Tartarus is a place of unending night where darkness reigns eternal.

Greek tradition includes mention of many sinners damned to Tartarus and describes some of its torments. SISYPHUS is sent to Tartarus for angering Zeus and outsmarting Thanatos, the deliverer of death. His punishment is to spend eternity rolling a boulder up a steep hill, only to have it roll back each night so that he must start his labor again.

TANTALUS is cast there after cooking his own son and feeding him to the gods to see if they could identify the unfamiliar meat. He is now eternally hungry, with a fruit-laden branch just out of reach, and thirsty, waist deep in a lake that recedes each time he tries to sip. (The word *tantalize* originates from this teasing tale.) The third man to retain his body in the underworld is TITYUS. In life, he rapes Zeus's wife and is punished by having his liver continually ripped out by vultures. The organ immediately grows back so his torment can continue unabated.

There are many souls in Tartarus who suffer psychological agonies. The Greek mortal Ixion, who tries to rape the goddess Hera, is punished by being tied to a wheel of fire that spins in the air. Also in Tartarus are forty-nine of the fifty daughters of Danaüs, called the DANAÏDS. These women murdered their husbands (the fifty sons of their uncle) on their wedding night according to their father's instructions. Only one renounced her father's evil plot, so she was spared from torture in the afterlife. The damned Danaïds are condemned eternally to try to fill a vase with water using a sieve.

Greek legends tell of other nameless souls who languish in the pit of Tartarus. Their torments include being burned alive, mutilated, whipped, and eaten by monsters. Images of such agonies are found in Homer's *ODYSSEY* and in Plato's *GORGIAS* and *REPUBLIC.*

TARTARUCHUS Tartaruchus is a fallen angel who rules hell according to several early Christian texts. In the APOCALYPSE OF PAUL, an apocrypha dating back to the first days of Christianity, Tartaruchus is named as the DEMON who holds dominion in the underworld until the LAST JUDGMENT, at which time SATAN will return as overlord. He is spiteful and cruel and takes great enjoyment in tormenting human souls. Another apocrypha, the APOCALYPSE OF PETER, tells that when the damned beg for leniency, Tartaruchus responds by taunting them that they should have begged for Christ's mercy, not his. The fiend gleefully reminds them that their fate is now sealed, and the days of finding relief are gone forever.

TATTOOS Among the most common graphics available at tattoo parlors are representations of SATAN, DEVILS, GHOULS, gravestones, and burning underworld landscapes. These are especially popular among BIKERS, who consider embracing the damned an integral part of their rebel image. Infernal symbols are also common among fans of HEAVY METAL MUSIC, as many bands and artists use demonic IMAGERY.

TERESA OF ÁVILA, SAINT

A Spanish nun and mystic credited with reforming corruption in Catholic religious orders, Teresa of Ávila (1515–1582) had numerous supernatural encounters during her lifetime. Most of these were joyous meditations in which she communed with the divine. However Teresa of Ávila also experienced a horrifying vision of hell. Church scholars have speculated that this image is perhaps the most accurate description of the inferno known to humanity. She describes the terrifying underworld in her book *Life,* the story of her spiritual journey:

The entrance resembled a very long narrow passage, like a furnace, very low, dark and closely confined; the ground seemed to be full of water which looked like filthy, evil-smelling mud, and in it were many wicked-looking reptiles. At the end there was a hollow place scooped out of a wall, and it was here that I found myself in this close confinement. . . . I felt a fire within my soul the nature of which I am utterly unable to describe. My bodily sufferings were so intolerable that, though in my life I have endured the severest sufferings of this kind—the worst that is possible to endure, the doctors say, such as the shrinking of the nerves during my paralysis—. . . none of them is of the smallest account by comparison with what I felt then, to say nothing of the knowledge that they would be endless and unremitting. And even these are nothing by comparison with the agony of my soul. . . . To say that it is as if the soul were continually being torn from the body is very little . . . in this case, the soul itself is tearing itself to pieces. . . . I felt, I think, as if I were being both burned and dismembered; and I repeat that the interior fire and despair are the worst things of all. . . . There was no light and everything was in the blackest darkness . . . and any burning on earth is a small matter compared with that fire.

After experiencing this apparition, St. Teresa lost all fear of human pains and afflictions, since she had suffered far worse agonies.

THEOPHILUS The legend of Theophilus dates back to the sixth century and is believed to be the inspiration for the story of FAUST, a conceited scholar who enters into a pact with SATAN. Theophilus was an arrogant monk who sells his soul to the DEVIL, then repents his wicked deed.

According to the account, Theophilus is offered a bishopric, which he declines, believing the new job will be too much work. But when the new bishop arrives, Theophilus becomes jealous and resentful of his new superior. The bishop, sensing Theophilus's hostility, treats him sternly and eventually forces him out of the abbey. The monk's loathing and self-pity grow so intense that he loses all interest in his clerical duties and becomes obsessed with revenge.

With the help of a sorcerer, Theophilus conjures the devil, renounces God, and vows allegiance to the fiend. He signs a pact in his own blood surrendering his soul to Satan. In exchange, the devil promises to humiliate the bishop and elevate Theophilus to a position of honor. Theophilus returns to the abbey, declares that the bishop is a liar unworthy of his office, and demands a formal investigation. Church authorities examine both men and decide that Theophilus is a more worthy candidate for bishop, and the former is stripped of his title.

Almost immediately, Theophilus begins to regret his infernal bargain. When Satan arrives to drag him into hell, he calls out to the VIRGIN MARY, mother of Jesus Christ, for help. He begs her to plead his case before God. Mary takes pity on him and intercedes, then travels to hell to retrieve the contract. Based on her mediation, God grants Theophilus a pardon, on the condition that he make a public confession and vow to live a life of virtue.

The story of Theophilus was circulated throughout Christendom and became a powerful tool in motivating the faithful. Fragments of the tale were interwoven into the Faust legends, MORALITY PLAYS, and the thirteenth-century French drama *Le Miracle de Theophile* (The Miracle of Theophilus).

THESEUS Theseus is a figure of ancient Greek myth who is damned for his heroic attempt to rescue the beautiful PERSEPHONE from the underworld. According to the story, Theseus and his friend Pirithoüs descend to the infernal kingdom of HADES to retrieve Persephone, whom the king of the dead has kidnapped for his bride. But before Theseus is able to accomplish his mission, Hades discovers the plot and has him chained and impaled in the depths of hell.

Theseus is eventually rescued from this vile place by HERCULES, who travels to the underworld as one of his legendary labors. He defeats the monster CERBERUS, guardian of the gate, and returns Theseus to the land of the living. Hercules is, however, unable to free Pirithoüs, who remains eternally in the pits of Hades.

THESPESIUS *The Vision of Thespesius* is one of the few examples of VISION LITERATURE that predate the Middle Ages. It was written circa A.D. 100 by Plutarch, a Greek author living in Rome. *Thespesius* is a frightening work of fiction that reads like a factual account, leading many contemporary religious leaders to use the story in sermons about the horrors of the afterlife.

As the tale goes, Thespesius is believed by all to be dead; however, he is merely in a deep comatose state. While unconscious, he "wakes" to witness the judgment of the dead. He sees pure souls rise to heaven, while spirits covered with scars and blotches are swept into a black chasm. Thespesius wanders among the damned and is sickened to find his own father in the depths of hell. His father admits that he has lived an evil life, betraying, robbing, and even murdering those who trusted him. As his father speaks, Thespesius is surrounded by DEMONS who torture the accursed souls. Unable to bear the spectacle any longer, Thespesius revives and returns home to warn others about the terrors he has witnessed.

TITYUS According to Greek myth, Tityus is among the damned in TARTARUS, the realm of the underworld HADES reserved for the worst sinners. Vultures continually rip out his liver, which grows back repeatedly so that the torture can continue. This punishment is for the offense of raping Zeus's wife.

In the *ODYSSEY,* an epic story involving a visit to the underworld, the hero Odysseus learns that Tityus is one of only three men in Hades who retain physical bodies. These three (SISYPHUS and TANTALUS round out the trio) are forced to keep their bodies in the underworld so that their agony can be felt in both the flesh and the soul.

TI YU Ancient Chinese myths describe the bleak underworld of Ti Yu, a subterranean prison for the dead. It is dark, cold, and barren. After death, souls are judged by supernatural magistrates, and the wicked are made to pay for the sins of their lives in this musty abyss. The dreadful abode of Ti Yu is located at the feet of T'ai Shan kun wang, the master of death, fate, and destiny. Like the Christian SATAN, T'ai Shan tortures the souls in Ti Yu's seventh hell, a brutal land of agony.

Specific details of the legend are unclear, since the texts referring to Ti Yu have come through so many copies, translators, and interpretations. But scholars believe this underworld to be similar in many ways to the Greek HADES.

TORCELLO The Cathedral of Santa Maria Assunta in Torcello in Venice offers several stirring compositions depicting CHRISTIAN HELL. A centuries-old mosaic shows SATAN as a fierce blue DEMON with unwieldy white hair and beard. Judas, the apostle who betrayed Christ, is seated on his lap, entwined in serpents. Around him in his hell, monstrous winged monsters torture the damned.

Also in the cathedral is a remarkable interpretation of the LAST JUDGMENT, the time of final reckoning prophesied in REVELATION. The work offers a legion of underworld fiends tearing at human souls. They are staging their last battle, determined to fill hell with accursed spirits.

TRADING CARDS In contemporary culture, trading cards depicting hell and the damned have become quite popular. Examples of these include pocket-sized pictures of FANTASY ART, television shows, movies, and GAMES relating to the underworld. Music buffs can likewise find hellish decorations on collector cards from HEAVY METAL MUSIC groups such as Black Sabbath, Iron Maiden, and Ozzy Osbourne. Typical cards of this type feature DEMONS, Satanic IMAGERY, or grisly scenes of underworld chaos.

Still photographs from "supernatural" episodes of the classic series *TWI-*

Assortment of trading cards incorporating underworld imagery.

LIGHT ZONE and *Outer Limits* have also been adapted into cards patterned after traditional sports memorabilia. Each card features a picture from the original production as well as information about the plotline, writer, and cast. This format has become a component of MOVIE MERCHANDISING, with such abysmal villains as Freddy Kruger (*NIGHTMARE ON ELM STREET*) appearing on cards purchasers are urged to "collect and trade."

The popularity of these infernal trading cards has led to a booming business. A 1995 show and sale in Boston drew more than twenty thousand patrons, many of whom came to view the supernatural wares. And periodicals such as *Sci-Fi* and *Trading Cards Magazine* regularly feature advertisements for memorabilia picturing the realm of the damned.

TREASURES OF SATAN

Symbolist Jean Delville painted the *Treasures of SATAN* in the mid-1900s, a time when traditional notions of the underworld were being replaced by modern interpretations or outright disbelief. Delville's vision of the underworld is one of utter despair, where all hope has indeed been abandoned.

Like many medieval visions of hell, *Treasures of Satan* incorporates heavy use of the familiar reds and oranges to suggest the unquenchable fire of the great below. Satan is portrayed as a loathsome monster with snakes for wings, gloating over his gain. The "treasure" of the beast is a myriad of damned humans, naked and writhing in agony. Hell itself, glowing in the background, is a jagged landscape of ruin that resembles an undersea wasteland, or perhaps the mangled remains of a countryside ravaged by modern warfare.

Treasures of Satan is important to the study of hell, as it blends traditional symbols of the abyss with contemporary images of nuclear devastation. The work suggests that the gap between the unseen horrors of hell and the demonstrable ugliness of humanity is closing. Perhaps in the third millennium, the atrocities of the two realms will become indistinguishable.

TRÈS RICHES HEURES DU DUC DE BERRY, LES *Les Très Riches Heures,* a BOOK OF HOURS composed for the Duke of Berry (brother of France's king) in the early 1400s, is considered the most luxurious and beautifully illustrated manuscript of its kind. Composed by the Limbourg brothers, the book offers dozens of miniature pictures of biblical events, including LUCIFER's fall from heaven and a frightening depiction of the DEVIL torturing souls in hell.

Unlike most portraits of the damned that use flaming reds and oranges to symbolize hell and SATAN, the Limbourgs employ heavy use of blues in their works. The miniature of Lucifer's expulsion offers a turquoise heaven lined with a legion of sapphire-robed angels. Lucifer himself is draped in royal blue garments, as are the rebel spirits who descend with him. These sinning angels are achingly beautiful, even as they fall from heaven to the inferno below.

Hell is blue, too: a cobalt cavern against the indigo sky. In the Limbourgs' vision, the devil reclines on a blazing grill, inhaling and exhaling the souls of the damned. A trio of DEMONS works the bellows to keep the flames burning. All around this infernal oven, winged blue and gray fiends strangle, mutilate, and choke their human prisoners. This horrific hell, inspired by contemporary examples of VISION LITERATURE, is considered a strong yet subtle warning to the infamous Duke of Berry, whose reputation for corruption was firmly established by 1413. He was encouraged to fear the underworld in this life so as not to experience it in the next.

TRICK OR TREAT The 1986 film *Trick or Treat* explores the relationship between hell and HEAVY METAL MUSIC. With cameos by such icons of the genre as Gene Simmons and Ozzy Osbourne, the movie vacillates between extolling the virtues of metal and condemning the whole industry as blatantly Satanic.

Trick or Treat opens with a passage from FAUST, the classic tale of deals with the DEVIL. The story then launches into the misadventures of an awkward teenager who seeks refuge from his miserable life in the music of heavy metal star Sammi Curr (played by Tony Fields). When the musician perishes in a hotel fire, the troubled teen conjures his spirit through a bewitched record album titled *Songs in the Key of Death*. What follows is a cinematic frenzy of hellish visions, gory mutilations, and demonic rape.

The hell of *Trick or Treat* is not a place for punishing moral offenses but instead a metaphor for teen angst and isolation. It is a realm that champions acts of cruelty and abuse, where the only sin is being "different."

TUNDAL The *Vision of Tundal* (Tyndal, Tundale) offers one of the most grotesque descriptions of SATAN and hell found in VISION LITERATURE. The work describes the afterlife adventures of Tundal, a depraved knight who has spent his life pursuing carnal fulfillment. According to the text, the dark hedonist "dies" and goes on a supernatural tour of heaven, purgatory, and hell. In the abyss of the damned, Tundal must face the dire consequences of his actions.

The manuscript of the *Vision of Tundal* originates from the mid-eleventh century, and though the author's name remains unknown, historians can trace the text to a medieval Irish monk living in Germany. Copies of *Tundal* were illustrated by hand and translated into at least a dozen languages, then distributed throughout medieval Christendom. Several of these early copies are still in existence, many of which contain elaborate pictures of the damned being tortured in hell.

The story opens as Tundal is bedridden with a severe illness. He soon falls into a comalike state and is believed dead. Tundal's spirit leaves his body and travels to the gates of the afterlife. But instead of ascending to paradise, the shocked knight learns the horrific price that must be paid for his indiscretions.

Tundal is met at the eternity's edge by a horde of DEMONS who prod and poke him, chiding, "Where are the good times now?" Terrified, Tundal tries to escape but is held bound until his guardian angel comes to claim him. The angel then takes Tundal on a tour of hell, showing him numerous monsters, torture devices, and pits of agony.

The angel explains that in the afterlife, souls must prove themselves worthy of salvation by negotating a number of obstacles. He takes Tundal to a narrow bridge over a fetid river. With great difficulty (and angelic assistance) he is able to cross. Tundal must then scale a treacherous cliff and face the demon ACHERON at its summit. As he clears the crest, the angel disappears, and Tundal falls prey to the fiends. He is chewed in the toothy mouth of Acheron, then torn at the loins as punishment for his sexual sins. A pack of mad beasts attacks him, and Tundal is further tormented by intense heat and cold that "no living man could stand." As the waves of pain overtake him, Tundal's angel reappears and retrieves him so that their journey can continue.

The next peril Tundal must face is a longer, narrower bridge spiked with sharp nails. He crosses, feet bleeding and scarred, only to be tortured by the demon Phristinus, who punishes those who have indulged in pleasures of the flesh. After this, Tundal is devoured by a steel-beaked bird and defecated in the form of a serpent into a lake of ice.

Tundal's angel takes pity on the man and restores him to his human form. The pair then travels to a fiery village where Tundal is melted in a raging furnace. His soul is melded with those of other sinners, and demons gleefully toss the damned blob around. Once again, the angel saves Tundal so that the trip through hell can continue.

Finally, the angel delivers Tundal to LUCIFER, who resides in the lowest depths of the abyss. The lord of hell is a horrid monster with a bird's beak, a beast's body, and thousands of hands with nails like razor blades. As Lucifer writhes on his bed of hot coals, his limbs crush and mangle damned souls around him. The pit is so crowded with the condemned that Lucifer continually breathes them in and out like smoke. Tundal, horror-struck, recognizes family and friends among these "unhappy spirits." While in the depths, he reports: "As the screaming souls were tossed into the cavernous pot, they bobbed and tumbled in the boiling mess . . . souls were suspended, impaled on hooks, lowered over the burning coals. Their piteous cries drowned out the sound of their sizzling flesh, as they begged the demons to release them."

Before restoring Tundal to life, the angel takes him to purgatory to show what spirits must endure in the mystic realm. In this PURGATORIAL HELL, souls suffer only the human pains of hunger, thirst, sorrow, and longing for God. The angel tells Tundal that these souls will eventually ascend to heaven once they have purified themselves and rid their spirits of the residue of their sins.

Tundal then awakens and resolves to change his ways. He dedicates the rest of his life to prayer, preaching, and performing acts of penance. And though he loathes having to relive his horrific vision, he repeats his story again and again to serve as a warning to others.

The manuscript recounting this supernatural journey inspired numerous artworks, including the *Vision of Tundal* painted by a student of HIERONYMUS BOSCH. The picture, which now hangs in the Museo Lazaro Gadeano in Madrid, depicts the horrors described in Tundal's account. Included are scores of snakes, rats, and other vile beasts torturing and eating the damned. Sinners are impaled on spikes, slashed with swords, and drowned in a pit of blackish green bilge. Others flail in a lake of fire. The painting's background is an ocean of fire against which the damned writhe in utter agony.

These images have also been incorporated into *HEROINE OF HELL*, a 1995 film about a young artist who, after witnessing a terrible car accident, becomes obsessed with this medieval hell.

TWILIGHT ZONE, THE During its 156-episode run from 1959 to 1964, the classic television series *The Twilight Zone* offered numerous interpretations of hell. These ranged from religious concepts to pop culture references and offered the abyss as a realm of justice, retribution, and even vengeance. Overall, series creator Rod Serling's message to viewers is that damnation is of our own making, and nothing conceived by saint or sinner is worse than the horrors of each person's imagination.

The first underworld episode to air was "Escape Clause" in late 1959. This update of the FAUST story stars David Wayne as a self-indulgent sadist who sells his soul to SATAN in return for immortality. Wayne quickly realizes that life without risk is too boring, so when his wife accidentally dies he claims that he murdered her in order to "give the electric chair a whirl." Confident that it will be unable to end his life, Wayne wants to satisfy his curiosity about what electrocution feels like. To his horror, however, his attorney is able to win him a sentence of life without parole, which in his case means an eternity of imprisonment. Defeated, he agrees to let Satan take his life and proceeds to the ultimate imprisonment: damnation in the depths of hell.

This story was followed a month later by "Judgment Night," a tale of divine retribution against one of modern history's greatest evils. It opens as a disoriented German, played by Nehemiah Persoff, finds himself aboard a British passenger ship in 1942 with no memory of how or why he is on an English boat. Persoff cannot shake the feeling of impending doom. When he spots a German U-boat about to torpedo the English cruiser, he looks through binoculars and sees *himself* at the helm of the Nazi submarine. The U-boat fires and sinks the British boat, gunning down the survivors as they scurry for the lifeboats. Suddenly, everything becomes clear: Persoff did indeed murder a boatload of civilians during World War II and now is damned to relive the fateful night for all eternity. His hell is having to face the reality of his own vile actions.

The philosophy of WILLIAM BLAKE is illustrated in a 1960 episode titled "A Nice Place to Visit." This theory, that heaven and hell are simply a matter of perspective, is artfully explored when cold-hearted criminal Rocky Valentine (played by Larry Blyden) is killed in a shootout with police. In the afterlife he meets Pip (played by Sebastian Cabot), who is assigned his mystic "guide." Cabot escorts Blyden to a world where the con man's every whim is indulged. Beautiful women fight over him, each gamble he takes pays off, and his every desire is immediately fulfilled. Blyden realizes that being assured "a sure thing" every time takes all the fun out of life. He hates being in the "dull heaven" and asks Cabot to send him to the "other place." Hearing this, Cabot laughs hysterically, telling him "this *is* the other place," and Blyden is condemned to a hell of nihilistic monotony.

In "Deaths-Head Revisited" (an episode quite similar to "Judgment Night"), *The Twilight Zone* offers a portrait of hell adhering to the DREAM MODEL theory, contending that in the next world we simply relive the goodness or evil of our lives. Those who have been kind will spend eternity buoyed by cheerful memories, whereas evildoers will be mired in ugly recollections of nefarious deeds. In "Deaths-Head Revisited," a former Nazi concentration camp commander must face the ghosts of those he tortured and killed during the Holocaust. The implication is that the soldier will be forever tormented by images of his hideous crimes.

Not all of *The Twilight Zone*'s forays into the inferno were so somber. In "The Hunt," Arthur Hunnicut plays an aging woodsman who drowns while hunting raccoon. He then travels, his faithful hound Rip at his side, along a bucolic road to a gate guarded by a smiling gentleman. The gatekeeper tells Hunnicut that this is the entrance to heaven and that the hunter is welcome but Rip cannot enter. Unwilling to abandon his canine companion, Hunnicut refuses the invitation and continues down the road.

The deceased hunter soon meets an angel who explains that first gate was actually the entrance to hell, and that a clever DEMON was trying to fool him into joining the damned. Rip smelled the FIRE AND BRIMSTONE, as can all innocent beasts, and was not allowed in since he surely would have barked a warning to his master. The winsome episode ends with Serling advising travelers to "take along the family dog" to unknown places to "save you from entering the wrong gate."

In addition to the previously mentioned episodes, *The Twilight Zone* probed hell in such segments as "The Howling Man," "Shadow Play," "The Thirty-Fathom Grave," "Of Late I Think of Cliffordsville," and a dozen other unique interpretations of the supernatural and its various creatures. When the show was dropped by CBS in 1964, Serling refused to continue the project—in slightly altered form—with NBC, telling *Daily Variety,* "I don't want to be hooked into a graveyard every week."

But the series was far from over. All but four episodes have been alive in syndication for decades. Creator-writer Rod Serling went on to numerous other screen projects, including the *NIGHT GALLERY* series that also featured numerous shows on the underworld. A new, slick color version of the classic series enjoyed a moderately successful run in the 1980s, often using material from collaborators who worked on the original *Twilight Zone* project. Many of these episodes likewise focused on hell, DEVILS, and damnation. *TWILIGHT ZONE—THE MOVIE,* released in 1983, was a commercial and critical success, although it lacked the eerie atmosphere that flavored the black-and-white TV series.

The cult classic spawned a number of literary projects as well. In 1982, Marc Scott Zicree published *The Twilight Zone Companion,* a comprehensive guide featuring detailed descriptions of each show, photographs, behind-the-scenes production anecdotes, information on the writers and guest stars, and an epilogue listing Serling's later television credits. A million-selling COMIC BOOK series and *TWILIGHT ZONE MAGAZINE* were also outgrowths of this phenomenally popular television accomplishment.

The Twilight Zone has recently been immortalized at MGM Studios in Orlando, Florida. One of the park's most technologically advanced additions is the Twilight Zone Tower of Terror, a high-tech haunted house that boasts allusions to many of the series's scariest episodes. The Tower takes patrons on a ghostly ride into the next dimension, while props, pictures, and other memorabilia of original programs adorn the interior. In the few years since its opening, the Twilight Zone Tower of Terror has become one of the park's most popular attractions.

Anthologies of *Twilight Zone* SHORT STORIES continue to be written, inspired by the original series. The show likewise has generated both serious and humorous copycats. Now a fixture of the American experience, *The Twilight Zone* has been parodied on everything from the *Jack Benny Show* in the 1960s to contemporary sketches on *SATURDAY NIGHT LIVE* and even the children's educational program *Sesame Street.*

TWILIGHT ZONE MAGAZINE

In April of 1981, almost two decades after *THE TWILIGHT ZONE* television series ceased production, Rod Serling's *Twilight Zone Magazine* premiered on newsstands. It was the brainchild of Carol Serling, widow of the series's creator, assisted by many of the talented artists who had made the show such a success. Montcalm Publishing's bimonthly periodical featured original SHORT STORIES of the macabre, supernatural movie reviews, interviews with horror mavens, synopses of cult classic television programs, and a wealth of spooky advertisements offering everything from "Voodoo Kits" to "affordable weaponry."

The prestige of the *Twilight Zone* name attracted some of the biggest names in contemporary fiction, including Stephen King, Joyce Carol Oates, CLIVE BARKER, Robert Bloch, Dean Koontz, Peter Straub, and Anne Rice, all of whom contributed to the magazine during its decade-long run. These writers, and many gifted newcomers, offered a variety of fascinating interpretations of the underworld, accompanied by FANTASY ART and eerie illustrations depicting the damned. Their visions were as unique as the authors themselves, and each issue painted new and innovative pictures of what terrors await the condemned in the world to come.

One of the first infernal stories published in *Twilight Zone* was Jonathan Carroll's "Jane Fonda Room." Carroll envisioned the great below as a multiplex cinema where damned souls could choose a favorite movie star and spend eternity viewing the actor's works. At first, this seems quite an enjoyable way to pass the aeons, until ticketholders begin realizing how monotonous this will soon become. As the reality of the situation sinks in, one condemned soul shudders at the thought of watching "*Barbarella, Klute,* all the others . . . over and over again" forever.

Over the years, hell tales covered a broad range of interpretations. Stories borrowed concepts of damnation inspired by the works of such philosophers as WILLIAM BLAKE, ST. AUGUSTINE, and EMANUEL SWEDENBORG. These compelling works ran the gamut between depicting the realm of the damned as an icy pit of desolation to sketching the dark abyss as a mystic supermarket where lost souls would pass eternity demonstrating cleaning products and offering samples of cheese spread. It was not uncommon for such mythical underworld figures as ORPHEUS, CERBERUS, and Sedna (goddess of Eskimo hell ADLIVUN) to appear in these modern afterlife tales, usually with updated bios and a wry sense of humor.

In addition to containing numerous short stories about Hell, *Twilight Zone* featured nonfiction articles about VAMPIRES, werewolves, and other supernatural creatures, as well as interviews with top names in horror films and fiction. The magazine devoted considerable space to the works of deceased supernatural artists such as H. P. Lovecraft, Edgar Allan Poe, and HIERONYMOUS BOSCH. With an eye on supporting the future of horror as well as the past, *Twilight Zone* sponsored an annual fiction-writing contest to identify new talent, in memory of an award won by then-student Rod Serling that helped launch his illustrious career. Winners routinely used hell as a backdrop for their eerie compositions.

Portraits of the grim realm of the damned were further developed in another *Twilight Zone* feature: the movie preview. *POLTERGEIST, HELLRAISER, NIGHTMARE ON ELM STREET, ANGEL HEART, TRICK OR TREAT,* and a host of other grisly cinematic forays into the unknown made their print debut in the magazine. These early behind-the-scenes looks included advance stills; interviews with the films' actors, directors, and writers; and anecdotes about production gaffes. (Because this was a *pre*view and not a *re*view, on several occasions *Twilight Zone* profiled a movie that died before release and never made it to the big screen. The only glimpses of these ill-fated projects ever seen by the public were contained on the magazine's pages.)

Fans of surreal productions could further feed their hunger by reviewing the "Show by Show" guide to supernatural programs in each issue. The magazine printed synopses of episodes of the original *Twilight Zone* series, *NIGHT GALLERY, Outer Limits,* and *WAY OUT,* all of which regularly dealt with "otherworldly" subjects. Descriptions of each program (many of which have never been seen in syndication) were accompanied by photos and filming credits. In some cases, the entire script—complete with stage directions—was reprinted.

Fascinating as all these features were, the most remarkable element of *Twilight Zone Magazine* was its truly bizarre assortment of advertisements. "Harness the power of witchcraft" a typical notice reads, "learn to place or remove spiritual curses." In addition to promoting an ocean of infernal MOVIE MERCHANDISING, the publication peddaled supernatural GAMES, underworld fantasy art and horrific GIFT NOVELTIES. One ad offered "Monster Paper Dolls" of Frankenstein's Monster, Dracula, and the Wolfman. The characters came in traditional garb but included football uniforms, Shakespearean theatrical costumes, and even Santa suits. Another pitch declared "Aliens Want Earthling Pen Pals" and listed an address to write for "space creature profiles" and "alien correspondence." Paranoid readers could even send away for "Halley's Comet Insurance," guaranteed to pay all expenses for anyone killed, dismembered, or severely disfigured in a mishap with the streaking comet.

Despite fierce loyalty of devoted readers, *Twilight Zone Magazine* began to falter by the late 1980s. The once-bimonthly gazette appeared erratically, sometimes months passed without a new issue. By 1989, publication ceased altogether.

TWILIGHT ZONE—THE MOVIE

Twilight Zone—The Movie tries to re-create the suspense and drama of the classic *TWILIGHT ZONE* television series. However, the 1983 film falls somewhat short. A compilation of four segments bound by riveting opening and final sequences, the anthology takes up the subject of hell and DEMONS with mixed results.

One segment stars Vic Morrow as a disgruntled bigot who blames minorities for his many problems in life. He vehemently denounces Jews, blacks, and Asians with ugly racial slurs. According to Morrow, they are responsible for his stalled career, his declining social status, and his overall malaise. But, as narrator Burgess Meredith explains, he has no idea what suffering is until he is "catapulted into the darkest corner of the Twilight Zone" from which there is no escape.

After loudly extolling his racist theories at a local bar, Morrow stumbles out onto the parking lot. But as he leaves the place, he is transported into realm where *he* is the target of hatred and hostility. Morrow becomes the innocent black man beaten by the Ku Klux Klan and the frightened Vietnamese refugee gunned down by trigger-happy soldiers. The segments ends as Morrow, now marked as a Jew during the height of the Nazi reign of terror, is loaded into a metaphysical railcar headed for the ultimate concentration camp. He peers out to see his friends leaving the bar; however, they can neither see nor hear him. Morrow has departed their realm. (In a sadly ironic twist, this film about departure to the next world was Morrow's last work; he was killed in a helicopter accident during filming.)

Other supernatural sections feature a depiction of hell in ANIMATED CARTOON form and the transformation of one of the main characters into a flesh-eating demon.

TYMPANUM RELIEF French sculptor GISLEBERTUS led a team of artists in carving the Tympanum Relief, a massive artwork above the doorway to the Cathedral of St. Lazare in Autun, from 1130 to 1135. Using images from the Bible as well as symbols from ancient myth, the composition shows the *LAST JUDGMENT,* the event prophesied in REVELATION when all will be consigned to heaven or hell. During the artist's time, paintings, mosaics, and sculptures depicting this theme became a common element in CHURCH ART AND ARCHITECTURE.

The Tympanum Relief shows the underworld and its many agonies. Gislebertus includes a hell littered with huge snakes, dragons, and DEMONS gnawing on human souls before thrusting them into a gaping HELLMOUTH. At Christ's left hand, the fiends use a scale similar to the one described in the Egyptian BOOK OF THE DEAD to weigh each spirit. Demons lean into the scale, trying to shift the balance in favor of damnation. A gallery of anguished faces surrounds the spectacle, as the accursed plead for relief that will never come.

The Tympanum Relief is one of the first artistic compositions of the Middle Ages that can be positively linked to its creator. Earlier depictions of this theme are anonymous or otherwise unidentifiable by artist. Gislebertus, who signed his tympanum relief, had a flair for creating ruffled textures and often depicted humans as elongated and out of proportion. His unusual style and innovative technique are easily identifiable.

This unique blend of underworld images from Christian doctrine, apocrypha, and pagan IMAGERY, greatly contributed to the advancement of religious art in medieval Europe.

U

UGBOGIORINMWIN
Ugbogiorinmwin is the seven-headed lord of the underworld according to myths of the Bini of Nigeria. He is a fierce monster who breathes fire, smoke, and blood and who has power over souls in the spirit world.

One legend describes the tragic journey of Igioromi, a rambunctious youth who travels to the underworld to show off his wrestling skills. In the land of the dead, Igioromi throws several spirits to the ground, killing them a second time. He then challenges Ugbogiorinmwin to a fight to the finish. But Ugbogiorinmwin revives the fallen spirits with a magic potion, then effortlessly crushes the boy. He orders the souls to gather herbs and spices to cook Igioromi's corpse for a communal feast.

UNCAMA According to the Zulu legend, Uncama is a farmer who unwittingly travels to the underworld while searching for a porcupine that has been devouring his crops. Unlike other African tales of the afterlife, this story is said to be a factual account of supernatural events rather than a fictitious myth.

The tale begins when Uncama, set on killing the animal that has been ravaging his garden, follows a porcupine down its hole. Expecting to find a short burrow leading to its lair, the passage turns out to be a long tunnel full of twists and turns. It takes Uncama several days to pass through it, his eyes becoming accustomed to the darkness as he continues. Finally, he emerges from the hole and discovers a dark, smoldering village where dogs howl constantly, children weep and wail, and people walk and talk backward.

Realizing that he has inadvertently reached the underworld, Uncama flees the village and makes his way back up the porcupine hole. When he returns to his house, his wife shrieks with surprised terror: for the man has been gone not a few days but several *years*. She, and the rest of the villagers, believed that Uncama was dead, and all his possessions had been burned according to funerary custom.

The story of Uncama's visit to the underworld was passed down for generations, originating with people who swore they knew the man and that every word of the tale is true. It was first published in 1868 in a volume of Zulu stories by British author Henry Callaway.

V

VAMPIRES Vampires, "undead" creatures with supernatural attributes, are tenets of many legends and myth systems from across the globe. Called "living damnation," vampiric existence is detestable to all, even to the vampires themselves. They are accursed souls, condemned and despised both in this world and the next.

Tales of these gruesome fiends date back centuries, to the oldest known civilizations. Strigoe, an ancient Roman god, was believed to prey upon infants, sneaking into nurseries in the midnight hours to drain the blood of children. Chonchon, the vampire of Chilean Indian belief, could fly using its oversized ears as wings. Greek vampires, called vrykolakas, could be used by evil DEMONS to terrorize the living. They are depicted as swollen, bloated bodies damned to a ghoulish existence of wandering eternity to finish unsettled business or as a punishment for unforgivable sins. The Maya fear Camazotz, a vampire deity depicted with a razor in one hand and a wilting victim in the other. And according to one Japanese myth, a vampire in the form of a cat launched a wave of bloody violence against the court of a legendary Prince of Nabeshima.

Throughout history, vampirism has often been linked to femininity. The Irish deargdue are seductive life-stealing vixens, human counterparts to the demonic SUCCUBUS. In Scotland, sensuous baobhan sith lurk in the mountains and move in shadows stalking their mortal prey. And Malayan mothers who die in childbirth are believed to become langhui, vampiric spirits who rise from the grave to suck dry the blood of newborn babies. (The word *vamp*—coined to refer to an unscrupulous woman who uses sexuality to manipulate and exploit men—is derived from the word *vampire.*)

Pre-Columbian South American vampire demon. ART TODAY

Belief in vampires has resulted in other traditions as well. The practice of holding a wake, where loved ones stand guard over a newly deceased corpse for several days originated out of fear of vampirism. In some South American tribes, the living periodically exhume the bones of their loved ones, rinse them in wine, and have them blessed and reburied to guarantee the deceased a restful afterlife. Another way to ensure that corpses do not rise again is to fasten them to the ground with thick poles. In Western cultures, wooden stakes are considered most effective, as Christianity teaches that Jesus was crucified on a cross of wood. Since he conquered death and overpowered hell, wooden stakes are thus believed to have great supernatural as well as physical strength.

This mingling of religious hysteria with pagan superstition made vampires as fascinating as they were fearsome. During the 1800s, literature exploring vampirism became quite popular. Such masters as Johann Wolfgang von

Goethe (author of the quintessential *FAUST* drama), Lord Byron, and CHARLES BAUDELAIRE composed brilliant works inspired by these diabolical fiends. By far, the most famous vampire of English literature is Irish novelist Bram Stoker's *Dracula.* Stoker's book is based on tales of the medieval Romanian sadist Prince Vlad Tepes, better known as Vlad the Impaler, who terrorized thousands with his brutal tortures, dismemberments, and mutilations. (The name *Drakula* is Romanian for "son of the devil.") Since its publication in 1897, *Dracula* has captivated the collective imagination and become synonymous with the word *vampire.*

Fascination with vampires and their gory practices remains steady. The undead creatures have inspired hundreds of novels, stage plays, artworks, movies, and other creative endeavors. A television series entitled *Forever Knight* features a penitent vampire who seeks to atone for eight centuries of killings by working as a policeman in modern Toronto. Contemporary novelist Anne Rice has built a career on relating the adventures of Lestat, a stylish New Orleans vampire. The last in this series, *MEMNOCH THE DEVIL,* sends Lestat to hell for a firsthand look at what SATAN has to offer. And cinematic adaptations of these bloodsuckers run the gamut from classic chillers such as *Nosferatu* and *Dracula* to modern comedic satires *Dead and Loving It* and *A Vampire in Brooklyn.*

Vampires are also favorite subjects for MOVIE MERCHANDISING, TRADING CARDS, and FANTASY ART.

"VATHEK" William Beckford completed his tale "Vathek," an exotic version of the FAUST tale, in 1785 after struggling with it for more than three years. By that time the author had become an eccentric nobleman obsessed with the occult. Beckford turned his massive estate of Fonthill Abbey into his own private hell, complete with hideously deformed servants. He also erected a wall around his Gothic mansion and six thousand landscaped acres that ran for fifteen miles, stood twelve feet high, and was topped with sharp spikes. Inside the gold-encrusted gates, Beckford kept sixty fireplaces burning at all times, even through the summertime.

Beckford retreated to this fortress after being shunned by decent society. His life had been marred by numerous scandals involving illicit business dealings, dabblings in witchcraft, and allegations of homosexual orgies. In his exile, he became fascinated with Arabian legends, especially tales of magic. From this odd synthesis came "Vathek," which many critics still consider the finest "Oriental tale" originally written in a European language.

The story describes the atrocities of a wicked caliph named Vathek who is fixated on indulging in sensual pleasure. Unable to satisfy his wanton cravings through excessive perversion, he becomes obsessed with gaining "forbidden knowledge" and enters into a deal with Giaour, an earthbound DEVIL. Giaour promises to deliver to Vathek wealth, power, and wisdom in exchange for his soul. Vathek agrees and is shown the "Palace of Subterranean Fire" below the earth in a "vast black chasm, a portal of ebony."

Vathek witnesses the horrors of hell but is unmoved by them. Despite the screams of agony and maniacal rages of the damned, Vathek believes that his soul will not suffer in the underworld, for it is already steeped in evil. The despicable caliph then meets Eblis (IBLIS), ruler of hell, who offers Vathek acceptance into the "fortress of Aherman [AHRIMAN]." Vathek shows his allegiance through an offering of "the blood of fifty children," all sons and daughters of those who loved and trusted him. He slaughters the innocents without a moment of remorse.

After his fate has been sealed, the condemned tell Vathek of their horrible torment. Many lament that for a few fleeting moments of pleasure, they now suffer unending agony. They bemoan losing "the most precious gift of Heaven: Hope." Dejected, Vathek joins the "accursed multitude . . . to wander in an eternity of unabating anguish." Too late, he realizes that hell is not a glamorous realm of unlimited indulgence but an "abode of vengeance and despair." The story ends with a warning against the petty pursuit of "empty pomp and forbidden power."

VAULT OF HORROR Vault of Horror is the follow-up to the 1972 horror film *TALES FROM THE CRYPT*. Like its precursor, *Vault of Horror* uses stories originally published in COMIC BOOKS of the 1950s to depict hell as a place of retribution where sinners can no longer escape justice. The film relies heavily on the DREAM MODEL of the afterlife, wherein souls spend eternity engrossed in memories of the past. Suffering for the damned is being trapped in the wretched recollections of their own hateful acts.

Vault of Horror opens as five passengers board an elevator that suddenly plummets to the basement. When the car crashes, all five are surprised to discover that no one has been hurt. The doors open to a comfortable room. They enter, sit down, and begin discussing their recurring dreams. But the nightmares they describe are dark and treacherous: A "neat freak" imagines driving his wife mad with his obsession; a magician kills a competitor for the "perfect illusion"; a brother slaughters his sister to gain the family inheritance. Each person offers a grisly tale of violence and deceit.

Disgusted with their companions and with their own ghastly images, the five try to leave but find that the elevator is not working. Their fate is then revealed: All have in fact been killed in the accident, and the "dreams" were actual events that resulted in their damnation. As punishment, these condemned souls must remain together for eternity recalling their atrocious crimes.

VICENTE, GIL Gil Vicente, (1470–1536), considered the "father of Portuguese drama," was among the first poets to write original religious plays in Portuguese. Vicente's works bear strong resemblance to traditional

MORALITY PLAYS yet add a touch of humanity and satire to teach religious lessons. His most famous work, a trilogy of dramas titled *The Ships of Hell, Purgatory and Glory,* has been called "the Portuguese DIVINE COMEDY." Like Dante's masterpiece, Vicente's *Ships,* written in 1517, describes the afterlife in lyric poetry.

VIRAF Legendary holy man Artay Viraf (c. 1000 B.C.) was reputed to be among the most virtuous men who ever lived. A text dating back to around 800 B.C. tells of his divine tasks, one of which was to discover knowledge through mysticism. In his quest to learn about the "other world," Viraf spent much of his time in trancelike meditation, often aided by hashish and other mind-altering drugs. Using this method, Viraf traveled out of body, investigating the supernatural and pursuing ultimate truth. In one such trance, he set out to explore the conditions of the underworld by paying a visit to hell.

According to Viraf, hell was a horribly desolate place like the inside of the grave, "cold and icy" and polluted by an unbearably putrid "dryness and stench." Beyond the immediate grave was a narrow chasm enveloped by blackness where "noxious beasts tore and worried at the damned." But this was not the worst of hell; Viraf was shaken by the numbing solitude of the realm, for "each soul thought 'I am alone.' " He determined that the true torture of damnation was the crushing solitude each soul experiences, being eternally isolated from his fellows.

However horrible, this suffering would be only temporary. Viraf's tale was eventually combined with the teachings of ZOROASTRIANISM, which teaches that at the end of time there will be an apocalyptic battle in which the underworld will be vaporized. Repentant sinners and souls in LIMBO will ascend to heaven after this LAST JUDGMENT. Paradise will be located on a renewed earth, where body and soul will be reunited for an eternity of spiritual and sensual pleasures. Those who refuse to renounce there evil ways, however, will face ANNIHILATION and be eradicated from existence.

VIRGIN MARY Roman Catholics believe that the Virgin Mary, mother of the Christian redeemer Jesus Christ, has the power to save doomed souls from hell. Her assistance is sought both for the living, that they may amend their lives, and for the dead who are languishing in PURGATORIAL HELL. The Hail Mary, a prayer to the Virgin, asks: "Holy Mary, Mother of God, pray for us sinners, now and at the hour of our death."

Some legends go even further, claiming that she can journey to hell to retrieve damned souls. Writing about the Virgin Mary, Saint Bonaventure notes, "He who honors thee will be far from damnation." There are numerous tales about iniquitous men and women being saved from hell through her intercession. A ninth-century account recalls a deacon named Adelman who died and "had seen Hell, to which he was condemned." But through Mary's urging, the deacon was restored to life to atone for his sins.

Even more extraordinary is the story of a Roman citizen who had died in a state of mortal sin. Years later, as Emperor Sigismund was moving his armies through the Alps, the man's skeleton came to life and asked for a priest. He told the astonished troops that Mary, whom he had always revered, had obtained for him this final chance at salvation.

A similar tale originates in early seventeenth-century Belgium. Two young men had been enjoying a night of drinking and debauchery, when one (by the name of Richard) left the party and went home. He mumbled his prayers to the Mother of God—albeit halfheartedly—before falling asleep. That night, Richard was suddenly awakened by a hideous monster who claimed to be his friend. "A DEVIL came and strangled me," his companion said. "My body is in the street and my soul in Hell!" Richard's deceased compatriot then opened his coat, and Richard could see the serpents and flames that tortured the man. Before returning to the inferno, the damned soul told Richard that it was his devotion to the Virgin that had saved him from the same fate.

The Virgin Mary has also been linked to visions of hell granted as warnings against falling to temptation. One of the most famous occurred in Fátima, Portugal, in 1917. Mary appeared to three young shepherd children and asked them to pray the rosary (a series of prayers commemorating Mary's role in Christ's life) over a period of several months. During one visit, she gave the oldest girl, LUCIA DOS SANTOS, a horrifying glimpse of the damned suffering in hell. The images were so disturbing that Lucia later stated that if the vision had lasted even a moment longer, it would have killed her.

A prayer card of *Mother of Perpetual Help* includes verbiage asking the Virgin Mary for protection from hell.
COURTESY OF THE REDEMPTIONIST FATHERS

Because of her significance in Christendom, Mary has become a prominent figure in Christian literature and drama. She is included as mediator in many variations of the FAUST legend and in MYSTERY PLAYS and MORALITY PLAYS. The Virgin is also frequently depicted in CHURCH ART AND ARCHITECTURE, often shown beside Jesus in renderings of the LAST JUDGMENT.

VISION LITERATURE Vision literature is a large, diverse body of works recounting the adventures of people who have "witnessed" afterlife events firsthand. Most originate from medieval Europe, although records of these supernatural journeys are also found in African, Asian, and North, Central, and South American Indian cultures. There are even contemporary examples of vision literature written in the past decade. These various texts share one thing in common: They are presented as fact, not fiction, and are fiercely defended by their authors as legitimate reports of the next world.

One of the oldest cautionary tales of this type involves a Burmese Buddhist monk who has become corrupt and self-indulgent. Upon "dying," he is damned to hell for his sins. There, the monk is immersed up to his chin in human feces while his face is gnawed by huge, toothy worms. He also witnesses other tortures, seeing his damned brethren being beaten, burned, and put through a gamut of thorny tasks that reduce them to mere ribbons of blood. The fallen monk offered his disturbing story as a warning to others tempted to abandon their vows.

The African legend of Angolan King KITAMBA's expedition to the land of the dead presents a very different message about mortality. When the king loses his beloved wife, Muhongo, he forces the entire village into mourning. Months pass, and Kitamba's subjects want to return to their former traditions of celebration, merriment, and festivities. Kitamba refuses to retract the order until a medicine man travels to the underworld to seek Muhongo's advice. The deceased queen tells him to relay the message that although the underworld is dark and monotonous, she not in any physical pain. When Kitamba hears this, he ends the

The Inferno, a sixteenth-century Portuguese painting, depicts many of the horrors described in Christian vision literature. GIRAUDON/ART RESOURCE, N.Y.

mourning and encourages his people to enjoy life while it lasts.

Vision literature from Christendom invariably stresses the need to reform and repent. Examples of this include the accounts of TUNDAL, FURSEUS, ALBERIC OF SETTAFRATI, BEDE, ADAMNAN, and DRITHELM, all of which describe horrible tortures inflicted on the damned. Torments range from being devoured by dogs to being forced to climb a ladder of razors barefoot. Most of these visions were experienced by peasants. However, since commoners were illiterate, clerics were usually asked to transcribe the tales. Colorful illustrations were often added to enhance the images, and these accounts were then widely circulated throughout Europe and its colonies.

These frightening medieval stories have a number of shared elements. The majority feature biblical DEMONS—SATAN, the DEVIL, BELIAL, LUCIFER—and a variety of lesser fiends as overlords of the abyss. Another common component is the inclusion of a supernatural "guide" to serve as escort and narrator for the tour of hell. Drithelm is accompanied on his afterlife journey by an angel, Furseus by a contingent of heavenly hosts. Christ's apostle and first pope of the Roman Catholic church, St. Peter, serves as Alberic of Settafrati's protector and mentor in the underworld. Other accounts refer to "benevolent spirits" and "steadfast shepherds" who usher human souls through the realm of the damned.

The popularity of vision literature peaked toward the end of the Middle Ages. By the time the genre went into decline in the fourteenth century, literally hundreds of people had claimed to have visited heaven, hell, and purgatory while "dead," only to be revived to tell their tales. Those who did not personally experience this phenomenon were eager to hear others' testimony. Sermons based on visions were commonplace: Priests drew on the riveting images for inspiration when preaching repentance, describing the afterlife, or trying to convert the unbaptized. Vision literature became so popular that many churchgoers began attending services just to hear the dynamic chronicles of hell.

The demise of vision literature can be attributed to several factors. First, the proliferation of these alleged journeys led to growing skepticism about their authenticity. Under the weight of so many conflicting and increasingly flamboyant accounts of hell's conditions, the fad eventually collapsed upon itself. This was hastened by scholarly debate over whether souls would be adjudicated immediately upon death, or would await the LAST JUDGMENT before entering heaven or hell. Many Christian philosophers taught that "visions" of spirits in the afterlife were impossible, since human souls would "sleep in Christ" until the end of the world. The final blow was the prominence of such fiction works as Dante's *DIVINE COMEDY: THE INFERNO,* which offer vivid, stylized descriptions of the underworld from the imagination of literary geniuses.

And though vision literature as an

industry died with the Middle Ages, it has by no means disappeared from the modern experience. In 1993, Mary K. Baxter published *A Divine Review of Hell* in which she describes a "40 day" vision of hell complete with odors, haunted tunnels, and torture chambers "like a horror movie." Other accounts of infernal NEAR-DEATH EXPERIENCES, also penned over the last few years, have likewise described a treacherous abyss where sinners will suffer for all eternity, even in this enlightened age. Like their medieval precursors, these contemporary tales warn readers that the day of reckoning is indeed on its way.

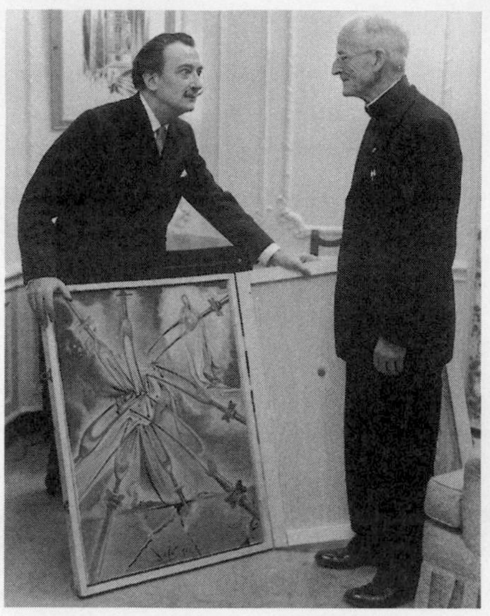

Salvador Dalí presents his interpretation of the *Vision of Hell* to Msgr. Harold V. Colgan of the Blue Army of Our Lady of Fátima. PHOTO COURTESY OF THE BLUE ARMY OF OUR LADY OF FÁTIMA, USA, INC. ALL RIGHTS RESERVED

VISION OF HELL, THE

Twentieth-century surrealist Salvador Dalí created a frightening depiction of the underworld with his 1962 *The Vision of Hell,* based on a supernatural experience of LUCIA DOS SANTOS in 1917. His painting shows a condemned soul being twisted and tortured with sharp forks in a desertlike inferno. In the background, fire, smoke, and DEMONS pour forth from a jagged chasm. Above, the VIRGIN MARY, mother of Jesus Christ, offers hope to humankind by encouraging them to turn to her son for salvation, thus escaping the bitter wages of sin.

The work was commissioned by an anonymous donor who feared that "Hell has ceased to be a reality to millions" and that this ignorance would lead to the eternal damnation of countless souls. Dalí presented the painting to Monsignor Harold V. Colgan, founder of the Blue Army of Our Lady of Fátima (an organization dedicated to spreading the message of sanctity, repentance, and reparation), in hopes that it would serve as a reminder of the "penalty of sin." *The Vision of Hell* was hung at the Blue Army's headquarters in New Jersey, where it remained in relative obscurity for more than three decades. The modern masterpiece was recently "rediscovered" by the organization's members and is now being exhibited throughout the world.

VIZARSH Vizarsh is the fearsome DEMON of ZOROASTRIANISM who seizes evildoers attempting to cross Cinvato paratu (CHINVAT BRIDGE). These damned souls are "followers of the lie" who have betrayed the truth.

As they try to navigate the narrow passage that leads to paradise, the weight of their sins causes them to fall into hell, where they are attacked by the vicious Vizarsh.

W

WANJIRU A legend from Kenya describes how the beautiful maiden Wanjiru is rescued from hell after being betrayed by her neighbors. According to the story, a severe drought has destroyed most of the village's crops and herds, and the only way to bring rain is to offer the gods a human sacrifice. The medicine man selects Wanjiru, a young virgin, and demands that she be brought to the sacred site for the ritual. However, he reassures the girl's family that she can be ransomed if everyone in the village brings a goat to exchange for her life.

The following day, Wanjiru is led to the field where she is surrounded by her friends and family. Each has brought a goat to appease the gods as substitute for the girl. Suddenly, the ground opens and begins swallowing up Wanjiru. Her loved ones rush forward and present their goats to the girl's parents in order to save her. But she continues to sink until she is emerged to her eyes. Then the clouds open, and rain pours down in a violent deluge. As Wanjiru's parents try to save her, the villagers continue to hand them goats in hopes of prolonging the rainfall. Before she can be pulled to safety, Wanjiru disappears into the earth, bemoaning that her people have abandoned her.

A young warrior who had long loved the maiden is enraged when he learns what happened. He vows to travel to the underworld to find out what has become of the girl. Dressing in battle costume, he stands on the spot where Wanjiru disappeared and prays to the gods. Soon he, too, sinks into the ground.

The warrior finds a subterranean road to the underworld that leads him to the maiden. When he sees her, he cries out in horror at her pitiful state. Wanjiru is naked and weeping, suffering from both physical and emotional pain. Her admirer carries the girl back to the land of the living, where he presents her to her elated parents. The two are then married and enjoy a long and happy life together.

WAY OUT One of the most embarrassing disasters in television history led to the creation of *Way Out,* a supernatural suspense series every bit as spooky as THE TWILIGHT ZONE and NIGHT GALLERY. After the abysmal failure of *You're in the Picture,* an asinine game show hosted by Jackie Gleason in which celebrities poked their heads through various works of art, CBS executives scrambled for something to fill the weekly thirty-minute time slot. Producer David Susskind proposed a program that would be "eerie, chilling, creepy" with "a netherworld sense to it." He hired English writer Roald Dahl *(James and the Giant Peach)* to write and host a series of macabre tales. In the spring of 1961, the resulting project premiered with a fiendish tale about a long-suffering wife who finally gets her revenge.

Over the next fourteen weeks, each Friday night brought a new twisted story to the airwaves. Roald Dahl opened each show with a grisly anecdote or tongue-in-cheek suggestion on how to get away with murder and closed by bidding viewers, "goodnight . . . and sleep well." In between, *Way Out* featured all manner of unsettling stories. One shows a vain actor becoming imprisoned in his Quasimodo makeup; another details the adventures of a loathsome boy (played by a very young Richard Thomas) who develops a formula for turning people into snakes. *Way Out* even aired a program about nuclear annihilation titled "Button, Button."

Among its terrifying tales, *Way Out* offers a number of frightening epi-sodes focusing on the afterlife and divine justice. "The Down Car" presents Frank Overton in the role of a corrupt businessman who murders his partner to mask an embezzlement scheme. On the day of the victim's funeral, Overton goes to the office to destroy evidence, and he feels a strange presence in the room. Unnerved, he runs down the hall and boards the elevator, which immediately begins dropping. The car pauses briefly in the basement, then plummets once again before safely coming to stop. When the door opens, Overton emerges without a scratch. He sees the silhouette of a man and remarks that he was sure the elevator was going to crash. Turning toward him, the mysterious figure tells Overton it *did* crash. Horrified, Overton sees that the man is actually a GHOUL with the face of his murdered colleague and realizes that the Down Car has delivered him to hell.

"I Heard You Calling Me" offers another cautionary tale about punishment of the wicked. The episode features a young American beauty who plans to run off with a married man. On the day of their intended departure, the girl receives unsettling telephone calls from a British woman saying, "You are not going with him tonight because you are coming with me." She tries to trace the calls, but the switchboard insists that there have *been* no incoming calls. The caller phones again, identifying herself as "Mrs. Rose Thorn" and laying out plans to visit landmarks that had been torn down decades ago. Hearing these details, the girl's lover rushes to her, only to find her dead body being examined by a doctor. But the physician is mystified at the cause of death; she seems to have drowned. The bewildered lover explains that Mrs. Rose Thorn was his mother and that she went down with the *Titanic* half a century ago. Disapproving of the American vixen's designs on her son, she has returned from the afterlife to drag the girl to hell.

Despite critical acclaim, good performances, and excellent scripts, *Way Out* was canceled just four months after its premiere. The show had done well in the ratings in large cities but was considered odd and distasteful in most smaller markets. Some episodes have been rebroadcast over the years, but *Way Out* never enjoyed the national syndication that cemented the popularity of *The Twilight Zone, Outer Limits,* and *Night Gallery.* In the early 1980s, Susskind donated tapes of the series to New York City's Museum of Broadcasting, suggesting that future viewers see the shows as lighthearted entertainment and "just enjoy them."

WITCHBOARD The 1985 film *Witchboard* depicts the misadventures of a group of friends who accidentally open the portal to hell with a Ouija board, a supernatural GAME. When Tawny Kitaen and Todd Allen unwittingly use the toy to conjure a damned spirit, they find that they have become the fiend's prey. Resurrected from the inferno, the evil being resumes his violent ways until a macabre ritual sends him back to the murky abyss.

Witchboard has been followed by two sequels; *The Devil's Doorway* (1993) and *The Possession* (1995), both of which portray the Ouija board as a gateway to hell. However, unlike the puzzle box that serves as an infernal passage in HELLRAISER, the Witchboard is a one-way conduit that allows the damned to escape their afterlife prison rather than an open channel allowing the living to visit the abyss.

WODEN Northern European myth features Woden (precursor of Odin, head of the Norse pantheon), god of war and guide to the underworld. He was a powerful deity who brought suffering and death to his soldiers and is frequently compared to the Roman god Mercury, a sinister being. Woden is depicted with a spear and is symbolized by a wolf or raven.

His fall from grace and banishment to the underworld bear similarities to the Christian tale of LUCIFER, the beloved angel who rebels against God and is sent to hell.

WORLD OF SHADOWS The Native American World of Shadows is a realm of impermeable darkness where disembodied heads, DEMONS, and other phantoms drift through eternity. Unlike HANHUA, a place of physical torture and punishment, the World of Shadows is a quiet place for the dead who were not considered evil. The greatest suffering in this realm is the bitter, unending gloom. It bears resemblance to afterlife concepts of Greek SHADES and of the Jewish SHEOL.

Y

YAMA Yama is god of death and punisher of evil found in many Asian religions, including versions of Hinduism and Buddhism. He is a green DEMON, often shown dressed in red robes and armed with a noose and a mace. Yama has red eyes and sharp fangs and is sometimes portrayed covered with open sores. Two hideous deformed dogs guard his palace in the depths of the underworld. Souls of the dead must cross the river Vaitarani and face Yama for judgment. Yama could send the spirit to a place of "21 hells" or back to the world for rebirth.

In hell, the damned face gruesome penalties that correspond to their earthly offenses. Blasphemers have their tongues ripped out, murders are drowned in blood, the frivolous are tormented with piercing knives. Yama has also been incorporated into Hindu religion, where he temporarily detains souls who must purge themselves of evil before being reincarnated.

The BARDO THODOL (Tibetan Book of the Dead) describes Yama as a fierce ruler robed in human skin and wearing a necklace of severed heads and a crown of skulls. In one hand he holds a sword ready to punish sinners. In the other he carries a mirror that reflects the actions of everyone. Departed souls must look into the mirror and face their evil, which is believed to be the worst torment of the afterlife. According to the text, "No terrible god pushes you" into hell; every wicked soul damns itself. The Bardo Thodol describes the DEMONS of "Yama, Lord of Death" who arise when a vile departed spirit finally recognizes its own ugliness: ". . . their fang-like teeth protruding over their lips, their eyes like glass . . . they carry punishment boards and shout 'Beat him!' and 'Kill him!' They lick up your brains, they sever your head from your body, and they extract your heart and vital organs."

Chinese belief teaches that there are many hells, each with its own Yama, or king. An ancient mural shows an underworld court where frightened souls awaiting judgment offer food and riches to the lord in hopes of winning his favor. Yama's court is a confused mass of bloodied bodies being chased and tortured by an assortment of green and red demons. Other spirits are being forced into pools infested with toothy serpents.

Yama is often associated with EMMA-O, another Asian deity of death and the underworld.

YAMBE-AKKA Yambe-akka (Jameakka, Jabmeanimo) is the goddess of death and the underworld of the Lapps of Scandinavia. She is a hideous hag whose name means "old woman of the dead." Yambe-akka guards departed souls in an endless pit of suffering and sadness, where she dwells in the shadows.

YEATS, WILLIAM BUTLER

Irish poet William Butler Yeats (1865–1939) was fascinated by the occult, mysticism, and metaphysics and dedicated much of his career to interpreting supernatural concepts through his poetry. Yeats came from a Catholic family but also grew up hearing ancient Celtic legends about FAIRIELAND and Druid rituals. As an adult, Yeats blended political dissent, Irish history, pagan IMAGERY, and religious themes into modern masterpieces.

One example, *A Vision,* contains an entire book dedicated to "The Soul in

Judgment." It was originally written in 1925; however, Yeats amended the work in 1937 after witnessing great personal tragedy and civil unrest. Another poem, "The Wanderings of Oisin," features heroes of Irish myth discussing philosophy with such Christian icons as St. Patrick in a mystic forum of information exchange.

In his FAIRIE *Tales of Ireland,* Yeats describes the fallen angels and their bleak underworld: "Some of the angels who were turned out of Heaven . . . landed on their feet in this world, while the rest of their companions, who had more sin to sink them, went down farther to a worse place."

Yeats also incorporates into his theories of mysticism the ideas of philosopher EMANUEL SWEDENBORG, who taught that heaven and hell are merely a matter of perspective. The poet likewise echoes ideas from WILLIAM BLAKE, an eclectic artist and visionary. Like Swedenborg, Yeats believed that souls are neither inherently good nor evil but exist temporarily in good and evil states. Thus each person defines his or her own salvation or damnation. This shifting definition of heaven and hell is evident in *Wanderings,* which describes a place of eternal youth and beauty called the "Island of Dancing." At first, Yeats's hero is enchanted with this paradise. However, the realm quickly becomes intolerably boring to adventurers seeking challenge. What seemed a place of ultimate joy has been revealed as a monotonous prison.

Yeats also believed that damnation was not a punishment for immorality but retribution for men who refused to live up to their artistic potential. In *The Hour Glass,* Yeats describes a dark abyss littered with the desolate spirits bemoaning their wasted lives:

Hell is the place of those who have denied;
They find there what they planted
and what dug
A lake of spaces, a wood of nothing,
And wander there and drift, and never cease
wailing for substance.

The torment of these souls is realizing that they will never be truly fulfilled.

Yeats's work also includes an allegory about damnation entitled "The Stolen Child." This cautionary tale follows an unhappy child (representing humankind) as he abandons earth (mortality) for the promise of a better world made by cunning fairies (demons). Too late, the child discovers that he has given up his humanity—and all its joys as well as sorrows—for existence in hell. He describes this Fairieland as a bleak realm of "unquiet dreams" and lost souls. The fairies mock their prisoner, reminding him of the earthly beauty he has forsaken. Yeats revisits this theme in "Valley of the Black Pig," which examines the last judgment, calling the devil the "Master of the Flaming Door."

As he grew older, Yeats became less interested in the supernatural and the afterlife, and his work centered more on real people, most notably deceased friends. His poetry also took on political battles and contemporary problems. In "To a SHADE" (deceased spirit), Yeats likens the Irish populist hero Charles Stewart Parnell to the suave DON JUAN. For such speculative works of poetry, Yeats won the Nobel Prize for Literature in 1923 and is credited with leading the Irish literary renaissance.

YELLOW SPRINGS Yellow Springs is the underworld of ancient Chinese myth. It is ruled by Yangwang, a mythical deity similar to YAMA, the god of dead. He punishes doomed souls in an indigenous hell that is very similar to earth geologically, located under the earth's surface. Yangwang's task is to enforce justice after death in Yellow Springs. He is a just overlord who administers pain in direct proportion to a person's immorality.

Relief from a Chinese Taoist temple shows souls being tormented in the underworld.
ART TODAY

YOMOTSU-KUNI Yomotsu-kuni is the Shinto equivalent of hell. The name means "land of gloom." It is a place of thick darkness populated by hags, thunder gods, and DEMONS. The ancient legend of IZANAMI, the first man, recounts how the father of the human race travels to Yomotsu-kuni in order to retrieve his dead bride, Izanagi, after she dies in childbirth. But the man discovers that she has begun to decay and he refuses to take her back with him. Izanagi sends a legion of demons after her husband, but he is able to elude them. When he returns to the surface of the earth, Izanami seals off the entrance to Yomotsu-kuni from the land of the living. After this, only the dead can enter Yomotsu-kuni, and neither deceased spirit nor demon can return to earth.

Z

ZAKKUM The zakkum is an enchanted tree in JAHANNAM, Islamic hell. The plant grows in the lowest depths of the underworld where the most egregious offenders languish in flames. Instead of blossoms, the tree is laden with the heads of shrieking DEMONS. Its sap is molten poison, and the fruit of the zakkum is pain and death.

ZOROASTRIANISM Many modern images of hell date back more than two and a half millennia to Zoroastrianism, a faith that predates both

Christianity and Islam. The ancient religion was founded by the prophet Zoroaster (Zarathustra, Zartust) around the sixth century B.C. and remained the dominant faith of the Middle East and parts of Europe and Asia for a thousand years. Zoroaster's concepts are detailed in the *Gathas* (Songs of Zoroaster) and the *Avesta* (sacred scriptures).

Zoroastrianism teaches that two powerful deities—twin brothers, one good and one evil—are constantly battling for control of the world. The "Wise Lord" Ahura Mazda dwells in paradise and sends good spirits to aid humans; AHRIMAN, the "Lord of Lies," lurks in hell where he is forever dispatching DEMONS to destroy humankind. Those who fall to temptation will be condemned to a subterranean abyss where they will suffer until the LAST JUDGMENT, when all souls will be called forth from the grave to give an accounting of their actions. After this occurs, Zoroaster assures his followers that Ahura Mazda will rule uncontested for all eternity.

According to Zoroaster, judgment in the afterlife is swift and decisive. When a person dies his soul remains beside the body for three days, then travels to CHINVAT BRIDGE, where angels balance the spirit's good deeds against his other sins. The soul is then forced across the razor-sharp bridge that leads to paradise. But if its evil outweighs its goodness, then the spirit falls into a deep abyss where it is seized by the cruel demon VIZARSH. There the damned soul is tortured until the apocalypse.

The ancient prophet Zoroaster. ART TODAY

Many of Zoroaster's beliefs were eventually absorbed into the Muslim and Christian faiths. Ahriman became associated with the Islamic IBLIS and Christian LUCIFER, and Vizarsh was likened to the vicious SATAN, wicked overlord of hell. Zoroastrianism also holds a place in the nativity story, as the magi (wise men) who visit the infant Christ in the manger were followers of the prophet Zoroaster.

illustration credits

pp. 3, 8, 26, 43, 45, 56, 119, 141, 146, 151, 159, 170, 182, 192, 194, 209, 213, 229, 230, 231, 237, 247, 262, 287, 300, 301 Art Today images courtesy of Michael A. Gariepy, CEO Zedcor, Inc. www.arttoday.com

p. 28. Photo of Clive Barker by Lance Staedler courtesy of Clive Barker, Joe Daley, and *Seraph Films*, Beverly Hills, Calif.

p. 39. William Blake's *Last Judgment* (1808) used with permission of Petworth House, Petworth, Sussex, Great Britain.

p. 41. The "Mouth of Hell" from *Book of Hours of Catherine of Cleves* used with permission of the Pierpont Morgan Library, New York, N.Y.

pp. 72, 117. Illustrations from *The Brotherhood* courtesy of John Schulte, John Besmehn, Cherly Ann Wong, and Pangea Corporation, Dana Point, Calif.

p. 81. Photo of Angel Featherstone from *Dark Angel: The Ascent,* by Charlotte Stewart, courtesy of Linda Hassani.

p. 100. Detail of Salvador Dalí's *Vision of Hell* and p. 294 photo of presentation of the work to Msgr. Harold V. Colgan used with permission of and by arrangement with The Blue Army of Our Lady of Fátima, USA, Inc. All rights reserved. No reproduction without the express written permission of the Blue Army of Our Lady of Fátima, USA, Inc.

p. 105. Japanese deity of hell with scroll used with permission of National Museum, Kyoto, Japan.

p. 125. Salsa from Hell courtesy of Southwest Specialty Food, Inc., Glendale, Ariz.

p. 185. Detail from Fra Angelico's *Last Judgment* used with permission of Museo di San Marco, Florence, Italy.

p. 201. *Charon Ferrying Souls on the River Styx* used with permission of the Vatican Museums, Vatican State.

p. 227. Francois Perrier's *Orpheus before Pluto and Persephone* used with permission of the Louvre, Paris.

p. 291. Prayer card of *Mother of Perpetual Help* courtesy of the Redemptionist Fathers.

p. ii, 292. *The Inferno* used with permission of the Portuguese School, Museu Nacional de Arte Antiga, Lisbon, Portugal.

selected bibliography

It is impossible to list every source consulted in compiling this book. The following works are suggested for further reading on matters relating to the afterlife.

Alfred Hitchcock's Witch's Brew. New York: Random House, 1983.

Alighieri, Dante. *Inferno*. Trans. Mark Musa. Bloomington: Indiana University Press, 1971.

Andersen, Hans Christian. *Andersen's Fairy Tales*. New York: Grosset & Dunlap, 1945.

Arberry, A. J., trans. *The Koran Interpreted*. New York: Simon & Schuster, 1966.

Baxter, Mary K. *A Divine Review of Hell*. Springdale, Pa.: Whitaker House, 1993.

Bernanos, Georges. *The Diary of a Country Priest*. Trans. Pamela Morris. Garden City, N.Y.: Doubleday, 1974.

Blake, William. *The Complete Poetry and Prose*. Ed. David V. Erdman. New York: Doubleday, 1988.

Boardman, Gerald. *American Musical Theatre*. 2d ed. New York: Oxford University Press, 1992.

Budge, E. A. Wallis, trans. *The Egyptian Book of the Dead*. New York: Dover, 1967.

Bugliosi, Vincent, with Curt Gentry. *Helter Skelter*. New York: Norton, 1974.

Byron, Lord. *The Poetical Works of Lord Byron*. Ed. Robert F. Gleckner. Boston: Houghton Mifflin, 1975.

Campbell, Joseph. *Oriental Mythology*. New York: Arkana, 1991.

Carey, Valeri Scho. *The Devil & Mother Crump*. New York: Harper, 1987.

Carola, Leslie Conron, ed. *The Irish: A Treasury of Art and Literature*. Hong Kong: Hugh Lauter Levin Associates, 1993.

Cavendish, Richard, ed. *Man, Myth and Magic: An Illustrated Encyclopedia of Mythology, Religion and the Unknown*. New York: Marshall Cavendish, 1995.

——. *Visions of Heaven and Hell*. New York: Crown, 1977.

Cotterell, Arthur. *The Macmillan Illustrated Encyclopedia of Myths & Legends*. New York: Macmillan, 1989.

Courlander, Harold. *A Treasury of African Folklore*. New York: Crown, 1975.

Crockett, William, ed. *Four Views on Hell*. Grand Rapids, Mich.: Zondervan, 1992.

Daly, Kathleen. *Norse Mythology A–Z*. New York: Facts on File, 1991.

Davidson, Gustav. *A Dictionary of Angels*. New York: Simon & Schuster, 1961.

Delaney, John J. *A Woman Clothed with the Sun*. New York: Doubleday, 1961.

DeMoss, Robert, Jr., host. *Learn to Discern.* Documentary. Colorado Springs: Focus on the Family, 1992.

Ebert, Roger. *Roger Ebert's Movie Home Companion, 1993 Edition.* Kansas City, Mo.: Andrews and McMeel, 1992.

Elkin, Stanley. *The Living End.* New York: Dutton, 1977.

Esposito, John. *Islam: The Straight Path.* New York: Oxford University Press, 1991.

Felleman, Hazel. *The Best Loved Poems of the American People.* New York: Doubleday, 1936.

Ford, Marvin. *On the Other Side.* Plainfield, Ill.: Logos International, 1978.

Gaskell, G. A. *Dictionary of All Scriptures & Myths.* New York: Gramercy Books, 1981.

Goldberg, Harold. "Pinhead's Progress." *Entertainment Weekly,* January 20, 1995.

Grimal, Pierre. *World Mythology.* New York: Excalibur Books, 1965.

Grossbach, Robert. *The Devil and Max Devlin.* New York: Ballantine, 1980.

Guiley, Rosemary Ellen. *The Encyclopedia of Witches and Witchcraft.* New York: Facts on File, 1989.

Halliwell, Leslie. *Halliwell's Film Guide.* 7th ed. New York: Harper, 1989.

Harper, George Mills, ed. *Yeats and the Occult.* Toronto: Macmillan, 1975.

"Hell's Sober Comeback." *U.S. News and World Report,* March 25, 1991.

Henry William A., III. "Having a Hell of a Time." *Time,* December 18, 1989.

Hitchcock, Alfred, ed. *Alfred Hitchcock Presents: Scream Along with Me.* New York: Random House, 1967.

Homer. *Odyssey.* Trans. Robert Fitzgerald. New York: Doubleday, 1961.

Ions, Veronica. *Indian Mythology.* New York: Schocken, 1967.

Janson, H. W. *The History of Art.* New York: Harry N. Abrams, 1995.

Jones, Stephen, ed. *Clive Barker's A–Z of Horror.* New York: Harper, 1997.

King, Stephen. *Nightmares & Dreamscapes.* New York: Viking/Penguin, 1993.

——. *Rose Madder.* New York: Penguin, 1995.

——. *Skeleton Crew.* New York: Penguin. 1986.

Knaper, Jan. *Kings, Gods & Spirits from African Myth.* New York: Schocken, 1986.

Konvitz, Jeffrey. *The Sentinel.* New York: Ballantine, 1974.

Koontz, Dean. *Hideaway.* New York: Putnam, 1992.

Langland, William. *Piers Plowman.* Trans. E. Talbot Donaldson, ed. Elizabeth D. Kirk and Judith H. Anderson. New York: Norton, 1990.

Larson, Gary. *Cows of Our Planet—A Far Side Collection.* Kansas City, Mo.: FarWorks, 1992.

Lee, Chris, narrator. *Fear in the Dark.* Documentary. London: BBC, 1991.

Leonard, Sue, ed. *Life Beyond Death.* Pleasantville, N.Y.: Reader's Digest, 1992.

Letterman, David, and Steve O'Donnell. *The Late Night with David Letterman Book of Top Ten Lists.* New York: Pocket Books, 1990.

Lewis, C. S. *The Great Divorce.* New York: Macmillan, 1946.

——. *The Screwtape Letters.* New York: Macmillan, 1961.

MacCana, Proinsias. *Celtic Mythology.* New York: Hamlyn, 1970.

Mack, Maynard, ed. *Norton Anthology of World Masterpieces.* 4th ed. New York: Norton, 1979.

Maltin, Leonard. *Leonard Maltin's 1997 Movie & Video Guide.* New York: Penguin, 1996.

McCarty, John. *The Official Splatter Movie Guide.* 2 vols. New York: St. Martin's Press, 1990, 1992.

McGinniss, Joel. *Cruel Doubt.* New York: Simon & Schuster, 1991.

McNamara, Robert F. "Hell Is Harrowed, Allelulia!" *America,* May 7, 1994.

Mercatante, Anthony S., ed. *The Facts on File Encyclopedia of World Mythology and Legend.* New York: Facts on File, 1988.

Moody, Raymond A., Jr. *Life After Life.* New York: Bantam, 1977.

Morris, Janet. *Rebels in Hell.* New York: Baen Books, 1986.

Nashawaty, Chris. "Devil Indemnity." *Entertainment Weekly,* January 20, 1995.

New Catholic Encyclopedia. New York: McGraw-Hill, 1967.

Ordway, Edith B., *The Opera Book.* New York: Sully and Kleinteich, 1915.

Paananen, Victor N. *William Blake.* Boston: Twayne, 1977.

Rawlings, Maurice S. *To Hell and Back.* Nashville: Thomas Nelson, 1993.

Rice, Anne. *Memnoch the Devil.* New York: Knopf, 1995.

Rimbaud, Arthur. *Arthur Rimbaud: Complete Works.* Trans. Wallace Fowlie. Chicago: University of Chicago Press, 1966.

Robbins, Rossell Hope. *The Encyclopedia of Witchcraft & Demonology.* New York: Crown, 1969.

Rushdie, Salman. *The Satanic Verses.* New York: Viking/Penguin, 1989.

Russell, Jeffrey Burton. *Lucifer: The Devil in the Modern World.* Ithaca, N.Y.: Cornell University Press, 1984.

——. *Mephistopheles: The Devil in the Modern World.* Ithaca, N.Y.: Cornell University Press, 1986.

Sartre, Jean-Paul. *No Exit.* New York: Vintage, 1989.

Schnindehette, Susan, and John Griffiths. "An Excellent Dude Goes to Hell." *People,* August 12, 1991.

Schouweiler, Tom. *Life After Death.* San Diego: Greenhaven Press, 1990.

Shaw, George Bernard. *The Portable George Bernard Shaw.* Ed. Stanley Weintraub. New York: Penguin 1977.

Simpson, Jacqueline. *European Mythology.* New York: Peter Bedrick Books, 1987.

Skal, David J. *The Monster Show.* New York: Norton, 1993.

Stern, Jane and Michael. *The Encyclopedia of Bad Taste.* New York: Harper, 1990.

Sullivan, Jack, ed. *The Penguin Encyclopedia of Horror and the Supernatural.* New York: Viking, 1986.

Sykes, Egerton. *Who's Who: Non-Classical Mythology.* New York: Oxford University Press, 1993.

Thurman, Robert A. F., trans. *The Tibetan Book of the Dead.* New York: Bantam, 1994.

Turner, Alice K. *The History of Hell.* Orlando, Fla.: Harcourt, 1993.

Twilight Zone Magazine. New York: Montcalm Publishing, 1981–1989.

VideoHounds Complete Guide to Cult Flicks and Trash Picks. Detroit: Visible Ink Press, 1996.

Willis, Roy. *World Mythology.* New York: Henry Holt, 1993.

Wright, Gene. *Horror Shows.* New York: Facts on File, 1986.

Zicree, Marc Scott. *The Twilight Zone Companion.* New York: Bantam, 1982.